FAITHING

FAITHING

A Reconstructive Method

A. Eugene Dyess

with an Introduction by
James W. Fowler, III

UNIVERSITY
PRESS OF
AMERICA

Lanham • New York • London

Library of Congress Cataloging-in-Publication Data

Dyess, A. Eugene.
Faithing : a reconstructive method / by A. Eugene Dyess.
p.   cm.
Includes bibliographical references and index.
1. Pastoral counseling.   2. Faith development.
3. Psychotherapy—Religious aspects—Christianity.
4. Meditation—Christianity.   I. Title.
BV4012.2.D87   1994   253.5—dc20   94–21259 CIP

ISBN 0–8191–9602–9 (pbk. : alk. paper)

IN MEMORY OF
JOHN J. EBERHART

AND TO
ROGER, STAN AND
SARAH JO

her job of the major editing of this manuscript. Actually, her work has almost been that of a translator, for she took the time and patience this effort needed in order to familiarize herself with all aspects of Faith Therapy. Additionally, I wish to express my gratitude to my wife, Sarah Jo and to my daughter-in-law, Sandra Napier-Dyess, for their help in editing at a number of vital points along the way. Also, I appreciate Molly Ozment, Hope Mooney and Cynthia Leonard for their word processing skills used in preparing the manuscript.

Finally, I must include the many special people who have contributed immeasurably to the establishment of Faith Therapy. They have been of invaluable help in incalculable ways over these years by aiding me to bring into reality this unique form of Christian ministry with its resultant manuscript on the method. These persons, who thus ministered to me, are members of my larger family, personal Christian friends, former parishioners, and clients. In countless ways their faith and their very lives are woven into the fabric of this work.

A. Eugene Dyess
Jackson, Mississippi

Figure Number 4, "The Self/Other Value Core of Trust," is based upon the work of Jim Fowler in "Life/Faith Patterns: Structures of Trust and Loyalty," in *Life Maps: Conversations on the Journey of Faith*, by Jim Fowler and Sam Keen, ed. by Jerome Berryman (Waco, Texas: Word Book Publishers, 1978), p. 20.

[1] John J. Eberhart, Letter to American Association of Pastoral Counselors, May 18, 1970.

state to stimulate conscious growth from unconscious origins. (The efficacy of this practice was discovered in dealing with suicidal patients.)

Part II is entitled "The Theory Framework" and discloses the theory from which this method was derived. The entire part presents the concepts constructed, developed and used by the method's originators and other contributors over the past nearly four decades of its successful practice but does not argue for these concepts—only presents them as a confessional offering.

Chapter V, "Theological Convictions," reveals the more significant Christian beliefs, convictions, and insights which undergird this specifically Christian therapy method. The approach taken to these convictions upon which this methodology was built is both subjective and developmental. The subjective approach presents the personal story behind the method's development. It tells of a pastor, a psychiatrist, and a psychologist, working out of the local church to help meet spiritual-mental-emotional health needs. Demonstrating the development of the method's origin will serve as testimony to the fact that the Church is a living organism out of which such a growth therapy method could grow. In this chapter the early conceptualizing which led to the founding of the therapy method is elaborated upon. The method was initially based on Paul's mystically powerful concept of the structure of the eternal life-giving process: the development of faith, hope and love, a process which leads to spiritual growth. The chapter also includes the theorizing which led to the development of the Intensified Faith Schema and establishment of the transcendent mind mood as well as the realization of Christian symbolism's efficacy.

Chapter VI, "Psychological Models" presents the reader with some additional contributions to the psychology of religion. The chapter explains the therapy's specialized constructs, concepts, and techniques as well as its topographical and structural construct of the psyche, with relations, operations, and their interactions. This chapter emphasizes those offerings to religious psychology which could be used, with minor modifications, by almost any Faith.

Chapter VII is entitled "Convictions and Models Structurally Synthesized: Faith is the Psyche's Primary Operation." This therapy's theoretical basis is that "faith" may be viewed as a structural process resulting in a unified whole. The chapter offers some essential concepts of faith and then draws them all together with recent findings of faith development as cognitive, hierarchical, and patterned stages.[9] For clarity, the material briefly gives the fundamentals of epistemological structuralism. Then the chapter elaborates on the three parts of the life development process: faith, hope and love. The author postulates that human life starts with the organism's original and self-limiting operation of faith as an attitude which immediately forms the attitude of hope as its own consequent and opposite limit. Love as an attitude and also as the basic affective and intelligent life-energy then becomes the third force in a triadic pattern of the life-forming process. However, the *modified* structuralist position presented posits that the faith process is *drawn* into life-action by cosmic intuition, a unitive perception or religious function which has a chemical-like, spiritual valence power. Though ultimately intended to lead life toward God, this intuition originally operates from God through the infant's mother as a graceful giver of love and vital satisfaction. This unitive perception may also be operative in human existence as that force by which life is constructed. It continually draws one onward to fulfillment of life needs—sometimes even erroneous ones if so chosen—that life may have depth and meaning.[10]

Next, the chapter suggests that all the basic psychic functions are rudimentarily present in this initial faith operation's triadic and socially responsive beginning. It is hypothesized that the more important psychic functions in primal form participate in leading up to life's first year trust-identity crisis. The predominant tone of feelings or emotions patterned in that first year (also probably well into the second) are indicated as life's fixed affective orientation which tends unconsciously to form and shape the general direction of the emotion flow of a person for the rest of his/her life. It is further postulated that overly severe relational negativities of this period (which include the necessary parental human imperfections) are often unconsciously and erroneously later projected upon God as the *parent of all parents*. Unless such severe negativities are subsequently overcome by a more correctly construed, direct experiencing of God's complete unconditional love, as concretely shown in Jesus Christ, they may cause an emotional restriction upon the normal development of life. Further, this blockage may also distort by fear normal spiritual dimensions of personality growth, transformation experiences in relating to God as "The Holy." This section then offers that the successes of this therapy model are due to its ability to guide one past such above negativities by activating one's "idealizing understanding" capacities.[11] Activating these abilities in turn may lead one into a possible *real* experiencing of God's presence—if both so will. Such relational restructuring of the primal love energy around God as Person in Christ opens the possibility for the client to move then into the transcendent mind mood where therapy work can be done in the presence of God's safety, the ultimate *safe-secure* affect.

Part III, "How to Practice This Method," consists of two chapters which provide instructions and advice on how to perform the method: Chapter VIII, "Pre-process Instructions for The Therapist" and Chapter IX, "Special Cautions for Therapist Consideration." This material, as already noted, is the product of more than thirty years of an evolving,, growing, and effective practice using this method of therapy.

The guidelines are readily available to those practitioners who may wish to use them.

Part IV, "Illuminating Transcripts", comprised of Chapters X, XI, XII, XIII, and XIV, are verbatims of actual illustrative therapy sessions with accompanying indications of the major important therapy points of note, procedures, and techniques demonstrated in each transcript. The live tapes of the transcripts (available from the author, 4251 Berlin Drive, Jackson, MS 39211) will also be accessible; however, names, some personal qualities, and voices will be changed or electronically distorted enough to conceal personal identity, but not important subtleties of the session. Additionally, there will be available from the author taped recordings of the Intensified Faith Schema, its Variations, Deschematization Exercises, the three Usual Positive Ideas and additions to the Intensified Faith Schema which are used with administering Special Positive Ideas so that the reader may also be familiarized with the special vocal style used by the therapist in guiding the client. This style is critical to the Schema's effectiveness as will be thoroughly explained in the first two sections of Chapter III, "The Intensified Faith Schema Exercise."

"Summarizing Conclusions" contains the author's ideas concerning Faith Therapy's potential for the future. These comments conclude the manuscript's contents with some final remarks.

Following is a glossary of terms to aid the reader in gaining a clearer understanding of the words and concepts used in explicating the therapy method. Also, an index will conclude the book.

The following diagram illustrates the infrastructure of Faith Therapy. It is designed to present the internal workings of the entire therapy method, the explanation of which unfolds in the main body of this book.

Figure No. 1 Faith Therapy Infrastructure

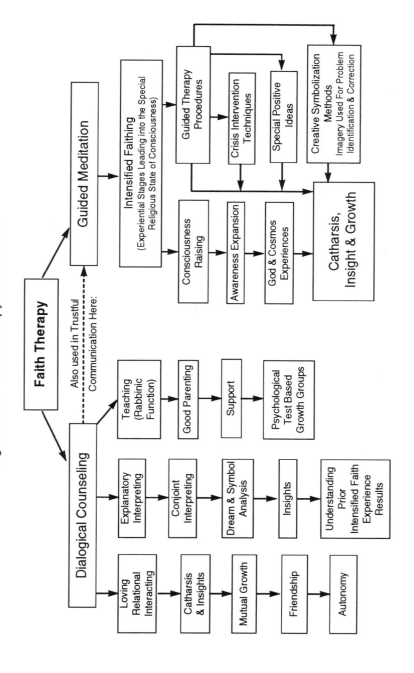

(A BRIEF BUT NEEDED ASIDE)

After reading this manuscript, a Christian female clergy friend pointed out that I am not a sexist and I needed to make that clear. With her helpful recommendation, here I would like to make an appreciative introjection; that is, I feel it is important for the reader to make a mental note that in this book my occasional use of the male noun or pronoun in reference to God is not intended to imply sexist orientation in my thought or life. Such thinking is primarily a habit of long standing in my writing style and very difficult to change, in every detail, at this point in life. My non-sexist attitude I believe to be borne out by my personal conviction that God is fully androgynous; and, therefore, we as human persons of one sex *must* also contain large mental-emotional elements of the opposite sex. Simplistically, sexually we are different but equal.

NOTES

[1] American Association of Pastoral Counselors, "The Efficacy of Pastoral Counseling," in *Pastoral Counseling: A National Mental Health Resource* (Fairfax, VA: *circa* April, 1993) pp. 9, 10.

[2] Edgar Draper, "Religion as an Intrapsychic Experience," *Cincinnati Journal of Medicine*, Vol. V., No. 5 (May, 1969), p. 111.

[3] Ibid., p. 112.

[4] Ibid., p. 112-118.

[5] Ibid., p. 118.

[6] Dictionary of Pastoral Care and Counseling, (Abingdon, 1990), pp. 769-71.

[7] Rudolf Otto, *The Idea of the Holy*, trans. by John W. Harvey, 2nd ed. (New York: Oxford University Press, 1950), pp. 5-7.

[8] John J. Eberhart, the psychiatrist and retired naval captain was my teacher, mentor, colaborer and friend over the years 1956-1970. Frequently he made this statement, in varying forms, but this is its essence. Like most great teachers, he had a way of reducing the things of great importance to powerful epigrams which for me tended to stick like mental glue.

[9] James W. Fowler, "Stages in Faith: The Structural-Developmental Approach," in *Values and Moral Development*, ed. by Thomas C. Hennessy, S. J. (New York: Paulist Press, 1976), pp. 1973-79.

[10] Jean Houston, "Foreword," in *Physicians of The Soul: The Psychologies of The World's Great Teachers* by Robert M. May (New York: Crossroad, 1982), pp. ix, x.

[11] Leroy T. Howe, "Piaget's Theory of Cognitive Structures as a Resource for Conceptualizing Religious Understanding." Paper presented at the Seventh International Conference on Piagettian Theory and the Helping Professions (Los Angeles, Calif.: *circa*. January, 1977).

PART I

THE METHOD'S
BASIC CONTENTS

I have chosen to begin my thorough explication of Faith Therapy with a discussion of the practical aspects of the method. Chapter I presents an excerpt from an actual case but with all identifying factors altered to preserve client privacy; however, none of the important content is lost. It also contains many of the therapy method's major procedures and includes a discussion of the main divisions of the therapeutic work. This opening section is intended to illustrate Faith Therapy in practice and to lay a foundation of familiarity for a later understanding of its theoretical and historical background.

A TRUE SHORT STORY:
A Clinical Case of Hearing and Experiencing the "Inner/Outer Voice" as God

I went into the waiting room to greet Mitchel, my next client. He was sitting there, sporadically coughing deeply and hoarsely, seeming almost to lose his breath at times. This caused even more curious, furtive glances from others sitting there. Such glances at Mitchel in the Counseling Center's waiting room were not unusual, due to the uniqueness of his appearance and something of the mysterious emotional aura which seemed to surround him. The coughing problem appeared only to add slightly to the glances.

Mitchel's visual impact was powerful. He seemed to loom larger than his small stature but well-proportioned, muscular build. The clothing certainly didn't account for the difference, for as usual he was dressed in boots, blue jeans, tee shirt, and a jacket—not unusual attire for a young man in his mid-twenties. Perhaps part of the impact was caused by the long, occasionally-present hunting knife, which hung in its scabbard on his belt, hanging only slightly below the short, open Levi jacket. Perhaps it was his head which most struck one's vision. His head was always erect and thrust forward slightly, hinting a subtle readiness to spring to the attack as though he were a bold, young, and able warrior ready to prove himself. His well-kept hair, shoulder-length and gently wavy, his neatly-cut, but slightly sparse, beard and mustache combined with his fair complexion to enhance this young Viking appearance. This impression was set somewhat askew by the hint of the pirate in his appearance, caused by the black patch worn over his vacant right eye socket, leaving one piercing eye. It seemed to stare at one with knowingness and defiant challenge. Yet, if the beholder were very perceptive he/she could detect a subtle yet deep sympathy, the result of almost unbearable physical pain in his past. If one were looking deeply, he/she also saw in Mitchel the keen intellect and the sensitivity and creativity of the artist. No wonder this mysterious looking young man compelled the eyes of those around him to cast hidden and darting glances in his direction.

"Gene, I almost didn't come tonight because I felt so bad," he said hoarsely in a near whisper as he rose and started with me toward the counseling office. As we proceeded to the room and were seated, and as I was preparing to turn on the tape recorder, he told me why he felt a driving need to have his session as scheduled. Two days prior he had contracted pneumonia and had seen the physician who gave him antibiotic injections and other medication; however, while the medication seemed to help, his dry coughing continued and seemed to clear none of the congestion from his lungs. The preceding night, as he had lain in bed with only sporadic dry coughing in a febrile, semi-delirious state, a formerly repressed memory came to consciousness. He remembered being five years old, lying in bed with an incessant cough, and his angry father came to his bed and beat him with a straightened coat hanger until he totally suppressed his coughing by a great effort of willpower. It seems important here to note that this memory concerned Mitchel's generic father. Indicative of the confusing, tense, early conditions under which Mitchel grew up before his real parents gave him up for adoption when he was age nine, along with a twin brother, younger sisters, and a younger brother. Fortunately, the oldest children were adopted by a successful professional man and his wife who were childless. The firm, understanding, loving care given by this adoptive father was truly a saving influence for Mitchel, but was brought to a tragic and highly traumatic end when the new father died three years later. It is an understatement to say this brought into Mitchel's life a great bitterness.

The coming to consciousness of the beating incident seemed to have brought with it the right to be aware of his body's soreness caused by the pneumonia. Later that morning, accompanying the pneumonia pains, he had begun to experience in his legs (where he was beaten with the coat hanger) the formerly repressed somatic pain of the beating. Later, his high fever had broken.

In order to put things into proper perspective for what happened in this therapy session, it will now be helpful if we digress briefly to understand something of Mitchel's background. I first met him and his wife, Evvie, when they came for marital counseling about four months prior to this session. They had a young son, Anthony, age three; and mother and son had been living separately from the husband and father for a number of weeks (she with her parents and he in an apartment). This was due to their inability to resolve satisfactorily relational problems between them. Love for their young son, as well as for each other, in spite of the difficulties, brought them to the pastoral counseling center for help. Mitchel's wife's background is almost as complex as his. As a matter of fact, the young man and woman had actually met and fallen in love while both were undergoing mental treatment in a local hospital while in their late teens.

Evvie's psycho-social background included a highly repressive childhood in a rigid, legalistic Protestant home in which there was also a mentally retarded sister. Although Evvie was a very attractive and intelligent woman, she had fought depression and withdrawal desires all of her remembered life. Her experience of nausea and vomiting in public school had continuously eroded any self-esteem she tried to build. From as far back as she could most easily remember, there was some association with community mental health workers, psychologists, and psychiatrists.

After their termination of treatment and a period of courtship they were married, and Evvie's self-esteem began to rise to such a point that she could deal with life on a more realistic level. The birth of her son lent further motivation for her to be responsible—especially in view of Mitchel's intermittent unreliability—and she had taken the General Education Development Test to receive her high school diploma. This motivation for self-sufficiency also led her to take licensed practical nurse schooling and training; she discovered that she truly loved this occupation although her self-doubt and authority problems stole some of the joy. At the time we began counseling, she had finished her training with high scores and was waiting to take her state licensing board examinations. In the meantime, she was also currently employed with a local clinic.

Following his adoptive father's death, Mitchel's bitterness and loss of faith in life caused him to become a severe behavior problem. Though he did graduate from high school, his high school career was interspersed with much drop-out and anti-social behavior. This behavior had gotten so bad that his adoptive mother had once legally committed him to a mental ward with the diagnosis of Acute Undifferentiated Schizophrenia with Homicidal and Suicidal Indications (though I noted at the time of our meeting no evidence of schizophrenic thinking or speech). Additionally, he had once become deeply involved in the drug culture and had tried most types of mind-altering drugs. At one point, his drug involvement had gotten him arrested and sent to prison, from which he was later paroled and returned to society; however, he had found it very difficult to adjust well, and his jobs were mostly of minor importance and of brief duration in spite of his intellect. To compound Mitchel's problems, he was hypoglycemic and intolerant of many medications.

One of the contributing factors in Mitchel's inability to relate well to Evvie was the fact that he had an out-of-awareness, strong symbiotic tie with his brothers and sisters (who also had very poor marriages), and he additionally felt a deep concern about the whereabouts and welfare of his other two siblings who had been adopted separately. This concern was a deep sense of responsibility Mitchel had somehow assumed for "all of us children" back beyond the time of easily accessible memories. Because of these multiple impediments in their marriage the couple came to the point of separation and from there to the counseling center for help.

In our first session, a conjoint one, as they unfolded the complexity of their lives, it seemed very evident to me that I would need to see them separately for hourly sessions weekly since the origins of both of their individual relational problems lay deep in the severe problems of each one's early childhood. The early traumatic childhood experiences were as yet too unresolved to make the marital relationship problems easily subject to more usual types of marital counseling. In the first session, I had instinctively liked this young couple and found myself admiring them for the nobility which lay behind their struggle for happiness. To use a Dialogical Counseling term, I found myself going beyond "affirming" them only and "confirming" them in their individual existences in all the polarities. After proposing separate sessions, I explained to them something of the nature, purpose, origin, and development of Faith Therapy with special emphasis upon the Guided Meditation with its state of consciousness elevation through the Intensified Faith Exercise which would then use the fantasy-like Guided Therapy Procedures. It was my hunch we would probably need to use the Guided Meditation components in the couple's sessions.

I must admit that I was somewhat hesitant in offering this

approach because of his intake interview sheet for the center. Mitchel had filled in the space for "religion" with words to the effect of "not interested *at all*." He further enlarged this position by stating that he had his own individual type of agnosticism, which contained openness toward perhaps the existence of some universal intellect but which was in no way personal in relationships with individual human beings. This agnosticism held true even though Mitchel had at one time worked with a minister in a religiously-sponsored drug redemption program. The failure of this program as a result of lack of concern by "religious people" had further alienated Mitchel from any interest in religion. However, as I explained my own early experience of atheism and my commitment to the rights of individuals to their own personal beliefs in such matters, he overcame some of his hostility at his wife's insistence that they counsel with a clergyperson. Curiously enough, Mitchel became convinced of my respect for his autonomy, he even became very interested in our using the Guided Meditation part of Faith Therapy. This interest arose as I explained to them the experiences and observations of people who had also had prior experience with mind-altering drugs, and thereby were acquainted with experiencing the strange powers of the unconscious, and had also used this part of the therapy. These people had unanimously described the transcendent or elevated meditative mind mood, in which the therapy work was done, as being closely akin to the type and level of consciousness state experienced with drugs, particularly LSD, but without distortion of unconscious images and symbols or the higher rational functions of the mind. Furthermore, these same persons reported they felt new feelings of enlightenment and enhanced problem-solving abilities accompanying the increased awareness which the Guided Meditation part of Faith Therapy had enabled them to develop.

Mitchel wanted to try the guided meditation in spite of the extensive use of religious symbolism and Christian belief-statements in the Faith Schema Exercise. On the other hand, Evvie was less open to this type of therapy and all future sessions with her were done with Dialogical Counseling and other more usual types of psychotherapy methods. The affective power of the unconscious symbols for her seemed to be anxiety-arousing. The other techniques helped greatly just the same to promote her growth and problem-solving abilities. She grew to the point where she could be supportive of Mitchel who appeared to have the more serious problem.

Surprisingly, with a minimum of explanation of technicalities used with this methodology Mitchel was ready to start at his first individual session with use of the Guided Meditation part of the therapy. Therefore, we proceeded straightway with use of the Intensified Faith Schema to Level III, Stage 9, Guided Therapy Procedures, Usual Positive Ideas, and subsequent Deschematizing Exercise. Once he had entered into the Transcending Level mind mood and explored it to his satisfaction, he was able to confirm for himself what he had understood this psyche state to be: it was highly akin to the consciousness level achieved when using LSD, but without any distortion of his rationality or symbolism; it was a very powerful state in which he was cognizant of his conscious control of the entire Intensified Faith Therapy experience. He explored this space in his own psyche without threat or fear but with a great deal of feeling, interest, and curiosity. According to the paradigm of process theology, in that session he seemed more oriented toward the mental pole of God, for at first his space seemed only to contain forms, e.g.: trying to describe his perception of this psyche space, Mitchel stated, "...the picture I get, I can understand, but it would be something like—just like Salvador Dali painted."

As I frequently do for a person who is a powerful, transcendent faith or elevated mind mood meditator, in this first session I suggested we might bring more unity to his personality by using some basic archetypal symbols and Guided Therapy Procedures. He was open to this, so we introduced into the situation for aiding his unity of mental functioning, three activating symbols to be visualized: the Plus-mark or Self Symbol, the Sword of Masculinity (a red rose for women), and the Tree of Life. He responded well to the affective power of each of these visualizations, especially the Tree of Life, a beautiful green maple tree which appeared spontaneously toward the close of the Guided Meditation's *therapy work* without my suggesting its presence. This maple tree seemed to have a very *special* archetypal symbolic power for Mitchel, but it was considerably later, after this initial session before he desired to introject this particular symbol; at this time, he felt that it was appropriate for this symbol simply to reside in his imagination. At the close of his first Guided Meditation session when the Intensified Faith

Deschematizing Exercise (used to return to the normal, everyday level of consciousness) was completed, Mitchel felt a new sense of self-confidence and psychic health. He had no further reservations about the use of any part of Faith Therapy. As is usual, however, there were resultant questions, dreams, memories, and insights needing additional clarification. Some could be briefly dealt with in the Dialogical Counseling which terminated the session. Most of the next few sessions were spent striving to understand the insights coming to consciousness from his own psyche's production of reconstructive and analytical grist due to use of this therapy.

Additionally, during this interval, he began to experience spontaneous new affect levels breaking into his consciousness. These were sometimes accompanied by awareness of his inner symbols and/or memories and were of a visionary nature, not hallucinatory! Using the Dialogical Counseling Method of explaining and offering insights, he and I worked through these breakthroughs and visionary occurrences. With this approach Mitchel steadily gained in his ability to accept this greater consciousness availability of painful, repressed matter from his own unconscious. Only one more session of the Guided Meditation dimension of Faith Therapy was used with Mitchel before the present. In the meantime, he had been increasingly able to produce a strong degree of transcendent or elevated meditative mind mood for himself in session without the Intensified Faith Schema being used. This self-induced production brought up plenty of material needing attention in the sessions. (The ability to achieve this meditation mood independently, but in the presence of the therapist, is not unusual for some clients after initial use of the full Faith Schema with the therapist's guidance and help.) No specifically religious symbolism was subsequently used in visual symbolic projection form. Rather, we simply explored—in a relaxed manner Mitchel's own self-induced elevated meditative state—the memories and feelings which he brought to consciousness. However, in one session, about three weeks prior to the current one, I had used with him that part of the Schema sometimes called the Beach Scene (Modified Level 1, Stage 1), which emphasizes concrete thought operation. Use of this level alone is very helpful if there is an indication that the client does not at the time need to get into profound states of transcendent emotion.

In that particular session we had explored a very threatening feeling which had come to his consciousness in a nightmare the previous night; but, even while in this lower level of self-activated meditation, Mitchel had much intense regressive material come to consciousness. (Apparently, of his own accord he had gone to that intensity of meditation more readily achieved at Faith Schema Level III, Stage 9.) As a matter of fact, he actually went back and re-experienced a series of associated memories from ages five down to two. These memories had led him back to an experience in which his father had deliberately beaten him so badly that he had broken Mitchel's collarbone. Before that session he had consciously remembered the broken bone and subsequent lengthy hospital stay but had not remembered how it had been broken: his father had brutally beaten Mitchel when he would not agree with a false view of an outer reality situation which his father had made real for himself.

As Mitchel had made contact with this feeling tone's structure and its stream of affective tone associations, this memory's feeling valence carried him from one experience to another down to age two. The one common core structural factor of all these feelings involved irrational parental thinking and emotional cruelty, which in Transactional Analysis would be called experiences with the "crazy child" in both parents. Fortunately, however, these traumatizing experiences were interspersed with some memories of good times together. While the good experiences probably accounted for some of Mitchel's ego strength, the bad ones were so irrational as to have caused childhood to be highly confusing—especially disconcerting to Mitchel who possessed superior capabilities of reason and logic indicated by his 180 I.Q.

The incident recalled at the close of that particular session was of his mother deliberately burning his twin brother's leg over a gas jet on a stove (the scar still remained but its cause had been forgotten). Mitchel visualized this memory as it had appeared to him as a two-year-old child. At this point he burst into crying over the formerly affectively unreleased and unconceptualized "craziness" of his early life's world caused by his parents' seemingly deliberate cruelty and insane actions. He had such a highly emotionalized abreaction caused by these early incidents that for several days ensuing he experienced some newly released physical pain resulting from the beating episode and specifically located in the area of his collarbone. Of course, the need for counseling through that experience and reorienting the new conscious emotions, thought patterns, and insights which became available caused us to consume several sessions.

In dialogical counseling the therapist participates with in-depth interrelating and offers [but does not dictate] his rational explanation of seeming non-rational material as a parent would do with a three-to-six-year-old-child. Early, healthy, rational explanations are often missing in the crazy childhood world of many clients, and their confused unconscious still hungers for such caring straight answers. Mitchel sorely needed some insight into his current inability to feel physical misery and its possible connection with this memory. Currently, as we counseled about the insights which flowed from such re-experiencing of his repressed memory and pain, we were able to arrive at the following conclusion: possibly the former ineffectiveness of his dry cough and accompanying apparent inability to experience his present illness might have been caused by his father's early prohibition of the coughing.

Further, this matter of denying the serious pain of physical illness because of financial costs to his father led Mitchel to associate with it the memory of the loss of his eye. Since he had never evidenced any desire to share with me the actual experience of losing his eye and since it seemed to be connected with his father's angry denial of Mitchel's legitimate body needs, I probed this experience for insights which might be strongly related to Mitchel's immediate physical condition. As he shared details of this painful incident, I was able to aid him in understanding that while there was indeed a great deal of parental cruelty experienced in childhood, there was also evidence of some loving care given to him by his father. I hoped that Mitchel would be able to clarify his current distorted view of reality which seemed to be caused by his emotionally experiencing early childhood in a way which constantly vacillated between strong feelings of safety and strong feelings of threat.

I had reason to hope for further insight because with each step Mitchel's accuracy of perception and intellectual interpretation of reality had increased, and he had subsequently developed greater abilities to be more responsible in interpersonal relations. Additionally, overall, his emotions had become more stable and loving, and his thinking capacities and conceptualization more realistic. These developments in adjustment, which began immediately

after Mitchel's first session with Faith Therapy's Guided
Meditation use,were evident in two major behavioral changes: (1)
Mitchel and Evvie had resumed living together, more easily
expressed their love to one another, and were beginning to resolve
their interpersonal problems; (2) Mitchel had held his last job for
the past three months and had even received two promotions on
the job because of his responsibility and work output.

As we arrived at the insights concerning the loss of his eye
Mitchel was now more aware of his physical tiredness and the tension which had caused him to pace back and forth, feel his sickness
throughout the day, and then come to the session in spite of his illness. I believed that this would be a good time to help Mitchel
release more of these physical and psychic tensions by again briefly
using Guided Meditation's Intensified Faith Exercise and one very
restful therapy procedure. This time I intended to guide him into
nothing more than imagining the Schema's Modified Level II,
Stage 4, which is also called the Mountaintop Scene because it
envisions life from the perspective of a mountain and inspires tranquility. It is also called the Transforming Level because usually all
Aristotelian or formal logic operations of consciousness and greater
ease of recall are readily available in this state of mental relaxation.
After arrival at this Schema Modification, I had planned to use a
simple therapy procedure. It is comprised of imagined creative
symbols which I refer to as the Sacred Circle, with the Knoll of
Light and Worship at its center, located in the center of the Forest
of Life. I observed with clients over the years that if they were
extremely emotionally and physically tense and were imaginarily to
place themselves in this Sacred Circle and rest while in the intensified meditative state, they would experience almost complete relaxation which would carry over later at home.

It is unnecessary with these particular therapeutic symbols, when
used for the above goal only, to do a great deal other than to make
sure the client imaginally corrects unhealthy aspects of the symbols
which can be present in the visualization. Therefore, they can enjoy
the pleasure, sense of well being, and rest which use of these
Guided Therapy Procedures brings them. I had only this intention
when I suggested to Mitchel that the remainder of the session be
devoted to undertaking this experience. Because he understood the
capacity of the exercise to reduce tension, Mitchel decided to do
this procedure even though he could only partially recline in the

chair due to his pneumonia and cough. What followed both surprised and greatly pleased me.

Usually a reclining chair is used for the Faith Schema Exercise. Reclining in a comfortable position facilitates body and psyche relaxation and enhances the Exercise's effectiveness. However, this night we were in a different counseling room with no recliner; but a tilting type of office chair was there, so Mitchel leaned back in it and closed his eye. Having him use his imagination, I led him through the Intensified Faith Schema, with its archetypal imagery and Christian belief-statements, exactly following Level I with Stages 1, 2, and 3 all a part of the Beach Scene. (The entire Intensified Faith Schema Exercise, Schema Variations, and basic therapist instructions, plus a brief explanation of its theory and use will be found in Chapter III.)

The first stage helped him relax his body and then mentally and emotionally accept his breathing in as an unencumbered gift of God's breath of life, the unqualified right TO BE, and his exhaling as a letting go of the natural exhausts of having to live a human level of life—exhausts God recycles into good for all. Next, Stage 2 led him to tune in on the eternal rhythms of the sea and contemplatively become at one with these rhythms of Nature. And then he let himself also become aware of the eternal spiritual rhythm from God pounding into him, God's special child, made in God's image as a person. With Stage 3, Mitchel contemplated space and then let himself become aware of God's individual love, so great for him that it held the stars in their place for his well being, safety, and security in life on this little planet.

Then Mitchel undertook symbolically flying to the mountaintop or elevating to Level II, Stage 4 as it was then in its modified form (for the Schema has since undergone even further refinement, and this modification was less thorough than now). Such a high place has always seemed to be a major spot for mankind to meet his gods. In this place Mitchel let himself identify with being archetypally in the spiritual space in his own psyche where he could accept God's unconditional love placed upon him. Then I offered the Prayer of Commitment. This act always comes at the end of any use of the Faith Schema in order to *set* or channel the psyche into a safe, Christian context of experience. It was unnecessary to have Mitchel check out the question of "Who is in charge, you or I?" The question is for checking out the person's assurance that while he is in this intensified faith or elevated meditative state, he is in full control of his own will with the therapist as a trustworthy guide only. This check had been done in the first meditation session, and Mitchel had no doubt that I was guiding only, so we proceeded to the use of the therapeutic imagery.

I asked Mitchel to imagine the Forest of Life with the Sacred Circle, with beautiful green grass and no scrub brush in the middle. And in the middle of that was the Knoll of Worship, which though it was conceived of as a natural phenomenon was also somewhat like an Indian mound because it was flat on top. This knoll was also envisioned as about as high as the treetops and had the Light of God's Presence, (though to the client it is not generally identified as such by the therapist) shining down on the knoll's flat top like a spotlight with an invisible source. These symbols tend to identify problem areas of life which then may be therapeutically corrected. One may correct revealed weak points by having the person imagine changing the symbols to a more healthy state. The theory is that this act of changing either builds or becomes a new brain-cell engram or psychic pattern which archetypally leads the client into an opportunity for healthier development. In this therapy this imaginal changing is conceived of as coupling imagination with *Logos-power*, that creative part of oneself residing within the Inner Self. The Inner Self is conceived as that part of God which is in every person and is Christlike in its creativity. This logos-power is construed as our image-making part of "the creative-person-thinking-feeling power of God."

As soon as Mitchel started to tell me the scene he imagined, his voice became very hushed. The pneumonia was not what was causing this tone. I had heard it before in many sessions; it was a client's voice when he was in the presence of *The Mysterium Tremendum et Facinans*. The forest was a huge unlogged and unending, pine forest with sunflowers growing in it and no breeze blowing anywhere. Also, Mitchel felt he knew someone else was there but didn't know who and neither saw nor heard anyone. But this type of forest is not a healthy forest for such a symbol because it is not very earthly life-supporting. Therefore, I had him use his logos-power to change it to one with more hardwood and undergrowth—one which could support more life as we know it.

He had no trouble doing this, and right away he heard birds singing and a squirrel chattering at him. With his strong self-determination, Mitchel immediately wanted to go up the knoll to investigate the strange light. But as he tried, he found that even in his imagination, it was too difficult. I thought perhaps he needed to imagine some type of person or thing to aid him because my therapist's insight-hunch was the Light was genuinely drawing him to it for rest's sake. So I made such a suggestion. He started to answer me, but something strange happened. Suddenly, Mitchel sat up, opened his one eye and looked around with a strange, startled gaze! Then looking at me said, "Did you say something?" I replied that I had not, but that sometimes people had this sort of experience in this therapy, and it was all right; he should just relax and allow his feeling to unfold. Mitchel seemed skeptical and was a bit reluctant to close his eye and re-enter the experience. So I reminded him that just prior to his sitting up I had said, "it's" (and was going to tell him to do something imaginatively that could be therapeutic). But he insisted that he had heard somebody tell him firmly, "No!" However, Mitchel alleged that the voice did not say it with finality, only more like "maybe later" but not "not ever."

He seemed so sure that I felt he was hearing what Jung called "The Voice" as a psychological Self-symbol, but which with this therapy may also sometimes be subjectively experienced as the voice of God. In either such event "it" needed to take its course then since spontaneously appearing like this and be further interpreted later. So I told Mitchel that in this therapy this voice was probably within himself and was a normal experience of his own mind, perhaps forbidding him to climb. He insisted, however, the voice truly seemed to be from an *outer somebody*. Later in Post-therapy Work Check-out, he was to tell me he at first feared he was hallucinating.

I determined about then that it might be wise for him to come down out of the meditation. So I got him to close his eye and lean aback; instead, in this state of consciousness he wanted to go on toward the Light in spite of the "No!" It was still hard climbing, and I suggested he could imaginally just sit down on the side of the knoll, rest a minute, and then try to decide what he wanted to do. As he did this, he said something I could not understand and then asked me, "...Have you ever been in a mangrove swamp just before a tremendous storm?" This was what he was feeling, for something had made the forest and everything totally silent. There was Nothing!

By now I was more aware of the apparent presence of his numinous feelings and asked him if the experience had an ominous feeling about it. He said no, that the feeling was more oppressing. Frankly, I felt the total silence was a symbolic presence of God as Void-like or impending Enemy (indications of the experiential presence of God as cited by A. N. Whitehead). And I was afraid Mitchel was physically overdoing himself. So I stressed to him that I thought it would be good now to come back down the knoll and rest instead. But typical of his strong will, imaginarily he tried to jump up and force himself on, but again it was too difficult. Therefore, I tried again to persuade him to come down the knoll, but he then determined on his own just to sit there. I tried to persuade him to sit there only and let himself become less sensitive to the threatening or oppressing feeling. My hope in doing this was to get him to some restful psychic state.

However, after a long silence, Mitchel broke in and said, "I felt a comforting love." I sensed it indeed may have been God expressing His/Her love to Mitchel, for he certainly was in need of it in order to obtain some rest. Then Mitchel noticed a bluejay squawking somewhere and "something else." He next became aware it was now all right to stay where he was but felt a need to be cautious. Again he was aware of a feeling that this was far enough for now. He then momentarily lost his imagery and seemed distressed about the loss.

Suddenly he said, "I feel like it's—somebody is with us. It's just like somebody was talking in my head, though. It's weird!" By now I personally felt assured "it" was God speaking to him and that Mitchel needed only to accept the fact of being comforted and loved and come back down out of the meditation. But as I was speaking of his being spoken to and restrained by a kind voice, Mitchel suddenly again sat bold upright and opened his eye! This time he carefully visually searched over the room. I asked him what had happened and what he was aware of now. And in an incredulous whisper he said, "Somebody said, 'Good!' That's enough for now!'" At this point I too sat up straight, leaned toward him—not without some awe myself—and asked him to repeat his whispered words. Mitchel again told me what he had heard, and that he knew it was not my voice because "it was the *same voice*." I remarked on the fact that all this sounded as though it were a good experience for him. This time he leaned back and closed his eye without having to be encouraged. Immediately he began to talk of the visual presence of the maple tree (his Tree of Life symbol which in the previous meditations had spontaneously occurred twice) being like one film transparency laid over another. This Tree was thus alternately overlaying his knoll experience and giving him some confusion in perceiving the *voice*.

However, he next added that it was all right because the deeper loved sensation was more powerful and had profoundly impressed him as though with a sensory experience. He not only felt loved but also comforted even to the point of sensing that he was being rubbed on the neck with warm acceptance. Then he added that he really felt good and that "everything [is] coolness inside."

Again Mitchel sat up, opened his eye, and expressed his need to quit leaning back and sit up. His lung fluid build-up was getting hard to take without sitting up so he could cough better. So I asked him if he wanted to come down out of the meditation mood, and he said he did. I immediately had him close his eye, and we deschematized the Intensified Faith mind mood, coming back to his usual level of consciousness functioning. The Deschematizing Exercise involved use of Usual Positive Ideas which are pre-fabricated concepts given the client with his prior approval. They allow the client to claim additional, immediate help in the unconscious but in Mitchel's current state were very condensed and shortened in order to quickly return him to his usual state of awareness. When asked to open his eye and sit up he really looked about the room with skepticism, amazement, and confusion. He seemed to be searching for someone else to be in the room where only the two of us were.

I paused a bit so he could better orient himself and then commented that he had had an interesting experience. After another long pause, in which I sensed he was really feeling a bit unsure within, I asked if he preferred to interpret his experience himself or to have me offer my understanding. (THIS OFFERING OF INTERPRETATION OF THE NON-RATIONAL ELEMENTS OF THIS THERAPY IS VITAL; OTHERWISE, A CLIENT IS LEFT IN CONFUSION.) He admitted that he was pretty confused, and I sensed he was having a somewhat slight aftereffect, an experience not unusual for a person with such natural capacities for profound elevated meditative abilities. So I reminded him of this same effect from his prior meditations and reassured him the confusion would clear shortly, and he told me it was clearing even then.

As I was further explaining that aftereffect confusion is not dangerous and is a limited simultaneous experience of both *inner* and *outer* world perception, he suddenly began to talk of his experience. Mitchel had been profoundly moved by the fact that in the knoll experience, as he sat there, somebody had said, "Good!" Then all he had been able to see was the forest trees, but he felt "comforted" and as if he had done "all right, or uh—." He seemed to be searching for exactly the right way to express his feelings so I suggested that perhaps he felt accepted, and while this seemed partially true, he still seemed to search. Then I added the suggestion that maybe he felt approval (confirmation) was the right word. He immediately pounced upon this term as exactly the one he sought. And his face lit up.

Next, he asked me if all he had experienced had "some significance or something?" I assured him it did, for I was speaking of such when I offered the explanatory interpretation of his experience. But before we could get into it, he remarked that he felt really weak, and I had to explain first that such weakness was often experienced by good meditators who had just done a lot of therapy *work* in this type of meditation. But I also felt his weakness was a legitimate tiredness due to his pneumonia, fatigue he had not been consciously able to let himself feel until the therapy procedure. I explained that this was exactly what I had hoped the Meditation Therapy experience would do for him—put him in touch with his body's tiredness so he could relax and later rest. He remarked that when he got sick he tended to become "real hyper like that." But now he was so relaxed he felt he could go home and sleep several days straight.

In spite of his illness and condition, Mitchel seemed to become excited by the concept of what could be done with the Imaginal Function and told me that changing his Forest had even brought an immediate, cooling breeze (God's breath, the pneuma?). Then I began to talk of the ancient meaning of the magic (sacred) circle which represents—in the middle of the life forest—the central peaceful feeling of God in our inner core and our place of contacting Divinity in life. And I added that even children, age three , the world over draw a circle as their first form. I went on to describe how at that age they next draw a plus-mark and then radials, and when one puts them all together he has a mandala-like centering and enclosing of consciousness and its healthy functioning. Mitchel affirmed this right away, for he had noted it in his three-year-old son. Next I pointed out how apparently using this (sun wheel archetype from the paleolithic age) mandala as the circle of safety in the life forest represented a healing dimension which was usable in this therapy. I added that the center of this healing, mental symbol was represented by the gods' high place of the central knoll with God symbolized there as Light.

I added that I thought it was the pulling force (valence-like) of this Light which had made him immediately want to climb, and he agreed. But I added that I thought his tiredness had begun to manifest itself physically at this time and was the reason the climb seemed hard. Right there, he disagreed with me. He said he had not been aware of being tired "until somebody said, 'No!' It was like I was excited or something!" His demeanor registered his disappointment. I reminded him that it was then he had the feeling of being in a swamp. He assured me that after that he had not wanted to go back down the knoll but wanted just to sit there instead. I told him that I felt he had not wanted to go back down because of the Voice. I also told him I thought the voice was God's, coming from his Self center. (This was an offering to him of my personal insight and was something he did not have to accept. For as stated, I had already agreed with him that in all respect to his agnosticism, I would always *share* with him my own particular religious views and interpretations. Therefore, I was in no way falsely trying to influence him.)

At this, Mitchel suddenly, strongly affirmed, "It was as distinct as if you said it yourself!" He again affirmed it was the same voice that had also told him, "*No!*" But when the voice said, "*Good,*" he had also felt comforted by it, and he again stated that he himself had received a personal feeing of confirmation from hearing the voice. At this point, I again explained how from clients' experiences I believed God personally *did* speak to us in this way; the Divine made direct contact with us through the Self. Although Jung, as a psychiatrist, would only affirm it as a psychological reality, he still held that the Voice as such was a verbal symbol of the Self; as the

God symbol it always spoke with profound authority and conviction. The concept, according to Jung, was that it was a communicating symbol of the Objective Psyche. Then I went on to explain
why I believed Mitchel's Tree of Life kept superimposing on the
knoll. This tree was sometimes also experienced as the father tree
and as such could also concomitantly appear because it, too, would
stand for God-like care and love. He was able to understand how
this symbol alternation could be true for him.

We went on a minute, elaborating on the goodness he had felt
with the voice experience and what it was perhaps trying to convey
concerning his need for care and rest. This again brought his attention to his current tiredness, and I further elaborated that the tiredness could also be due to the sort of chemical change in the blood
that usually seems to appear after about two hours of meditation. I
believe the change appeared after only a few minutes for him
because of his current condition. We briefly discussed how everybody could benefit to some degree from such experiences, if they
would try them.

As we talked, Mitchel began to get a profound, pensive look
indicating an insight. Suddenly, he said, "You know, I—I can't be
positive, but it seems like that was the same voice!" He then repeated to me an account of his once working under a car of his which
suddenly fell off the blocks upon him. As told to me before, he had
said only that he happened to look up and see the car falling as
though in slow motion. He decided that he was *not* going to die,
pressed upward with his hands in a supreme effort of will, lifted the
car some, turned his head sideways so it would not be crushed, and
then let the car back down on himself. It put a dent in his skull but
did not cause severe damage, though he did pass out from the pain.
The entire incident was witnessed by two policemen who happened
to be standing nearby, and one was able to lift slightly the car's
body weight by the bumper. But the other was able only to pull
Mitchel out from under by his heels before the other had to let go
of the weight. They got him to the hospital immediately and the
amazed doctors had chalked it up to one of those bursts of superhu-
man energy which sometimes come to people in life or death emer-
gencies.

I listened to Mitchel's account as though he had never told it to
me, for this time he said that just as the car had started falling, he
heard the same voice say, "Look!" Now he grew very excited. This

voice had caused him to notice the car's falling. When he finished, I told him he had not told me of the voice before. He snapped his fingers and said he had not remembered it until now and that it must have been hearing the sound of the voice again that caused him to remember it.

I believed him completely! His account had been too spontaneous, the story exactly the same, and too sincere for me to question. I was again filled with awe and told Mitchel that it seemed to me that he was a special person in God's sight for God to communicate so lovingly and caringly. Reminding him that I was a preacher and tended to interpret such incidences in this manner, Mitchel immediately kindly replied, "O.K.! Yeah, I understand!"

With this permission from him, I again explained to him the basic, underlying theory of the Guided Meditation dimension of Faith Therapy: if we were fortunate enough to have some genuine love like from his father and my parents—imperfect as that love had been—it gave us a basic paradigm for understanding some degree of dependency. In turn, that gave us a framework with which to understand such experiences of God's care, such as the one he had. We were then able to build upon this framework a higher love relationship with God which could enhance our present adult lives with meaning in spite of all our suffering. I added that even in his parents' craziness, they had apparently at least given him some needed love upon which he could build an awareness of God's type of person-parent love. Further, if we were to get to do more therapy work, he, like other clients had, might discover that he had heard God's voice very early in life—guiding him even then. To this Mitchel replied, "Could be!"

After the session Mitchel went home and indeed was able to relax and sleep for nearly forty-eight hours. The medicine now could do its work, and he recovered quickly from the pneumonia. Due to the pre-planned brevity of my stay at this particular counseling center, I was unable to follow completely all the way through with Mitchel on his therapy. But in the next few months he grew considerably in the positive aspects of his personality, was better able to relate to and interact with his wife, and more realistically cope with his life and work situation constructively. I never pushed the religious view of life at him, but simply continued to share. However, I do know he also privately went on to some more intense transcendent experience on the knoll, using his own power-

ful meditative experiences. Perhaps one of the most fulfilling incidents for me came one day when a fellow clergyman at the center
asked him if the Guided Meditation part of the Faith Therapy had
done him any particular good. Mitchel, looking intently into the
man's eyes with his own good one, very positively and without ran-
cor stated, "Well, now I believe in God!" That seemed to say it all
for me. Is not that what pastoral counselors are ultimately trying to
help people find, the inner peace of belief in God and Eternal
Goodness?

Chapter II

THE DIALOGICAL
COUNSELING METHOD

Origins and Orientations

This Faith Therapy technique of counseling through dialogue just grew up supportively beside the Guided Meditation with its Intensified Faith and Therapy Procedures because the whole therapy approach is by nature interactional. The counseling method construction simply flowed from the maturation of the whole approach. The manuscript's theory section, Part II, will cover the broader perspective of the counseling, so in this chapter I will largely give the component parts, concepts which were assimilated into the structure of the Dialogical Counseling Method. As is pointed out and further elaborated upon in Chapter V, "Theological Convictions," the counseling technique shaped itself around the sincere belief that Christian love is the center of any healing ministry of the Church. Later this concept of love was seen as a process pattern which was somehow intricately tied to faith and hope. Paul's explication of faith, hope, and love as outlined in I Corinthians 13 became the underlying and guiding illumination for the development of Dialogical Counseling.

The counseling method originated from an insight concerning the incident near the end of his ministry when Jesus called his disciples "friends" (John 15:15 RSV). This statement suggests that Christians are equals in relating to each other and should minister to the other in love. This idea was further amplified by Jesus's telling Peter to feed, i.e. lovingly take care of his sheep's growth (John 21:15-19 RSV). The ministering person was, therefore, also to have a loving pastoral orientation. He/she was to be a caretaker. Another early contribution to the development was the concept of the teacher, the rabbinical or educational function of pastoring, drawn from Christ's parting commission that the disciples go into all the world and teach his way of love (Matt. 28:19, 20 RSV). These scriptures formed the basic pastoral convictions that led to the pastoral counseling approach I called Christian Friendship Counseling.

However, this information represents only part of the background. The other part came from collaboration with Dr. John J. Eberhart. His psychiatric orientation was around love as the basic healer. Having started as primarily Freudian in approach, he had become increasingly Jungian because of what he felt was that school's more realistic view of the psyche; its beliefs allowed for some ultimate reality in spiritual matters. However, Eberhart found his theory of the counseling type of therapy best expressed in the purely psychoanalytic method of Sandor Ferenczi, a technique Eberhart had followed for some time. He called Ferenczi's technique Good Parenting.[1] These approaches formed the other major contributing insights in the origin of Dialogical Counseling.

Ferenczi's approach was to become personally and fearlessly involved with his patients. Such active participation was so radical in the early days of psychoanalysis that it almost caused Freud to break with Ferenczi. This innovative psychiatrist believed that in order to heal the patient, it was necessary to relate to him/her with the type of parental love and acceptance which was lacking in his/her infancy and childhood. This missing love was to be given therapeutically in a natural but wise, safe, and appropriately limited way.[2] From this idea of active participation grew other techniques in Dialogical Counseling. These practices are still central to this method, though some, like the good parenting, are prudently hidden or tacit. The reason for this subtlety is that generally speaking, most adults do not consciously want to be parented.

Ferenczi's method was also influential in the formation of Dialogical Counseling because it was extrovertive in procedure. The therapist was to move out and meet the client's problems. This outgoing approach fit both originators. From this concept of active participation grew the position that the therapist is to relate honestly to the client by being open and expressive. Additionally, the therapist needs to be willing to expose with discretion his own failures and weaknesses. When the therapist thus exposes his/her humanity, he/she accomplishes two necessary objectives: first, he/she reveals him/herself as believing in and living by his/her own awareness of God's grace; second, he/she proves to the client's unconscious that this intimate association is entirely different from the negativities of the early relationship of parent and child with its forbidding and unrealistic nature.[3] Whether this negative view of his/her childhood is actually valid or has been mentally constructed by the client is not necessarily that relevant in therapy work. The client's perception of childhood is how memory has processed and symbolized it and is thus real to him/her.[4] Some of his/her negative perception must now be unlearned. By traveling the client's unconscious route with him/her and helping one reenact the emotionally debilitating experiences of childhood, the therapist is able to provide the necessary good parenting in the present.

Good Parenting

The overall task of this approach to good parenting is two-fold. The first is to help unlearn the inadequate way of living assimilated in childhood, by dealing with the psychically predominating principle of repression. Repression in reasonable amounts is necessary to keep consciousness uncluttered. but repression is capable of being a very traumatizing, heavy handed, *law and order* force which can become so powerful that it shuts away the ease of life-energy flow from the instinctive life sources of the unconscious. The first phase of therapist orientation then is to reparent childhood's false law and order demand, thus enabling the unconscious sources of abundant life to become free to operate.[5] Second, the therapist is now ready to guide the client toward the next step: to lead the person to express this newly-released energy as growth toward its highest healthy expression in peak and meta-peak experiences. But this cannot be done unless one first tends to the "necessary substructure" of undoing false repression.[6] After the therapy work on repression is completed, the next goal becomes the task of helping the now freed client to fulfill the peak experience of simply being his/her best human self. With this opportunity for new individuality, the client now needs to awaken to the existential fact that one's highest expression of meaning *for* oneself is that he/she can be meaningful *to* him/herself in relation to community. He/she is to activate his/her *higher* social nature. One's personality can become meaningfully fulfilled by doubling back upon oneself in his/her uniqueness with a desire for service to humanity in a profound, ethical, and responsible way.[7]

In this growth context, a spiritually ministering therapist needs to keep in mind that human beings have a will-to-meaning for the entirety of life. The pains of existential anxiety easily fold in upon one since one lives and knows beyond the instincts. It is not enough to have meaning and purpose for daily and yearly living. One must find ultimate meaning in life itself. The counselor who uses this dialogical method will find that his/her psychotherapy, theology, and metaphysics meet as he/she strives to help clients separate and deal with both their neurotic and existential anxiety.[8] When doing reconstructive work, rather than crisis intervention, such an overall healing and growth-centered therapy is time-consuming. Therefore, this orientation, like that of a good parent centering on a child's long term development, refuses to set its goal upon quick returns. As in Freud's therapy work, the time needed is the time taken. Doing so assures the client of his/her individual human worth.[9]

Because of its good parenting orientation, Dialogical Counseling also takes into special consideration the concept of the transference. There is much controversy about this term's descriptive validity. Nevertheless, it is a reasonably accurate name, for the feelings involved are normal human emotions but which were only poorly handled in childhood growth. Jung described the transference as the projection upon the therapist of an image of one of the more powerful universal archetypes—the hero, goddess, wise old man, great earth mother, etc. In all probability the transference's true source can be found in these images. Using this approach and thus naming it enables the client to see the problem of these feelings in a more realistic, less threatening, and sometimes less embarrassing perspective, thereby giving greater ease in handling it.[10] On the non-archetypal level, Assagioli had an insight into how to handle the transference feelings. He held that the therapist is indeed fulfilling a parental function and so must be willing to accept this task of "protector, counselor, and guide." Therapist acceptance of this role was necessary to the task of helping the client develop autonomy. In Dialogical Counseling this technique is predominantly used in dealing with the transference because it meshes well with Ferenczi's overall approach of growing through the problem. Additionally the dialogical model tends to favor Assagioli's technique a bit because it seems to end therapy more realistically and agreeably. He believed the transference problem should not conclude in "termination" but in "resolution" with the new positive relationship continuing afterward. Therapist and client could choose to continue to retain the friendship and even become collaborators.[11] Jung's and Assagioli's methods of dealing with the transference are adequate for most cases in Faith Therapy, but much usual transference material is totally avoided because such feelings are typically placed upon God as Central Person both in Dialogical Counseling and Guided Meditation. However, if one encounters the transference in its more childish or psycho-sexual form, the slow, in-depth approach of Ferenczi's parenting model works better.[12] In this religion-centered counseling model, continuing awareness on the part of the client and therapist of the presence of the Transcendent Third helps greatly with transference problems. This growth therapy's basis is that God can help bring equilibrium in such cases if both therapist and counselee endeavor to be responsible toward Him/Her. Both strive to keep in mind that He/She is present in any crisis for the specific positive purpose of transforming this energy. God intends these problems ultimately and evolutionarily to become a part of a higher resolution of the energy, one which arrives archetypally from the unconscious, bringing with it good moral order.[13]

In all this work the therapist seeks to evidence his/her own faith in God as an attitude of encompassing transcendent optimism. The counselor helps him/herself as well as the client be aware that God is Friend. This expectation makes itself known as faith being born from the inner Self and strengthening the ego, conscious center, to know that God is a dynamic, imminent Presence who wills good—even beyond life's evils—and acts for good. This dynamic faith brings its counterpart, hope, which together can start the healing love-power flow.[14] Clients must be encouraged to envision life holistically as a meaningful experience. They need to be led to the faith that in each existential crisis there is a rebirth opportunity. However, this rebirth can occur only when they become attuned to the inner Self, for rebirth arrives "from the spirit."[15] Some such crises will be caused by the client's normal need to work through problems caused by growth. There are continuous stages and sub-stages of normal development in the biological life process of every person. These stages recently have been validated and shown to have certain characteristic crises at each transition point. It is wise for a therapist to be aware of these biologically determined stages so that he/she can consider their possible presence in the problems the counselee presents. Roughly, the findings indicate more severe negative stress times to come in the transition periods which are approximately from adolescence to early adulthood, ages 17-22; early adulthood to middle adulthood, ages 40-45; middle adulthood to late adulthood, ages 60-65.[16]

In Dialogical Counseling, even if done by a therapist who is not a member of the clergy, the position of counselor is unashamedly theistic.[17] However, this orienting affirmation is not dogmatically, or totally inflexible and acknowledges that God has meaningfully revealed Him/Herself to all people and all tend to have varying traditions of faith interpretation and value which they bring to the therapy session. The therapist honors a person's right to that sacred autonomy while insisting that the client, even if an atheist, acknowledge the counselor's autonomy in a similar manner as he/she declares his/her convictions in the therapy situation. As does Jung, the method holds the position that "The seat of faith...is not consciousness but spontaneous religious experience, which brings the individual's faith into immediate relation with God."[18] While this experience needs to have rational interpretation applied to it for conceptual clarity and understanding, the faith experience comes from unconscious sources and its feelings of certitude are acknowledged as self-validating for the counselee.[19] The position that there is an inner Self which is the source of this experience is also largely oriented around Jung's concept of the Self as both the center and circumference of the psyche.[20] However, this Self is envisioned as a *real* (not psychological only) spiritual entity, as in Psychosynthesis.[21] In Faith Therapy this center is sometimes also called the Soul-center, "God-spark,"* (See End Notes) or High Self; it is understood as the *imago Dei* and is eternal. The center is considered as beyond the ego and is superordinate to it, "a person-ality which we *also* are."[22] The therapist considers the client's Self as constructing an ego, a spatio-temporal extension which has eternal meaning. This ego is said to be developed by the Self in order to learn experientially value versus disvalue and order versus disorder for eternal life's sake. It is from this theological and metaphysical position that the therapist views the client's problems and their best resolution as of lasting importance. The ego and its character derived from life's experience is seen as assimilated back into the Self at death; that is, God's aim is that the ego is to be *saved*. For this reason, the inner Self is considered the source of transformation power for the ego's problems. In Dialogical Counseling the therapist depends upon this higher Self to lead the client ultimately toward growth, intended increasingly to orient his/her personality around this new Self-center.[23]

The religious process-oriented counselor needs to be particularly alert for the types of more intense spiritual growth problems and crises which develop in the middle-age period of life and are called by Assagioli "crises of spiritual awakening." These crises are caused by the Self beginning to press for the spiritual growth of the personality. Crises of this type are often deeply disturbing and produce seeming neuroses which can flood the ego with such spiritual power that inflation, depression, moral crises, and sometimes even delusions may occur in personalities who are without sufficient ego strength or adequate spiritual development. The therapist needs to be aware when this kind of crisis reveals itself, so he/she can recognize its type and guide the counselee through to an adequate resolution.[24] In essence this seems the same type of spiritual drive problem Jung also found as belonging to the second half of life. He referred to this drive principle as the process of individuation. Jung so named it because its purpose seemed to move one toward becoming a distinctively different yet spiritually deep person whose new center was the Self and not the ego, though the ego still maintained its task of keeping the person properly related to spatio-temporal or outer world reality.[25] A good acquaintance with Jung's observations concerning the Archetypes of Individuation is of immense help in guiding a client who is striving to deal with these spiritual drives. These archetypes, feeling-thought pictures or symbols, are superb indications to the therapist of the client's present unconscious condition. They are also of great help in dream analysis.[26]

Having briefly covered the major component parts contributed to this counseling methodology from its early psychiatric source (and some items which thereafter flowed from subsequent interest in this source field) we turn now to the other central source of Dialogical Counseling's components.

Christian Friendship Counseling

These contributions to the method grew out of pastoral convictions drawn from the teachings of Christ. It seemed to me that Christ's relational approach to people demanded a somewhat more active approach than was generally prevalent in pastoral counseling at the time the concepts forming Christian Friendship Counseling were shaped. Two major concepts contributed to the basic shaping. They were drawn together into the pastor who is a true friend and also a religious teacher, rabbi. *Friend* meant one who cares and relates to another as a close equal. *Pastor* meant one who embodies the full range of the Christian concept of the *rabbinical function* of the ordained, trained, and educated expression of Christian ministry. However, it must be kept in mind that this entire method of therapy praxis is not *confined* to clergy only, but also may be used by those who choose to express their Christian ministry this way and are otherwise qualified.

Pastor-Friend

At the heart of Dialogical Counseling was the theological concept of the pastor as a counselor/psychotherapist. There are certain qualities either lay people or clergy will need within him/herself to carry out the job successfully. To practice this method from the core of being, he/she needs to be one who knows and loves the things of God and that which is of God in every person. He/she is a shepherd type of person who recognizes the seamier side of life as somehow a part of God's beloved world. Such a servant of Christ needs to understand the spiritual crises which befall good people as they strive to grow in faith and to understand that all of life is somehow also encompassed by God's care. As a clergyperson this therapist endeavors to be aware of constantly living within a framework of divine grace, a continuing manifestation of God's unconditional love personified in Jesus Christ. The therapist's effectiveness is grounded in the fact that he/she is inwardly convinced that the primary goal of life is ultimate meaning—in, with, and through God.[27] For a pastor-therapist practicing this method, the foregoing conviction constantly orients him/her in every daily task. The entirety of Faith Therapy grew from professional awareness that clergy had as much responsibility for curing souls as did psychiatrists,[28] so this work is simply a special expression of ministry.

This type of clergy-therapist also needs to have a genuine concern to fill the pastoral role lovingly for the sake of society's needs. As a committed medical doctor must acceptably fulfill a social role, so does the pastoral counselor need to give of him/herself. This is not to suggest complying with an image falsely and rigidly but rather being openly a person of faith, providing society with those things that as a whole it hopes to receive from such a servant. In reality, this requirement is simply an appropriate and healthy pastoral persona, one which can be healthily slipped into for the sake of the comfort and need of others.[29] However, if one who practices this method lacks inner depth of commitment to God, it cannot be concealed. The counselee will quickly, tacitly perceive this void because his/her perceived need is for a counselor who is a person of God; he or she needs a *pastor*. The counselee's hope is for help from a human pastor first, then from a *psychotherapist*. In spiritual turmoil one needs a therapist who can mediate God's grace for him/her.[30]

This emphasis on fulfillment of the pastoral role does not mean the pastoral counselor is locked into a narrow existence with this mode of expression. As just indicated, the pastoral counselor extends this role into two other vital life-areas. Since there is a decided tendency for society to stereotype the clergy into a stuffy role, this pastor needs lovingly and subtly to disprove it. Not much meaningful interaction and mutual growth will take place if the stereotype is not eliminated or if the minister remains aloof, nearly super-human in the client's eyes. Although Dialogical Counseling was an extrovertive method in origin, this fact does not confine the counseling to use by extrovertive therapists. An easygoing and warm personal approach to the client can be used by the clergyperson or another whether he or she is an extrovert or not. The pastoral therapist takes the initiative in breaking down barriers. He/she moves toward establishing equal friendship by striving to get the entire relationship on a first name basis immediately. In this

method, use of titles, whatever their cause or origin, only furthers
fear and alienation. The Dialogical Counseling therapist endeavors
to arrive at the point of common humanity with a client.[31] Here the
aim is for pastor and counselee to come to *know* one another first as
friends, then as counselor and client.[32]

Pastor-Teacher (Rabbi)

The second tributary of Christian Friendship Counseling is the
pastor as rabbi or teacher. Teaching does not mean preachy lectur-
ing, but it does mean the pastor-therapist is properly qualified to
use the authority vested in him/her by the Church. As much as possible, the therapist needs to be theologically prepared to explain
things of a perplexing religious nature, just as though he/she were
pastoring a church. A client who is given help in acquiring needed
theological and/or related metaphysical information can often get
many insights into his/her own problems, thus increasing self-
esteem. While such authority has been vested in a pastor by the
Church and society, he/she will wisely go no further with such
direction than is needed to aid a client who personally grants that
authority in trust. This trust requires the therapist not to take an
authoritarian approach. The counselor may, however, proceed
authoritatively with the client and thereby relationally hope to give
over to him/her the authority of the counselor's pastoral convictions about God as seen in Christ.[33] In the personal interaction the
client will perceive that the therapist can love and accept him/her-
self as the "*object* of His/Her transforming grace." Because the therapist constantly tries to live in this consciousness, or frame of reference, his/her life is centered within faith, hope, and love; this
lifestyle will be a model. In relating with the client, the counselor
will evidence that life is to be centered practically in relating to
God. This fact will be reflected in the shared realities of the counselor's life as "neither private nor otherworldly." It is a social and
ethical approach to life that is fulfilling now and reaches forward to
a future as God wills. This "lived faith" is the true authority for
teaching one to live a vital, dynamic existence. It is the greatest gift
the pastoral therapist offers the counselee.[34]

The Dialogical Approach Further Discussed

Good Parenting Therapy and Christian Friendship Counseling joined as a medical psychology and a pastoral counseling method and became Dialogical Counseling. The personal interaction which informed and steered the Guided Meditation part of the entire therapy method became greatly clarified and enhanced by the relational insights put forward by Martin Buber. Buber taught that God, the Eternal Thou, who is person but greater than person—indeed is even Absolute Person—forms us all as spiritual Thous through relationship. If the inner Self and Thou concepts are viewed as equivalent, then what was being observed in both the meditation and counseling parts of the therapy began to bear out Buber's theory. This Soul-center seemed always in some sort of connection/relation with God and also seemed constantly seeking to grow in power to have a positive effect upon the ego, the spatio-temporal center of usual awareness. In this understanding, person seemed to belong to both God and people.[35] This concept of God and people as alike in some measure certainly makes it clearer for clients to build for themselves an intelligible therapy construct. Because they experience themselves as a person, they can with some ease also understand God as the Eternal Thou and Absolute Person who calls them into being in relationship. The concept is fairly easy to grasp because a person's first awareness of his/her individual centrality of being is manifest through the person nature in the mother-child interaction.

From the absolute existence of the Thou-world, God creates the It-world of space and time. In this object world our ego and personality are built because the spirit can enter this world and change it.[36] The theological paradigm of Faith Therapy takes the position that God personally and physically encountered and related to the It-world as the "I" (ego) of His Jesus-ness flowing from the special Thou (Soul-center) of His Christ-ness. Jesus Christ was and is that special commitment God made of Him/Herself from His/Her absoluteness into the process world of space-time, an evolutionary pattern to bless and aid us in our growth encounters. At some point in the counseling process it will become necessary to present the client with this position as the background theological and metaphysical orientation of the whole therapy method. This type of intimate relating greatly reduces fear and anxiety, and such open-ness enhances personal problem solving capacities, further improv-ing self-image. The entire therapy process is conceived of as simul-taneously working in the polar relations of the Thou and It worlds. When we conceive of a person's Thou self as the eternal inner Self and his/her I self as the It-world spatio-temporal ego, we are in a position to encounter and relate healthily to a client.[37] The thera-pist must be able to *see with the eyes of Christ* into the client's Self where potential health for the disturbed ego resides. The therapist does this in emulation of Jesus as he looked into the soul of Mary Magdalene. While acknowledging the real negatives of the It-world in her ego, Jesus saw her Thou which was intended to become more evident. He saw her in her total polarity and called forth into space-time being the greater and more positive expression. She thus became St. Mary of Magdala. Buber calls this process of seeing the Thou and relating to the I as if it were the Thou "imagining the real" in another person.[38] The therapist may help a client's more positive dimension of being become reality in space-time by seeing the potential for this positive existence. This I-Thou mode of relating to all that is, is man's most basic epistemological method. This dialogue is man's way of knowing all things in a holistic approach. But truly to know a client the therapist must keep in mind that there must be an interplay on the part of the counselee and him/herself. The relating must flow between I-Thou and I-It and back again (repeated distancing and relating), but remembering that to relate only in the world of It is to use another and "not be a *man* [*person*] at all."[39] If the counselor treats a client as an ego only the therapist reduces the client to an object, violating the basic position of this counseling method.

To avoid this sort of reduction of a counselee, the therapist must "image" the realness of the Thou of the client in a Christlike man-ner. If the effort is successful, both counselee and counselor will be in a situation in which the therapist's empathy will allow him/her to feel the depth of the other's emotion and being. Although there is the interplay of the distancing and relating of the two in this situa-tion, they are not, however, lost in union. The therapist sees the real good and bad polarities which are present. He/she does not avoid seeing the client's negativities, but by realistic choice, holds to the belief in the ultimate good within the client, even if sometimes the bad wins out. Such is the therapist's risk in this method with its in-depth relating to others, where one works in loving trust and optimism rather than constant despair and pessimism.[40] Buber has called this sort of relating to another "confirming" that person. This realistic but optimistic acceptance of another in his/her total good/evil polarity preserves the client's right to be in the relationship—even if for some reason the client must be opposed. Thus *confirming* someone goes a step beyond *affirming*.[41] In this sense, confirming one is the way God treats us as sinners. "He/She confirms us in our right to be here in this life and be sinners—that is, not be able to be the more perfect thing we can see and even *sometimes* want to be."[42] The confirming therapist emulates the Person nature of God and His/Her grace-filled love given the world.[43]

Buber's work contributed further to this method. It took its name from what Buber referred to as the "dialogical method." The name Dialogical Counseling Method precisely designates the final distilled construct. As with Buber's dialogical method, the speaking in Dialogical Counseling must be honest, holding nothing back surreptitiously.[44] The counselor and client must build up a common world of understanding between them. Such speaking is in accord with the "thoroughly sensuous living speech" which Heraclitus taught was the "word common to all, speech-with-meaning, logos," which all men understand from within.[45] This type of vocal communication is needed for mutual depth understanding between client and therapist as they interact in the Intensified Faith's Guided Meditation and Therapy Procedures. Such speaking simply means they are communicating freely, openly, and spontaneously, following life-logic, using feeling-thought, (terms clarified in Chapter VI) and as much as possible envisioning with archetypal imagery. The counselor will be aware that the communicating is actually taking place in "the between" of the client and therapist when they are in dialogue. Therefore, it is vital to realize that both speak and both listen. The dialogue is a shared living process, not primarily a technique of listening and clarifying only.[46] In the midst of this, both will sometimes sense the presence of the Transcendent Third in this space of "the between."

The sort of in-depth knowing that goes on in this dialogical method involves great mutual trust. In some measure at times this open and spontaneous living communication seems somewhat mystical, not sounding very coherent to others. The total object is mutual loss into knowing communication between therapist and counselee. Here again the therapist takes the initiative of striving to establish such a common language for them both by moving toward use of the client's *version* of the common tongue they both speak (to the degree the therapist's standards permit). This is an additional means of confirming the client and eliminating barriers between them. Sometimes this means that *the preacher's language isn't so preacherly* if we judge by some social standards of what is proper rather than that which establishes a common bond between two people. However, if the counselor is successful in establishing such a dialogue, he/she will be rewarded by the client's beginning to trust the therapist with any "crazy" thoughts and feelings. These are matters which before now the counselee had been too inwardly frightened and secretive to share with another. Such lack of defensiveness indicates the therapist has accomplished the dialogical goal.

Other Accoutrements

Often a client who is having difficulty initially conceptualizing and stating his/her problem can be helped to do so. The therapist invites the client to use the device of circumambulation, or "beating around the bush." This method takes pressure off the client. As the client describes his/her problem many relevant aspects may be illuminated, and the therapist may detect the basic patterns as well. This method is not to be misconstrued as a sort of free floating directionless approach; rather it is a non-linear method of arriving at the source of a problem. This strategy follows in reverse manner, the abstract and archetypal growth pattern evident in many places in nature, and thus it seems to aid the client in presenting the counselor with a holistic description of what is troubling him/her.

In the process of all Dialogical Counseling, the therapist needs to make notes of *triggers* for use in the Guided Meditation dimensions of the therapy. Triggers are situations, insights, memories, or dreams with strong, disturbing, negative affect charges. However, it is best to make the list of triggers in final form for therapy work by using the client's own images and words. The final notations can best be done—with client approval—as the initial counseling is being concluded in a session but before the related Guided Meditation is begun. These triggers will be worked with in the Guided Therapy Procedures by using Crisis Intervention Techniques, Special Positive Ideas, or Creative Symbolization Methods. In the prior counseling the therapist will need to stay alert for insights into such emotionally debilitating factors as the client expresses them in the interaction.

A very important item in the counseling will be the therapist's directive task of rational explication, an important rabbinic function. Our God is the God of reason as manifested in space-time, so it is the job of the ministering therapist to help a client strive ultimately to find reason even in the so called *non*-rational, that which at times seems the *irr*ational. Human need for ultimate meaning forces this point; the dedicated ministering Christian therapist needs to be prepared to help a client fulfill this soul hunger.

The longing for understanding usually will make itself known in two ways: first through the desire for metaphysical-theological explanation of the problems of life in general and those of the client in particular. In order to best meet what is hoped for here, the Dialogical Counseling therapist needs to consider that we understand God in a limited, paradoxical way. In some manner He/She is the Mysterious Absolute, but God has also at the same time committed something special of Him/Herself into the spatio-temporal process.[47] The mystery of the Absolute remains exactly that— though He/She may be thus experienced through Guided Meditation's Intensified Faith Schema, there is nothing beyond this *faith-knowing* but revelation and speculative fantasy, so far as this methodology can probe. However, process thinking reveals much to us about God and reason as known in space-time, culminating in the life of Jesus Christ.[48] More can be understood of God and reason if one views reason as serving the forces of life. First, reason manifested itself as *practical (pragmatic) reason* to serve species survival. Then reason transformed itself so as to criticize itself and became *speculative reason* which opens new and more satisfying choices that life may advance fulfillingly.[49] Practical reason may be roughly paralleled to what we mean by the quality of God known as Mother Nature. Speculative reason may be viewed in a similar manner. It is a quality of the God the Father/Mother exponent who historically came into His/Her fullness in spatio-temporal, Person development. Then He/She most completely and intimately revealed Him/Herself to us in Jesus Christ, who embodies His/Her ultimate intentionality.

The second point at which the client will manifest need for understanding is through presentation of dreams. Relatively recently, neuroscience has uncovered the somatic source of this interpretive need; it is no longer a *hypothetical* psychotherapeutic function. Many early learned unconscious problems are presented for solution in dream and symbol form. They have been locked into current adult behavior by the brain's childhood interaction with the environment. The brain's information processing through the limbic system, hippocampus, and prefrontal cortex establishes lasting behavior patterns which evidence themselves in dreams occurring in REM (rapid eye movement) sleep. Such sleep is characterized by the brain's theta rhythm, a rhythm evolutionarily developed in the problem solving activity of mammals but specifically present in human sleep.[50] (It is also of special note that theta rhythm is one of the major components of Guided Meditation and therefore important to the Dialogical Counseling process in rationally interpreting reality.)

Both the Freudian and Jungian methods of dream interpretation are viable, the Freudian for its psycho-sexual maturity information and the Jungian for its spiritual personality growth indications. Also, there will be times when some dreams and visionary experiences will have only a rational explanation if considered from the parapsychological or Christian spiritualist viewpoint. Since this therapy model is admittedly theological and metaphysical in orientation, the ministering therapist will find persons turning to him/her for help in gaining a reasonable explanation for such unusual human transpersonal psychic experiences, but the therapist will also need to be cautious that such experiences are not hallucinatory or delusional. However, many sane people harbor such non-psychotic experiences, failing to share them or search for any reason in them for fear they will be thought crazy by those who hear them—especially some who work in the mental health field.

Growth group therapy is also very helpful in this counseling method toward offering rational explanation of difficult questions. From early existence we are both one-to-one and one-to-group people, the experience originating in the matrix of self-to-mother and self-to-family relations. Thus it is important experientially to learn in both circumstances. More intimate matters can best be dealt with in private sessions and the more common material in public with the groups. Group sessions more easily allow the therapist to use teaching techniques part of the time. Also, this will increase insight and understanding in private sessions because concepts and vocabulary have been explained more thoroughly. In addition, if psychological tests are being used and if the results are mutually shared (read within the group—the ministering therapist's included), God's grace experienced through group acceptance becomes more real. The Birkman Method is one such personality inventory which seems to be ideally suited to this purpose and also to the entire therapy method. The individual test returns also include the client's highly significant conscious *and* unconscious personality component statistics which offer powerful help in private sessions.[51] A number of personality inventories may be suited for such use as well as different types of growth groups may be utilized for this teaching and social learning experience. The individual therapist will need to determine the type of group to be used with the decision based on individual group needs and the therapist's ability to work freely with a particular type of group.

Professor James W. Fowler recently made the vital discovery that faith develops in stages. There are six hierarchical and sequential stages. While transitional periods between stages are sometimes disturbing periods, in general the stages themselves offer more stability in one's life and faith. Some of the crises of these transitional growth periods could bring believers to practitioners of this therapy method because of its also being oriented around help in problems of faith growth. The ministering therapist is most needed at such times of faith crises and struggles for growth.[52]

Surroundings

A comfortable ambience is very effective if not necessary for this type of therapy. The client sits in a reclining chair during meditations and may perhaps also recline partially during Dialogical Counseling. (The therapist may also recline as much as seems appropriate, keeping in mind that mutual eye level makes a great deal of difference for some clients and therapists.) The meditation is greatly facilitated by the client's being in a partially supine position. Muscle relaxation and mental receptivity is more complete, and the intensification of the faithing ability is enhanced causing guided therapy work to be more productive.[53] A recliner is a more effective choice than a couch because the chair does not allow the counselee to slip into sleep quite as easily and thereby to disturb his alpha-theta brain wave pattern needed for the better Guided Meditation.

A Recommendation

Since this therapy model is religiously oriented the therapist, if a pastor, does well to close the session by subtly laying on hands and praying with the client. This ancient ritual may be done unobtrusively while praying by holding both hands of a woman or by continuing a handshake and grasping the forearm of the same hand of a man. This act is taken seriously as a symbolic ritual from the long tradition of the church. The gesture certainly fills a touch need, but it also is a vehicle of power. Many times both persons experience the Transcendent Third in "the between." This act is highly meaningful to most clients. However, if the privilege of a closing prayer is sought and yet denied (as sometimes happens), this pastor accepts the refusal as an expression of a client's special needs. Rejection is the risk one runs when extending him/herself toward anyone in need. Very few clients however, refuse or prefer the ordained minister not to pray, and most of those who deny the privilege for themselves have absolutely no objection if the pastoral therapist asks to pray for God's guidance in the therapy process for him/herself. The few who are unyielding will express their preference with understanding of the pastor's subjective position. No clients have ever seemed to take offense about being asked to enter into prayer, and many will give expressions of gratitude for going before God together. A mutually fulfilling and enriching experience, this act of joint prayer redirects transference feelings—strange and powerful numinous activity occurs.

A Concluding Note

Since this method of relational pastoral counseling was first conceived of as a ministry for the Church, presently it generally needs to be seen as a "subdiscipline" of ministry as a whole. It is obviously a specialization within the broader concept of the religious vocation. The method's major thrust is not "cheap psychotherapy" but more one of spiritual growth facilitation.[54] The focal point of this ministering counseling method is one of meaningful interpretation of life's disorienting experiences, offering understanding to clients which enables them to reconceptualize life in a holistic metaphoric structure. Thus a counselee experiences him/herself to be part of a "battleground of titanic forces" and linked to suprapersonal powers. This cosmic participation concept is highly significant for religious growth and healing.[55]

NOTES

[1] Dr. John J. Eberhart led the author into the concepts of Sandor Ferenczi as seen through the experience of one of his disciples, who also had trained under Erich Fromm. Eberhart loaned the book to me, and I was to find it a powerful resource for pastoral counseling. The book is Izette de Forest, *The Leaven of Love* (New York: Harper and Brothers, 1954).

[2] Izette de Forest, *The Leaven of Love* (New York: Harper and Brothers 1954), pp. xi-14. See also, Brenda Schaeffer, *Is It Love or Is It Addiction?* (New York: Harper and Row, 1987), pp. 3, 4, *passim*.

[3] *Ibid.*, pp. 15-131, *passim*. See also, Martin Stanton, *Sandor Ferenczi: Reconsidering Active Intervention* (Northvale, New Jersey: Jason Aronson Inc., 1991), pp. 135-141.

[4] Jean Piaget and Barbel Inhelder, *Memory and Intelligence* (New York: Basic Books, 1973), pp. 1-26.

[5] Erich Fromm, *Psychoanalysis and Religion* (New Haven, Conn.: Yale University Press, 1950), pp. 97, 98.

[6] Abraham H. Maslow, *Religious Values and Peak-experiences* (New York: Viking Press, 1970), p. 7.

[7] Viktor E. Frankl, *The Doctor and the Soul* (New York: Alfred A. Knopf, 1955), pp. 80-88.

[8] *Ibid.*, pp. IX-XXI, 213-215. See also, Gerald D. May, *Addiction And Grace* (San Francisco, 1988), pp. 64, 65.

[9] Fromm, *Psychoanalysis*, p. 98.

[10] C. G. Jung, "The Transcendent Function," in *The Portable Jung*, trans. by R. F. C. Hull, ed. by Joseph Campbell (New York: Viking Press, 1971). pp. 273-300. See also, C. G. Jung, *Analytical Psychology: Its Theory*

and Practice (New York: Random House, 1968), pp. 151-204.

[11] Beverly Besmer, "An Interview with Roberto Assagioli," "Psychosynthesis: Height Psychology—Discovering the *self* and the *Self*" (New York: Psychosynthesis Research Foundation, 1975), pp. 21, 22.

[12] de Forest, *The Leven*, pp. 20-75, *passim*.

[13] C. G. Jung, *Modern Man in Search of a Soul*, trans. by W. S. Dell and Carey F. Baynes (New York: Harcourt, Brace and World, 1933), pp. 193-95, 200, 242.

[14] Frances G. Wicks, *The Inner World of Choice* (New York: Harper and Row, 1963), pp. 297-311.

[15] Frankl, *The Doctor*, pp. 213-15.

[16] Daniel J. Levinson, *et. al.*, *The Seasons of a Man's Life* (New York: Alfred A. Knopf, 1978), pp. 3-39, ff.

[17] The position taken regarding *non-clergy* practice of Faith Therapy, in its entirety, is that the psychotherapist, additionally should have a reasonably good working acquaintance with theology and metaphysics, and have a sense of *call* or commitment to the field of *ministry* as his/her vocational orientation.

[18] C. G. Jung, *The Undiscovered Self*, trans. by R. F. C. Hull (New York: New American Library, 1957), p. 100.

[19] Ibid., pp. 101-03. See also, C. G. Jung, *Psychology and Religion* (New Haven, Conn.: Yale University Press, 1938), pp. 113, 114.

[20] Jolande Jacobi, *The Psychology of C. G. Jung*, (New Haven: Yale University, 1962), p. 125.

[21] Roberto Assagioli, "Dynamic Psychology and Psychosynthesis," (Greenville, Del.: Psychosynthesis Research Foundation, 1959), pp. 1-8.

*The term "God-spark" is a vital part of this Therapy's Crisis Intervention Technique's "Key-word Desensitizing Exercise" where the self-command word "Kindle" is used to image the *imago Dei* as re-energized by Christ. Its original concept dates back to the metaphysics of Leibniz and is neither divinely reductionistic nor Gnostic. Use of the term will be fully explicated in Part II, Chapter VI.

[22] Jacobi, *The Psychology*, pp. 125-28, ff.

[23] Assagioli, "Dynamic," pp. 8-20.

[24] Roberto Assagioli, "Self-realization and Psychological Disturbances," (Greenville, Del.: Psychosynthesis Research Foundation, 1961), pp. 1-22.

[25] Frieda Fordham, *An Introduction to Jung's Psychology*, 3rd ed. (Baltimore: Penguin Books, 1966), pp. 76-80.

[26] For a brief but thorough explication of the Archetypes of Individuation, their accompanying process, and their results within and upon the psyche, see Jacobi, *The Psychology*, pp. 103-47. Additional help may be obtained by reading John A. Sanford, *Dreams: God's Forgotten*

Language (New York: Crossroads, 1984). *Passim.*

[27] Wolfhart Pannenberg, *Metaphysics and the Idea of God*; trans. by Philip Clayton (Grand Rapids, MI: William B. Eerdmans, 1990), pp. 165-70.

[28] C. G. Jung *Modern Man*, pp. 221-44.

[29] Jacobi, *The Psychology*, pp. 26-30.

[30] See also Carrol A. Wise, *Pastoral Psychotherapy* (Northvale, NJ: Jason Aronson, 1983), pp. 175-77.

[31] Carl R. Rogers, *Becoming a Person* (Austin, Texas: University of Texas, 1956), pp. 1-7.

[32] See also, James W. Fowler, *Stages of Faith: The Psychology of Human Development and the Quest for Meaning* (New York: Harper and Row, 1981), p. 185.

[33] Stanley C. Russell, M.D., *Mental Illness: A Conceptual Model*, Prepublication Manuscript (Jackson, Miss.: University of Miss. Medical Center, 1986), pp. 4-10.

[34] Albert C. Outler, *Psychotherapy and the Christian Message* (New York: Harper and Brothers, 1954), pp. 180, 181.

[35] Martin Buber, *I and Thou*, trans. by Ronald Gregor Smith, 2nd ed.; (New York: Charles Scriebner's Sons, 1958), pp. 131-37.

[36] Ibid., pp. 100, 101.

[37] *Ibid.*, pp. 83-90.

[38] Maurice S. Friedman, *Martin Buber* (New York: Harper and Brothers, 1955), pp. 60, 61.

[39] Friedman, "Introductory Essay." pp. 11-25.

[40] Martin Buber, "Distance and Relation," in *The Knowledge of Man*, trans. by Maurice Friedman and Ronald Gregor Smith, ed. by Maurice Friedman (New York: Harper and Row, 1965), pp. 59-71.

[41] *Ibid.*, pp. 70, 71. For further enlightenment on the dialogue between Carl Rogers and Martin Buber concerning the affirming and confirming concepts, the reader is referred to the book's "Appendix" for the verbatim transcript found on pages 166-84.

[42] This quote is taken verbatim from Chapter III. "The Intensified Faith Schema".

[43] Buber, *I and Thou*, pp. 135-37.

[44] Buber, "Elements of the Interhuman," in *Knowledge*, pp. 72-86 ff.

[45] Buber, "What is Common to All," in *Knowledge*, pp. 89-98-104 ff.

[46] Buber "The Word that is Spoken," in *Knowledge*, pp. 110-112 ff.

[47] Pannenberg, *Metaphysics*, pp. 41, 42.

[48] A good in-depth insight survey into this more recent development in theology may be gained by reading the book, *Process Theology; Basic Writings*, ed. by Ewert H. Cousins (New York: Newman Press, 1971).

[49] This concept of reason is well explicated by Alfred North Whitehead

in his book, *The Function of Reason* (Boston: Beacon Press, 1929), *passim*.

[50] Johathan Winson, *Brain and Psyche: The Biology of the Unconscious* (New York: Vintage, 1985) pp. 241-43.

[51] More and in greater detail will be said about this unique test in Part II, The Theory Framework.

[52] James W. Fowler, *Stages of Faith: The Psychology of Human Development and Quest for Meaning*, (San Francisco: Harper and Row, 1981), *passim*. I believe it imperative that the Dialogical Counselor be familiar with Fowler's theory. It will help greatly with faith-growth problems. His more recent relevant publication *Faith Development and Pastoral Care*, Philadelphia: Fortress Press, 1987) is even more helpful for a pastoral counselor.

[53] Authur Deikman, "Bimodal Consciousness," in *The Nature of Human Consciousness*, ed. by Robert E. Ornstein (San Francisco: W. H. Freeman, 1973), pp. 68, 69.

[54] John Patron, *Pastoral Counseling: A Ministry of the Church*, (Nashville: Abingdon, 1983), pp. 10, 11.

[55] Jerome D. Frank, *Persuasion and Healing: A Comprehensive Study of Psychotherapy*, Revised ed. (New York: Schacken Books, 1974), p. 232.

Chapter III

∾

THE INTENSIFIED
FAITH SCHEMA EXERCISE

A Brief Glimpse of Its Theory and Practice

The Intensified Faith Schema Exercise lifts one into the special psyche state of consciousness in which the Guided Meditation Therapy Procedures are carried out. One of the best answers to how this consciousness elevation occurs comes from the French psychotherapist, Robert Desoille, who offers a very thorough explanation of the power in language. His understanding of the psychotherapeutic efficacy of his Guided Daydream Technique was not even clear to himself until the relatively recent translation and release of the later work of the great Russian psychologist, I. P. Pavlov, and his disciples. Pavlov's work indicates that humans, unlike other animals, have two signal systems which work through the neurological system itself. The first signal system is perception by the senses. Desoille writes, "In man only has there been added to this a 'second signal system' which consists of words, either spoken, heard or read." Concerning the relational power existing between the image and the word, Desoille says:

> There is a strict bond between words and their images; the two are inseparable. Experiments conclusively demonstrate that if a subject thinks a word, its verbal image is very frequently accompanied by other images. These are usually of a visual character, but sometimes olfactory, auditory, and motor imagery, all of which are closely linked to the first signal system, are also evoked. All of the images which can be evoked by a word can also, in their turn, function as signals, thereby supplementing the second, characteristically human, signal system. This fact is extremely important, for in it lies both the explanation of how psychotherapy acts and the justification for its use.[1]

More recent brain and neurological research has revealed additional insights about Desoille's observations and how this representation function works. Part of the explanation lies in the existence of the special functions of the left and right hemispheres of the brain. The left places its information processing emphasis upon the verbal-linguistic orientation of speech and analytical thinking while the right emphasizes the holistic, analogical-metaphorical function with its stress upon color, emotion, and images.[2] The corpus callosum, a bundle of nerve fibers, joins these seemingly almost separate brains at vital points of connection and apparently causes them to function in a feedback manner, giving the person more complete mentation, much as our two eyes, controlled by each hemisphere separately, give more realistic, complete vision. Inasmuch as the brain, through the prefrontal cortex and hypothalmus, physically incorporates sensory input, memory, and emotion via the hippocampus and limbic system, then it should be no surprise that these images should be so mentally and physically powerful.[3] Therefore, both in the Faith Schema and Guided Meditation Procedures much stress is placed on right brain metaphorical imagery and emotion functions in order to encourage right hemispheric functioning and thus stimulate more balanced, truly lifelike, and holistic psychic experiencing, lifting mentation into its religious awareness state. Also one can now see why *preaching the Word* has been so effective over all these centuries. It blesses mankind by giving the brain a total pattern by which to give coherence (comprehensibility, manageability, and meaningfulness) to his/her universe. The schema exercise is only an intensified and specialized present day effort to activate this ancient practice of faith. It is spellbinding to consider that some images are also powerful symbols. In the Schema this concept of words and beliefs having power to communicate and change even the cells and chemicals within them and of some images having great symbol power helps one further understand the vocal thrust in intensifying the faith operation (the life-moving, advancing pattern), even from infancy. I believe the Christian Faith to be life's best orientation to the brain's emotion and thought feedback system which gives us our essential safe-secure appraisal and reappraisal approach to life.[4] It eventuates in a needed overall metaphorical vector to our existence which is adequate for the full living of human life.

The theory underlying this therapy sees a person as in the Psychosynthesis concept of the mind, as having two centers of self awareness, the ego, I, and the Self, Inner Self. (At this point of *brief* explication of our psyche construct, if the material below seems confusing, the reader may find help by looking at the diagram of the psyche construct found in the first part of Chapter VI "Psychological Models", [Figure 3]. While the diagram is particularly relevant to that chapter's material, in lesser measure it also may be enlightening here.) The ego is the center of human consciousness and is primarily attuned to our daily level of functioning in the outer world of reality. This center is the usual focal point of our perception, and our higher logical thought capacities operate through it. The Self, though, also reaches beyond space-time and is a "pure center of self-awareness." The Self's chief orientation is around transcendent, transpersonal, altruistic, and spiritual existence. As a unifying center of being and psychic transformation, it conceptually bears very close resemblance to Jung's understanding of the *self*, the awareness of which is arrived at by the "process of individuation."[5] From the theological position of Faith Therapy's metaphysical construct, this same Self is considered the eternal Soul-center or focal point, the soul itself being construed as the person's life-giving, animating, spiritual force-field, the soul's circumference. Since this Self is only partially in space-time as well as into the eternal, it can create and extend an ego center from itself into spatio-temporal reality in order to grow correct feeling-and-thinking valuing experience. In the ego's daily reality framework this center usually retains only a vague awareness (if any) of its connection with the Self until after death. Both centers possess parts of the total will and unitive or cosmic intuition capacities of the person. As a result when Self and ego are drawn into closer harmony and connection by using the Intensified Faith Schema, their combined functioning greatly amplifies the higher psychic faculties.

The construct of the individual unconscious views the psyche as having arisen from the collective unconscious, as Jung conceived it, with its Self and structure-forming archetypes. These archetypes are usually forcefully manifested in myth and symbol form, though at times they may also be more abstract patterns.[6] Use of archetypes is central to the intense activation of the faith operation through use of the Schema Exercise. This paradigm also follows

Assagioli's division of the individual unconscious into three parts: the lower unconscious, containing the libido or life-energy source and also very akin to the general concept of the subconscious; the middle unconscious, which approximates Freud's concept of the pre-conscious, and at the center of which is the superego surrounding and protecting the circular field of consciousness with the ego as its center; the upper unconscious, containing the altruistic or spiritual qualities and drives and the Self, which is construed as partly within this psychic area and partly outside, into the cosmos and collective unconscious, and in direct contact with God.[7] The faith operation is activated within the newborn infant's body as its basic aim-directed and life-giving scheme. This initiating point identifies the origins of both faith and consciousness with the deeper levels of the affect-laden knowing or cognitive structures of the lower unconscious, as indicated by Piaget.[8] The daily exercise of the faith attitude, produced by the faith operation, even makes all human life possible by concomitantly creating and using the hope attitude—as the faith attitude's feedback mechanism—in order to shape and make available life's attitude and energy of love, eros. While such a knowing structure of faith builds all life for persons through its relational nature, it is ultimately oriented toward religion.[9] This ultimate orientation of the faith-hope-love process structure, with its conjoint emphasis on volition, affection, and cognition, originates with activation of the faith operation. This process structure is the psyche's dynamic which through its transformations elevates consciousness and further amplifies its religious functioning through use of the Intensified Faith Schema. It is activated by using suggestion, Christian belief statements, and symbols in a non-violatory way with the client. Robert Ornstein has stated, "We live in a sea of suggestions, symbolic messages, which shape beliefs and in turn, [even] influence our physical well being."[10] This Exercise makes positive use of this psyche function in order to enhance this religious experience.

Guided meditative use of this Schema temporarily lifts the ego and field of consciousness into or nearer the upper unconscious and stronger, conjoint functioning with the Self. The elevating and unifying action results in varying intensities of transcendent and/or mystical religious experience. Charles Tart has called such experiences a "state specific state of consciousness." He has further suggested examining such states to find their universality for humanity, though he expressed doubt that the pre-disposition of minds caused by the many religious belief systems would make such scientific investigation of them possible.[11] Though this Schema's concepts and symbols are directively Christian, the arrived at state of consciousness, sometimes at its greatest intensity, seems also to be somewhat akin to that of the Zen *Zazen* and Hindu *Samadi* mystic states. However, the Schema's primary development actually took its religious orientation and developmental clues from Christian mystic practices of prayer, contemplation, and meditation. This faith intensification uses both the *set* (emotional pre-disposition) and *setting* (environmental orientation) to help produce a specifically Christian religious interpretative experience. However, even within the experience, and even though a Christian committing prayer is used in the Schema, those whose belief system is not Christian, as a rule, do not necessarily interpret the experience as specifically Christian. There seems to be no inner force compelling them to do so. Nevertheless, persons with a sincere Christian commitment usually have a profound experience which fits perfectly and comfortably within a broad context of Christian understanding.

The client entrusts the therapist with the role of spiritual guide and the therapist uses the power of suggestion so that he/she may help the person activate this special religious experience. A guide is necessary for a subject whose background is based in our Western culture because one is apt to drift off into sleep after the meditative state is first entered and as the faith intensification begins elevating consciousness. Further, as a rule Western culture based clients who desire to reach as high as Levels II or III of the meditative faith intensity are usually unable to do so without a guide. Individual and solitary use of auto-suggestion powers do not seem to work very easily beyond Level I. Instead, one usually enters into a prayerful, peaceful and inspiring rest state with a mild awareness of God's presence. But as a rule, in this mind mood, or state of consciousness, not much reconstructive psychotherapy or spiritual growth imagery work can be done by oneself. In addition to being a qualified psychotherapist, the minister guide needs to fill two other major personal requirements: he/she must have a reasonable, broad familiarity with metaphysics and theology; and he/she must be spiritually mature enough not to violate the sacred autonomy or faith development of his/her client. The guide's role is to facilitate the counselee's experience, not try to cause him/her to have a religious experience as dictated by the guide's faith convictions.

The ministering therapist will want to keep in mind that there are also two goals for which the Faith Schema may be used: as a Level-by-Level worship experience only, or its resultant transcendent mind mood may be used as a "safe-secure" background awareness of God's love (like a theatrical stage setting) for use with the Guided Meditation Therapy Procedures. The Schema intensely activates a subject's greater immediate awareness of the unconditional love of God and is thus, effective in aiding with problems. In the ambience of this accompanying unequaled safe-secure affect powerful therapy work can be conducted. These two goals are not truly separate, for in some measure each use interpenetrates the other. The Schema has a religious healing effect in its use alone, and the Therapy Procedures are frequently very worshipful. Being in the presence of God's love in Christ has a wholeness producing effect. The biological basis for this psyche state is probably to be found in Hans Seley's discovery of the general adaptation syndrome indicating that threat, negative stress, activates the sympathetic nervous system while challenge, eustress, activates the parasympathetic. In healthy religion nothing could be more nonthreatening than the ambience of God's unconditional love.[12]

The therapist's use of the mental faculty of suggestion does not appear to lead to hypnosis and trance but to production of a state of intense meditation or profound contemplation, identified by amplified and intensified alpha and theta brain waves.[13] Alpha is indicative of the relaxed but alert creative mental faculties. Theta is associated with the psyche's strong symbolic activity and personal problem-solving insights.[14] As in some types of meditation, Guided Meditation is done with the person's eyes closed in order to facilitate better and greater production of these brain waves. However, no special body posturing needs to be done. The client is probably most comfortable in the Exercise simply leaning back in a reclining chair, to the degree he/she feels most at ease. Also, it is vital that the client realize he/she is to enter the passive mode of being and to be receptive. If he/she has any trouble understanding this mental attitude, two illustrations may be given: the receptivity is that attitude which the Bible speaks of when it directs us to "accept" Christ—not "strive for" him; the mind mood is also like that of a child lying in the grass and watching the clouds form butterflies, toadstools, fairies, etc.[15] The counselee is requested to keep his/her eyes closed until asked to open them again because alpha waves are very hard to produce consistently unless the eyes are kept closed. Additionally, the counselee is assured that he/she will be in ultimate control of the experience at all times because the Exercise will amplify the total will power. The client is also assured that this fact will be checked out to his/her satisfaction at the end of the use of the Faith Schema by being asked who is in charge. Usually the answer is that God or the client is; even then, to reassure, the therapist says, "If I asked you to say or do anything you did not want to, would you have to?" The adamant negative answer usually comes quickly, but at the same time it is good to clarify that in the transcendent psyche state *the person will probably feel trustfully cooperative,* and this puts upon the therapist the obligation to be trustworthy in order to continue therapy. If at any time the trust feeling is disturbed, the client can and quickly needs to clarify the issue with the therapist so that the work continues to flow easily. The therapist must keep this trust factor intact.

The Three Usual Positive Ideas (which will be found at the end of the Schema verbatim) also need to be explained and checked out with the counselee for approval and understanding before use. These Positive Ideas are used at the close of the Therapy Procedures and just before returning to the client's usual mind mood and attunement to the outer world of reality. Before using the Ideas, the explanation needs to be given that unlike use of posthypnotic suggestions, the subject will feel no frustration if he/she does not follow them. Positive Ideas are simply prefabricated concepts which are of special help to the whole therapy process and which are dropped into the preconscious, much as a small child unconsciously learns a language. The first is to encourage the unconscious to be open to being as much help between sessions as possible, as God directs. The last two are feedback learning loops which are given in order to help produce the greatest subsequent immediate comfort and recall. The second Positive Idea is to dispel or prevent mental fuzziness caused by the quick shifting of stages of consciousness and to give a little mood boost instead. The third, the quick recall idea, is also helpful in the immediate post meditation analysis of what transpired in the transcendent state.

The Schema is written to convey a specifically vocal style. The human voice richly conveys many different shades of meanings, feelings, and thoughts. When we consider that words and much of their perceptual nuances of meaning (especially emotional) are being learned throughout the critical period of phoneme categorization in life's first two years and that these neocortical areas still are decreasingly affected until puberty, it is no wonder that the spoken word has power of which we are frequently unaware.[16] This vocal style reflects my attempt to capture language's largely unconscious spoken power. In a way the style is only a dramatic manner of *preaching the Word*. In the Schema, which follows an upward-moving or life-logic pattern, the vocal signs and symbols are used by the therapist to "paint a picture" with feeling-thought.[17] Some aspects of the picture are deliberately left vague so that the client is unconsciously caused to use his/her personal experience to complete the image, thus activating the psychic power of his/her own imaginal faculty. The Schema cumulatively recycles the contents of lower stages in order to help produce the same experience more transformingly at a higher stage and with richer content. All these patterned activities are archetypally oriented around our primary relation, God. This whole faith exercise also increasingly calls forth the collective unconscious archetypes which themselves bring about the higher structuring of the faith operation until the symbols and Christian belief-statements lift the ego and consciousness into closer proximity to Self and the higher, religious qualities and characteristics of the upper unconscious. Many times correct use of the Exercise in and of itself helps reform or recharge the client's old or sick religious symbols which have been overlaid by negative personal life experiences or understanding. Such symbol recharging becomes a very advantageous therapeutic side benefit for the counselee. An idea of how to use this vocal style of presentation may be found on the tape demonstrations, if the reader desires and procures them. The strength of the Schema, however, is in the overall pattern and correct use of the vocal style, not in the voice of the therapist. Other therapists have used the Schema, imitating the vocal accent style, and consequently found the Schema equally effective for them in use with their own clients.

Some concluding matters need to be considered before closing this section: first, the Schema's three Levels and nine Stages are in reality three stages with three sub-stages between each stage. The idea of levels and stages has to do with the archetypal dimension of

UP. In leading the imagining of the average client, it is more help-ful thus to "picture" the structuring action. Second, this chapter's verbatim transcripts will present not only the Schema's experiential structures on all Levels and Stages, but also its suggested Variations and their Instructions for Use, Deschematization Exercises, and the Three Usual Positive Ideas. Next, there is the matter of naming the client's relation to God in the Schema. Such naming helps us form our identify in our daily life. Naming aids in shaping our self-con-cept and is, therefore, a vital part of the intensification of the faith operation in the Schema. The term "responsible and adult-level, free child of God" is described in the following manner: *responsible* means complying with one's sense of obligation in social relations to his/her best current abilities. *Adult-level* means one willfully tries to act from an adult position in problem-solving and reasoning. However, when one relates to the total majesty of God, he/she is certain to feel inconsequential, little, and much like a dependent child. But as God's child, one is not that (perhaps) parentally-pos-sessed person of real childhood but is God's *free child*, set free by Christ to experience the abundant life. In effect, God as the *good parents perfected* relates to His/Her child in the present moment with total faith, hope, and love instead of conditional love. This naming is to relate to God from His/Her viewpoint and in trusting dependency, as shown in the Parable of the Prodigal Son (Luke 15:11-32 RSV). And thus naming his/her relation to God, the client is also learning the reality of what Jesus meant by, "Verily I say unto you, whosoever shall not receive the kingdom of God as a little child shall in no wise enter therein" (Luke 18:17 RSV). As Friedrick Schleiermacher so piercingly saw, relating healthily to God in this life involves a "feeling of absolute dependence"[18]

Ultimately, the therapist can never adequately explain the Intensified Faith Schema's experience. Like so many living things, it must be experienced first but with as much preparatory explana-tion as can be given. As Otto pointed out about experiencing the Christian knowledge of God, "...it can only be evoked, awakened in the mind; as everything that comes 'of the Spirit' must be awak-ened."[19]

In conclusion, at this point it seems appropriate to ask why a person would even want to reach or get into this intensified faith state of consciousness. Certainly, not everyone does or is con-sciously unaware of such a desire, but in general there seems to be an inner human longing to experience different states of consciousness. This fact manifests itself all around us in the widespread social use of alcohol, marijuana, L.S.D., cocaine, and other substances which will produce varying pleasant consciousness states. In reality it would seem that such a common hunger, which is variously expressed, may be seen as manifesting one central inner drive for the ultimate in all sources of pleasure. The facts indicate this ultimate source drive started immediately after birth with our first act of aim-directed reaching (faithing) toward the previously totally experientially unknown source of continuing life and pleasure, mother's nipple and breast. Thereafter all our existence is spent in reaching, or faithing, toward various life-giving sources of pleasure which the universe generally makes available. It seems rather natural we should long and reach for an ultimate goal, or as Augustine beautifully stated long ago, our hearts are restless until they find rest in God. Certainly no one can grab a handful of Him/Her and sensately give it to us, so we faith toward some sort of inwardly satisfying union with God. The fact that there has been some sort of subjective satisfaction for this goal the world over witnesses that the varying religious systems are searching for the one Central Truth which none alone can totally contain. However, these powerful intuitions lead humanity close enough to that Truth that there is enough satisfaction to sustain the systems which have the higher ethical longings. This Faith Schema is a Christian path for reaching a fuller, more satisfying and helpful measure of pleasure's Source-of-Sources through this special state of consciousness. It leads one worshipfully and therapeutically to experience briefly the reality of the fulfillment of this ultimate life-hunger.

As Buber indicated, we need to enter relationally the "Thou-world" of spirit and then return lovingly to the "It-world" of space-time to build within it. The Intensified Faith Schema helps us more fulfillingly carry out our desire to achieve this goal. We can come to know with the self-validating "I-Thou" and "I-Eternal Thou" relation, as it is made possible in right use of this Schema—further assisted by the relational reasoning of Dialogical Counseling—that our "I" existence is not in vain. [20]

An Overview Outline of the Intensified Faith Schema

FOREWORD: In considering the Schema outline, it should be obvious to the reader that the aim in upward progress is that of balancing the functioning of both hemispheres of the brain, the left with its logical emphasis and the right with its metaphorical. The right, however, with its aliveness of imagery and feelings has first to take the lead in order to help the client arrive at a new balance point since in our Western culture we daily tend to overemphasize the left. It appears that full and equal functioning of both hemispheres allows us to process information concomitantly both sequentially and simultaneously.[21] In so doing we arrive at a state of intense creativity in which we are apt to sense a reality more real than usual reality, one that is ineffable, a mystical state. There are those who hypothesize that in this state, more fully reactivating the "now" of early childhood experience accounts for the "eternal now" of the religious mystic. This may be true for some "peak experiences;" however, my observations of others' experiences at Schema Level III, Stage 9, seem to vary. If both "nows" are the same but amplified, in a Guided Meditation in which one imagines him/herself in the archetypal "Childhood Meadow," he/she would experience the state as the "eternal now." This is simply not the case. The uppermost Schema experience of the "eternal now" certainly seems best described as experiencing God's presence as the Absolute of the Thou-world spiritually interpenetrating and interacting with our spirit in our spatio-temporal It-world. Perhaps there are lower and higher mystical states according to the faith development stage of the meditator. I believe the reader needs to be aware of all these factors in considering the following material.

EXPLANATORY STATEMENT: To give an orientation for perceiving the faith-hope-love process moving within the Schema, I will begin by presenting the structure in outline form.

LEVEL 0. The Imagination Only: This is used with eyes closed, the chair reclining (if desired by the client) and use of the committing prayer. (This Level mostly is used for some children and also for highly disturbed clients.)

LEVEL I. The Concrete Level or Beach Scene (at this point the emphasis is upon the concrete operation type of thought). It is much centered upon body-relaxation, activation of the parasympathetic nervous system, and some numinous feeling. This begins the procedure eventuating in the hypometabolic state of meditation.[22]

Stage 1. Life Principle Acceptance: here the emphasis is upon the ancient knowing of God as the Pneuma (Wind or Breath Giver) in the evolutionary pattern. The meditative mind mood is entered here, emphasized through body relaxation response.

Stage 2. Unity with Nature and God: here the emphasis is upon the life rhythm oneness both as a part of nature and as a special child of God, a *different*, god-like creation.

Stage 3. Acceptance of Universal Value: here one sees him/herself as *infinitely* important to God in the vast scheme of the universe.

LEVEL II. The Transforming Level or Mountaintop Scene (at this level the emphasis is upon the transforming function of the *formal operation* type of Aristotelian logic thought process in an intensified manner so that the higher logical operations of the ego are accentuated). Yet, one is also at an archetypal position (visually) which quiets and then amplifies the numinous emotion flow accompanying the thought. A mountaintop has always been an archetypal place for this type of thought and/or a meeting with the gods.

Stage 4. Acceptance of Safe Becoming: here one accepts his/her position of individual *safe-secure affect* because his/her self-image now also bears the imprint of Christ.[23] One comes to experience that he/she is unconditionally *accepted* and *confirmed* by God with that right as is a newborn infant who must first BE totally loved this way in order to live and grow to GIVE such love. However, this is not to be construed as cheap grace, for as a good mother has *hopes* for the child to be a good person, thus God has hopes for the person to bear Christian life fruit for *his/her own* sake.[24]

Stage 5. Acceptance of World Perspective and Ego-Self Existence: here one puts him/herself into the larger perspective of his/her perception and amplifies his/her *reality frame of reference* as he/she surveys the position of his/her meaning to the existence of the planet and as he/she looks into two valleys below which bring him/her into confronting the paradox of good and evil existing concomitantly; he/she then places him/herself into the position of discovering his/her inner soul-fortress or strength of inner Self. [25]

Stage 6.Reality Acceptance with Trust and Commitment: here one makes real for him/herself that he/she is assuming a different perspective of the world being evolutionarily, at present, a transcending thing led by a caring God he/she can and does accept as ultimately willing good for him/her and all creation. He/she then commits him/herself to this new depth insight and lets go to existence in trust, as an action of thus committing him/herself, doing so and psychologically setting him/herself into the intensified faith psyche state of trust in God as a perfect androgynous Parent, making a commitment of him/herself in absolute trust—as though an infant—to God for this experience. He/she lets him/herself become aware of entering a new space in his/her psyche, the "eternal now".[26]

LEVEL III.The Transcending Level or Universal Center Aim (at this level the emphasis is the unitive experience with God and transcending the former limits of intensified faith so that the client may experience more of the love of God and have better insight into his/her own ultimate existence and its meaning). This aims to find one's ultimate center as a person and his/her real child relationship to God.[27] Both numinous emotion and abstract thought patterns are most highly emphasized here.

Stage 7.The Spiritual Word-stairs of Ascension and Existence: here one elevates the faith mood by use of imagination and moving upwards towards God's perfect love. Also, he/she is affirming his/her ultimate trust rights as a Christian by utilizing the archetypal Christian importance of the conceptual thought meanings of Peace, Joy, Faith, Hope, Love.

Stage 8.Abstracting the "Not-I" and Accenting the Self: here one is eliminating the contents of consciousness as they usually occupy the ego and at the same time beginning an accenting of his/her innermost selfhood, the Self.

Stage 9.Conjoining Ego and Self with God by Affirming Ultimate Identity: here one is affirming the totality of what he/she is not and affirming "Who I Am" and have a right ultimately to be—and is affirming who he/she is as a Center of Will, I Am-ness, Knowing, an Eternal Child of God and of paradoxical connection/relation with God. [28]

APEX OF EXERCISE: For the final psychological set of the

mind into a *Christian* experience, the therapist now gives the Prayer of Commitment, "In the name of the Father, Son, and Holy Ghost. Amen."[29] (Or if preferred: "In the name of our Creator, Reconciler, and Sustainer. Amen.")

After the transcending mind mood has been reached and the Prayer of Commitment has been offered, the ministering therapist uses with the client the Pre-Therapy Work Check-out and then proceeds with the appropriate Guided Meditation Therapy Procedures. At the end of the therapy work and returning to the Beach the Usual Positive Ideas are given. Afterward the person is led back down to his/her usual spatio-temporal frame of reference or state of conscious and logical rational functioning by use of the Intensified Faith Deschematization Exercise (to be explicated in the next section). Finally the Post Therapy Work Check-out is given for the sake of clarity and comfort of both therapist and client.

The Intensified Faith Schema Verbatim

THERAPIST'S NOTES AND USUAL POSITIVE IDEAS

Introduction

Below is the procedure for elevating and intensifying the psyche's religious operation of faith, by use of Christian belief-statements and archetypal symbols, into some dimension of objective, mystical mind mood with a raised state of consciousness. As will be further clarified in Chapter V, this intensified faith process uses "life-logic" and "feeling-thought" to emulate and evoke the spoken quality of life; thus the wording and typing is written in a special deliberate vocal style for the therapist.

Notes to the therapist, frequently concerning voice quality, style, and sound are inserted at appropriate points. They will be identified in two ways: when applying to a major section they are indented, bracketed and denoted by the sign *TN*: (Therapist's Note); when applying to a smaller part (a word, phrase, etc.), they will be *bracketed only* with the *TN*:, plus a brief explanation; e.g. [TN: softly].

The Complete Schema, Itself [30]

Level 0: Imagination Only

[TN: This is chiefly used in special cases and instructions for it are to be found in this chapter in the section following The Complete Schema and entitled "Schema Variations And Instructions for Use."]

Level I: The Concrete Level or Beach Scene

Stage 1—Life Principle Acceptance
Now, let yourself lean back in the chair. *Do not* cross any part of your body because it interferes with your energy flow. Now, place your hands and arms comfortably on the arms of the chair, and using your imagination, let all of your feelings, sensations and emotions be present—just as though you were *actually existing* in the following situations as you imagine them. Do not TRY to concentrate! Just let yourself get into a daydream-like mood. Now imagine yourself in a bathing suit, walking along a beautiful, sandy, ocean beach on a nice warm, sunny day. The sky is a beautiful deep blue overhead. You are alone—but not lonely—just enjoying being "with yourself" and God. And there is *no* one or *no* thing about anywhere which can harm, hurt, or bother you—under any circumstances. As you walk along the beach, imagine the ocean breeze gently caressing your body, whispering in your ears, tossing your hair in a carefree way—imagine the waves swashing up about your feet and ankles coolingly—the sand trickling from under your toes, as the waves go back to sea. *Now* imagine looking up toward the shore and seeing there a spot of *beautiful, crystalline, white sand* which has at the edge of it a great big old driftwood tree—washed up there by some extremely high tide way back in the past, with a couple of gnarled, broken-off old limbs sticking out from it—casting mottled shade here and there, over the sand. [TN: Enticingly] It looks so comfortable and inviting that you decide just to go up and lie down there on your back and rest. [TN: Comforting]

Imagine yourself doing so, putting your head in the shade of one of the driftwood tree limbs, and just *giving* yourself over to the comfort of the sand—*hot*—but not too hot-*just* right!

Now, using your imagination, just let yourself become aware of the radiant warmth of the sand and of the sun [TN: Drawn out] *slowly permeating your body* as though your body were made up by layers. NOW, FOCUS YOUR AWARENESS: *first,* upon the warmth as it *slowly* soaks into your body—so saturating your skin that it loses its [TN: Staccato] *drum-head-like tightness*—[TN: Slowly, lazily] so that now your skin gets a sort of *melted, folded-over feeling*—until it just seems to *hang loosely* over the top of your body, as though someone had floated a sheet down over your body and it just draped itself there, lightly, clingingly. Now, again using your imagination, let yourself become aware of the *same warmth* as it continues to radiate inward—sort of *seeping* into your muscles. And where they feel as though they were rubber bands wound tight upon themselves—as the warmth saturates them—[TN: Running, rhythmical] they suddenly just RELEASE and UNWIND *and* dangle *and* flop—*limp*-loosely within. Again, using your imagination, feel the warmth permeating right on through every nerve bundle and cell throughout your entire body. [TN: Clipped] Where your nerves feel as though they were raw, sore, irritated, [TN: Soothingly] the warmth soothes their pain as though with an ointment or balm. {TN: Firmly, authoritatively] *or,* on the other hand, if your nerves feel as though they were a military guard on a military post gate on a cold, dark, winter night—*standing rigid, stiff, and at attention*—[TN: Gently, then lazily] NOW imagine the warming sun has risen over him/her—it's light, and he/she can see better, he/she is aware of the warmth seeping into him/her—and—he/she begins to *relax—stand at ease,* and even becomes a little bit drowsy. Again now, let yourself imagine this same warmth permeating on down—into your bones and bone marrow. [TN: Clipped] Where your bones feel brittle, fragile, breakable—[TN: Slowly] now imagine the warmth causing them to become *rubbery, malleable, and flexible,* [TN: Comfortingly] so that now *you* can imagine *cradling yourself warmly, heavily, deeply, and at ease* into the sand—just as though you were a pat of jelly or warm candlewax *comfortably* conforming to the sand—[TN: Gently] but noticing the *cooling* ocean breeze blowing across your shaded forehead—feeling as though someone had just placed a cool, wet cloth there with great care and tenderness.

[TN: Firmly] *Now, actually breathe* THREE TIMES *ONLY*—in the following manner—using your lower gut muscles *only*: using your lungs and abdomen as though a bellows to *suck* the air into your lungs, *inhale very deeply* with your gut muscles only—*to the fullest extent*; and holding your breath, *bear down very hard for a moment*—with the gut muscles *only*—then suddenly EXHAUST and EXHALE all your breath! Hold your breath out just a moment, long enough to break your breathing rhythm; then focus your attention on the limp-looseness which comes over your musculature. Now, as you do this three times *ONLY*—[TN: Serenely] let yourself imagine inhaling *fresh, clean, salt air*—*air washed clean by God* with His/Her rains over the ocean. *And*, as you *exhale* notice how your internal organs *relax and dangle limp-loosely* within.

Now, let these thoughts and feelings come to you: [TN: Firmly] this is like INHALING the life-giving breath of almighty God—taking into myself *new life*, new right to *existence daily in power, pleasure, meaning, and purpose*! EXHALING is like letting go of the natural exhausts of any level of living thing God has created—*exhausts* which He/She *recycles* into good for everyone and everything. So that now—as I exhale—I can imagine releasing *my* exhausts of *having* to live human life because it is all the life God has given me to live in the first place—letting go *my sins, mistakes, shortcomings, false fears, false hates*, false feelings of actually *being* a failure—instead of like all humans, ONLY *failing at doing some things sometimes*—letting go for God to recycle them into good!

[TN: Happily] So that *now* with each inhalation I can imagine a wellspring of *new life* surging up *within me*. And with each exhalation I can imagine God *tenderly removing* the *clutter* and *exhausts* of having to live a human level life—to recycle them into good for me, everyone, and everything!

Stage 2—Unity with Nature and God

Now once again, using your imagination, let yourself focus your awareness upon the *eternal rhythms of the sea*. Imagine *hearing* them come in wave upon wave—with a [TN: Loudly, firmly] CRASH-H-H upon the beach—and a gentle [TN: Nearly a whisper] SIGH-H-H as they go back to sea. *And now* let these thoughts and feelings come to you: "As I contemplate these eternal sounds of the sea, I imagine not only *hearing* the sounds but also feeling the vibrations of these rhythms traveling all the way up into my body from the sands of the shore. *And now*, I let myself imagine becoming so attuned with these rhythms that I *myself* begin to feel a sense of [TN: Sounded rhythmically] *unity* and *harmony* and *oneness* and *peace* with NATURE and *all* her *power*! [TN: Excitingly, assertively] But now again using my imagination, I let myself become aware of A HIGHER RHYTHM—a spiritual rhythm—eternal in nature—POUNDING into me from GOD HIM/HERSELF—upbuilding all these lesser forces within me, and bringing ME God's GOOD WILL for ME as His/Her responsible and adult level, BUT free child—MADE IN HIS/HER IMAGE—as a PERSON!

Stage 3—Acceptance of Universal Value

Now, again using your imagination, let your attention wander off into the vastness of the sky above you. Notice the puffy, white clouds drifting [TN: Slowly, draggingly] *lazily*, *sleepily by*; but letting your gaze travel beyond this—[TN: Mounting awe] into the *vast infinity of the space overhead*—wondering what lies above and behind and beyond it! Now, let these thoughts and feelings come to you: [TN: Great awe] "God loves me so much, as His/Her *individual child*, that He/She even holds those *far-flung stars in space in their place* so that I might live life—right here on this little insignificant speck of cosmic dust—this planet—but live it with reliability and dependability and experience my feelings of living here as being *safe* and *secure*!"

Level II: The Transforming Level or Mountaintop Scene

Stage 4—Acceptance of Safe-secure Becoming

[TN: In these earlier mountaintop scenes imagined by the client, the therapist's voice should be of a lower modulation meeting and harmonizing with the client's basic need for soothing feelings.]

Now, again using your imagination, stand, and spreading your arms out by your sides [TN: Excitedly] with a LEAP—FLY—as though by magic—up—up to the tiptop peak at the top of a range of mountains—where you alight and stand in a safe place where you cannot possibly fall—one which is plenty large enough to feel *comfortable*—and now, let these thoughts and feelings come to you. [TN: Solidly] As I stand here, I am very aware of the *SOLID, ROCK CORE* of the mountain supporting me underneath—*buoying me up—holding me up! I imagine a pinnacle of that core-rock, jutting up beside me—to hold to if I wish.* [TN: Lightly, airily] I let myself become aware of the *freshness and freedom of the mountaintop breezes*—gently caressing my face and body! [TN: Exultantly] And now, I let myself become *aware of feeling HIGH, EXALTED, LIFT-ED-UP*—feeling as though I were an *EAGLE*, soaring with wings of strength, power and freedom—HIGH overhead! *And now,* I imagine becoming aware of a sense of GOD'S PRESENCE standing right here beside me—*so real,* that it feels as though He/She were actually standing here in an *invisible but human body,* with His/Her arms around my shoulder as though I were only a little child—aware of His/Her love, *so great,* that now I know it is all right to be me. It always has been—and it always will be! And it is all right consciously to know all my little child thoughts and feelings—aware God is *filled* with MERCY and FORGIVENESS for me because HE/SHE KNOWS HOW HARD IT IS TO BE GOOD in this *imperfect* world, living in a human body. He/She *understands,* because He/She lived it HIM/HERSELF—in JESUS CHRIST! [TN: With great kindness] And because of this experience He/She is filled with *mercy—forgiveness—compassion and grace for me—HOPES, that I might bear Christian life fruit for my sake and well being but no demands. He/She accepts me and confirms me "Just as I am!*"[31]

Stage 5—Acknowledgment of World Perspective and Ego-Self Existence
[TN: Now, the therapist's voice should increasingly become more strongly, and somewhat threateningly emotional until the therapist has led the client completely through the intensity of the emotion of the storm up to the point of the *contemplation of the good/evil paradox,* safely, from atop the mountain, where again the soothing tones of voice should be used—*but, with greater serenity and deeper profundity.*]
[TN: Somewhat dreamily] Again now, using your imagination, let your eyes drift away to the horizon's curvature—imagining the air to be *crystal clear* so that you can see the earth *falling away into*

the emptiness of space in all directions! Now, let these thoughts and feelings come to you. [TN: Authoritatively] God, in His/Her great *power,* created this *ball of matter and set it spinning through space; BUT, in His/Her great love for me He/She has given this planet laws it has to follow—which make it meet every need I have!"* [TN: Gently] And again, let yourself become aware of God's spiritual presence with you—His/Her care, concern, acceptance, forgiveness, support, and *confirming-love* power.

Using your imagination again now, [TN: Somewhat dreamily] let your eyes *lazily* wander down the mountainside—seeing (as though through a telescope clearly and distinctly) on one side—the *beauty* of a valley below, which *sparkles with sunlight.* Notice the puffs of various shades of green that are the treetops stacked edge on edge, all the way down the mountainside into the valley below— broken only here and there by the jutting forth of mountain rock— exposing multitudinous hues of color. Imagine seeing the mica— exposed here and there—glistening in the sunlight, as though some giant had playfully tossed a handful of diamond chips over the stones as he leisurely strolled this way. Imagine the *soft, velvety green* of the pastureland in the valley below—with the cattle standing there *contentedly* grazing—looking no larger than specks. Imagine the black-brown patches of fertile, plowed soil, growing *abundant* crops, scattered over the valley floor. Imagine a yellow, ribbonlike road ambling lazily, almost *meaninglessly* along the valley floor, bordered helter-skelter by rainbow colored houses and barns, *looking no larger than pencil erasers.* Imagine a *beautiful,* crystalline, little brook—meandering here and there—gently elbowing and nudging its way across the valley floor—*peacefully* on its way to the sea. Now, let yourself become aware—*way down deep* inside yourself—of a sense of *luxury—beauty—well-being—tranquillity—serenity—PEACE and GOODNESS* about *all human life* in THIS VALLEY!

BUT NOW, [TN: Somewhat ominously] imagine shifting your attention so that you look down into *another valley*—on the other side of you—(and again seeing as though through a telescope clearly and distinctly) where there, far down below you, [TN: Increasingly ominously and threateningly] *RAGES A VIOLENT THUNDERSTORM—with black clouds boiling angrily within themselves—the lighting flashing vividly—*[TN: *Add* sustained staccato] *repeatedly*—with BOLTS of *green-blue-lavender!* Notice the *white-*

hot-heat—where the bolts *STRIKE* the earth and (in spite of its heavy wetness) throw up puffs of *dust—dirt—and particles of rock!* Where the bolts *STRIKE* tree trunks and *SNAP them off like match sticks—leaving smoldering stumps instead*!! *Imagine the WINDS— whipping the trees—torturously twisting—snatching—R-R-RIPPING one out of the earth—BURSTING it into pieces upon the surrounding rocks!* Imagine the *RAINS—blown* in *solid sheets* of *heavy, leaden wetness—bending the trees almost to the S-SNAP-PING point—washing away the EARTH—carrying the very earth itself away in a muddy flood*—which joins with other waters to become a *mighty—massive— muddy—seething—frothing—angry—WALL OF WATER—SWEEPING MADLY DOWN THE VALLEY—HURLING HUGE BOULDERS— GRINDING! CRUNCHING! CRASHING! SMASHING! DESTROYING!!* Now, let yourself become aware of the *suffering— turmoil—strife—vicissitude—trouble—THE EVIL OF ALL HUMAN LIFE IN THIS VALLEY!*

[TN: Use a quiet, serene, calm voice now.]

YET—here you are *high and lifted up—far above it—removed from it and objective to it!* Now, let these thoughts and feelings come to you: [TN: Affirmatively, factually] "I live life right here on this earth *everyday* with my *consciousness* caught up in living life in *both of those valleys below*—constantly alternating and shifting back and forth between them both—*knowing both good and evil—experiencing both pleasure and pain!* [TN: With awe and amazement] *And yet—at the very same time—IN THE INNERMOST—HIGHEST RECESSES OF MY BEING—I AM REMOVED FROM IT—AND OBJECTIVE TO IT—EVEN THOUGH CAUGHT UP IN THE MIDST OF IT!* And, I feel *within myself* as though I were a MIGHTY FORTRESS of strength and power—*atop this mountain*—and UNASSAILABLE! *A soul-fortress out of which, however, I CAN AND I DO reach forth in POWER—to participate fulfillingly in life all around me.*!

Stage 6—Reality Acceptance with Trust and Commitment
[TN: With *much awe*.]

And now, let these thoughts and feelings come to you: "I am looking at things *as though with the eternal viewpoint of Almighty God*—seeing *His/Her* meanings, plans, purposes, understandings, acceptance, and forgiveness—wrapping everything that exists together—under the great mantle or cloak of His/Her love, wisdom and power—*so great, that HE/SHE EVEN BRINGS GOOD OUT OF EVIL—SOMEHOW!* [TN: Dumbfounded] And, as with the psalmist of old, I feel, "Such knowledge is too high for me. I cannot attain unto it!" Yet, with my own eyes *I SEE AND KNOW* the eternal truth and reality of the fact that God ultimately converts even evil into good! FOR, as I look into the stormy valley below— where EVIL is at work with all its destruction—*at the very same time*—I see *God* at work—*beyond the power of Evil*—to use even the storm and its results to form the fertile soil of the valley below— out of which the very food I *must* have for energy *and* pleasure to eat daily grows! *And, though I do not understand or comprehend this truth—HOW* God can bring good out of evil—I know it—and accept it—as the eternal truth of the nature of the God who rules this universe! For, I see it with my own eyes! *And, I accept it and its reality!* And with this truth, I also accept the peace, comfort, and support it brings to me *to know* God is also at work within ME— with what I often feel is *the great evil within* me—to convert it toward GOOD for ME and OTHERS!

[TN: Continue dumbstruck] But that is not all—*for,* as I look into the other valley—where all the beauty lies—I see that *God is so good* that He/She is *even better than my wildest imagination*—that as Christ said, "My Father worketh still." For, I see Him/Her actually evolutionarily *perfecting PERFECTION—making the good better* for me and His/Her other children. And, *I do not understand or comprehend* HOW it is that God can make the perfect more perfect—*nor do I understand* how I can know this! Yet, SOMEHOW *I do see it, and I do know it!* And I accept this eternal truth about the nature of the God who *runs* this universe—and with it I accept the meaning, peace, comfort, and support which it brings to me to know God is at work within me to *evolve and magnify* what I often feel is *the little bit of good within me* so that it will bless *me* and *others* even more.

[TN: Serenely and with profound awe] And now, with this *NEW DEPTH INSIGHT INTO GOD'S GREAT LOVE AND GOOD-NESS*—I *now* let myself go into a *new, more far-reaching and profound DEPTH OF FAITH AND TRUST IN GOD'S GREAT GOODNESS—DEEPER THAN EVER BEFORE IN MY WHOLE LIFE: "LETTING GO OF"*—floating upon—*TRUST* IN GOD— yielding up—turning loose of—releasing to—resting upon— *TRUST IN GOD—very aware of His/Her undergirding,* supporting, upholding, underpinning, care, concern, acceptance, forgiveness, and power—*letting go just as though I were only a little*—tiny—baby— who doesn't have to *UNDERSTAND*—because he/she is held in the perfect, loving arms of the one perfect parent—*THE FATHER AND MOTHER GOD!* I am letting myself *go* to exist in the "ETERNAL NOW"—that place in my *own psyche, where the present moment of my life meets God in His/Her eternity—just accepting God's non-demanding love—without expectations or requirements*—like a little newborn baby, *who has a right to be UNCONDITIONALLY LOVED*—in order that he/she may GROW—AND LATER BE ABLE TO RETURN LOVE! AND NOW, tranquility and serenity—more beautiful and quiet than a mountain lake—*steals* over my Being and the mood of elevated meditation and intensified faith descends upon me.

Level III: The Transcending Level or Universal Center Aim

Stage 7—The Spiritually Significant Stairstep Words
Now (name) we are going to use five spiritually significant stairstep words: *Peace, joy, faith, hope, and love*—spoken in that order—(with descriptive accompanying thoughts)—to help elevate and further intensify your faith mind mood. These words and belief-statements have great archetypal and collective meaning (especially for those of us who are Christians) built into our collective unconscious over these hundreds of years and help draw us closer to God. Pictorially, think of these words and thoughts as being cloudlike stairsteps—up which you walk imaginally into greater *closeness and communion with God* as each *word*, with its accompanying thoughts and feelings, is spoken. Therefore, let these thoughts and feelings come to you:
[TN: Brief pause. All stairstep words and statements are said with a contemplative firmness.]
PEACE! Peace means to me—being at ease with everything that *IS*—because God created it and me, and He/She loves and cares for us all! *LET* THE MOOD ELEVATE AND INTENSIFY!
[TN: Brief pause.]
JOY! Joy means to me—God's gift of *laughter and humor*—given to me that I may have fun in life—even in the midst of *suffering!*

LET THE MOOD ELEVATE AND INTENSIFY!

[TN: Brief pause.]

FAITH! Faith means to me—the wonderful power of knowing the Mind, the Love, the Force, the Power of all the far-flung universe—at its very core—*as a Person, Jesus Christ*—my personal friend—who knows me, loves me, understands me, accepts me, forgives me, and gives me strength and guidance when no one else can or will! *LET* THE MOOD ELEVATE AND INTENSIFY!

[TN: Brief pause.]

HOPE! [TN: More forcefully] Hope means to me—that I keep my attention *FIXED upon the* good things *the good God IS DOING* for me in the present—AND, with happy anticipation—upon the good things He/She WILL do for me ahead in the future—NOT FIXING MY ATTENTION UPON THE EVIL WHICH IS PRESENT AND WILL BE TO THE FUTURE—SOME OF WHICH *WILL BEFALL ME* IN A LESS THAN PERFECT WORLD—*AND SOME* OF WHICH *I WILL DO* BECAUSE OF MY HUMAN IMPERFECTION—*BUT*, REALIZING AND ACCEPTING THE *FACT that I CAN choose to use evil and its results—transforming it into stepping stones or building blocks toward GREATER GOOD for myself, others and God—all together and all at the same time to the best of my ability!*[32] *LET* THE MOOD ELEVATE AND INTENSIFY!

[TN: Brief pause.]

LOVE! And in this case *love means to me—THE LOVE OF GOD*—BEING TOTALLY WRAPPED UP IN HIS/HER GREAT *all-embracing arms—drawn into His/Her very bosom—into His/Her heart of hearts*! *And,* [TN: Very firmly and assertively] *there MADE* to feel accepted and confirmed—not just with my positive points—but even with my negative points—in this less than perfect world— [33] *LOVED IN SPITE OF MYSELF AND BECAUSE OF MYSELF*! In *spite* of myself, FOR I do not *have to prove to God that I am sinless—good—worthy—or righteous—AND because of myself.* FOR there are great well-springs of *good deep* within me—and I am not even aware they are there—because they are yet deep within my unconscious. But God knows that they are there and that they are to come into being and do their good in space and time *through me.* So I am *loved, accepted and confirmed—in spite of myself and because of myself*—simply because *I AM, I EXIST!—AS GOD'S RESPONSI-*

BLE AND ADULT-LEVEL BUT FREE CHILD—BORN INTO THIS WORLD AND THIS UNIVERSE BY HIS/HER WILL AND HIS/HER WISH—AND THEREFORE WITH A RIGHT TO BE HERE—AND TO EXIST—IN POWER—PLEASURE—MEANING AND PURPOSE—aware God has good HOPES that I might bear Christian life fruit—*but* with *no demands* and *no conditions* laid upon me by Him/Her—*just loving me, accepting me, and confirming me*—causing me to feel *SAFE—SECURE—SAVED—LOVED— now—and into eternity—JUST AS I AM!" LET* THE MOOD REACH ITS GREATEST HEIGHT AND ITS GREATEST INTENSITY!!

Stage 8—Abstracting the "Not-I" and Accenting the Self[34]

Now let these thoughts and these feelings come to you: now, I use these CENTRALIZING THOUGHTS AND FEELINGS to unify myself with my *innermost* SELFHOOD—my *soul-center*, my *Spirit*, my *Inner Being and Becoming*—my very *INNER "I-AMNESS!"*

[TN: Pause. Wondering and contemplatively.]

I have a *body*, but *I am not my body!* It is a *good* body—given to me by God—that I might enjoy the good awareness of living life on earth within it. *But, I* cannot *be* my body, *for* when I was smaller (or a child) my body was *smaller*—and now that I am grown (or older) my body is *larger*—yet, I have remained *the same.* SO, I—who amUNCHANGING—*cannot BE* the *changing, growing body* in which *I* live!

[TN: Pause. Contemplative wonder increasing with each new "Not I" abstracting statement.]

I have *feelings, emotions, sensations*—but *I am not my feelings!* They are *good* feelings which God has given me—that I may experience the *pleasures* of life and be aware of the *pains*—lest I hurt myself overmuch. And, I am *free*, in God's grace and goodness, to experience *any feeling* which *needs* to come to my conscious awareness. *But, I*—who am always CONSTANT—*cannot be* my feelings! For my feelings *change constantly*—swinging back and forth as though a pendulum on a clock. Sometimes I feel happy—sometimes I feel sad—sometimes I feel optimistic—sometimes I feel pessimistic. So, *I—who remain CONSTANT—cannot BE* these constantly *changing—swinging—alternating feelings* which *I experience!*

[TN: Pause.]

I have a *mind, thoughts, an intellect*—BUT, *I am not my mind!* Again, it is a *good* mind—given to me by God—that I might INCREASE my knowledge, wisdom, and understanding about life! And, *I am free in God's grace and goodness to think any thought* which *needs* to come to my conscious awareness. But, I—who am *always at the center*—cannot BE the *constant FLOW of thoughts* moving through my mind—which *I* utilize!

[TN: Pause.]

I play roles in life! And, I choose to play *good roles*—which will be good for me, for others, and for God all together and all at the same time to the best of my ability—*but*, since *I choose* to play these roles—*I cannot BE* any role which *I have chosen TO PLAY!*

[TN: Pause.]

I experience troubles, hardships, suffering—in life! But, I—who con-*tinuously exist*—cannot BE any suffering—*which I UNDERGO!*

[TN: Pause.]

Stage 9—Conjoining Ego and Self with God
by Affirming Ultimate Identity35
[TN: Authoritatively, assertively.]

Then, if I am NOT the body in which I live—NOT the feelings which I experience—NOT the mind which I utilize—NOT the roles which I play—NOT the suffering which I undergo—WHO AM I? I AM MYSELF! I AM A SPARK OF LIFE—STRUCK FROM GOD—YET IN CONSTANT CONNECTION/RELA-TION WITH HIM/HER—who lives eternally! I AM A RESPONSIBLE AND ADULT-LEVEL, FREE CHILD OF GOD! I am a center of pure self-awareness—a center of decision—a center of KNOWING! I AM I!!

[TN: PRAYER OF COMMITMENT, reverently offered now—"]

Now, in the name of the Father, and of the Son, and of the Holy Ghost. Amen." (Or if preferred: "In the name of the Creator, Redeemer, and Sustainer. Amen.")

[TN: There are four items which are repeatedly found in any use of the Intensified Faith Schema. I want to highlight them because of their importance and because they are also used, at times with clinically indicated pragmatic alterations or dis-missal altogether (if appropriate), in the following Schema

Modifications. Because of their consistent use and positioning they are called The Four Standard Use Schema Referents and are designated by capitalization as follows: PRAYER OF COMMITMENT, PRE-THERAPY WORK CHECK-OUT, USUAL POSITIVE IDEA USE, and POST-THER-APY WORK CHECKOUT.]

[TN: PRE-THERAPY WORK CHECK-OUT—At this time of completion of the intensification and elevation of the psyche's faith operation, the client should have entered his/her maximum meditative or transcending level of the raised and unified state of consciousness (of which he/she is currently capable). He/she should now be ready to proceed to the Guided Meditation Therapy Procedures. BUT IN THE FIRST FAITH SCHEMA EXERCISE it is vital for the therapist to have a client check his/her feelings to be sure he/she is the one ultimately still in command of the therapy situation with the therapist only in the position of a helpful guide while the client is in the transcending mind mood (or only elevated, whichever may be the level he/she has achieved for him/herself). Next, the client's present awareness of God and His/Her love should be checked. If there is no such awareness, ask the client to focus on his/her reflexive breathing as God's breath given to him/her moment by moment of life—as a free gift. This usually brings an awareness of the unconditional love, even if not personal. This ambience is needed for best therapy. However, if it is not felt, do not force the issue! Accept the feeling of relaxed peace and work the therapy from there. It is good to remember God can take care of Him/Herself.]

[TN: USUAL POSITIVE IDEA—After terminating the Therapy Procedures and just prior to deschematizing or total descending from the transcending mind mood, the therapist should give the prearranged Usual Positive Ideas to the client. They are listed after this paragraph and should be used before completing Deschematization. However, I must re-emphasize that ethically ALL Positive Ideas, as described in the Therapy Procedures Section, should be discussed, clarified, and mutually agreed upon with the client PRIOR to entering the Intensified Faith Schema Exercise itself!

1. The first is called Unconscious Help Between Sessions:

"you will have dreams, memories, and insights which will reveal to you the causes of your problems and the good solutions to them, just as soon as you are consciously strong enough to accept them this way, as God sends them to you in this manner from unconscious to consciousness—but NOT to control you—rather to set you free with the right to be yourself" This Positive Idea SAFELY stimulates the client's private growth and work on solving his problem. Furthermore, it places this unconscious work under the control of God through His/Her constant relation to the client, on a personal level, through the Self.

2. The second is called Positive Feedback in Affect Result. It is as follows: "You will have no bad aftereffects from the elevated, meditative, faith session—but rather will feel refreshed, alert, optimistic—with a sense of well-being, power, and new self-confidence." Use of this Idea has a tendency to enable the client to change his/her state of consciousness more quickly back to the usual state without the mental fuzziness which usually accompanies such rapid consciousness state changes. Also, it gives a nice little extra, a slight mood boost. This prefabricated concept additionally prepares the way for more constructive use of material gleaned from the Guided Meditation part for use in the immediately following Dialogical Counseling.

3. The third, called Easy Recall and Positive Gain, says, "Also, as you return, you will immediately be able to remember all that you experienced while in this meditative or intensified faith psyche state so that you may gain from it all the insights God wants you to have for your growth and fulfillment—as you contemplate them on your own or as we may need to talk about them." This positive idea adds to the client's sense of reality about the contents which were revealed, gives a sense of God's presence and approval of the new knowledge, and also facilitates the client's out-of-session growth.]

Deschematizing the Intensified Faith or Transcendent
Mind Mood into the Usual or Everyday Mind Mood, the
Usual State of Consciousness
Now you are ready to come back down—out of this prayerful,

religious, elevated mind mood—with its attunement to your inner world of reality and its frame of reference—back down into your usual and everyday mind mood and usual frame of reference with its atunement to the outer world of reality. In order to avoid any mental fuzziness caused by too quick a change in levels of consciousness, let yourself come down out of this transcending psyche state using the five spiritually significant stairstep words IN REVERSE—so that, at the sound of the word PEACE—its accompanying thoughts and feelings—and the request that you open your eyes and sit up—you will be completely out of your present religious, meditative mind mood and back into your usual and everyday mind mood and frame of reference.

[TN: All spoken liltingly, optimistically, powerfully, flowingly.]

LOVE—God's love—totally accepting without demands—hopes—for my sake—but no demands or conditions on His/Her part!

[TN: Pause.]

HOPE—I keep my attention FIXED upon the good things the good God is doing for me—NOT fixed upon the evil—Knowing I can even strive to transform evil and its results toward good!

[TN: Pause.]

FAITH—The wonderful POWER of knowing the mighty GOD of all the far-flung universe as a person—my personal friend, Jesus Christ!

[TN: Pause.]

JOY—And joy means to me the joy which was in Christ and which he said he wanted me and all his disciples to have—the joy which is a special gift from God in the Holy Spirit—coming into my inner soul-fortress of strength, power, and selfhood—and there the joy elevates the level of the cycling of my feelings—so that my high points are higher, happier and longer lasting—and my low points not so low, nor long lasting—thereby, enabling me to reach out of my inner fortress to participate fulfillingly—in all dimensions of life about me!

[TN: Pause.]

PEACE—"The peace that passeth understanding"—illogical—unreasonable as the world sees it—because it does not come from the surrounding circumstances of life—NOR from its past habits and conditioning—BUT comes instead as a special gift from God in the present—through the Holy Spirit—to my inner lighthouse-like tower of strength and Selfhood. And, there the peace abides—a radiant, gleaming, golden nugget of light which BEAMS well-being to me and all people and things around me! PEACE.

[TN: Pause.]

Now, please open your eyes and sit up.

[TN: POST-THERAPY WORK CHECK-OUT—After completing the Guided Meditation Therapy Procedures and Deschematizing, any points which are confusing should be discussed immediately with the client by the therapist; and insofar as these may be urgent or demanding (anxiety producing) they must be clarified before the next therapy session! The suggested rule is for the therapist to give a brief recapitulation of the therapy work, especially where it has revealed either highly numinous or traumatic matter. This also should be accompanied at the session's end by a brief explanation and/or exploration of the symbol meanings (both universal and personal) which were used or which emerged. Also, the therapist should encourage the client to discuss briefly his/her own insights received or important things experienced. Some rational interpretation of seemingly otherwise non-rational matter is absolutely necessary, or the client may leave in a somewhat disoriented state with considerable confusion which will not be helpful to the next session.]

At the next session the same contents may need to be more carefully examined, if the client suggests it or if the therapist feels further amplification is advisable after the materials have remained on at least a somewhat conscious level (in varying degrees of intensity) for this period of time. Often additional insights and further archetypal material will have come to consciousness, including significant dream material, for analysis by that time.

Occasionally some experience in the transcendent state itself, or experiences due to material elicited in it by use of the Guided Meditation Therapy Procedures, may be so disturbing if consciously pressed that the therapist should avoid (as much as possible) too much immediate analysis of this material until the next session when the client will have expanded his understanding or built sufficient ego strength to withstand better the insights and affects accompanying the analysis of the traumatic material. Here the therapist must use his/her own perception and good clinical judgement!

Also, after the first session, the client needs to be advised never to reveal or discuss with anyone else any universal symbols (or their meanings) which have been used in his/her session. The reason for this request should always be shared with the client: it is the fact that once the meaning of an archetypal symbol is consciously known, its effectiveness may be more limited and its helpfulness somewhat curtailed—if not eliminated at times. This point needs never to be overlooked by the therapist as he/she deals with a new client.

Schema Variations And Instructions For Use

It is neither necessary nor desirable always to use the entire Intensified Faith Schema in helping a particular client. The entire Schema was given first for clarity of all components in the exercise. This presentation makes the following modifications easier to understand according to the various Schema parts they contain. We also needed to get the larger view of the Schema's use. I will elaborate on this and offer related material for general use with any part of the Exercise.

This entire faith intensification system seems to be safe in its use with most, even with those who have a mild PSYCHOSIS, but he/she should be adequately medicated in order to maintain reasonable ego contact with outer reality. The rationale behind treatment of paranoid or schizophrenic disorders is that the deeper personal unconscious symbols of these people are very confused. In the period of unconscious symbol formation making up the primary mentation capacities, they developed some highly confusing feeling-thought patterns in personal symbols. Such distortion profoundly inhibits their ability to do the healthy secondary mentation needed in this growth therapy.

The deeper archetypal symbols of psychotics are basically healthy and productive of spiritual—mental—emotional growth. However, these symbols have been so experientially overlaid with distortion that their frightening or thought confusing capacities are strong. They lack the deeper, clear thinking operations needed for true rationality and will not have the symbol clarity needed for good therapy work. This is more true of the even more distorted primal symbols formed in the first one and one-half to two years, the critical period or psychomotor development period of life. If the healthy archetypal manifestations of the symbol are to be tapped, care and skill in symbol use is demanded of the therapist. The preferred procedure followed in the Guided Meditation part of Faith Therapy centers around first building an adequate usual state of consciousness and a certain strength of ego in order to deal with outer world reality. Thus it is often more productive to use only the imagination. The client may not wish to recline or close his/her eyes, but the committing prayer is always used. This is the first type of Schema variation and is called use of the Imagination Only or Level 0. In cases where ego strength is greater, the therapist may start with Intensified Faith Schema Level I. Stage 1— AND NO FURTHER. As the counselee gets stronger, other Stages, perhaps even Levels, may be added as clinically indicated. From this basic point of faith intensification only certain Therapy Procedures are done. Here the relaxation response techniques and building adequate ego strength are foremost. The foundational Schema archetypal symbolizing is of the primary God-given right to existence. The participant inhales God's gift of life, affirming the grace-filled gift of breath, and exhales the natural exhausts of life, physical and spiritual. The gift is being accepted as the basic principle of God's love for all living things. Before proceeding any further than the end of the stage where therapy work is to be done, the PRAYER OF COMMITMENT is used.

This prayer is always used upon reaching the goal of a Schema Level or Stage because of the archetypal therapeutic power produced. This is not based on superstition but is a proven aid determined by clients who have remarked that this offering of prayer was a clincher point in feeling there was Another present directing both therapist and client, bringing safety and good.

It is then best with children and psychotics to work with the more concrete level of thought and dream material. Also, Crisis Intervention Techniques may be very helpful in such cases, particularly the Desensitizing Exercise with intense fear problems, giving more realistic perception through better perspective. The Switch Technique for energy transformation to higher levels at times may also be used to great advantage with these individuals. Additionally, use of the Plus-mark Creative Symbolization Method is highly advised because of its integrating power upon the entire personality. (The above mentioned Guided Meditation Procedures are clearly explicated in Chapter IV.) Use of more advanced Schema degrees and Therapy Procedures thereafter should only be used as the client's condition and trust level increases. Much skill and good clinical judgement is required in dealing with such immature or poorly structured types of personalities, so use of this therapy is not indicated for beginners in the practice of psychotherapy or those without adequate psychiatric assistance and/or guidance by a skilled supervisor.

Use of this method with an affective psychosis should also be approached in the above manner. If the person is in a highly manic state, he/she is apt to let this Schema Exercise and/or Therapy Procedures give him/her intense overly-optimistic feelings or in hidden anger self-destructively, unconsciously resist help so that the method can do no good; thereby advanced levels of Schema use could become an excuse for increasing self-defeating attitudes. However, this therapy dimension can be highly beneficial in these affective problems if the client unconsciously truly wants help and the therapist proceeds with caution. Again, the chief matter is the therapist's use of good clinical judgement; nothing can replace it. Differing Therapy Procedures and Schema Levels and/or Stages can be used under certain circumstances, but proper familiarity with the methodology is a must if the client is to be done no harm.

I would in no way recommend use of this methodology in cases of pure paranoia or organic brain syndrome. In such cases the therapy may be applicable in some controlled situations, but I have had neither cause nor opportunity to use it in such circumstances and would advise such problems be approached with extreme caution, probably in an institutional setting, making use of the total team approach. The delusional system or non-functional psychic operations in these problems is so intricate and complex that to use less caution in any future unfolding use of this methodology would be unethical.

For the client lacking psychological illness who nevertheless is deeply disturbed by his/her mental-emotional-spiritual problems, the ministering therapist will find use of the Schema's Modified Level I, Stage1, Plus the best place to start with the Guided Meditation part of the method. This approach to the Schema Exercise's use has been of more recent development; coming about with recognition of the need to keep consciousness nearer its usual level of functioning, yet still gain some of the benefits of a more intense faith mood. The aim was to arrive at the psyche space where one was still aware of God's unconditional love and presence, was not quite as bound to space-time awareness, still felt in charge of the therapy situation, but was not quite as caught up into transcendent awareness. Also the modification was so structured as to reduce the anxiety accompanying initial use of the full Schema. The verbatim for establishing the Schema's Modified Level I, State 1, Plus will be found in the next section of this chapter.

After a client begins to feel secure and trustful with this modification, the next step is Modified Level II, Stage 4, which may be used with greater effectiveness and client satisfaction. This modification was the first Schema alteration, and when it proved viable for its intended purposes (see Mitchel's story in Chapter I), this outcome naturally led to consideration of the briefer and more down to earth approach described in the previous paragraph. Modified Level II, Stage 4 use is indicated when the client has reached a strong enough sense of selfhood that he/she is ready, without coercion, to increase his/her religious perspective of life. Or he/she may deeply desire to move on to the more worshipful, mystical, fully transcendent experiences usually made available through Level II, Stage 6 or Level III, Stage 9. Use of any modification should be determined by client need or desire and the trust relationship in Dialogical Counseling.

The client should determine the intensity of the Schema to be used with him—once he/she is familiar with the procedure. Some few clients so develop this ability that they can enter the state on their own with only the therapist's presence but will ask for additional reinforcement from him if they need it. In such event the therapist should be on standby in order to immediately assist while the client does his own symbol work. However, the advantage of allowing the client to do the meditation work using his own intuition also should not be underestimated. Such desire represents developing consciousness stability, increased ego strength, and deepening trust. It is to be held in utmost respect and sincere response-ability by the therapist.

In all Schema use, the essential element is the client's developing trust in the therapist. It is indeed a holy place where one stands with another in his/her transcendent psyche space and should be honored by the therapist, for this therapy method is a Christian ministry. At some points in the Therapy Procedures very sacred spots are reached. If the therapist is a good shepherd, at such times he/she perhaps will find him/herself empathetically weeping with shared joy, even in some measure feel a sense of being with his client in the presence of the Mysterium Tremendum et Facinans. Figuratively speaking, here one may find him/herself like Moses feeling a need to remove his/her shoes. If so, the therapist should openly, quietly share these feelings with the client, honoring his/her worship and in no way be condescending toward the private experience. This sort of personal ministering intimacy is demanded by Faith Therapy.

One of the more vital points of instruction for using the Schema Exercise has been saved until last for greater emphasis. This item has to do with all Level II work because the client imagines him/herself atop the Cosmic Mountain. The person's sense of safety here is of utmost importance. Such things as too little room, the mountaintop crumbling away, etc., tend to indicate that the client's needed strong father figure was missing or inadequate. Since this guiding image helps provide confidence and trust about moving out into the world with courage, it is also a part of the poor parental trust experience erroneously projected upon God and must be corrected before the Schema and Procedures can move ahead effectively. The solution is twofold: first, develop client trust in the therapist; and second, work with any fantasy or imagination technique which may make the mountaintop feel more secure. Any idea from client or therapist can be helpful. Some suggestions for imaginal help are boring a hole down the center of the mountain to the earth's mantel and pouring it full of concrete with much steel reinforcement, shoring up the mountain with steel, imagining the corerock being solid, imagining the place upon which one stands as being larger and "not scary," etc.

It would be difficult to list further variations and helpful instructions for modification use. More detailed help will be given in Part III about practice of this method. These variations and enlightening comments are adequate for beginning to understand use of this therapy model. Other such variations are best determined through familiarity with the method itself, and the therapist with good training in healthy empathy will know when and where to vary and apply the differing subtleties.

The Modifications And Variations Themselves

Modified Level II, Stage 4

[TN: Faith Schema Level I, Stages 1, 2, and 3 should be carried out in the usual manner first. Then as the client is ready to intensify to Level II, Stage 4, the modification given below should be added instead. The Intensified Faith Level is usually less profound (not always) and therefore less threatening or disturbing. The resulting mood seems more warmly emotion-charged and somewhat more personally experienced. This may be due to the more person-centered, imaginal relating with which this modified Schema version concludes the faith intensification. The modification from Level I, Stage 3 begins as follows:]

Now, again using your imagination very vividly, stand—spread your arms straight out by your sides, and with a leap, transfer yourself—as though flying by magic—to the tiptop peak at the top of a range of mountains—where you alight in a safe place where you cannot possibly fall, and which is plenty large enough for you to feel comfortable. Now let these thoughts and feelings come to you. [TN: Firmly] I am very aware of the SOLID ROCK CORE of the mountain supporting me underneath—buoying me up—holding me up! I imagine a pinnacle of that core-rock jutting up beside me to hold to if I wish. [TN: Lightly, airily] I let myself become aware of the freshness and freedom of the mountaintop breezes gently caressing my face and body. And now, I let myself become aware of feeling [TN: Strongly, powerfully] HIGH—EXALTED—LIFT-ED—UP—FEELING AS THOUGH I WERE AN EAGLE soaring with wings of strength, power, and freedom—HIGH overhead!

[TN: Pause. Spoken gently with some awe.]

Now, I let myself imagine becoming aware of a sense of GOD'S PRESENCE—standing right here on this mountaintop beside me—so real that it feels as though He/She were actually standing here in an invisible but human body—with His/Her arm about my shoulder—so aware of His/Her love—that I know now that it is all right to be myself—it always has been—it always will be! And now I am aware that I am at a special religious space in my own psyche—feeling like a little, newborn baby—who must first BE UNCON-DITIONALLY LOVED—in order to grow and be able to give love ALSO! So I accept the love. Standing here, I am very aware of

God's love—mercy—forgiveness—all flowing from His/Her unparalleled UNDERSTANDING! Understanding that is so great because God Him/Herself knows just exactly how hard it is to HAVE TO live life here on this imperfect earth in a human body. HE/SHE DID SO IN JESUS CHRIST!!

So that now I am aware of God's loving me—accepting me—and even confirming me, in my right to exist—NOT just for my positive points—but even existing here in this imperfect world with my negative points! So that I am aware of God's loving me, accepting me and confirming me—IN SPITE OF MYSELF—AND BECAUSE OF MYSELF! for God knows there are great wellsprings of good deep within my unconscious, and that they are yet to grow into conscious awareness and do their good in space and time through ME—and I do not even know what they are yet. [TN; Powerfully, with certainty] But God knows! So I am loved, accepted, and confirmed, in spite of myself and because of myself simply because I AM! I EXIST!—AS GOD'S RESPONSIBLE AND ADULT-LEVEL BUT FREE CHILD—BORN INTO THIS WORLD AND THIS UNIVERSE BY HIS/HER WILL AND HIS/HER WISH—AND THEREFORE WITH A RIGHT TO BE HERE!! AND TO EXIST—IN POWER—PLEASURE—MEANING AND PURPOSE—aware God has good HOPES for me—that I might bear Christian life-living fruit—for my well-being and fulfillment—but no demands and no conditions laid upon me—just causing me to feel SAFE—SECURE—SAVED—LOVED—now and into eternity—"JUST AS I AM!!"

[TN: Pause. Then give the PRAYER OF COMMITMENT.]

And now, in the name of The Father, and of the Son, and of the Holy Ghost. Amen. (Or if preferred: In the name of the Creator, Redeemer, and Sustainer. Amen.)

[TN: PRE-THERAPY WORK CHECK-OUT—Now check the client's present God awareness and his/her own condition by asking: How do you feel with where you are in your psyche? After checking out the general psyche condition and God awareness, if it is of a positive nature, it is now all right to proceed with whatever work had been previously decided upon. It is only necessary to check out the issue of "Who is in charge?" with the use of any new and higher Level of Schema use.]

[TN: Next use the Guided Meditation Procedures.]

Brief Deschematization for ModifiedLevel II, Stage 4
[TN: This Modified Level of intensified faith may be deschematized in the following manner:]

Now, transferring yourself back to the mountaintop, stand there and absorb all the good feelings while I give you the Usual Positive Ideas.

[TN: USUAL POSITIVE IDEA USE—These should be given here. Then the client is told the following:]

Now again spreading your arms—fl[y as though by magic, back down to the ocean beach—where you alight and settle yourself back into the sand in the same spot. And now, [TN: Lightly, self-assured] let yourself become aware that you have been lying there—resting, renewing and restoring yourself—and feeling new feelings of power, self-confidence, optimism, well-being, and rested alertness—just open your eyes and sit up.

[TN: POST THERAPY WORK CHECK-OUT—Most people will immediately feel this well-being. But some are a little slower than others, and still others will have a mild, residual fuzziness which they may be assured will leave shortly. This usually happens as the contents disclosed in the Transcending Mind Mood or Guided Meditation Therapy Procedures are "counseled through." This concludes the Guided Meditation part of the Faith Therapy Session.]

Modified Level I; Stage 1, or Stage 2, or Stage 3
[TN: This modified Level is done exactly as the Stages of Level I are carried out in the full Schema verbatim. The meditative faith intensification is simply terminated with the desired Stage, the PRAYER OF COMMITMENT is said, and the Christian mind set is thus established. Children ages five or six through eleven or twelve generally should use this approach.

Next the PRE-THERAPY WORK CHECK-OUT is used. How to do this and other Standard Use Schema Referents for the therapist's use will be found marked by their capitalization at the close of both the full Schema Exercise and the first modification in the prior two sub-sections.

For Deschematization the person is simply asked to "Use your imagination now to return to the same spot on the beach and get ready to accept the Positive Ideas." Now comes the USUAL POSITIVE IDEA USE, perhaps avoiding "Help Between Sessions" if the client's condition indicates having such dreams, memories, and insights would be too disturbing. Then the deschematizing is brought to closure with these words, "Now, focusing your imagination—become aware that you have been lying on the beach—long enough to have rested, renewed, and restored yourself—and feeling all the good feelings of optimism—self-confidence—and relaxed alertness—just open your eyes and sit up."

Now the POST-MEDITATION CHECK-OUT is completed. It concludes the items related to the Guided Meditation part of the Faith Therapy session.]

Modified Level 0

[TN: This variation of the Intensified Faith Schema is also called the Imagination Only Stage. It uses fantasy with such Guided Meditation Therapy Procedures as are considered appropriate according to the therapist's good clinical judgement. As indicated, it is for the highly disturbed client and children under age five or six. He/she may lean back in the recliner only to a comfortable degree. Also he/she may or may not choose to close his/her eyes. Use of the imagination proceeds from that point after the Prayer of Commitment is used to give the Christian set for the mind prior to the therapy work.

Any adult having difficulty holding a grip on outer world reality at the beginning of work with Faith Therapy will do better work overall by use of this Schema modification. After comfort has been established at Level I, Stage 1, appropriate advancement to each sequential, hierarchical Stage is done as it seems in keeping with client safety.

Deschematization is accomplished by asking the client to bring him/herself back into the room (as in concluding a Fantasy Therapy session) with his/her imagination. If any Positive Ideas are used, they are given here. Then the client is asked to focus awareness on the fact that he/she is now back and sitting in the reclining chair. After that he/she is asked to open his/her eyes and sit up.

At this Modified Level, the Standard Use Schema

Referents are somewhat limited: the PRAYER OF COM-
MITMENT remains the same; the PRE-THERAPY
CHECK-OUT only checks for total client comfort; the
POSITIVE IDEA USE totally avoids the one on Help
Between Sessions with its stimulation of the dreams, memo-
ries, and insights; and the POST-MEDITATION CHECK-
OUT is a bit more cautious but again concludes the Guided
Meditation.

Modified Level I, Stage 1, Plus
[TN: This is the most frequently used variation of the
Intensified Faith Schema. It best accomplishes the needed
faith intensification degree which is most adequate for first
time Schema use, usual needs for help, or most problem-solving assistance. The time in faith intensification is long enough
to establish adequate alpha and theta brain wave flow. Yet at
the same time its transcendent mind mood is simultaneously
into enough residual contact with spatio-temporal existence
that daily life conflicts are frequently best worked with in this
consciousness state. The Christian belief-statement concepts
of this modification are gleaned from some of the most powerful parts of the Stages in Levels I and II, but only hints at
Level III material. Also, the archetypal imagery used is very
efficacious. This combination of belief-statements and images
provides optimal Schema Level help with the chief aims for
which most people seek therapy.

In this Modified Level I, Stage 1, Plus version, the verbal
patterns of many parts from Stage I are almost exactly as in
other variations but are somewhat less elaborate and more
directive (by prior client agreement). This modification is
given in the following way:]
Just lean back in the recliner. Close your eyes, and do not open
them until I ask you to do so. Also, do not cross any part of your
body (it interferes with your energy flow). Now, do not try to concentrate—just let your mind get into a passive, receptive state (like
a child lying on his/her back in the grass, watching the clouds form
bunnies, butterflies, birds and such).
Now imagine yourself in a bathing suit, lying on the warm,
sandy ocean beach—on your back, with your head in the shade of
the driftwood tree limb. [TN: With the first such Modified Schema

Exercise the therapist should use the ocean beach scene more completely. He should start with the completeness of Stage 1 up to the "lying in the sand..." part. Thereafter, this detailed, lengthy part may be left off.] There is nothing there that can hurt, harm, or bother you in any way. Now just using your imagination, focus your awareness upon the warmth of the sun and sand s-l-o-w-l-y permeating your body—HOT, but not too hot, just right—as though your body were made up by layers. Imagine the warmth so saturating your skin-that it loses its [TN: Staccato] drumhead-like TIGHTNESS [TN: Slowly, lazily] and begins just to hang loosely over the top of your body—just as though someone had floated a sheet down over it—and it just draped itself there lightly, clingingly.

[TN: More crisply and tightly] Now, imagine the same warmth soaking on down into the next layer—your muscles. Where your muscles feel as though they were rubber bands—twisted so hard— they are TWISTED AGAIN IN ON TOP OF THEMSELVES— as the warmth saturates them—[TN: Running, then limply] they suddenly UNWIND—and RELAX—and FLOP—LIMP-LOOSELY, WITHIN. Imagine the same warmth permeating the next layer—where all your nerves are, [TN: Tightly] and where your nerves feel RAW, SORE, IRRITATED [TN: Calmly] now as the warmth seeps into them, they begin to feel s-o-o-t-h-ed and comforted as though with an ointment or balm—so that now they feel g-o-o-d to the touch. [TN: Very firmly] OR, if on the other hand—if your nerves feel RIGID—STIFF—AND AT ATTEN-TION—as though they were a military guard on a post gate—on a dark, cold, wintry night—now imagine the sun has risen over him/her in the morning. [TN: Lightly down to slowly] Now he/she can see better, and as he/she begins to feel the warmth he/she begins to r-e-l-a-x, stand at ease—and even get a little bit d-r-o-w-s-y. [TN: Tone lower] And now the warmth soaks on down into the very core of your body—down into your BONES and bone marrow—so that your bones lose their [TN: Rapidly, clipped] BRITTLE FRAGILITY— [TN: Softly, lazily] and become rubbery—malleable—and flexible. So that now, you can imagine cradling yourself—warmly—heavily—deeply and at ease into the sand—like warm candle wax flowed out conformingly against the sand. But focusing your awareness on your shaded forehead—[TN: Comfortingly] where it feels as though someone just placed a cool—wet cloth there with great care and tenderness.

[TN: Authoritatively] Now, do your deep breathing exercises—using your lower gut muscles ONLY—in the following manner: let your diaphragm and lungs act like a bellows—sucking air into your lungs to the fullest extent—BEAR DOWN ON YOUR GUT MUSCLES VERY HARD and hold your breath for a moment! Then suddenly, explosively, EXHAUST and exhale your breath—and hold it out for a moment—until you feel a little limp-loose feeling come over your musculature. Repeat this breathing exercise—in the same manner—TWO MORE TIMES ONLY—after which, let yourself return to normal, reflexive, gut-level, relaxed breathing. [TN: Lightly] As you do these exercises—imagine inhaling—fresh—clean—salt air—air washed clean by God for you PERSONALLY with His/Her rains over the ocean. And as you exhale—notice how even your internal organs relax—limp-loosely within.

[TN: Firmly] Now as you return to deep, relaxed, reflexive, gut-level breathing—let these thoughts and these feelings become yours. This is like breathing the life-giving breath of Almighty God! With each new breath I am taking into myself—a new right to live for the next few moments—breath by breath given a right to be—to exist with no demands—no requirements—no expectations—so freely given to me that even if I tried to punish myself, kill myself by holding my breath—I would only pass out, and God's breath would breathe itself again through me—through my autonomic nervous system—absolutely refusing to make demands upon me, or take payment for LIFE!! It is a completely free GIFT!

[TN: Assuringly] So that I am aware that God loves me with an UNCONDITIONAL LOVE—the sort of love a little—tiny—newborn baby MUST HAVE a certain amount of in order to live and grow and learn to love. But I am aware NO parent can give this love. They can only point toward it or indicate it briefly—for they are human and imperfect. [TN: Very firmly] But also, this is God's space in my psyche, and only He/She can fill it—and He/She does fill it—as He/She proved in Jesus Christ—and as He/She continues to prove—BREATH BY BREATH that gives me life in unconditional love.

[TN: Firmly with assurance] And this awareness makes me feel so SAFE AND SECURE—that I am aware that I have moved to a new spot in my psyche. I am now at the point where the present moment of my life—meets God in His/Her Eternity. I am in the "ETERNAL NOW" —where all Christians live at all times in TOTAL SAFETY—at their Self-center or Soul-center—even while at the same time their ego—everyday "I Am", is caught up in space-time living—learning the lessons of value versus dis-value and right thinking for eternity's sake—for whatever reason God may have there for me.

So that now, I am aware God loves me unconditionally—accepts me without any demands—[TN: Gratefully and awe-filled] aware He/She even CONFIRMS me in my right to be here—and be a SINNER—that is, it is O.K. for me to be here and be unable to be the more perfect thing I can see—and even SOMETIMES WANT TO BE. [TN: Softly and gently] I am aware He/She can do this because of His/Her own experience here in the imperfect world and living in a human body! He/She did so in Jesus Christ! And out of this subjective suffering and sorrow He/She experienced first hand, flows His/Her understanding, which is filled with mercy—kindness—forgiveness—compassion, and grace.

[TN: Acceptingly] And I am aware all this LOVE is mine IN SPITE OF MYSELF and BECAUSE OF MYSELF—in spite of myself because I cannot do anything good enough—sinless enough, or righteous enough to make God owe me life. It is a free gift! Because of myself, for there is good in me, I know from past experience. And, there are yet greater wellsprings of good—deep within my unconscious—which are to grow into consciousness and do their good in space and time through me. And I do not even know what they are yet. But God knows!

So now, I am aware God loves me, accepts me, and confirms me—in spite of myself—and because of myself simply because I AM!—I EXIST!—as God's responsible—and adult level—but free child—[TN: Firmly, stridently] BORN INTO THIS WORLD AND UNIVERSE—BY HIS/HER WILL AND HIS/HER WISH AND THEREFORE WITH A RIGHT TO BE HERE—AND TO EXIST IN POWER—PLEASURE—MEANING—AND PURPOSE! [TN: Softly, amazingly] I am aware God has good hopes for me that I will bear Christian life fruit—but no demands—no conditions laid upon me—just causing me to feel safe—secure—SAVED—LOVED—NOW AND INTO ETER-NITY—"JUST AS I AM!"

[TN: Pause. Calmly, accepting contemplatively.]

Exhaling my breath—on the other hand—is like letting go of the natural exhausts of any living thing God has created—exhausts He/She automatically recycles into good for everyone and everything. So as I exhale my breath, I imagine letting go the exhausts of having to live a human type of life. That is all the life God gave me to live in the first place. But as I exhale—I imagine not only releasing my physical exhausts—I also imagine releasing my psychic exhausts: l-e-t-t-i-n-g go my sins—mistakes—shortcomings—false fears—false hates—false tensions—false feelings of actually being a failure—instead of only like all humans only failing at doing some things, sometimes. [TN: Exhilarated] So that now, with each new breath—I imagine a wellspring of new life surging up within me! And with each exhalation I imagine GOD Him/Herself—tenderly removing life's clutter—to recycle it into good for me and all. [TN: Give the Prayer of Commitment] And now, "in the name of the Father—and of the Son—and of the Holy Ghost. Amen." (Or if preferred: In the name of the Creator, Redeemer, and Sustainer. Amen.)

[TN: Next do the PRE-THERAPY WORK CHECK-OUT, and if everything is all right now is the time to move ahead to the therapy work itself using the Guided Meditation Therapy Procedures. After closure with these having been satisfactorily completed, it is time for the Deschematization, which in this Schema Modification is relatively simple. It is done as follows:]

Now, with your imagination, return to the beach and settle yourself into the sand in the same spot you were before—and get ready to receive the Usual Positive Ideas.

[TN: This is the place for using the USUAL POSITIVE IDEAS. After the presentation, Deschematization continues: "Now, focus your awareness on the fact that you have been lying there long enough to have refreshed and renewed yourself and feeling optimistic and alert—just open your eyes and sit up."]

[TN: At this point the client is given the POST-THERAPY WORK CHECK-OUT and this concludes the Guided Meditation part of this particular session of Faith Therapy.]

SPECIAL NOTE: There is one further slight Faith Schema

Variation. Briefly, it uses the exercise for Schema Level I, Stage I, Plus; plus the Prayer of Commitment, but the nature of its therapeutic value is specifically connected to "Guided Meditation Procedures," Chapter IV. Therefore, this variation will be more appropriately dealt with at that time in the section on Special Positive Ideas.

NOTES

[1] Robert Desoille, The Directed Daydream, trans. by Frank Haronian (New York: Psychosynthesis Research Foundation, 1966), pp. 13-33. Note: The current address by which one may order Psychosynthesis reprints of booklets is Psychosynthesis Institute, 3352 Sacramento St., San Francisco, CA 94118.

[2] Ernest Lawrence Rossi, The Psychobiology of Mind-Body Healing: New Concepts of Therapeutic Hypnosis (New York: W. W. Norton, 1986), pp. 30, 31.

[3] Winson, Brain, pp. 18-34.

[4] Robert Ornstein and David Sobel, The Healing Brain, (New York: Simon and Schuster, 1987), pp. 251-53, 103, 104, 68.

[5] Roberto Assagioli, Psychosynthesis: A Manual of Principles and Techniques (New York: Hobbs, Dorman and Co., 1965), pp. 17-25.

[6] Richard I. Evans, Jung on Elementary Psychology: A Discussion Between C. G. Jung and Richard I. Evans (New York: E. P. Dutton and Co., 1976), pp. 65-74.

[7] Assagioli, Psychosynthesis, pp. 17-25.

[8] Richard I. Evans, Jean Piaget: The Man and His Ideas, trans. by Eleanor Duckworth (New York: E. P. Dutton and Co., 1973), pp. 15-23, 48.

[9] James W. Fowler, Stages of Faith: The Psychology of Human Development and the Quest for Meaning (San Francisco, Harper and Row, 1981). pp. 292, 293.

[10] Ornstein and Sobel, Healing Brain, p. 98.

[11] Charles T. Tart, "States of Consciousness and State-specific Sciences," in The Nature of Human Consciousness, ed. by Robert E. Ornstein (San Francisco: W. H. Freeman and Co., 1973), pp. 41-60.

[12] Rossi, Psychobiology, pp. 20-27, 57-60, 18, 19.

[13] Akira Kamasatsu and Tomio Hirae, "An Electroencephalographic Study of the Zen Meditation (Zazen)", in Altered States of Consciousness,

ed. by Charles T. Tart (New York: John Wiley and Sons, 1969), pp. 489-501.

[14] Elmer and Alyce Green, "Update from Elmer and Alyce Green," Association for Transpersonal Psychology Newsleter (Summer, 1977), p. 8. See also, Winson, Brain, pp. 42, 44, 186-87, 189-90.

[15] Deikman, "Bimodal," pp. 68-73.

[16] Winson, Brain, pp. 163.

[17] A. Reza Arasth, "Final Integration of the Adult Personality," in Frontiers of Consciousness, ed. by John White (New York: Julian Press, 1974), pp. 34, 35.

[18] Friedrich Schleiermacher, The Christian Faith, trans. by H. R. MacKintosh and J. S. Stewart (New York: Harper and Row, 1963), pp. 12-18.

[19] Otto, Holy, p. 7.

[20] Buber, I and Thou, pp. 100, 101.

[21] Robert Ornstein, The Evolution of Consciousness (New York: Prentice Hall, 1991), pp. 133-38.

[22] Robert Keith Wallace and Herbert Benson, "The Physiology of Meditation," in The Nature of Human Consciousness, ed. by Robert E. Ornstein (San Francisco: W. H. Freeman, 1973), pp. 255-68.

[23] See also, Paul Tillich, The New Being (New York: Charles Scribner's Sons, 1955), pp. 15-24.

[24] Dietrick Bonhoeffer, The Cost of Discipleship, trans. by R. H. Fuller, 2nd ed. (New York: Macmillan, 1963), pp. 45-57.

[25] Jolande Jacobi, The Psychology of C. G. Jung, trans. by Ralph Manheim, 6th ed. (New York: Yale University Press, 1962), p. 130.

[26] Paul Tillich, The Shaking of the Foundations (New York: Charles Scribner's Sons, 1948), pp. 34-37.

[27] See also, Paul Tillich, The Courage to Be (New Haven: Yale University Press, 1952), pp. 186-190.

[28] Psychosynthesis Research Foundation, "Introduction to the Techniques: Working Draft," (Greenville, Del.: Psychosynthesis Research Foundation, circa. 1955), no page numbers (3 pages total).

[29] In the Committing Prayer throughout the Schema or any variation of it the therapist may say instead, "In the name of our Creator, Reconciler, and Sustainer. Amen."

[30] Throughout the Schema or its variations the therapist may prefer to use the feminine pronoun for God, provided a preference for this useage is indicated by the client in Dialogical Counseling prior to Schema use.

[31] Charlotte Elliott, "Just As I Am," The Cokesbury Worship Hymnal (Nashville: The Methodist Publishing House, circa. 1938), No. 151.

[32] Tillich, The New Being, pp. 3-14.

[33] Maurice Friedman, "Introductory Essay," in Martin Buber, The Knowledge of Man, trans. by Maurice Friedman and Ronald Gregor Smith, ed. by Maurice Friedman (New York: Harper and Row, 1965), pp. 29-31.

[34] Psychosynthesis Research Foundation, "Introduction," no page numbers (3 pages total).

[35] Ibid.

Chapter IV

❧

GUIDED MEDITATION
THERAPY PROCEDURES

Introductory Considerations and Other Symbolism Resources

It is vital that the therapist use these procedures *only* in accordance with the correct, indicated Schema Levels and Stages as pointed out in the preceding chapter.

Since the inception of using projected symbol psychotherapy methods, much similar fantasy and imagination material has additionally come to light. Insights from these methods dealing with reverie have been an aid in guiding the further development of this specifically Christian religious method. In my opinion, the religious experience psyche space is universal, but herein entered by using Christicized archetypal symbols and belief statements, and the procedures are interpreted under this basic assumptive framework. Unfortunately, since the death of Dr. John Eberhart, the psychiatrist who was my mentor and early co-laborer in founding this entire method, I have had no way of knowing the origin of some of the techniques of this religious growth and psychotherapy methodology. Some may have come from his own original, problem-solving contemplation, surfacing from somewhere in the back of his mind; some may have creatively arisen from his many years of experience in the fields of medicine in general and psychiatric specialization in particular, or they may have unconsciously structured themselves for him from his intense personal study of religion, particularly the more mystical parts of Christianity, in the latter years of his life. By and large, the techniques presented here originated from my own private work and creative attempts to help distressed persons, but some were conjointly, or partially developed with Eberhart.[1] Many fantasy techniques are usable—though not all totally appropriate or helpful—with Guided Meditation and its transcendent or elevated meditative psyche mood produced by the Faith Schema. However, most fantasy methods using archetypal symbols have in common two characteristics which were mentioned in an early Psychosynthesis research publication: "Initiated Symbol Projection (ISP) is both a *psycho-diagnostic* and *psycho-therapeutic* technique"[2] (Italics mine). These same techniques listed in this early article will also be found in Assagioli's book. In his discussion of Robert Desoille's use of this type of methodology, Wolfgang Kretschmer has written, "The technique is, in a unique way, both diagnostic and therapeutic and the *seemingly irrational* procedure is worthy of note"[3] (Italics mine). With more recent right brain discoveries this function is seen as increasingly important; in my estimation, it has been generally and seriously overlooked by the lack of a deep Christian-experience based reconstructive psychotherapy and spiritual growth methodology. The therapist using Faith Therapy will increasingly discover that indeed certain archetypal symbols do have, as pointed out, both diagnostic and therapeutic value and that the meditative therapeutic value is amplified in this intensified faith-produced psyche space. An excellent demonstration of this element (which so far as I have been able to discern, Eberhart and I discovered and developed) is illustrated in the manuscript's opening chapter about the true clinical case history where Mitchel, at my guidance, changes his completely evergreen Forest of Life to a largely hardwood forest, one which can support more life. To those interested in such an approach, I would suggest that careful distinction be made between archetypal and therefore collective unconscious symbols and those symbols which have their origin in the person's own private unconscious symbol formation arising *only* from his/her personal experiences. The best suggestion I can make for doing this is careful observation of dream material from a Freudian and Jungian viewpoint. However, one really needs to make Jungian dream interpretation a specialty, if he/she intends to uncover some of these sick archetypes, images which have become overlaid with unhealthy personally experienced matter. Such archetypes can then be changed therapeutically and aid in spiritual growth and/or needed restructuring of the psyche.[4] However, such changed archetypes do not always take *immediate* effect but are like newly planted seeds which take varying periods of time to germinate. Some seeds even take a long period of incubation before germination begins. Here the therapist needs to hold tight to his/her faith and keep working, for such life-growth is ultimately activated by God alone, in His/Her time frame for each individual life. Also, a client's *unconscious willingness* is a factor under his/her control. To undertake this generally Jungian approach effectively, one must also give very serious attention to the Freudian interpretation of dream content. Otherwise, much vital growth material will be overlooked or misinterpreted. While Faith Therapy emphasizes Jung's total approach, like Jung himself, it insists on the fact that this religious method still rests upon the basic foundation of the psychic truths which Freud first uncovered. These have recently been indicated actually to have a biological base, as Freud postulated. In the last decades brain research has borne out the validity of the existence of the unconscious and its use of images and symbols in the representation function in dreams and problem solving.[5]

Placing emphasis upon dream interpretation provides the therapist with significant triggers which will prove highly beneficial in a number of the therapy procedures presented here. Triggers, as briefly mentioned before in the chapter on Dialogical Counseling, are highly emotionally charged dreams, concrete situations, or memories containing an identifiable, distressing emotion or feeling tone (similar to a Jungian complex). They are often intensely anxiety-arousing in nature. Many times they are of traumatic memory foundation, having an early unconscious origin, and indicate the need for reconstructive work.[6] The therapist will need to make lists of such items, with the client's help, while they are working on dream interpretation, generally engaged in Dialogical Counseling, or otherwise doing varying types of therapy work. Fortunately, as therapy progresses, the therapist will find that many of these triggers are no longer of their former intensity. Apparently in dealing with the client's growth problems on many differing levels, including energy transformation procedures or desensitizing to other items, many of the formerly disturbing structurally related situations which set him/her off, almost like pulling the trigger on a loaded gun, are no longer of that intensity. As client and therapist survey from time to time these triggers, they rather objectively measure client progress. Of greater importance, the counselee's self-image improves as many former triggers are eliminated.

I also want to emphasize that the client (though he/she may seem to be so from bodily stillness) is not at all in a truly trance-like, cataleptic state while in the transcendent mind mood (and in using these Procedures) for independent will and thinking capacity are very active; and conscious, concentrative abilities are exceedingly high. The client is into a more *zazen*-like state instead. This state is very clearly indicated by the level of intelligent problem-solving he/she is able to do and tell the therapist about while *in* the transcendent mind mood. The client may have to be stimulated to talk from time to time because there is a tendency to lose contact with the usual sense of the passage of time. Sometimes one may even drop off to sleep, but it is most important that he/she stay awake, at least *after* Schema use, so he/she can talk with the therapist. (Intervening sleep while using the Schema itself seems not to hurt since the Self seems to be in charge: The *ego* needs waking only when the PRE-THERAPY WORK CHECK-OUT is done.) The client needs to be awake in ego in order to remain in tune with outer world reality and also to achieve more conceptual concreteness and clarity of memory. Otherwise he/she will have difficulty recalling any accomplishment in the transcendent psyche state upon return to a usual level of conscious awareness. If he/she cannot recall what happened there will be difficulty in making these new insights immediately available for use in the Dialogical Counseling afterward or for putting into effect in daily living. Also, in the immediate counseling after the Meditation, if there is any need to gestalt residual levels of the problem or to use body work (such as Bioenergetics or Psychomotor Therapy) for a fuller resolution, this opportunity will be lost.

There are times when therapy work is progressing well in the transcendent state when the therapist may use what I call a Therapist's Insight-hunch. Use of this device is indicated when the client is having some problem conceptualizing what is happening in his/her transcendent space. Language in this state of consciousness frequently is inadequate to express the client's experience, although the imagery may be going well. If the therapist is perceptively staying with his/her client's experience, a sudden flash of intuition or an insight into what is going on in the client's psyche may suddenly, sympathetically burst into the therapist's mind. If this happens, it should immediately be *offered* to the client—not coerced—as such an insight-hunch; and the client is reminded that if it offers no help or enlightenment, it should be rejected. The therapist will probably be surprised by how often such hunches are helpful, but getting the right feel is both intuitive and carefully learned.

The therapist who wishes to minister must keep in mind that because the Faith Therapy's Guided Meditation is oriented around the metaphysical and religious components of the psyche, God at times may be experienced in the therapy work, as Whitehead has indicated, as Void, Enemy, Companion,[7] or (as many times experienced in this therapy) *Friend*. Such awareness of God may evidence itself at any particular point in the Schema's transcending psyche state. It seems this experiencing of the nature of God stems from the fact that as one grows spiritually, he/she may increasingly uncover deeper memories and get new insights into life and his/her time identity. This stimulates him/her to repeat his/her experience of God again and again on higher levels of understanding until one truly comes to know: "God knew all this incompleteness and error in me all along—long before I recognized it—and He/She loved me even then." With enough of this sort of experiencing of God's graceful love, the client will probably settle increasingly into a subtle sort of usual conscious awareness of God as constant Companion and/or Friend. Thereafter, a client may not frequently go through the intensity of the more negative aspects of experiencing God as he/she continues therapy and growth in faith development.

Two very important and purely metaphysical (in origin) experiences force themselves upon us now. They are the experiences of *Spinning or Spiraling*, and the *Void*: in some measure they may have presented themselves for consideration in the Schema Exercise itself as items for the PRE-THERAPY WORK CHECK-OUT because they are often mentioned there. However, since the citing of them by name introduces the possibility of their being experienced by the power of suggestion, it is better to deal with them only if they occur spontaneously and the client mentions them. (For those who suppose the Faith Schema to be overly influenced by *Christian beliefs* as a mode of entering a *universal transcendent state of consciousness*, I might ask why is it that in this Schema's experience such neutral religious state universals as the Void and Spinning should thus arrive non-directed?) At times it may even be after the Guided Meditation part that the client may mention experiencing these strange phenomena but was not disturbed enough by either occurrence to ask the therapist about it at the time.

The Void may be experienced as total blackness alone and is usually not threatening to clients (if it is threatening, it is desensitized to). Also, the Void sometimes seems to be out beyond space-time, though space-time additionally may be envisioned. The experience of the void may be simply waited through until the person grows weary with waiting and wants to move on to other things. Spontaneous imagery most often eventually appears; or the therapist may ask the client, if he/she is comfortable, to move ahead into the therapy work.

Spinning or Spiraling, the other major spontaneous experience, is so realistic at times that it must be immediately dealt with before any progress in the session can be made. Sometimes the movement is experienced more as a swinging but eventuates in Spinning. Also, there are times when, on one level of consciousness, the person experiencing the Spiraling feels the recliner moving too, though he knows it is not actually happening. Again, the Spiraling experience may be dealt with, if not too distressing, by simply *staying with the feelings* until the spinning abates itself. Another way of dealing with it is by repeated desensitizing until it is no longer distressful. Then the therapy work may proceed as planned. Significantly in my experience, never has a client's Spiraling feeling been sensed as vortex-like or truly fearful. And contrary to Desoille's usually correct construct of mental experience, in these metaphysical events, there has been neither prior "primary signal system" sensory experience nor "secondary signal system" work or image which would causally relate to these spontaneous experiences.[8] My empirical conclusions have led me no closer, after all these years, to offering a solution to the questions of the Void and Spinning than to venture a guess that this is the human monad, or Self, manifesting its eternal nature as *life* and *motion*. It could also be a focal-point of self-awareness which is presently caught up into being at a specific position of spatio-temporal process. The therapeutic value of these experiences is awe.

Further, clients in this elevated psyche state are likely at times to have sudden bursts of insight on the unitive level of their shared existence in a mystical participatory way. All sorts of even formerly noxious things, i.e. weeds, worms, feces, etc. may occur in these insights. In such events my advice is to let the clients *stay with* the experience until they gain the insight their psyches need from such experiences. This seems to presage a much needed modern method which could encourage us to return to living with a feeling of participation mystique if we are to preserve our species and planet. Laurens van der Post's lifetime work among the tribesmen of Africa's Kalahari desert seems to prove that some measure of such unitive feeling (though not in such primitive manner) is increasingly becoming a necessity for psychosomatic and spiritual health.[9]

It is most likely that the client's own psyche generally knows best what he/she needs. However, there are also times in which the therapist will become aware a client is dodging dealing with issues which have consciously otherwise manifested themselves as problems. In such event, the therapist needs to confront the client gently about the resistance. He/she may either admit the avoidance and choose to proceed with working on that problem or will honestly confront the issue privately and tell the therapist that the problem no longer exists. However, a client may also plainly state unwillingness to deal with the problem. This indicates serious resistance, and further related counseling is first needed.

Psychobiological Factors Present in These Procedures

Since the use of suggestion in healing and growth is common to both Faith Therapy and hypnosis, it seems correct to start with the work of Milton H. Erickson, M.D., who was probably one of the most effective hypnotherapists in recent times. He concluded that some major problems were caused by "...learnings that we acquire at various levels of awareness...." As they are synthesized they establish for persons a particular frame of reference (a general attitude) which may manifest itself as a pattern of maladjustment. In order to correct this, one needs to mentally "...establish a different frame of reference so that he/she can function in that regard."[10] These *we* would refer to as "affective tone structures," a subject to which we will later return.

Ernest L. Rossi, a clinical psychologist, has also developed some vital contributing insights. He has found that due to the brain's interaction within the hypothalmic-limbic system, since the latter involves the amygdala and hippocampus, there is an encoding of information which allows for mind-body transduction (energy transformation) into communication between the various components of a person. He/she, thereby, is really considered as a single information complex. Through its interactions, the hypothalmic-limbic system causes the production of messenger molecules which are sent to all major functions which control systems of the body— the autonomic, endocrine, immune and neuropeptide systems (all of which also intercommunicate by messenger molecules). The messenger molecules are like "keys" which have designs only fitting certain receptors, "locks," on cell walls and with varying processes change cell functioning—even down to gene material by affecting the RNA and DNA protein molecules. Interestingly, the hypothalamus itself is not easily identified, as are other parts of the body; but it is an important center of tissues with seemingly vague boundaries, located at the base of the forebrain, with which it has rich connections. Its small size belies its great importance in body-mind transduction.

Having established the body-mind information transduction factor, let us proceed to another important finding of Rossi. He studied under Erickson and has enlarged on and clarified the "frame of reference" concept. Due to the hypothalmic-limbic encoding caused by transduction, he contends that *all* like memory, learning, and behavior becomes "state-dependent," which has a more specific meaning than "frame of reference." He holds that these state-dependent matters are held together unconsciously by the fact that they are of the same psychophysiological origin due to their happening in the alarm reaction of Hans Seley's "general adaptation syndrome" and the accompanying pleasure/pain factor. These similar amalgamations gain their general affective structuring by the response to some threat caused by activating the sympathetic nervous system and usually become amnestic upon reactivation of the parasympathetic system and usual consciousness functioning. Rossi further holds that each time we access this state-dependent material we reframe it because memory is always a "constructive process" in which we synthesize subjective experiences each time we recall them.[11] It is obvious, therefore, that the following Procedures participate in this reframing of state-dependent experiences and change them.

The more specific functioning of the hippocampus, limbic system, and frontal (or pre-frontal) cortex is at the core of information processing by body-mind transduction as it accesses state-dependent material. Therefore, we will examine this functioning in further detail. According to a leading neurological scientist, Jonathan Winson, "The key to understanding the brain mechanisms underlying the psyche lies in the means by which the hippocampus, limbic system, and prefrontal cortex process information and build behavior strategy."[12] In these Procedures the central ingredient responsible for their success is the production of theta brain wave rhythm first induced by use of the Intensified Faith Schema. Theta wave production indicates that the hippocampus is at work integrating new behavior patterns with the basic schemes for survival, mostly formed in the prefrontal cortex in the critical period of life's development. These schemes seem to be predominantly structured for survival, in one's personal unconscious, in a given environment by conforming to expectations of parenting figures. While the first two years of this period are the most important time of scheme formation, the period is still active, diminishingly, until puberty. These schemes then become the primary behavior patterns which determine the structuring of basic conduct throughout life. Also it appears that information related to present experiences is processed within the hippocampus using critical period structures as a primary map by which subsequent behavior is plotted. Interestingly, there is a three year period before hippocampal memories are somehow more permanently incorporated into the neocortex.

Reliable experiments indicate that the signals directed to the limbic system by hippocampal action—with its input from the amygdala (with emotion infusion), neocortex (with memory and sensory input), motor action signals (with their behavior potential—temporally action-blocked by the Schema meditation or REM [rapid eye movement] sleep)—are making associations which later will be offered to consciousness as alternate solutions for problems presented by life. Central to this processing is hippocampal neuronal gating (signal selecting and directing) which apparently has a highly discriminating routing of possible behavior inputs to select groupings of certain limbic structures which will best produce the action models presented to consciousness. The limbic system seems to be an important core information processing system which is interposed between sensory input and motor output in an indirect manner; that is, the limbic system seems to be involved in a cognitive solution presenting process within the brain after the problem is sensed but before action is taken.

These potential behavior solutions caused by the brain's associational capacities probably go on all the time on a level below consciousness but are particularly evident in the symbols used in dreaming—especially in REM sleep.[13] As Freud, Jung, and others have discovered, the symbolism taking place in dreams, when interpreted and brought to consciousness, has great meaning for deciphering life problems. At this point the cognitive structuring becomes comprehensible enough for the person to take actions willfully which better positively unify the objective psyche needs with wise ego functioning. This chapter's Procedures (especially with their symbol use) apparently help the process by effecting the hippocampus and limbic system's better structuring of behavioral options, impacting unconscious problem processing.

IMPORTANT TIPS FOR PROCEDURE USE

When doing Guided Meditation therapy with a client, a good general rule of procedure for the therapist is the advice we frequently give a client searching for solutions: "stay with the feeling." After all, they are the individual's feelings, and knowing them cannot really hurt him/her so it is mostly by identifying and enduring these feelings that breakthroughs will occur. Next, if this procedure does nothing to introduce *some* positive change, the therapist should use either of the two immediately following Crisis Intervention Techniques of this therapy method. One or both will probably quiet the anxiety enough that the therapist may proceed with the session.

Also, *central to all these therapy techniques and procedures is the awareness of a client's need for the SAFE-SECURE AFFECT in any highly threatening situation. This unconditionally loved feeling should be readily available after having done a prior Schema Exercise in which one focused on awareness of God's unconditional love. The client also needs to keep in mind that he/she may at any time call upon the LIGHT OF GOD'S PRESENCE to bring a greater awareness of God's love.*[14] Finally, we again remind the therapist that it helps if the ministering person analogically thinks of all procedures used as carried out as though acting upon a theater stage where the backdrop and props establish the location as taking place in the safe-secure presence of God's unconditional love.

Guided Therapy Procedures
Crisis Intervention Techniques

Introduction
Some explanation of these particular Guided Meditation Procedures being separated and called Crisis Intervention Techniques is in order here, since we have differentiated them from Creative Symbolization Methods and Special Positive Ideas, although they all at times intermingle. A crisis may be better understood through the metaphor of two high speed trains headed toward each other on the same track. A wreck *will* occur unless something is done immediately. Some of life's crises have a comparable intensity. However, if there is another parallel track at the point where they will meet, one train can be switched off onto that track, without losing speed or time and then switched back on to the main line after they have sped past each other. This is crisis intervention. In this way neither would lose time nor collide destructively. Later, after the danger is past it could be decided what destructive error was made, and steps could be taken to prevent further trouble. The Techniques usually immediately stop the psychological distress of the emotion and pave the way for new insights and behavior—arising from newly established brain engrams (electrical pathways) utilizing preconscious imagery patterns. These new successful patterns tend to work their way into consciousness and become a part of the person's permanent behavior—if they answer a true need. [15]

It should be evident that the central focus of both these Techniques is the "Relaxation Response" amplified beyond the degree caused by use of the Schema alone. The new level apparently is a higher baseline functioning plane of relaxation brought on by intensified faith and the meditation mood. Against that background a more intense activation of both the sympathetic (loud voice and clapping) nervous system as well as the parasympathetic (pleasant images and concepts) becomes a powerful therapeutic psychic intervention implement.[16]

Key-word Desensitizing by Sensitizing Exercise

Prior to use of this intervention technique, the therapist should make sure the client has no heart problem, for body stressing plays an important part in this technique. This exercise is also carried out by therapist use of the vocal style as in the Faith Schema. Let me first describe this Technique's setting, then perhaps an understanding will be easier to grasp: we will suppose the person is imaginarily in contact with some tense feelings, situation, or troublesome thought to which he wishes to desensitize (a trigger situation—preferably imagining the scene). First he/she is asked to get the feeling with his/her imagination. Perhaps the client can only think of it (obtain it intellectually) at first, but if one will *image* the situation in which one was last aware of it, then he/she probably can become aware of the *feeling* again now. (*Throughout this technique's use, the clarifying of feelings at their base as sad, mad, glad, scared, or excited is very helpful.*) If one cannot get the feeling, one is to imagine "feeling" it when he/she affirms he/she is "into it," ("into it" usually means he/she has imaginarily "slidden into" his/her own body in the scene in order to get maximum results) the following procedure is taken *immediately*. The therapist then commands with the word, *STRESS*!! At this command the person is supposed to hold the breath, tighten every muscle in the body, clinch the fists, grit the teeth, and pinch the face (scowl) thus causing activation of the sympathetic nervous system. While holding him/herself in this fixed state, the *Key-word command* is given: *Relax, (Preferred name)*! [This is the initial stimulus which starts a series of signal words, phrases, and images designed increasingly to implement the calming power of the parasympathetic nervous system.] Following this Key-word the following six *Self-command Words* (ego self) are given. At first use their full explication, but possibly later reduce them to a few words and phrases; perhaps, further along, even reduce them to the Command Words alone:

EXHAUST!——— all your breath and hold it out a moment

until you feel a limp-looseness come over your musculature. Then resume normal, deep, gut-level, easy breathing. Let every muscle flop—like a wet sheet *blown* by the wind on a clothesline.

SMILE!——— *relax* and let go all your *scalp* muscles—as though you had a wig on five sizes too large, and it's about to slide off, and you don't care! *Relax, and let go* all your *neck* muscles—so that it feels like your head would roll off in your lap if it weren't propped up on the chair pillow. But if it did, you wouldn't care; it wouldn't bother you! *Relax, and let go* all your shoulder and back muscles—so that it feels as though your *arms* are only tied on your shoulders with little pieces of kite cord and would *dangle and flop*, instead of swing rhythmically at your sides, if you were walking around. *Relax, and let go* your face so that it becomes like the smooth surface of a mountain lake. *Relax, and let go* all the *tightness* in your *forehead* so that every tension line and worry line s-m-o-o-t-h-s out. *Relax, and let go* all the *tense tightness*—the *knottiness* in your *temple muscles* so that they become *soft—loose—and just hanging*. *Relax, and let go* your *eyes* so that they just lie there in their sockets like marbles, placidly lying in pockets—with your lids lying over them lightly—like a blanket lightly over your body on a cool night. *Relax, and let go* the muscles which try to hold your *nose* in place on your face—so that your nose just *sits there* like a knot on a log. Now *relax, and let go* your *cheek muscles* so that they lose their taut-tightness and *hang*, loosely and so floppy that they feel almost as though they would just hang down over your jaws. Now, *unhinge your jaw* so that your teeth are about an eighth or quarter of an inch apart. And let yourself smile a gentle pleasant look for your own self's sake. *You do not have to feel happy*; it is mechanical but is to help yourself, and if someone wonders why you are smiling, that's their problem—not yours! Just let the muscles smile in order to help your brain change its center of operation from the agitated to the peaceful center.[17]

ERASE! Now, imagine Jesus Christ with an eraser standing at *the blackboard of the mind*—just behind your forehead—upon which all this jumbled-up stuff is scribbled and scrawled. (And since He is God's son, it is permanently erased.) Let Christ *erase* all these *conditioned into you, trained into you—habituated into you—false feelings, false thoughts, false perceptions*—but if they are correct, let him erase the *false perspective* you may have taken on these perceptions—which leads to *false interpretation* of the data—and a subsequent *false*

understanding of everything. Also, let him erase the *false behavior
(action or reaction) patterns* coming from the past. Let Christ erase
ALL these things which no longer apply to the *here and now of
today*—safety, salvation and freedom!

Let Christ *erase* the false feelings of fear—terror—panic—
tense—scared—threat—anxiety!

Let Christ *erase* the false feelings of
*little—weak—powerless—helpless—
hopeless—hurt—inferior*! Let Christ *erase*
the false feeling of guilt!

(You ought to *be damned or die—or punished!*)

Let Christ *erase* the false feelings of

"*Shamed* of yourself!" Belittled—ridiculed—laughed at—embarrassed—humiliated—almost non-existent—wishing a hole would
open up and you could *disappear into it and not be for a while!*

Let Christ *erase* the false feelings of self doubt!

Worthlessness—unimportant—insignificant—of no account—
no value—unlovable—stupid and ugly!

KINDLE!——————— *Now on the clean mind's blackboard* let
Christ *kindle* your God-spark Self-symbol—by drawing a tiny,
white circle on the board which immediately begins to gleam like a
brilliant new star in the heavens, as God's vertical gift down to you
from eternity—signifying to you *your right to be a focal point of life,
being, "I—amness"—independently of anyone—anywhere—anytime:
though you may choose to relate to them positively—not letting THEM
determine who you are—ONLY YOU AND GOD DEFINE THAT!*

BEAM!——————— AND SMILE FORTH from your eyes
and face an *all accepting*, non-threatened, invisible light—as though
you were a *lighthouse*, which light—like that of God's all accepting
non-threatened love—as it falls on anything which exists—even the
evil, hurtful, painful and suffering—allows it to have existed in the
past, rather than to have to destroy us as His/Her children because
He/She destroyed space-time for us—but beaming and smiling it
right up to the *present moment only!* Where *now* because you have
the Spark of God's life in you, and you are in charge of this particular space-time situation, and it is distressful to you,—*you may*
CHANGE IT!—IF ONLY TO CHANGE YOUR ATTI-
TUDE—CHANGING IT BY YOUR *CHOICE—YOUR DECI-
SION—YOUR ACTION—AND CHANGING IT SELFISHLY—as*

God's responsible, adult-level, but free child—who has a *right* to love him/herself, and give him/herself the basic *good* needs and wants of life—*enough to make life pleasurably DESIRABLE!*

FORTRESS-POWER!(You are) atop the mountain-within your soul-fortress, *unassailable—undefeatable! MASTER/MISTRESS WITHIN!*

After the exercise I pause for a moment or two and then ask the client (if desensitizing to the feeling is the goal) how he/she feels different or what he/she is now aware of as he/she imagines him/herself back in the same situation and circumstances. (The word *different* is used to help re-direct attention by aiding in overcoming self-defeating tendencies.) The person may reply that he/she feels the same, and nothing is different. In such an event, I am apt to try next the Energy Transformation Switch Exercise (the other Crisis Intervention Technique—to be explained fully further in this section). However a successful outcome is usually the case. The client may feel less fear or anxiety, or have changed his/her attitude toward the whole situation or thing because of new insights of which he/she immediately becomes aware, or he/she may be able to see and choose alternatives, options which did not seem available before; he/she may also now even imagine him/herself responding in an *active* manner, different and more satisfying. Perhaps most powerful, he/she may immediately associate a long train of similar memories within the affective tone of the previous structure. This usually brings abreaction, new insights, and new behavior. In the event desensitization is the aim, but if the person is feeling only a little less of the anxiety or fear, the therapist is to repeat the Key-word Exercise until the problem no longer disturbs the client (or has minimal intensity) when returned to in the imagination. (Some residual dimension of the feeling, however, may be desirable.) This imaginative confrontation, in all likelihood, will make a decided positive impression in actuality the next time the client faces the same or similar circumstances. Of course, the Technique does not work that lastingly or that well for all, but it does work for the majority—often even with severe phobias. Overall, the least help received from this Technique is by persons with severe obsessive-compulsive disorders, personalities with such leanings, or passive dependent problems.

The most important contribution of this Key-Word Exercise is its power in aiding regression work. The discovery of the various parts of this exercise extend back to my own *de facto* becoming consciously aware of having overcome a long-standing spider phobia while I was in the rain forest jungles of Dutch New Guinea in World War II. When I discovered the phobia was gone, I knew somewhere there had to be a total pattern for overcoming phobic fear levels. It was worth the twenty-five years it took to find the last piece of the puzzle, for in its final form, the Key-word Exercise works.[18] Although I explain this Technique to the client in the following way, *this* Exercise is essentially experiential, and no one seems really to understand it until he/she has actually done it. It is the whole person who is in one way or another upset. He/she is seeing with tunnel vision due to some past training or traumatic experience structure which limits and unconsciously focuses his/her awareness. The person is caught into what cognitive therapists would call *automatic thinking*. Therefore, what we try to do is stop the tunnel vision (automatic thinking) by expanding awareness so that the whole context may be seen and adjusted to differently. Afterward, in all probability, there will not be that much to be concerned about because the entire perceptive field and awareness will be broadened. In other words we are actually sensitizing the whole person to the whole environment to give him/her a truer perspective. He/she may appear to desensitize but it is actually only an appearance with the person continuing to appear to focus his/her entire attention upon the formerly disturbing situation or object.

To proceed with the explication of this Technique's rationale: it is explained to the client that this Exercise involves the whole person—body, thought, emotions, soul, and spirit. The person's name is used in order that he/she may affirm personal integrity and also learn to do the exercise alone using the Key-word and Self-command Words in proper order.[19] In this way the client can use the Exercise privately, even in a crowd, when such (or similar) feelings arise. The effectiveness, however, is lessened when the client is not in the transcendent mind mood. The reason for thinking and feeling "*STRESS*" (can even be done silently with the body in public) is that this brings almost the total body into the situation and further drives the entire emotion or feeling tone up to near maximum tension within the whole organism, thus *fully* activating the body's sympathetic nervous system. The command "exhaust" is used because by exhaling the breath and holding it out, the person will cause his/her body naturally to reach a point of slight relaxation of the muscles, which the client enhances using the imagination to evoke a picture (the sheet blown by the wind) thus activating the parasympathetic nervous system with its breaking effect on the sympathetic. While the sympathetic system is centered in the brain, the parasympathetic is decentralized with its activating neural system located in close proximity to the organ it is to effect. This sets the pattern for the following self-command word procedure as sequential and oriented about the face which in all primates is a primary focal sign center of emotional communication, particularly among humans, though much of signing may be effectively out of conscious awareness for many observers. The perception of these signs may be unconsciously denied out of fear or anger by both sender and receiver.

Next, the "smile" command is explained: the threat response of all mammals shows in the tense look upon their muzzle or face.[20] Also, a person's mind will begin to believe the signals his/her body is acting out. Further, it requires nearly fifty muscles to get the slightest frown of tension upon the face (and one can even self induce a migraine-like headache just keeping a tense face for a while). A perpetually sad or depressed *look* is socially self-defeating; the same is true for an anger-arousing, fear-causing, or sad human *voice*. The unconscious motivation behind these visages and tones is to CONTROL OTHERS, usually originating out of awareness and learned in childhood from parental modeling. The controlling expressive look or special voice sound can be effectively dealt with by the therapist's mimicking the client's expression for a few minutes and asking how the client feels confronting a person with such a visage or tone. Then the client is asked to mimic his/her own or the threatening look or sound of others, turn attention inward, and observe his/her own feelings while in it. A small hand mirror and a tape recorder will facilitate getting both the vocal and/or visual expression. Actually, this calling attention to some special look or sound and mocking it is a very helpful technique even without use of the Key-word Exercise. I also point out to the client that a gentle human smile is as meaningful to others as a dog wagging his tail in friendship; they both are positive feeling signs to others. It is simple to relax the face by use of the polar opposite muscle group from those which cause the personally unhappy look because it requires only about fifteen muscles to smile. *The point must be made that one does not have to FEEL happy in the smile command action, for he/she is only changing a set of muscle groupings for self help.* These groups of involved muscles will be relaxed in proper general order, ending with the dropping of muscles around the jaw. This last act is vital in order to have the necessary gap between the upper and lower teeth, under normal or relaxed circumstances. A rigid jaw is a manifestation of supposed hidden anger. Additionally, one cannot give anything but an obvious *fake* smile through nearly or completely clinched teeth; such tension will be perceived by others subliminally. Having dealt with the body, we are ready to proceed with the psyche; though this too is actually primarily a result of body and brain functioning, it is not generally thus conceptualized by the average client.

The next step is to explain to the client the self-command word "erase" and its accompanying feeling-thought pictures which enable us to make more real to ourselves the concepts we need. Therefore, the *scribbled upon* blackboard of the mind is a picture used to begin the activation of the symbolizing function of a Christian's religious belief system about God's forgiveness. Imagining Christ erasing the chalkboard will help eliminate false guilt or other such threat feelings which do not actually have anything to do with one's Self's safe-secure position in the *"eternal now"* in which Christians live. Further, one may not be troubled by all the feelings which he/she imagines Christ erasing, but most of us have some of these components present in any tense situation; and this symbolic scene will help us make more real to ourselves our belief in divine forgiveness. At this erase point, we are beginning to deal with the spiritual dimensions of one's psyche's problems.

Next the "kindle" concept is explained: while we have dealt with many negatives, we have yet to affirm one's basic right to BE. The fact that a single star is a universal spiritual Self-symbol is explained—perhaps even pointing out that we symbolically envisage an inner image of that totally independent right to existence gleaming down as a vertical gift given from God only, a basic existential individual human right. This position reinforces the archetypal sense of one's God-given right to be. Others only help me understand my personality, but they have no right to define me. Because of necessity I am a socially responsive being, however, I can and do choose to relate positively to them.[21] This basic inner

Self affirmation is a part of our total sense of loss in every threat experience, so it is given a rekindling by the Son of God himself.

The "beam and smile forth" self-command is next explained. Christ said that we were to "resist not evil...." (Matt. 5:39 KJV). He spoke truths we are only now psychologically comprehending; thus we can now realize that a person who goes about with a threatened look on his/her face, as though there were something to fear all the time, is indeed going about constantly on guard against evil. (This insight came in a personal conversation with a paranoid schizophrenic friend who told me this visage kept people on guard around him. It was why he kept such a look, and added, "The best defense is an offense!") Then it is to our great personal advantage to beam and smile forth in a relaxed way at all creation around us: by doing so we bring ourselves and all others a sense of blessing. However, as children of God created in His/Her image, when evil does suddenly confront us, our person nature has a relatively basic right to self-preservation and may choose at that moment to deal with the evil in a Christ-like way. That right demands we take certain things into consideration: we recognize we are adult-level and responsible to God for that which we change or do; and yet, we also are God's free child, set free to our existence by Christ himself. Thus we also have certain God-given needs, and some wants, which are inalienably ours, that is, a minimum right to love ourselves or preserve our own life by giving ourselves enough pleasure to cause us to continue to find life desirable. (As Christians, we are NOT TO KILL OUR DESIRE. Killing desire is Buddhist teaching! Desire, love, is the life-juice.) Furthermore, it takes this self-love to be able to continue to exist in order to love God and neighbor. Nor will we be able to do *any* good if we allow everyone to walk all over us in our false humility.

Last, the hyphenated command word of "fortress-power" is explained: the client is led to see that one must have some inner feeling of adequate power; this has been the secret of Christian ability to stand and even live under the most adverse circumstances. The key to such stamina is that we have an inner soul-fortress, the Self, which is able to withstand almost any onslaught. This fortress is our inner image of selfhood and power given us by God, and we can know its inner secrecy of retreat and self-protection if we turn our mind to its symbolism. Thus we end the exercise on the high point of the gifts of eternal life and God's type of safety and security again. The explanation does not take as long to provide as one might think. After the *experience* of the exercise, the client generally readily grasps the significance of the parts of the exercise.

Of course, there are those who *cannot* trust the therapist, or anyone, very quickly. The trained therapist will recognize those clients almost immediately, know to take more time, and first give the needed intellectual details. Thereafter, the therapist may persuade this type of client to try the Exercise with imagination only. Even then the therapist takes the time needed before moving ahead to using the technique on the transcending level. The lower the trust level, the more slowly one should take the entire procedure. However, even the most avid clients generally do not need to do this Exercise more than three or four times in one session; it is too exhausting.[22] After experiencing this total technique once or twice, the client will tend to respond well to briefed-down uses of the exercise i.e.: Stress! Relax (name)! Exhaust; Smile; Erase; Kindle; Beam and Smile; Fortress-power. It is important to note, however, this briefed-down version rapidly tends to lose its symbol-based power and brief return to use of the full Exercise must be done every so often as the therapist notes the loss.

The Switch Exercise For Energy Transformation

Although I cannot claim credit for the origin of this exercise, I developed it within the framework of Faith Therapy. Dr. Martha Crampton of the Canadian Institute of Psychosynthesis in Montreal as guest speaker for the April, 1973 meeting of the Psychosynthesis Seminars in New York, addressed the group about some principals and techniques of energy transformation in the psyche and told of her recent discovery in that area. She had found that great catalytic force lay within the Self and Will (in our paradigm, the Self and Will-of-wills). She also discovered she could get people to let themselves "wallow around in" the negative energy of such feelings as "hatred, dependency, self-pity, resentment, etc."; then she could audibly clap her hands, turn a light switch (or say "switch" in groups), use small cymbals, or snap her fingers and the Self and its Will-center would begin a natural transformation of the negative energy into its polar opposite. (It was fascinating to me that another had independently come upon the discovery that clapping and finger-snapping had power to affect the psyche positively. This led to further, later amplification in my own development of an enlarged concept of the Switch Technique.) Her findings indicated that one defeated this energy transformation when one consciously tried to think instead of only becoming aware of exactly what the polar opposite would be. The individual unconscious was the only faculty which *knew* such personal exact opposites, so the ego was more or less to observe and experience the transformation of the negative feeling into the positive energies. The more frequently one used this energy transformation approach, the more positively it reinforced itself because of the great satisfaction it brought.[23]

The Crisis Intervention Technique which I call "Switch" developed through my own theorizing and application of the switch idea as used in this religiously oriented therapy. Since the person in the transcendent mind mood is in closer connection with the Self and Will-of-wills (Dr. Crampton's "Will") and is concomitantly in closer connection with his usual willpower (our usual "will") centered in the ego, the total power available to effect the energy transformation from the negative to the positive pole is greater because the will centers operate together. Will power (sometimes becoming a will-to-power) wears out very easily and needs to relax and cooperate with the Will-of-wills if life is to be lived with some comfort. In my approach, I get the person who is into his/her trigger to use the imagination to slip into a memory of a true scene for which he/she had a lot of negative feeling. (In order to do so, one may need to imagine his/her spirit slipping into his/her body.) When the client feels saturated with it, I clap my hands, an act which seems to shake the individual up, physically and psychologically, and simultaneously I loudly say, "*Switch!*"[24] My theory is that the startling sound activates the primitive threat response centralized in the sympathetic nervous system, with which we are born—jarring free the frozen energy to establish a new alternate neuron pathway through which the soul may thereafter function. Following this, the old energy may be lifted to upper unconscious expression through religious imagery and concepts. I immediately continue to guide the client in the following manner (again written in vocal style, including bracketed TN:'s for the Therapist's Notes of instruction): [TN: Sharply, commandingly] *SWITCH!* (**CLAP**) *Don't think! Don't think!* [TN: Now only forcefully] Just *release* your energy—and *be aware of and experience it* almost *objectively*—almost as though it were happening to someone else—*releasing it* from its more *negative polarity* within your being—*your ego*, everyday "I am" center—with its "will-power core" of *will-to-power*—*must control*—*must be perfect*—*must please*—*must do everything just right orientation*! So that the energy *floats free*—like a bar of soap slipping out of your hands in a bathtub and *floating away* from you. So that *now* the energy becomes sensitive to its natural, inner—chemical-like—but *SPIRITUAL VALENCE*, which orients it toward the more natural home it should have gone to in the first place before your false ego defenses got in the way! So that now—the energy becomes *switched across and UP* (Clap)—to your God-spark center—the more *positive polarity, I am-ness center*—*the larger center* within your being—with its Mother Nature side of God within you [TN: Easily]—with its *easy—flowing—growing* orientation. This polarity has as its will-core a [TN: Firmly] *TRANS-FORMING CENTER OF POWER* (*power* being the ability to change, transform, convert, or use energy)—*THE WILL-OF-WILLS TO ULTIMATE GOOD*—the best good *possible—for you*—*God—and everybody* (or *name of the disturbing person*)—*equally—alto-gether—all at the same time—to the best of your IMPERFECT human ability!* Where *this core* takes the energy—and transforms it *UPWARD*—like electricity converted *upward* into *heat* and again changed *upward* into *light*—as this core takes your (name of negative feeling) and *transforms* it *upward* into whatever for *you*, under these circumstances, is the *GOOD* (Clap)—into whatever for *you*, under these circumstances, is the *FREE* (Clap)—into whatever for *you*, under these circumstances is the *POWERFUL* (Clap)— [TN: Pause adequately] Now, return to the same scene and see how you feel different. If there is *no* change, tell me that, too. What pleases me is what you *truly* feel.

At times the therapist will find this Switch Exercise may produce results if it is repeated several times successively, like a railroad switch engine needing to bump repeatedly the same freight car down the track until it hooks on to the other cars forming the train. Such repetitions of the Technique shorten the verbal part increasingly but *not* the shock effect of the hand claps. The action stops the client's mind from returning too quickly and obsessively to the old electrical neural pattern which is stubborn and hard to break in the first place.

Sometimes an immediate energy transformation appears, complete, and subsequently proves itself in the client's life. At other times, the process may have to be repeated several times, as is done with Key-word Desensitizing by Sensitizing, in order to get any results with which the client is satisfied. A briefed-down approach may also be used with the Switch Exercise for Energy Transformation, i.e.: Switch/"Clap;" Release energy from Ego's Will-to-Power...; Sensitive to spiritual valences...; Switched across and up/"Clap" to God-spark center and into Will-of-wills...; Transformed into your good/"Clap," free/"Clap," powerful/ "Clap." Also, there are times when the Switch Procedure shows absolutely *no* positive results, and another method will have to be used. Upon occasions the Switch Technique seems beneficially interchangeable with the Desensitizing Technique; their physiological mechanisms are somewhat alike but the concept and imagery is different. However, the differences are very decided in many cases; for example, I have not found the Switch Technique to aid but slightly, if at all, in regression work. In such cases, Switching apparently does not really bring to working availability the negative energy blocks which, in the first place, prevent the switching of the energy into a higher, positive structure. However, most of the time the Technique is a very effective energy transformation tool.[25] [An example of its use will be found in Chapter XIII, "The Client With 'Burn Out'."]

Creative Symbolization Methods

Experiencing "The Holy"; God, Light, Knowing, Time
Stop/Start Watch, and Objective Observer
In the light of God's Presence the client may temporarily stop time and all action as though everyone and everything else in the area were frozen unthreateningly in statue-like form. Further, the client may even spiritually step out of him/herself for greater objectivity. By so doing the client may then come to discover that which was perhaps in awareness (possibly it was subliminal in the first place) and which he/she had falsely and unconsciously refused to acknowledge. In using this device, the client can often make better and more accurate judgments which use sympathy wisely, empathetically, and which provide understanding and forgiveness. He/She agrees to become the Objective Observer, as an operation of the Self.[26] At times I find this to be more easily done by the use of an imaginary Time Stop/Start Watch which one may conceive of being with him/her at all times, pulling or pushing the stem to

start or stop time. God's presence as "Light brighter than day—but not blinding—coming like a spotlight from somewhere above, you cannot tell where" can be caused to shine revealingly and protectively around the person and the situation, penetrating through any layer of earth, ceilings, etc. This symbol of the presence of The Holy provides the safe-secure affect and enhances perception. However, the therapist will also occasionally find the need to remind the client, when re-experiencing formerly threatening experiences, that in God's Light it is *now* O.K. to let oneself know anything which he/she had formerly hidden from consciousness.

Black Light

A strange phenomenon connected with the Light of God's Presence and which may occur anytime the Light is experienced is that it may appear as Black Light (or as Light with quanta or blobs of alternating blackness within it). The actual rate of occurrence is rare, however. Highly perceptive people are more likely to have this experience; if by chance they were exposed to a lot of emotionally arid early life and/or much hell-fire and brimstone type of early religious training, the blackness could indicate a false fear, identifying it with evil. Probably in this blackness, God is symbolically presenting Him/Herself to them in the pairs of opposites— Female/Male, Ying/Yang, Good Dark/Good Light aspects of Him/Herself; therefore to allow the fear to continue is a major ministering therapy error. The person has probably refused to consider this metaphysical fact deeply and earnestly before. I have noted that these people also tend to be those who, in the Jungian sense, have striven to live too much of their lives on the light, or ego, side of their existence and have almost stifled the positive power aspects of their shadow side. My experience is that this fear, if present, may be explained to them simply: of necessity as Creator, God contains both sides of the pairs of opposites. The Bible creation story indicates this fact, for He/She even divided the darkness as His/Her first act of creation and named *both* sides of existence, night and day (Gen 1:1-5 RSV). It may be necessary to remind them that not all dark is bad nor all light good. Most important, they should not get the mistaken idea that dark has no good in it. And they need to become aware that the evil spoken of biblically was mostly that of *non-good done in the hiding of darkness.* Most often the symbolism of the black is only the presence of contrast which *must* be (all sticks must have two ends). Or, the black may represent avoidance of the more (traditionally thought of) feminine aspects of oneself which have been falsely evaded. Interestingly enough, with one client the Black Light, of its own accord, entered the skull and seemed to divide it into four equal parts, after which the person began to gain access to more positive feelings, repressed in the past.

Transforming, Clapping, Finger Snapping, Holy Spirit,
Asking God, the Voice of God, Introjecting (or Assimilating),
and the Sweat-out

Again, in this exercise the Light is used. At any time one has a highly negative or personally unpleasant feeling, such as a false guilt feeling, he/she may call for the Light to shine around him/her, imagine the feeling as being a *black fluid of feeling* mixed in with the bloodstream, and alien. (Here black *is* conceived of as something unwanted and personally discomforting.) In the Light the client may sweat out the blackness of feeling by lifting his/her hands and arms upward, palms out, in an act of dedication and consecration to the Light and letting the blackness sweat out through the palms and fingertips, watching it come out in a smokey, dark, vaporous form. It is simultaneously drawn upwards by the power of the Light, disappearing into the Light. If the person conceives of this feeling as sinful, he/she may not wish to do this, feeling that sin is unworthy to offer to God. In that event one has to be reminded that God wastes nothing, not even material energy, and that humans are supposed to make a complete offering of themselves, even their sins. When the client indicates that it is all gone (individual time periods vary and some residue *may* remain), he/she is requested to bow his/her head, close his/her eyes, and cup his/her hands and arms down in front of him/her in order to receive back from God that which He/She has now converted to a higher form. The client is to wait until he/she feels something appear in his/her hands or arms coming down from the Light. The client then imagines opening his/her eyes and describes the transformed gift sent by God. At this point it is often necessary for the therapist to snap his/her fingers, or clap, in order to break over-concentrative thoughts, coming from the left brain, which delay the spontaneity of the right brain creation of the returned symbol. For some reason, perhaps inadequate childhood right hemisphere stimulation, a few clients have trouble imagining seeing a symbol; in such event simply repeat the reverent waiting, repeat the finger snapping, or clapping, and proceed as before. Repeating several times will usually ultimately produce an acceptable symbol. If for whatever reason a transformed symbol is negative, return it to God, letting it float upward out of sight into the Light, and then repeat the dedication until an acceptable symbol returns. Sometimes nothing transformed is seen, though it is felt in the hands. If so, ask the client to stare at it until it takes form. Or it may be a feeling of some sort of power which flows into the hands. In that event it will be necessary for the therapist to ask the client how he/she now feels different or to ask God concretely to symbolize it. Also at times a returned symbol may come from the collective unconscious and be cross-cultural. In such an event, the therapist does well to research the symbol later for additional nuances of meaning.

When the symbol appears in the hands, the client should then look up into the Light and ask God, "What is this supposed to mean to me?" Usually, the Voice occurs.[27] It may seem the quiet inner knowledge, or it may be actually experienced as though outwardly heard, but it will almost always reveal the personal meaning of the symbol. If the symbol seems too unclear or even negative, another way of dealing with such confusion is for the therapist to ask the client to become aware of "the Light intensifying inside itself like a laser beam—but without losing any power—with the power of the Holy Spirit, and lightning-like, but not painfully nor destructively, striking the symbol and again Transforming it." This process should be repeated, if necessary, until a positive image occurs. When it does, the client should ask God (after asking Him/Her for personal meaning) whether he/she is to "absorb it (like a sponge, a drop of water) and let it fill the places where the other was sweated out (Introject or Assimilate it) or if he/she should keep it exteriorized in an imaginary way." Usually the person is told to absorb it; but one way or another, the client should now be asked how he/she feels different in order to conceptualize the symbol's personal effect. If there is no answer from God, the symbol may be Introjected, and if it is unpleasant it may then again be Projected and imaginarily kept with the client (or released to go its own way) along with the request of the Light that somehow the symbol soon become clarified in its meaning. In such cases the answer may come as a later sudden insight or clarifying dream, often before the next session. Interpretation of such sought-for dreams and insights should be given a high Dialogical Counseling priority. One way or another, it is the therapist's job to make sure the client is currently reasonably comfortable with the symbol.

It is vital in all transcending sessions that a Christian therapist be constantly aware of and guided by the concept that *God is Good!* Self-defeat is so strong in some clients that the therapist, if an ordained member of the clergy, must use the authority vested in him/her at ordination to keep the client from utilizing the deep, and sometimes skillfully hidden, determination toward self-defeat, self-destruction and feelings of personal worthlessness. It is, I agree, an awesome responsibility. But if pastors do not authoritatively speak for the love of God made real in Christ, who will? The clergy have authority in these areas, but it must be used without manipulation.

The Spiritual Recharge

A person may, using the same technique, get a Recharge (like charging up a discharged battery) of his/her own spiritual level of life-energy. When a client feels his/her spiritual batteries are dead, the therapist tells him/her to hold his/her hands up to the Light in an act of dedication and consecration, asks the client to watch as the Light surrounding him/her intensifies within itself (as the Holy Spirit) and laser-beam-like with power like lighting, but painlessly, strikes the fingertips. This light continues to stay in contact with the fingers and charges the person up until he/she feels full and invisibly radiates love as the power of light to all around. The therapist should give the client time to experience this feeling and the client should tell the therapist when the process is complete. The ministering guide again aids the person to conceptualize any new feelings by asking how he/she now feels different. To repeat for emphasis, this asking how the client feels *different* is not a manipulative gesture. It is simply that the client has been frequently conditioned to look for negatives (even *expect* negative feelings), so finger snapping and asking the client to focus on different feelings is a therapeutic tool to aid in recognizing that one can and does at times in life have positive feelings and that all emotion is cyclical. Also, the instrument helps a person realize it is his/her own task virtuously to create for oneself as many honest good feelings as one can. This is particularly true for a person who grew up in a highly depressive environment, was constantly criticized, or had to be (hysterically) the family entertainer.

Quieting the "Foundry Noise"

This Procedure is done largely and almost solely by reaching the transcending level of mind (preferably using Schema Level III, Stage 9) and staying still. Prior to entering the Schema Exercise, this practice is described in the following manner: "Living in a body which preoccupies the psyche with constant sensory input signals may be likened to trying to hear birds singing outside when one lives and works constantly in an operating foundry. Therefore, we are going to quiet the noise of the senses in order to be aware of things beyond their input." Once the client is into the transcendent mind mood he/she is asked to become open to new insights while in this holy place in his/her own psyche. The person's awareness is to be directed toward insights concerning whatever problems or issues he/she had listed to the therapist before the Intensified Faith part of the session began. The client is to verbalize all awareness flow as insights occur so as to enhance personal conceptual clarity and later recall. The therapist's chief concern will be to keep the client conceptualizing and talking aloud at times due to a problem of time-sense distortion. The spiritual guide may need to keep asking and prodding. It is nevertheless amazing what solutions and positive insights into perplexing issues and problems a client may get while doing this Procedure alone in his/her own psyche. Also, suggesting that the client ask for God's Light to shine around him/her throughout the Procedure brings additional benefits for some.

Unwinding

This method helps relieve much diffuse body tension and anxiety. The exercise is particularly effective with persons who have a tendency to somatize emotion, convert all emotion—usually fear, anxiety, or anger—into neural energy which is stored up in the form of warehoused sensation in a particular spot within the body. The client is asked simply to stay in the Light and focus awareness upon the spot or spots in which the tension or pain is centered. At the same time, the client is immediately to focus awareness on the freely given and reflexive *God's breath that breathes itself* (further activation of the parasympathetic nerve system) until he/she can let go of fearful chest muscle breathing. When the client can keep steadily "breathing God's breath reflexively," he/she is ready to turn attention to Unwinding. If tension should again take hold at any point in this Procedure, the client should immediately return to the breathing exercise. Each time the client turns attention to a tense spot, as a rule, there will be a slow unwinding in the form of a pleasant, warm feeling in the area of the somatized pain or tension. People prone to tension may be asked to put the tense feeling into their fists. Simultaneously they are asked to tighten the fist as though to strike something. (This is an accurate archetypal picture of what is probably the truth within them, but they cannot let themselves consciously know it.) When they feel that all the energy is now in the fist, as a symbol to them of the tension they feel all over, they are asked to let the fist go slowly, with the aid of the Light's relaxing warmth and love until the fingers even hang limp-loosely. This exercise is repeated a number of times if needed, and then immediately one is given a Specific Positive Idea that one will clearly remember how to do this exercise on the everyday mind mood level and carry it out immediately in an appropriate place. This auto-suggestion idea of Desoille's is particularly helpful for persons who have difficulty in getting much elevation or intensity of faith's transcendent mind mood.[28] After deschematizing and for reinforcement, it is important immediately to check out the client's ability to use this technique by having him/her try it out several times, using his/her own imagination.

I strongly suspect that this and other Creative Symbolization Methods may be very helpful in getting the immune system's power into more active participation in healing the body. Many of the Methods tend to *further relax* the brain's emergency operation system for the body. This means more positive emotion flow, which in turn releases a more natural enhanced flow of the immune system's power, for somatic healing.[29]

Logos-Power

This practice may be inserted anywhere in the other Procedures. It is defined this way to the client: "Logos" is used in the Gospel of John in speaking of Christ, and it is translated from Greek into English as "Word" because we do not have an adequate single

English term with which to translate it. If we put it into English, we would have to hyphenate a group of words to communicate the entire concept. Logos is the creative-person-thinking-feelingness power of God. Now, since we also have *some* of the same God-spark power as Jesus, we also have some Logos-power, power easier to use in a transcendent mind mood. This force also seems a little like magic because by coupling Logos with imagination we can creatively change things, even destroy constructively. We can also conceive of this Power as being FLASHED like lightening from our eyes to cause powerful changes. In fact, Buber calls Logos' verbal use the speech with meaning. In short, Logos-power is a spiritual force inside ourselves with which we can imaginally change and create things. The advantage of giving this force a name is to give it more credibility than mere imagination, which one tends to identify with child's play. Therefore, Logos-power used in conjunction with other Therapy Procedures seems also to have a therapeutic validity which most often later manifests itself in desired behavioral change.

Also, I believe Logos power to have to do with the strange phenomenon of "the look," one of those frightening (archetypal) experiences children tend to have early in life. Even as adults we may experience the strange power of the look when we see it directed at us by another person. This can sometimes cause a shudder sensation in us. We make a grave mistake ever to think an archetype, in reality, has no unconscious, universal power, because it is *never* that logical by Aristotelian standards of reasoning. The archetype's source of reason, meaning and purpose lies deeper; it is at the root of all things in their instinctual, psychoid base within the collective unconscious or objective psyche.

The Key-word and Consciousness Raising

Many times it will be wise after use of the Key-word Desensitizing Technique merely to ask the client to return to the envisioned scene and check his/her present awareness. This almost simplistic re-imagining will likely allow the client to now expand awareness of the situation and receive insight into the formerly troublesome threatening incident. Desensitizing is really of less concern in this situation, for the depth spiritual growth and elevating of consciousness are the real gains. (This is well illustrated in

Chapter XII where Speck, while in his transcendent space, has an encounter with God as Center of Light, Person, and Communicating Presence!)

If the insights are accompanied by profound emotional reactions, such as weeping, the ministering therapist must allow reasonable time for the reactions of the client while still in the transcendent state. This will enable the client to abreact as much of the traumatic emotional matter as possible and assimilate the new insights gradually. The therapist may empathize even to the point of tears if the feelings are genuinely overwhelming. It is also appropriate for the therapist to kneel beside the client and perhaps put a comforting hand on his/her hand, arm, or shoulder. Because the client's grief in some situations may be tremendously intense, the most needed response may be a comforting *human touch*, perhaps accompanied by some *thou-words* spoken softly: "I know—it really hurts, doesn't it?" "Yes, it was a crazy way to treat a child!" This too, spoken by the therapist, is "logos," the word-with-meaning.

In such an event of depth abreaction, it is very important to try to allow a bit more time at the end of the session itself for the Dialogical Counseling in order to explore new insights in the Post-therapy Work Check-out and to place these insights logically. The client needs an opportunity to "talk it out" with the therapist as a sounding board and form the insights into firm concepts. Considerably more growth time is needed to integrate this new material into the usual mind mood of everyday, ego-oriented life so that it may produce positive change in his/her experience of faith. The client's main need at this time is for social reassurance that this emotionally charged knowledge indeed makes the sense he/she found it to have in the ultimate reality of the transcending mind mood. This same need also manifests itself in the Regression Procedure.

Regression and Relating (Including Mind Screen, "Floating Back" [in time],New Decisions, Two Levels of "Now" Awareness, Self-affirmations,Time Stop/Start Watch, and Positive Assertions)
So far as I can tell, there are two central differences between a regression exercise in most other psychotherapies and in this religious therapy: the first is that one regresses not by associated thoughts or ideas, unless they are the first items presented. In Faith

Therapy, however, the primary emphasis is upon regression by a definite, but perhaps only vaguely felt, cognitive structure noted primarily by its association with similar emotion or affective tone. The second difference is that this regression exercise, done principally by following a feeling tone, at times indicates that the uncovered material is so consciousness threatening it must otherwise be done with deep hypnosis, a method in which the client is apt not to have as quick or easy recall upon return to his/her usual state of consciousness. Significantly, regression done with this religious psychotherapy is accomplished with the full cooperation and assistance of consciousness, for the Exercise is done with the ego in service to the Self. I believe the fact that the client's awareness is being directed by his/her Self is a major reason for this method's success, inasmuch as the Self is the Soul-center and has always been present from some point of womb existence although there is no way of proving at what point. (Further elaboration of this theory will take place in Part II.) Although one can only speculate about womb awareness, the eyes—or perhaps only archetypal symbols or eternal forms which are already active in the mind do seem to be functioning, and some sort of feeling-centered awareness does appear to occur in utero.

One thing of which I am reasonably certain is that the discriminatory clarity of regression with the Self leading the way for the ego would probably not be possible except for the symbolized presence of God as the Light. This Light seems to give the regression its needed sense of safe-secure affect which then allows the person to know on the ego level things the Self has known all along. The superego, thought of here as only similar to conscience, refused to allow this knowledge to be present in consciousness and to be available to the ego because the knowledge seemed threatening to continuing existence. Even in the Light, from time to time it is necessary for the therapist to remind the client that this safety provided by the Light means it is now all right to let oneself come to know the formerly ego-denied material. This reassurance by the therapist is also needed in Key-word Desensitizing and consciousness expansion, but the repeated reassurance is even more often called for in regression work.

A very good illustration of this Guided Meditation Therapy Procedure and its accompanying practices appears in the following actual case history. (The names and enough details have been changed to disguise the characters, but the basic material illustrating the Procedure has been kept intact.) In this particular case there was so much obvious, constant disagreement, even dislike, between husband and wife that I wondered how they had managed to stay together for nearly fifteen years. So far as I could discern, the only real reason was the depth of Christian conviction about the sacredness of marriage and the sense of duty to the three children. Since this particular regression was done with the wife, I shall largely keep my comments centered upon her; however, it should be noted that the husband had some deep emotional problems, which stemmed from his childhood characterized by emotional neglect, in which both parents worked and were filled with tacit hostility which largely went unexpressed and unresolved, fostering a rigid, polite, home environment. The maternal grandmother, who lived with them, only presumably looked after the child up to age six. Apparently, she primarily used him to gain her own ends. Therefore, in childhood, this husband learned very little personal value put upon him for his sake alone.

On the other hand, the wife had before marriage been a sort of selfmade, successful business woman. She had grown up in a largely semi-rural situation where there were a number of other sisters and brothers, of whom she was the oldest daughter. She had early been given the responsibility of doing much of the housework by a whining and complaining mother, who seemed to shirk as much responsibility as possible. However, the mother seemed to enjoy her sex life with her husband, a fact not hidden from the children. The greatest negative factor was that the father had occasional bouts of acting crazy. The episodes finally became so bad after most of the children left home that my client, as one of the older children, had to take the initiative in having the family institutionalize the father, who was diagnosed as having severe paranoid schizophrenia from which he never recovered. He later died in the institution.

Most of the early memories of her father of which my client consciously had awareness were fairly good ones, except for his displays of temper. But she (let us call her Nell) had no conscious memories of his actually ever hurting her. Nell had a certain combination of anger and fear concerning her husband at times, however, which led me to suspect a deep structural link to early childhood experiences with her father. At times her husband had a way of treating her which reminded her of feelings she had when her father was in a "crazy bout." At these times she feared that she, too, would go into a rage. The particular way in which he looked at her and treated her at these times was the trigger situation which resulted in my asking her to make a two-hour appointment for plenty of time to undertake a regression to seek out the unconscious source of the distress and begin some work on coping with the feelings.

Nell's regression work began with the Intensified Faith Schema in which she proceeded only to Modified Level II, Stage 4, for she was as yet not ready to go to the Transcendent Level. With the problems she apparently grappled with it was wise not to move any higher. Being a deep Christian on an experiential level, she had no trouble getting the sense of the transcending mind mood from the mountaintop and an experienced level of the Presence of loving acceptance. I then asked her to imagine the last time that her husband, Sam (another fictitious name), had acted in the way which she had defined as the trigger. I then asked her to be sure she noticed his "look" and "sound," to be aware of where in their home the incident had taken place, and to notice who was present. She was to verbalize it all to me as she imagined the situation. When Nell arrived at the point where she had the full awareness of her feelings about Sam, I had her use the Key-word Desensitizing Exercise. (i.e. Stress! Key-word [Relax Nell]! Smile! Erase! Kindle! Beam and Smile! Fortress-power!) As soon as she had completed it, I requested her to return imaginarily to the scene and see how she felt different. In a few moments, she reported that while she no longer felt the same anger toward her husband, she was now vaguely aware of something back there in the back of her mind, a similar feeling which she had never noticed before. I asked her to stay with the feeling and ask for God's Light to shine upon her in the situation. She did so and felt the immediate increase in safe-secure feelings of God's graceful love.

I then asked Nell to amplify the *back-there* feeling as much as she could, to follow the feeling backwards in time into the blackness of the past—supported by the Light. (For some very strong meditators, the therapist may safely merely ask them to let themselves become aware of their earliest situation in childhood in which these feelings occurred and they can find it with the Self's help.) I directed her to let the feeling draw her to the earliest similar incident she could safely let come to her awareness. Nell felt herself floating backwards in the darkness. As she was experiencing this I suggested to her that she might even feel somewhat as though her body were becoming smaller, as though she were a child. She was to remember however, that even if she had a sensory impression of a smaller body she still had her current adult ego going back with her so that in God's safety she could let herself know things she had hidden from herself before. Additionally, I suggested that she imagine she had a Mind Screen upon which the incident could safely appear out in the darkness and that the incident she saw might even appear to be happening to someone else. She was to tell me when she saw some picture appear. I suggested that the Light would stop moving when a scene did appear.

There was a long silence, into which, however, I occasionally dropped relevant questions concerning what was happening. After a few minutes she said she saw a picture of herself, on the Mind Screen, in a temporary house in which her family had once lived while they were building a new one, and a school friend seemed to be with her. I then asked her to step into the Screen and slip into herself, bringing the Light with her; and I reminded her she had her Time Stop/Start Watch with her, so she could pull its stem to stop time safely until she became aware of what was going on and how she felt.

She immediately stepped into the scene and did as I had suggested. This action made her instantly aware of the increased strength of the trigger's affective tone which she had been letting draw her backward in time. When asked how old she was in the "back there, *now*," her reply, in her adult voice, was that she was somewhere around eight years old, and the girl was a friend whom she especially liked and whom she wanted to like her; but Nell's father was there with that strange "look." I asked her how she felt or thought she would feel if she started time again with the watch in order to see what was really happening. She felt she would be safe in doing so and started the time. Immediately her father assumed an odd appearance and behavior, strangely teasing the friend who had come to spend the night. As she again looked at her father, the surge of the trigger feeling became stronger, and she was aware of her fear. We again used the Descensitizing Exercise(i.e.: Stress! KeyWord:[Relax Nell]! ....Exhaust! ....Smile! ....Erase! ....Kindle! ....Beam and ....Smile! Fortress-power!....) while she imagined looking at her father. Afterwards the feeling was not present anymore, but she was aware that this behavior was "sort of crazy-like" and was threatening her friendship. But she had a stronger hunch that its source was further back.

So I had Nell step out of the Mind Screen memory and back into the darkness, bringing the Light with her to see where the feeling would now carry her. The device of floating backward was reactivated, and this time she saw a picture of a little girl who looked about four-and-a-half years old who was on the back porch of her family's old house. Again I asked her to step into the picture, slip into the little girl to see what was happening taking the Time Stop/Start Watch with her, and let the Light go with her for safety. She did so and instantly recognized the little girl as herself and was very frightened. I asked her to remember that the safety of God and His/Her Light was with her. As she focused her awareness upon herself, she felt the full intensity of the trigger feeling but also realized she was safe and wanted to know where this feeling came from. Sensing that she was at the structural heart of the matter, I reminded her that the Light was with her; and she, therefore, could not get hurt in what was about to happen. (The therapist can even have the client reverse the situation [as in reversing movie film] in order to get out of, desensitize to, and dismiss an impossible situation.) It was O.K. to let herself consciously know what she had kept hidden before now; and if she wanted to, she could now start time again to see what would happen. She did this and became immediately aware that her father had a funny (strange) look and was coming toward her. Her father seemed to be going to do something to entertain other people on the porch. Nell was experiencing increasing fear as he came toward her and picked her up in a jerking manner. I had her stop time immediately, look at him, and desensitize (i.e.: Stress! [Key Word:] Relax Nell! ....Exhaust! ....Smile! ....Erase! ....Kindle!.... Beam and Smile!....Fortress-power!....). When we were through, she knew she was not only terrified but also rigidly angry. Additionally, she knew he was going to dangle her over the reportedly bottomless well at the edge of the porch. Nevertheless, she wanted to re-experience all this in safety and come to know more about it. We started time again, and her father proceeded to do exactly what she had known he would do. At the maximum of the terror of being held over the well, she could also experience her fear and anger at her helpless situation. (Oddly enough, no one on the porch came to her rescue or defense at any time.) As she let herself feel the full terror and rage, she also looked at her father full in the face. We again stopped time and used the Desensitization Exercise three times, until she experienced complete calm. Ultimately, she was able to become rationally aware of her father's paranoid nature even in the re-experiencing of that early time in her life.

With time stopped, God's Light surrounding her in safety, and her "present now awareness" of everything, she stayed in the "back there *now*" letting her adult ego rationally establish the Relations and come to know what she fully believed God wanted her to know. (Notice the two levels of *now awareness* running simultaneously.) As she began to feel she currently consciously had the knowledge of how crazy her childhood situation had been and the total confusion she had often felt, I asked her again to remember and re-experience the feeling she had when her father was still holding her over the well. Then I asked her the clincher question? "While in the 'back there then, *now*,' notice how these feelings you have been experiencing relate in some manner to today." "Oh Lord," she said, "that is the way I felt with Sam the other night!" Again, I asked her to search fully for any further connections between the two experiences. (Often such early negative emotional experiences become an unassimilated basic core in the unconscious which has a valence-like pull, erroneously drawing into its affective structure and consequent behavior attitudes toward persons, situations, things, and surroundings. Consciously the person has no awareness of how it is poisoning the whole cognitive structure toward anything unconsciously associated with it and its early affective roots. It is like an unassimilated and encapsulated piece of baking powder in a good "scratch" cake. The cake looks and tastes good until one bites down on the piece of baking powder, then the entire mixture seems to taste terrible. Apparently, such was the case in this incident of relating to close male figures.) This time she related the early well experience feeling-tones to a number of experiences of this seemingly irrational type which she had gone through and which she identified with her husband over the years of their marriage. While she had thought there were absolutely no connections or similarities between her father and her husband, actually there were a great many. So we now desensitized in the present day to these related reactive feelings toward her husband.

When she had completed them, I had her see if she wanted to

make a New Decision that she would never let Sam, his actions, and looks, affect her that way again.[30] She said yes to the idea, so we proceeded to have her imagine looking Sam in the face again and telling herself that he was not her father and she was not a little girl anymore but an adult and could take care of herself.[31] I asked her to speak this statement out loud several times, with a one minute pause between for more complete assimilation. (Speaking aloud this way helps to make the language-thought pattern firmer to the brain.) She then said it with self-affirmation and strong conviction, actually so strong that she laughed out loud with the good feelings she was giving herself.[32] (This incident, then, is also an illustration of Self-affirmation and Positive Assertion.)

At the close of this part, she spontaneously became aware of a vague dislike toward a son (another matter valence-like drawn into the negative affect structure). She saw that this dislike was also caused by a relationship which reminded her of her father in very minor ways. Largely, they had to do with the son's poor school and play behavior and his reactions to these problems. However, she felt she did not need to desensitize to these feelings about him in these matters. With this new knowledge she felt she could now help him more and understand his maladjustive actions better. Nell was ready to end the regression part of her therapy so I guided her to return to the "back there then, now"—to imagine her father putting her down on the porch, her stepping back out of the Mind Screen and into the Light in the darkness, and letting the Light bring her all the way back up to the present, with no false impressions left over such as littleness. She then let the Light bring her back to the mountaintop and disappear into the heavens. All this she did quickly. We then used the Usual Positive Ideas, and deschematized her intensified faith level to her usual level of awareness, or usual frame of reference.

Finally, I asked her to open her eyes, sit up and explore how she felt. We briefly reviewed all she had been through as I had written it on my chart. (Note: in using this method, it is an excellent idea to record briefly and quickly the major events of any such session so that one can discuss them with the client in the event he/she does have any left over vagueness about important details of his/her experience. The record should be again reviewed together at the next session, at which time the client will have better assimilated it and may have had additional related insights.) As we discussed what had happened, and where it all came from, she grew even more consciously cognitively aware of how all these matters had been related in many intricate ways, and how she had let them nearly wreck her marriage because of her individual views. The marriage improved immensely from that point, and her husband began also to change and work harder at making the marriage work. He further began to take his own therapy more seriously and work on his problems more honestly. Nell was also able to change her relating to her son; and he, too, began to improve in school and in his other relationships.

The Redream

The idea behind this exercise is to solve problems and stimulate balance between conscious and unconscious. Dreams present the therapist with the client's own unconscious symbolism, which has the most fruitful information for helping consciousness and bringing growth[33] In this procedure, the person re-imagines and gets into the dream. Then he/she slips into each character or object in order to discover the symbolism there. The dream may be one in which all characters and things are some form of representation of an *outer world* problem, or it may be also an *inner world* representation of a heretofore consciously ignored part of him/herself.[34] Or it may be that the dream elements (people, living creatures, things, situations) have to be analyzed for any symbolic quality of their positive or negative aspects, such as unresolved life problems, past or present relationships, or neglected growth. Once into the dream scene, if he/she cannot let him/herself know what its symbolism is, God's Light may be called upon for the Voice to disclose it. However, God does not always tell the person, and that has to be accepted as some mutually determined growth point which as yet has no relevance for present spatio-temporal reality.

The main point in this method is to let the person come to know, as well as one can, what certain strange dreams mean to him/her, what the threatening but consciously unaware problems are, what his/her positive and negative personality potentialities are, and what other missing information the figures originating in the personal unconscious or the objective psyche are representing. In this manner the client may come to know some strengths and

weaknesses within him/herself so that he/she may deal with things
to his/her best advantage. This Procedure is excellent for relieving
anxiety aroused by any dream. There are also a number of other
Procedures which can accompany this one in order to help understand and deal with the dream's preconscious symbolism whether
of personal or collective unconscious origin. Among these procedures are: the Light, Introjecting, Switch, Key-word, Sweat-out,
and, most powerful, the presence and action of the Christ-symbol
(a matter more thoroughly dealt with later). My pointed recommendation is that the therapist who wishes to use this Method first
learn as much as possible about Freudian and Jungian approaches
to dream interpretation.

Depression Relief, Personality Fragment (or "Multimind")
Integration, Use of the Redream, and Objective
Observer Procedures
Probably the best way to clarify the Personality Fragment
Integration Procedure is to illustrate through an actual case history,. It is a story of a talented, well-educated young woman in her
mid-twenties. She had hoped to teach college-level courses in her
field, but only high school teaching opportunities were available
when she first went job hunting. The job finally became so unre-
warding (indeed personally punishing) that she took the wise
approach of not returning the following year in order to look for a
better teaching opportunity. However, no other teaching jobs were
quickly forthcoming. She was a perceptive, idealistic, richly emotional and sensitive young woman, and the negative effects of the
lack of suitable jobs brought her to therapy with depression, loss of
self-esteem and self-confidence. This background should illustrate
the sort of self-doubt and unconscious personality fragmentation
she was experiencing. She did well in therapy, and worked hard on
her problems with ultimate success in the midst of a bout of depression and just prior to getting a sought-for position, she had the following dream:
     She saw three young women and one young man in a setting of
school classrooms. One woman was defeated and depressed and
went running into an adjoining small room and collapsed into a
hopeless, weeping heap. Another young woman was attempting to
explain to an uncomprehending young man why the other woman
had run from the room and was behaving as she was. The third

woman was standing off to one side of the room and seemed simply to be watching and surveying the whole scene.

In view of the client's depression it seemed wise to do a Redream with her, to which she agreed in Dialogical Counseling. Therefore, to get better insight we used the Guided Meditation at Schema Level I, Stage 1, Plus, since this seemed to be her optimum therapy work point. After the Pre-Therapy Work Check-out, I asked her to get into the dream again. She had no trouble doing so (apparently people are viewing from their Self's position at such times), and she immediately saw that the three young women, as well as the young man, were all manifestations of herself.[35] She had now been in therapy long enough to be acquainted with the concept of personality fragments (seemingly closely akin to Robert Ornstein's "multiminds"—later "simpletons") and the Jungian concept of the animus (woman's unconscious dominant male traits) so in her present negative stress, this didn't surprise her too much. I asked her to slip into each person and be aware of his or her feelings and thoughts. The weeping, depressed person she immediately identified as the part of her personality which now was giving her the most difficulty. The male side of herself, as she entered it, was not unkind but could not with thinking's ordering rationally *only* understand why the hopeless feminine other part was acting that way.[36] This is a typical problem for men, ignoring the logic of feeling's rational function of valuing by degree of emotional importance. As she became that part of herself which was trying to explain the depressive action to the male side, she felt she was into the rationality of her feeling-centered feminine side. When she slipped into her self who was leaning against the wall taking this all in, she felt more balanced. This was undoubtedly the part of the Self (perhaps the Moral Self symbolized) which is frequently called the Objective Observer,[37] and which is often caught in the position of judging and integrating the varying parts of the total self. This Observer usually offers the most hope for equitably balancing all personality fragments; she agreed with me that this fragment seemed to be the most hopeful personality dimension of all those present, so we had her stay within it. Then she called for the Light to surround her as she strengthened this Observer part. She then brought all the other personality fragments into the Light and introjected them one by one. She immediately felt more unified and centered and was ready to terminate the Redream.

During the next few sessions she had to accept realistically that part of her personality which tended toward hopeless feelings and to deal with it (it had in childhood been rejected by her father). In the Dialogical Counseling we were straight about it, admitted its right to be, but recognized its ultimate self-defeating qualities, if allowed to take control. This fragment then seemed to take a back seat to the more outer-world-attuned parts of herself. The integration's final result was a stronger, better functioning young woman.

Self-directed Therapy with Free-floating Fantasy

An excellent illustration of this entire Procedure is to be found with Denny's work in Chapter XI. The illustration serves as adequate explanation when one considers the accompanying commentary in the verbatim. Further elucidation here would probably complicate. For the therapist, the main emphasis of the Procedure is to have the client stay with his/her feelings and images. The guiding therapist should also "stay with" the client for quick guidance and help when and if needed.

The Forest of Life, Sacred Circle, Knoll of Light and Worship, and Ego Inflation Correction

Most of these elements are also well demonstrated in the true clinical story presented in Chapter I and the verbatim transcript of the same session in Chapter X. The ministering therapist should make sure the Sacred Circle is large enough so that the person does not feel trapped, but not so large that it is overwhelming. It should be tailored to the client's individual needs. Also, the clearing should contain nothing but grass—about upper calf to knee high—and perhaps a few wild flowers, and it should have nothing of a threatening nature within it. A healthy Forest of Life should be predominantly hardwood with a *few* evergreens and plenty of undergrowth. A totally evergreen forest is too threatening and not life supporting while a totally hardwood forest lacks the few needed evergreens scattered about to help the person keep an eye on eternal life goals. Avoid allowing the Forest to remain like a park, lacking normal undergrowth, or to be like one in a fairytale. The Forest of Life *must* be natural. With the trees representing people as they do, obviously, the Forest should contain all sizes, types and varieties. Tree trunks almost impenetrably close together tend to represent the client's feeling crowded by life and people, or they could mean the client depends too heavily upon others for support. Additionally, the circle of trees beginning the Forest needs not to be too far away, for this tends to represent a false need to keep people at a great distance out of fear. Neither does the Forest need to be autumnal or in winter, for again there is little or no active life; everything is in suspension. Also in this context, correct any swamp or jungle images since these tend to represent the immediate pressure of a too primeval or primitive level of the unconscious threatening to break through.

Finally, the Knoll with Light at the top represents the High Place of Worship, as it always has to the collective unconscious. But here it certainly needs to be not too high or impossible to climb. Having it about as high as the tops of the healthy Forest's trees is a good suggested picture. Also, the Light needs to be as it has been depicted in the prior descriptions. A client may have a good experience by standing in the Light atop the Knoll and letting him/herself simply become aware of the power of the Light, which penetrates like X-rays but harmlessly. Some persons who tend to deal with life a little too concretely, instead of reflectively, may be aided by suggesting to them that they let themselves become aware of the Light's power (God's power) in this succession: its *cleansing* power through and through, like the best bath one ever had; next, its *healing* power so that all parts of oneself function properly and harmoniously; last, the *abundant life-giving* power saturating one and bringing a healthy child's feeling of life. The Knoll, further, is a good place for the Sweat-out Method and the Recharge Method. It is also a place for identifying and correcting Ego Inflation. Persons with this problem sometimes will envision themselves as being giant size when arriving at the top of the Knoll and stepping into the Light. Correction would consist of having them grow in reverse, back down to normal size.

Tree of Life, Plus-mark Spiritual Personality Center,
Sword of Masculinity, or Rose of Femininity
These symbols are particularly good for a first experience with Guided Meditation Therapy Procedure sessions because of their usually immediate positive and healing contribution as well as their personality problem identification. They may be visualized alone and against an emotionally neutral background in the case of the Tree, Rose, or Sword. The Plus-mark should, however, be against

a black background unless too threatening. It should, also, be described by the therapist in some of its details. Once the person has the huge, white plus-mark, the following procedure takes place: (For a good illustration, refer to Chapter XIV where Mitchel's first Guided Mediation session demonstrates the Plus-mark Procedure and seems to bring centeredness and attunement to the Universe for him.) Ask the client to visualize blue-white lines which extend all the way across the mark at each of the four corners; these separate lines are like the leading-edge of a sliding door; and they all begin slowly, simultaneously, and at the same speed, to move from the outer edges toward the center. However, while the leading edges are vividly bright, they are transparent behind and leave behind them a trail of blue-white light which continuously zips (in blurbs or quanta) from the outer edges of the plus-mark toward the centers of the lines as they move toward the center of the Plus-mark, moving about as rapidly as lightening's repeated flashes. (Note: the client should be checked from time to time in this exercise to see how he/she is doing with visualizing such an abstract, geometric, archetypal symbol.) Now the person is asked to watch as the four lines slowly move to the center of the mark and arrive there at the same time. Then the therapist may say, "At this point all four lines overlap, and they form a brilliant core of churning—transforming light—which suddenly *sunbursts* forth with constant transforming radiance, like a star!" So that now the client should have a picture of a huge white plus-sign with blurbs of blue-white light constantly zipping from all outer corners to the center which is a churning, transforming core of power and which is also constantly radiating forth like a star.[38]

Now the client is asked to absorb (Assimilate or Introject) the symbol until it is all gone, and its entire essence flows through the bloodstream to every part of the body. The client indicates when this is completed, and the therapist then asks the client how he/she feels different. As a rule, this highly abstract symbol is difficult to describe in its effects upon a person, who may require some descriptive questions for direction. However, for the one who does accomplish it with no trouble, the description of his/her feelings is usually of a center of rhythmical and/or melodious warmth and glow which usually feels as though it were centered upon the heart but which spreads over the whole body with a sort of harmonizing and wonderfully unifying feeling. The therapist may ask the client to put a hand over that part of the body at which he/she feels the center to be. Usually, it is over the heart but may also be at a number of other places, or one may become aware of strangely concomitant centers, such as, the back and top part of the head, behind the forehead, in the middle of the viscera and near the pelvic area, the heels or the entire foot, and the hands or arms. (I describe these experiential points as simultaneous *soul hook-on points*, if needed, because the client is usually curious as to the reason his/her center or centers have such multiple points of positive feelings.)

Some persons need help in describing their feelings because, like most mystical happenings, this experience caused by an abstract form is one for which it is hard to find words. If this is the case, the therapist should ask him/her if he/she would like some help in trying to describe it; and if the answer is yes, the following may be asked: "If you imagine your entire personality as being the white plus-mark, do you feel that you could take whatever might strike you from the outside world and, by the spiritual power within you, *zip* it to your inner Soul-center, there transform it, then sunburst it forth in positive, constant radiance and pleasure to yourself and all around you?" (It is good to tell him/her this is not your own description but is the general description of many clients with whom this has been done.) Often the reply is an almost surprised or incredulous sounding, "Yes! That is it exactly."

The curative power of this symbol is tremendous most of the time, but at times it is not so noticeable. However, for most persons with confused feelings and thoughts, it seems to have an immediate unifying effect upon the thoughts, emotions, and whole sense of personal centeredness. A curious thing about this archetypal symbol, which is really a very abstract and geometrical Self symbol, is that it has a tendency to elongate at one end and become a cross shape for Christians. It is advantageous to talk with people about what they may feel such a specifically religious meaning of the experience has added to the therapy; thereby, one may be led into clarifying some of the deeper experiential dimensions of his/her faith. However, if this symbol does not assume a cross shape, seemingly no negative psychotherapeutic effects occur.

Similar to the Plus-mark is the Tree of Life,[39] ideally for a European collective unconscious, the tree should be the following: a strong hardwood tree in full, green, summer or late spring growth, anchored by an excellent root system claiming as far into the earth as the branches reach above ground. The tree's trunk should be large and sturdy, the limbs reaching into the sunlight and highly flexible out toward the ends so that they could withstand summer or winter storms without breaking. The tree should have no knot holes, rotten spots, broken limbs, or parasites. (If any of these negatives are present, they *must* be immediately healed or positively changed by using Logos-power and imagination so that complete balance and health are present in the tree.) Also the tree should have a smaller amount of this year's new growth of green twigs with slightly lighter colored tiny leaves at the very tips of the branches. Finally, it should be a kind tree—one in which squirrels and birds could make nests and beneath which people find shelter and comfort. If the tree is something other than a *strong* hardwood, such as, an evergreen, weeping willow or fruit tree, the client should change it along with any defective features. If the tree appears dead or only a stump, a change is required immediately. A stunted or dead tree tends to represent a strong suicidal feeling within the client, one of which the client is probably preconsciously aware. Additionally, the evergreen seems to symbolize an over-emphasis upon eternal life, to the sacrifice of any personal enjoyment of life now; and the weeping willow tells its own story of current depressive life orientation, while the fruit tree tends to indicate too much emphasis upon the reproductive function of life to the sacrifice of other sources of fulfillment. Any necessary overall change is made by having the Light shine around the tree and reverse time so that the tree grows backwards and even disappears into the earth and becomes a seed again. At this point the laser beam-like power of the Holy Spirit strikes the earth and the seed, harmlessly, with transforming power. Time is then again reversed and sped up. Then *by the therapist's suggestion*, some type of strong hardwood tree springs up from the transformed seed and grows to the appropriate maturity for the individual client. The Light then disappears, and the Procedure moves forward in the usual manner. (Some may only grow the Tree into a sapling, which according to the client's actual emotional age may represent real, inappropriate clinging dependency, so he/she may have to be encouraged to grow it to its full maturity.)

After corrections have been made, the essence of the Tree of Life must be absorbed into one's bloodstream. (Some have trouble with *Introjecting, Assimilating, or Absorbing* anything, but this can usually be helped by the therapist's suggesting that it is like the childhood game of pretending you are a tree, house, stone, etc.) After Introjecting, the client is again asked to describe how he/she feels different. When this has been discussed, the therapist may again offer the client a check-out about having all the good feelings to which he/she is entitled by the Tree of Life. If the client agrees, the therapist may ask the following (and also ask the client to imagine strengthening certain inadequate feelings): Does he/she feel the root system's strong anchor, and his/her right to feel one with the earth, like Jesus as a little boy squiggling his toes into the mud with pleasure? Next does he/she feel the great might and strength of the tree trunk? Then, does he/she feel the flexibility of the limbs which will allow one to bend before the storms of life without breaking? Does he/she feel the rich, growing life of the leaves, especially the tiny new growth? Next, does he/she feel the tree's perfection (one should as a helpful idea)? Following this, the client is asked if he/she feels the reaching out and up of the limbs to take in all the power one is due in his/her space in life. Finally, the client is asked if he/she also feels the tree's kindness. When all the feelings are blended (as with a food blender), the client should feel abundantly alive (Abundant Life). The idea of this Tree of Life is found in the first and last books of the Bible and also can be traced to the collective unconscious as the Cosmic Tree. In the collective, it was one of humanity's early customs, particularly among the Celts, to believe the life in a person was somehow strangely connected to the life in a particular tree. Therefore, this is a helpful ancient archetypal image one can re-imagine from time to time (as is also done with the Plus-mark). Holding the image in the mind one can re-experience the accompanying feelings in a contemplative state.

The final exercise to consider here involves two archetypal symbols of healthy sexual identity as I believe God intended for man and woman. A man is asked to envision a Sword (a symbol of Masculinity).[40] The sword should not be broken, rusty, bent or dull. It should be unsheathed and of high quality steel. Also, the sword should be as equally ornamental as it is a good battle weapon, having excellent balance with which to acquire that which rightfully belongs to him and to defend that which is entrusted into his care. The client is asked to change all the negatives, using Logos-power and imagination. This is done in the following type of questioning: Is the blade clean, sharp, and of the finest steel?

Does the blade have a shaft on the end which runs up through the hilt? Is the hilt itself of solid gold studded with jewels, rubies, emeralds and blue sapphires; and is there a large diamond imbedded in the pommel of the hilt? Any inadequate or missing elements should be altered or added. Then the client should imagine picking the sword up to test its balance, which must be perfect. After Introjection, he should be aware of the golden ideals represented by the hilt, the Wisdom represented by the diamond, and all the rich feminine feelings represented by the jewels; the man should experience a sense of non-threatened guidance (symbolized by the diamond of wisdom in the pommel) in using the power of his total masculinity, the blade. The therapist aids him to check his feeling of possessing all the above symbolized qualities. If he does not feel them, then, of course, he should use Logos-power and *imagine* feeling that way to its maximum. He is also asked to keep the image of balanced power and inner handsomeness available for contemplation when he needs, and it is explained to him that this archetype is God's image for a man, the way He/She wishes for a man to feel. It seems to me that the problematic interpretation dimensions of this symbol are self-evident.[41]

The complementary symbol for a women is a single rose, growing atop a bush, the Rose of Femininity, which has good roots in nutritious dark soil.[42] Ideally, the Rose should be a rich (but not nearly black) red rose. The archetypal image needed is as follows and if not, it should also be corrected with Logos-power and imagination: the Rose itself should be near the color of the American Beauty Rose and opened just about right, (that is, at its maximum beauty for the individual woman, but certainly not totally opened, petals about to fall off, or still a tightly closed bud). Next, the stem should be long and graceful with a few large thorns so that it is self-protective enough, but the rose should not have so many thorns that it is untouchable. The bush should have a healthy stalk with no disease and good green leaves; the root system should be drawing all this health, strength, and beauty from the rich nutrients within the soil, in the Jungian understanding, symbolic of woman's special connection to earthiness. Once the observable negatives are changed, this entire Rose and its bush should be absorbed so that its essence flows throughout the blood stream and becomes part of the woman. Then the following questions should be asked, and, again, any negative element should be eliminated by Logos-power and imagination; also all positives should be amplified if they are not strongly felt: Does she experience the richness of her *feeling nature* as symbolized in the deep redness of the Rose. She should be asked if she feels the slender grace of the stem (if she is not actually slender, she may possess some inner negative feeling and should be assured by the therapist that this archetypal image relates to the inner feelings which God intends for all women to have, whether it corresponds exactly with outside appearance or not). She should be asked if she feels the adequacy of the self-protectiveness of the thorns (male thrustingness). She should be asked if she feels the vitality of the green leaves and strong stalk symbolizing her right to woman's earth processes. She should feel all this strength and beauty being drawn up within from the nutrients in the rich earth itself. The final question directed to the woman is: "Do you feel *beautiful* as a woman person, as *God* would have your feel?" Even if of poor stature, crippled, ugly, or old, all women are supposed to let themselves have this *inner* beauty. If the woman will allow herself to feel like a beautiful woman (and some will have to be urged), she should be encouraged to soak up and enjoy the feeling and remember the true image so that anytime afterwards she may recall the feelings as she contemplates the picture. (Note: the condition of the bush itself tends to indicate a woman's feelings about womanhood as a whole.)

These procedures originated largely in what is called Initiated Symbol Projection. The source for these phenomena is found primarily in Assagioli's *Psychosynthesis*. The only exception is the Rose of Femininity, which to my knowledge Eberhart designed and developed.

Push-Pull Will Development

This Procedure works by the concept of neuron motor pathway training. One of its aims is the client's learning to choose to be assertive against some perceived overpowering force in his/her past or present by imaginarily thrusting it away from him/herself. The other aim is to learn to choose to be assertive against the same inhibiting force by rightfully taking something unto oneself. Since the client is reclining with eyes closed in the thrust-away training, he/she is asked to get an image of the force overwhelmingly pressing in upon him/her and to experience the feeling which this produces. The client then puts his/her hands up, palms out and bent at the elbows, as though trying to hold something away which is pressing in upon him/her. The therapist leans over the chair, palms out, places his/her hands against the client's, asks the client to imagine the therapist as the overwhelming force, begins to press the person's hands back, and with acted anger begins to say something to the effect, "You *will* do what I say!" The client is to push back simultaneously with all his/her might (even though reclining and feeling weaker and more vulnerable) against the therapist's power and also with feigned anger to say something like. "Get *AWAY* from *me*! or, *NO! I WON'T!*" Frequently, the therapist may have to coax the client in order to get him/her to put power into his/her muscles and voice. When the client assumes adequate force, the therapist deliberately begins to weaken his/her push-power and repeatedly pleads with the client, "*No! No, please don't!*" Then the therapist acts as though actually thrust away by the client, and with a cry of "Ah-h-h-h!" rapidly steps away and immediately, noisily slaps his/her desktop—simulating some effect of being pushed down. This action and sound may have so startling an impact on the client that at times he/she will immediately open his/her eyes to see what has happened and will have to be assured that everything is all right before resuming the procedure. Then the client is asked to return to the overwhelming feeling and check his/her responses now. Often, a spontaneous smile spreads over the person's face, as he/she reports a more powerful and capable feeling now.

The assertive *pull-toward* training is done with much the same approach. The therapist hands the client, seated in the chair with eyes closed, one end of a twisted, small hand towel and then tries to take the entire towel away from the client saying such words as, "*Give* that to *ME! I want it!*" The client counters similarly with, "*No! It's MINE! I WANT IT!*" Again the therapist ultimately responds by weakening, letting the towel slowly slip away, and giving in noisily as above; and the client's feelings are again checked out afterward. Either or both of these exercises in this Procedure may need to be repeated several times for the client's feeling of closure. The true reward usually comes in the next session as the client shares a sense of growth in use of his/her Total Will and an accompanying better self-image.[43]

Negative Overlay-image Structure Separation
This device is most helpful when a client's emotional reaction is inordinately negative toward someone of a close relationship—*often*

a spouse. This distressing person is imaged as though in a bust shot photograph with the disturbing nuances of facial expression and the appropriate, negative voice sound which often accompanies the expressions. The client focuses on this visual and auditory representation. Then the therapist has the client imagine a color slide overlay now over the person's face, or perhaps a color print at the side, an overlay or comparative bust shot of someone from childhood who probably looked and sounded the same way and caused a very similar negative emotional effect upon the client. (The therapist may even suggest a specific person for the photograph or overlay, provided he/she has a reasonable theory of who the original person was.) Frequently, the similar image or overlay brings a startled response of realization, for it may be an unexpected image such as a father, mother, grandparent, brother, etc. If an overlay, the client is then asked to slide it to one side as though there were two color portraits. The client is asked then to spend some moments in the transcendent mind state contemplating how past unconscious negative perception structures (or automatic thinking) have contaminated his/her current conscious perception structures. Usually these past highly-charged negative perceptions have unrealistically affected current intimate relations with a loved one. The client is asked to relate these insights to the therapist as they are recognized; then either or both the Crisis Intervention Techniques are used in order to remove the threat or transform the fear or anger upward so that it may be rationally talked through with the disturbing person rather than escalated. A Specific Positive Idea is then given the client to remember these particular insights clearly after deschematizing so that he/she will behaviorally and spontaneously put the new knowledge into effect immediately. Frequently this procedure produces an immediate improvement in communication within the relationship and consequently improves its positive emotional quality.

The Circular Love-cycle Flow, Playing With a Pet,
or Feeding The Monster

Many times personally distressing images will appear in some of the Procedures. Such impressions at times have disturbing archetypal symbol content relative to a part of oneself or a close other (e.g. acquaintance, father or mother). Many of the images will need to be related to positively instead of fearfully and negatively and will have to be therapeutically dealt with. In such cases the client is to imagine a powerful Love-cycle Flow energy beginning to emanate from the heart—Logos-power may be called into play to effect it—melting the hardness of the heart of the other, thus causing the symbol or person to flow love back to the client's heart. This energy may be envisioned as like a rainbow going to and from both hearts (with the return being like an inverse rainbow). The circular flow is maintained until a standing, loving attitude is experienced by the client. In order to relate more positively to the archetypal image, if it is in animal form, a pet may be imaginarily made of it; and the two may even play together in order to establish a more permanent, accepting bond.

There are also times when such elements may appear as monstrous. In such event the monster may be fed until full from an imagined inexhaustible picnic basket or some such source—after which a positive element emerges either outwardly or inwardly.[44] This Procedure is helpful in cases where great fear or anger separates two people or the client has similar feelings for denied and rejected parts of himself.

Transforming A Negative Reaction to the Watchfulness of God and People (The Big Eye and Many Eyes)

For people who have a tendency toward a painful or even near paranoid fear of society and/or God, the following Procedure is often helpful. The client imagines him/herself being in a long, hall-like room which is totally dark (the walls, ceiling, and floor are even painted a flat black). The client is standing with his/her nose against the wall at one end. As his/her eyes become accustomed to the dark, the client becomes aware of an eerie, weird glow from behind. He/she wheels around to see what is causing it and sees a single, huge, living Eye embedded in the wall at the opposite end. The Eye is staring at the client with a weird light, like a spotlight, coming from the iris and focused upon his/her viscera (focusing here accents the emotions). Asked what the client feels at this point he/she usually responds "fear" or "terror." At this time the Desensitizing Technique (i.e.: Stress! [Key Word:] Relax (name)! Exhaust! Smile! Erase! Kindle! Beam and Smile! Fortress-power!) is used to relieve the emotion, after which the client is asked to zig-zag—the Living Eye stays focused on the client's viscera—from wall to wall, walking toward the Big Eye (God's, though the client is not told this until after the deschematization) and comes as close to the Eye as possible until the emotion become unbearable. As that time the desensitizing exercise is repeated, and the client again resumes zig-zagging toward the Eye. This procedure is repeated until the client is able to walk right up to the Eye. The object of this maneuver is to promote a feeling of friendly acceptance of the Eye. If the client does not feel it coming from deep within the Eye, the client uses Logos-power to flash or beam this transforming power into the Eye's depths and transform the Eye's feelings into friendly acceptance. Fear of God tends to decrease afterwards.

When this part is completed, the exact, same exercise is carried out in the same manner for fear of people in general or in groups but with one exception: the far wall this time is embedded with pairs of living eyes, Many Eyes, with pin-point beams of light coming from their pupils, all acting in perfect concert (like spotlights at night converging on a single plane in the sky), and all focused on the client's viscera. Of course, these Many Eyes represent society's negative watchfulness, as perceived by the client (again, the client is not told this until later) in the same manner that the Big Eye represents the client's erroneous perception of God. This Procedure tends to produce more background, long range, back-up symbolic power for growth in these areas. Immediate change from this session is *not* to be expected.

Letting Non-being Give Birth to Being

There are times when a client feels very fearful because he/she imaginarily envisions him/herself as totally into the nothingness and blackness of the Void. Usually this feeling comes at a time of great depression, hopelessness, and desire to withdraw from life-involvement. If the mood is experienced by a person whose psyche problems go no deeper than a *disorder* level this Procedure may be helpful. *Use of this Procedure with a psychotic person is negatively indicated.* The client may experience him/herself as being in the Void or have a feeling and vision of *nothingness* after entering the Faith Schema's transcendent psyche space where he/she sinks completely into his/her feeling. The use of good clinical judgment is strongly advised here, but the therapist may ask the client to stay with the feelings and let happen what will. The client may have further sinking but more peaceful feelings and remain psychically still for a while afterward. This experience is waited through with the ministering therapist occasionally asking the client to keep describing any imagery or feeling change which occurs. Eventually, life and growth imagery will tend to appear or perhaps even in some instances Christ Himself will simply appear there with the client. Of course, the client may also ask for Christ, or any other trusted helper for that matter, imaginarily to be there as comforting or encouraging company. By staying with the feelings Non-being will ultimately disappear, overcome by Being, and Becoming (as life process will increasingly, growingly appear with feelings of a more positive life). After deschematizing, the new positive affect tends to remain for a while with the client. It seems to me that some kind of *ultimate fear* has been more permanently overcome in the client's psyche. This Procedure also is more productive of a positive, long-range growth stimulation.

Growing Up and Down

Many times a client may get a better growth producing perspective on feelings toward some person from the past or someone who currently arouses either great fear or anger by using this method. The fear or anger feelings which have been conditioned into the client may even have been desensitized to, but they are of such severity and power the client may remain nonplused. Even the Energy Transformation Switch Exercise (i.e.: Switch/"Clap;" Release energy from ego's Will-to-Power...; Sensitive to its spiritual valence...; Switched across and up/"Clap," to God-spark center and into Will-of-wills...; Transformed into your good/"Clap," free/"Clap," powerful/"Clap") may have been used to change the client's feelings to a higher level so that he/she can find some positive way currently to deal with the person, yet Crisis Intervention Techniques will have been of no avail. At such times the Growing Up and Down Procedure is frequently of great help. If the client, upon introspection, currently experiences him/herself as being like a powerless child in the intimidating person's presence, the client should imagine growing him/herself up and growing the other down to harmless child size. Then the client imagines the other acting in the fear-arousing, anger-producing, obnoxious manner while the client observes it from this safe and different perspective. Usually the formerly threatening behavior is now clearly perceived by the client as non-threatening, as a childish temper tantrum, or perhaps as caused by the other's inferior feeling and attention-getting needs. The now unthreatened client is then asked to imagine relating to the formerly threatening person in a way which will allow the client to deal with the intimidating person in the most constructive way possible, in view of the circumstances. Such imagining tends to create a new psychic pattern which gives another behavior option when needed, and usually the client has no great problem in imagining this more satisfying action. He/she is then given a Specific Positive Idea to attempt to put this new perspective and more positive action into effect in his/her daily interaction with the person. The interpersonal relationship tends to exhibit more satisfying behavior soon.

Protection by the Spiritual Shield

There are times when a client cannot avoid facing threatening people in difficult circumstances. Again, it may be that Crisis Intervention Techniques do not help or will not answer the client's need for realistic feelings of adequacy with which to deal calmly and powerfully with the situation. Using the imagined threatening circumstance, in this Procedure the client may pull the stem on his/her Time Stop/Start Watch to stop all action except the client's own, like a frame in a moving picture, until he/she is ready to let time move again. Also the client asks for the Light of God's Presence to shine around him/her and goes through the Spiritual Recharge Procedure. However, this time the client asks for the power of the Light to fully charge him/her in such a way as to cause the person's light to radiate out from him/her forming an invisible and protective Spiritual Shield which almost magically insulates him/her from the power of harmful attitudes emanating from others. The client should imagine these attitudes bouncing like daggers or poison darts off a shield of impenetrable but invisible material. When this sort of shielding is completed to the client's satisfaction, the Light of God's Presence returns to heaven, and the Time Watch stem is pushed for the scene to continue. Now though, the client imagines being protected by the invisible Spiritual Shield of light and fully capable of dealing powerfully with the formerly frightening situation.[45] Again, a Specific Positive Idea may be used that the client when actually threatened is to envision him/herself protected within such a shield and to proceed normally in the actual situation. Indeed, thereafter the client usually deals with the real situation better, especially if he/she continues to use the Shield image in any actual threatening environment.

Spiritual Personality-growth "Journeys"

Many healthy people today wish to get help with personality development, stimulation for growth impetus leading toward higher levels of life and faith development. They may not have anything of great evil or emotional pain bothering them but simply as Christians wish to make life fuller by encouraging psychic growth or removing psychological blocks which prohibit growth. Since this religious therapy is primarily aimed at giving such support and growth help, many of the procedures for evaluating and correcting problems in the personality which are present in the work of Roberto Assagioli, Robert Desoille, and Hanscarl Leuner may be slightly modified and used for just such a specifically religiously oriented purpose. The chief difference added by Faith Therapy is that the work is carried out in Intensified Faith's transcendent psyche state, *and* the Procedure's imagining most usually starts from the Sacred Circle. The Circle is envisioned as having paths leading away from and back to it like spokes from a wheel so that any therapeutic Growth Journey into the Forest of Life usually returns the client to the same Circle bringing with him whatever gift, treasure, or person the Journey's encounter has yielded. The client then takes his/her accoutrements up on the Knoll and into the Light of God's Presence. There the client lifts these up into the Light for Transformation: the Holy Spirit (laser beam-like) may powerfully strike the elements (like lightning but non-destructively) and cause them to disappear or transform. Or the source of the Light may take the item or person up and return it in a positively transformed state to the client. As in the Sweat-out Procedure, in whatever nature the transformed item or person returns, the client asks God what it is to mean to him/her. After the client receives God's reply (most usually intuitively, the Voice, or a feeling to which the client must put words), also as in the Sweat-out Procedure, the person may Introject the symbol or imaginarily keep it with him/her somehow. Or the client may totally release it if thus directed by God. It is easy to see that in Faith Therapy these Journeys begin in God's safety and end in His/Her transforming Presence.[46]

The Christ Symbol
Introduction

Because of its importance and the delicacy of its proper use, this Creative Symbol Method has been saved until this special place in the conclusion. *This symbol could very easily be used inappropriately or too frequently, if the therapist is not spiritually mature and sensitive enough.* When Christ appears in this manner it arouses such numinous feeling that the therapist needs the presumed sensitivity of a member of the ordained Christian clergy even if the therapist is a non-ordained person who thus ministers. If a client is caught up into any seemingly impossible situation, he/she may be asked to imagine the physical presence of Christ with him/her, for the Lord can bring some sort of good or peace out of the blocked and distressing situation. However, the therapist must be cautious not to let the client inject desires for magical properties into this type of religiously symbolized therapeutic situation. Also, the person may be asked to listen inwardly to see if Christ has something to say to the client or anyone else involved in the situation. Usually Christ's words are conveyed by feeling or thought. This Procedure is quite powerful and numinous, the ministering therapist will need to attend to his/her client's experience with honest reverence. The therapist may lay a hand upon the arm or hand of the client at such times to add the comfort and understanding of *the touch*. The presence of the Transcendent Third is usually evident for both client and therapist at such a time. This experience often leaves both in a state of awe from having profoundly worshiped.

Anxiety or Depression Release

Let me illustrate this procedure in this manner: suppose a client feels overburdened but also feels a sense of dedication to keep putting one foot in front of the other in life. Yet, due to fatigue, tension, and emotional burden, he/she feels unable to continue. The therapist leads the client into the transcendent mind state where he/she is to participate imaginarily in one of the Gospel stories (Mark 4:35-41 RSV). The client envisions him/herself in the storm-tossed boat with the disciples. The wind and water are raging around them, and they are about to be swamped; yet Jesus is asleep on the cushion in the stern. Then the client uses the psychological device of identification to feel *his/her inner emotional storm unify with the outer storm.* Next the client uses imagination to hear someone angrily say, "Teacher, don't you care if we perish?" Then he/she envisions the Lord waking, surveying the situation, rising, and then with arms outstretched, with palms down as though softly touching the wind and sea, saying, "Peace! Be still...." At this point, the therapist, using the vocal style, says [TN: softly and quietly], "*Listen*—as the wind stops its H-O-W-L-I-N-G AND DROPS TO A GENTLE BREEZE. *Feel*—as the boat stops *wildly pitching* and now begins to rock gently. (TN: Quiet awe) Hear—in the calm and quiet—someone speak, 'Who then is this, that even the wind and sea obey him?' Now, in the stillness, become aware of how *your* 'inner storm' feels." And if it has calmed, as it usually has, the therapist gets the client to remain still in order to soak up the calmness.

Grief Resolution

Also the Christ Symbol may be used with clients confronting a bedbound, terminally ill, or deceased loved one. In the confinement or hospital room, Christ may be envisioned as spiritually standing there with his loving hand of strength upon the patient, bringing peace. Or if death has ensued, one can imagine Christ's presence entering and lifting the loved one's spiritual body out of the material one to accompany him. Before the departure the client may be asked if the deceased has some last words for him/her. Often the words, "*It's* all right" or other similar statements of peace are heard. It is not unusual for the client to cry or softly sob with such verbal comfort.

Specific Positive Ideas

These are simply instructions, which will be of help afterward, given a client in the use of any Guided Meditation Procedure. They are used to assist the client in remembering clearly any matter needing to be dealt with for greater clarity of interpretation and/or contemplation later. Or, the Idea may be instructions to the unconscious to work on further clarification of confusing material between sessions. Explanation and use of this device, used at the therapist's discretion, should be obtained in advance and after mutual trust has developed.

Special Positive Ideas

Introduction
This special Guided Therapy Procedure originated from the theory behind the use of all Positive Ideas given during therapy work. This advanced concept and more effective method was designed originally to aid a client with profound suicidal feelings. It initially addressed one person's serious suicide attempt while on weekend leave from a mental hospital. This attempt resulted in his being transferred for similar hospitalization to another larger city and undergoing over a month's milieu therapy but which also had been unsuccessful in rectifying the unconscious suicidal causes. The serious urges the client had toward self-destruction remained strongly present even with consciousness (using conscious cognitive and behavior therapy methods) firmly set against his desire to end it all. The solution to this problem came as an insight gained through prayer of concern and petition for help in the face of the need.

The success of this approach led to its successful use with other clients with a variety of stubborn problems, some of suicidal depth and for which medication and other psychotherapy had been inadequate.

This procedure is a variation of the use of the Intensified Faith Schema and proceeds following use of the Modified Level I, Stage 1, Plus; then the exercise is carried out after the Prayer of Commitment in the following manner.

Time of Meditation's Intensification and Faith's Profundity Growth
[TN: With calm, soft assurance] Now just let yourself relax in this time of quiet ahead—while of its own accord your MEDITA-TIVE MIND MOOD *coasts* on upward by its own impetus to a position of greater power and openness for reception of these Special Positive Ideas—which you want to work—and which together we have composed for the help you desire. *And they will work—because you want them to work.* Without you having to *consciously think* about them—AND AT THE APPROPRIATE NEEDED TIME—they will SPRING FORTH into your BEHAVIOR as *new attitudes and habits* with which you approach and deal with life. After you have utilized them, you will CON-

SCIOUSLY NOTICE YOU HAVE dealt with things in a more satisfying way so that you feed back to your unconscious—*positive reinforcement* to continue using this more satisfying approach to living—which *God* wants for you.[47]

Now, in order to facilitate all this—*at the same time, you will let your FAITH EXPERIENCE grow in its profundity (faith experiencing being you and God interacting in mutual love and appreciation for one another.)* But now focus your attention upon God's initiating the whole process—HIS/HER PLACING SPECIALNESS—IMPORTANCE—VALUE BEYOND VALUE— UPON YOU—INDEED PLACING PRECIOUSNESS UPON YOU—in the same manner we as humans *place preciousness* upon a newborn infant—*and the baby can do nothing either to merit or stop it*—THUS DOES GOD PLACE PRECIOUSNESS UPON *YOU!* AND YOUR PRECIOUSNESS TO GOD IS A FACT OF ULTIMATE TRUTH—AND THIS IS A STRONG PILLAR OF CHRISTIAN BELIEF TO WHICH YOU CAN AND WILL HOLD CONSCIOUSLY AND UNCONSCIOUSLY IN ORDER TO MAKE LIFE MORE ENJOYABLE AND LIVE-ABLE. It is also true that you are precious to God even in the midst of life's evils—that God is somehow at work with you in them—*converting them somehow toward good*—AND THIS IS TRUE EVEN WHEN EVERYTHING SEEMS TO BE GOING TO THE CONTRARY![48]

Again now, in this period of silence ahead—you will ignore *all sounds*—even the sound of my voice—*unless it is addressed to you by name*—just as though you were too tired and sleepy to pay attention to *anything.*

[TN: Softer, comforting] In order to implement this whole process, now imagine yourself, though grown (adult/youth/child) as a tiny infant—*who doesn't* HAVE TO **UNDERSTAND** anything because he/she is both held and upheld in the perfect loving arms of the one perfect parent, the father/mother God—[TN: Very comforting] letting go to—resting upon—floating upon—*trust in God, very aware* of His/Her peace, safety and security. Now rest.

[TN: The client is now allowed to rest undisturbed for approximately twenty minutes (according to clinical judgment, perhaps as little as ten minutes) in the recliner. During this time the therapist should make as little noise as possible. (It is of note that this psyche state sometimes has a sort of mental contagion similar to infants in a hospital nursery all beginning to cry at the same time once one starts. Therefore, the therapist may have to guard against dropping off into a sleep-like state in this interval, especially if he/she is tired.)

After the quiet time the Special Positive Ideas (which have been formerly conjointly composed in Dialogical Counseling) are given. The therapist's voice tone for this should be clear, caring, and *firm*, but with no hint at being authoritarian or forceful. *Also, the client is to be addressed by name.*

After this, the entire Procedure and Intensified Faith mind mood is immediately deschematized in the following manner:]

Now, using you imagination—bring yourself back to the beach and open yourself to receive the Usual Positive Ideas. [TN: Here give *only* the *first* two Usual Positive Ideas: Unconscious Help Between Sessions and Positive Feedback in Affect Result.] Again now, use your imagination to look around the beach, notice that you have been lying there long enough that you feel alert but well rested and restored—and feeling all the good feelings—just open your eyes and sit up.

Rationale

My theorizing about Special Positive Ideas and their effectiveness came, as already stated, from the sudden prayerful awareness that many times a particular client had a difficult time allowing imagery work to be effective in overcoming a particular problem. Perhaps these are people not adept in right brain use. This also seems to be especially true for persons who take a concrete and action-oriented approach to living and dealing with life and its problems. (However, reflection-centered persons also respond well to this newer procedure.) It appears to me that the tangible-oriented and action-centered person seems to deal with life and things predominantly using the left hemisphere brain's linear emphasis on numbers, thoughts, words, and Aristotelian logic. This may indicate why the needed imagery use with such clients is sometimes more effectively approached obliquely with word use and counting on the corpus callosum, with its feedback effect between both brain hemispheres, to rouse such imagery and emotion as possible in the right.[49]

As pointed out previously, the concept of tailor-made positive ideas was a part of the early beginnings of this therapy method, but their use (other than the three usual Positive Ideas) was rather minimally effective. Clients frequently did not let some such *Specific Positive Ideas* work into behavior from the unconscious. The problem facing me with my suicidal client seemed to have the above negative qualities along with inadequate effect with imagery use. Prayerful concern led me to remember a religious hypnotherapy technique once used in my early conjoint work with Dr. Eberhart. It was that about twenty minutes of additional quiet rest time after the trance induction phase could sometimes deepen the hypnoidal or even light trance state. This approach was used with the hope of getting a somnambulistic or more profound depth trance in which the person's will apparently was seemingly no longer present or at least was less active and resistant to the therapeutic work.

My insight was that if such a quiet period worked for *deepening a hypnotic trance*, with its orientation toward the giving up of individual will and control by proceeding in an archetypal **DOWN** direction, then a similar but opposite approach theoretically should work in *meditation*. If there were a coasting effect for hypnotic trance deepening, there certainly could be such a coasting psychic elevating tendency which would cause the meditative and intensified faith mind mood (where will was accented) to become more effective by using its archetypal **UP** direction. Further increasing the intensity of the meditative mood could provide the power needed to help the client place greater emphasis upon his/her Intensified Faith Exercise as it is experienced as safe-secure affect. Centering upon awareness of God's placing preciousness upon one—a belief central to Christianity—could open the client's receptivity to his/her own Special Positive Idea. This openness takes place on a more highly suggestible level of the mind such as that of a three-to-five-year-old.

The Procedure has worked well for a large number of people. The Ideas are repeated in a meditation weekly or bi-weekly, even monthly toward the end of the therapy period,, as the effect on behavior becomes more permanently established. Through repetition, these Ideas become reinforced often and long enough that the rewarding behavior becomes automatized and more permanently establishes itself through positive reinforcement as feedback. Interestingly, I have observed that the client seldom seems to go to sleep in the quiet period. This is indicated by the person's tendency to hear everything but choose to ignore it (as in *zazen*). Even if he/she starts to snore, the client tends to become immediately aware and stops before the special faith space is lost.

In some ways these Special Positive Ideas seem to bear a strong similarity to what Robert Ornstein has called "hot ideas." He speaks of them as being large positively charged emotional patterns which bring a good mood and more favorable interpretation of our necessarily limited (by our simplifying and organizing) perception of the world. When brought to consciousness, these "ideas" bring with them "all associated ideas." In turn, this enables us to perceive our world more positively, which then profoundly affects our physiology in like manner. Special Positive Ideas also tend to deal with problems centrally oriented around emotionally distressing matters so that the "associated ideas" are all brought to bear on the identified problem. In a sense we are priming life's pump.[50]

More recently I have observed that persons with passive dependent problems generally respond poorly to this Procedure. This is probably because the basic maladjustive patterns leading to this trouble happened within the "critical period" of the brain's first two years of development. These unconscious patterns are difficult or nearly impossible later to change.

How to Formulate the Special Positive Ideas

The client and therapist together compose Special Positive Ideas which are tailored to the client's highly individualized needs. There are several precautions, however, which *must* be taken into account. Remember that the wording of any Idea must be clear, sensible, and appropriate to the particular client. One should especially consider that some words can have a very different meaning to another person or even to the individual's preconscious. The more concrete logic wording gives best results. Also, since these are prefabricated complete thoughts, or whole concepts, which the client wishes to make effective in his/her unconscious mind, everything should be thoroughly rational and in complete accord with the client's usual, honest, conscious AND unconscious (where these may be made aware) desires, so that the two psyche centers are not in conflict. With this approach, Special Positive Ideas may help form adjunctive aids which assist one in reaching his/her goals. In the conjunctive composing of the Idea, it is often wise for the client to make an exact copy of the special concept for personal and conscious use.

The therapist should suggest that the client place a number of these copies in prominent places (mirror, desk, etc.) for daily help in keeping these ideas in consciousness.

Another serious warning must be given: the unconscious of the client simply may not choose to cooperate because out-of-awareness desires run contrary to those of consciousness. If the client's unconscious does not wish to cooperate, the particular Special Positive Idea will not work and may become an irritant; therefore, it should be discontinued or changed to fit the whole person's desires more realistically, as they become clearer. If it becomes evident that the person is making no gain with the Idea's continued use in his/her sessions, persistence will probably harden the unconscious against any such future change or set up specific resistances to the therapist. Further, the Special Positive Ideas are articulated firmly but gently so that the preconscious will listen as if hearing the directions from a kind authority (Good Parenting) rather than a command from a stern disciplinarian—against whom the unconscious will likely rebel. The Idea has no more power than the Self chooses to give it.

The main point I wish to make about formulating and using Special Positive Ideas is that while in some instances they may be very helpful to the client in achieving goals, they also may be equally ineffective if they are not in accord with the ultimate good which the whole person seeks through the equilibrating work of the Self and Objective Psyche. Also, some problems will not yield to this procedure for indeterminate reasons, such as the satisfaction of a well-automatized, primitive, survival need. In such event, the entire problem must be dealt with by using some more totally behavioral or conscious cognitive oriented therapy approach.

Examples

Two examples using specially-formulated tailor-made Special Positive Ideas are given below. These originated as frequently used Specific Positive Ideas and in a general form such as this (perhaps with certain individual variations) still seem to be helpful to people who have these problems.

Sleep—When you get ready to sleep, you will simply "take off" your troubles, fears, anxieties, and worries (as though taking off clothes to be laid aside and then picked up at a more convenient time). Then you will just totally relax (like on the Meditation

Therapy Beach and breathing God's breath) and give yourself over into the arms of *deep, restful, restoring, and renewing* adult-level sleep which will allow you to awaken later refreshed, alert, and optimistic.

Study and Tests—when you need to study, you will structure or organize yourself in such a way as to develop good study habits, so that *when* you study you will immediately relax, grow calm and concentrative, *losing* your attention into interest in the material you are studying. Then you will let your unconscious help you by *letting* it grasp the materials studied in complete associated units (or wholes) and relating the important *details* to these units. You will allow yourself to enjoy this process and afterwards feel proud and good about accomplishing your goal. Then, in any *test or stressful situation*, you will immediately relax—grow calm and concentrative and just *let* the needed material flow up into your consciousness in a creative, logical, coherent and holistic way.

NOTES

[1] I shall not try to elaborate on the many types of creative fantasy techniques developed by others, for there are many good books and journals on the general subject now. However, I will suggest that an excellent overall understanding of these methods may be gained, beyond the works of C. G. Jung, by the reading of Roberto Assagioli's work, especially his book, *Psychosynthesis*, which will also provide the reader with a helpful bibliography from which to do further study. Some suggested helpful books are: Roberto Assagioli, *Psychosynthesis: A Manual of Principles and Techniques* (New York: Hobbs, Dorman and Co., 1965): John A. Sanford, *Dreams: God's Forgotten Language* (New York: Crossroad, 1968); John A. Sanford, *Dreams and Healing: A Succinct and Lively Interpretation of Dreams* (New York: Paulist Press, 1978); Joseph E. Shorr, *Psycho-imagination Therapy* (New York: Intercontinental Medical Books Corp., 1972); Martha Crampton, *An Historical Survey of Mental Imagery Techniques in Psychotherapy and Description of the Dialogic Imagery Method*, Rev. ed., (Montreal, Quebec, Canada: Canadian Institute of Psychosynthesis, Inc., 1974); *The Potential of Fantasy and Imagination*, ed. by Anees A. Sheikh and John T. Shaffer (New York: Brandon House, Inc., *circa* 1979). The efficacy of symbolism has also been recognized by the psychoanalytic school of thought; for example, see F. Paul Kasbab, "Imagery Techniques in Psychiatry," in *Archives of General Psychiatry*, Vol. 31 (September, 1974),

pp. 283-90. There are two journals: *Journal of Mental Imagery*; Brandon House, Inc., P. O. Box 240, Bronx, NY 10471; and *Spring: An Annual of Archetypal Psychology and Jungian Thought*, Spring Publications, P. O. Box 222069, Dallas, TX 75222. Overall, this chapter's Procedures have been well worked out over the years, and parts of many people's concepts have been incorporated. Most of the material is original. Although some were sparked by the ideas of others, I am not aware of any procedures which attempted to work psychotherapeutically in the ambience of an intensified awareness of God's unqualified love manifested in Christ. The books listed above by no means suggest that these are either all or the best materials in the field, but they will give the reader a good start.

² "Initiated Symbol Projection" (Based on Unpublished Manuscripts by Hanscarl Leuner, M.D. and H. J. Kornadt, Ph.D. of the Psychiatric Hospital, Unviersity of Marburg, West Germany), trans. ed., and amplified by William Swartly, Ph.D. (Greenville, Del.: Psychosynthesis Research Foundation, *circa* 1959), pp. 1-5.

³ Wolfgang Kretschmer, Jr., "Meditative Techniques in Psychotherapy," *in Zeitschrift Für Psychotherapie und Medizinische Psychologie*, Vol. 1, No. 3 (May, 1951); trans. by William Swartley (Greenville, DE: Psychosynthesis Research Foundation, *Circa* 1956), p. 5.

⁴ Akhter Ahsen, "Image for Effective Psychotherapy: An Essay on Consciousness, Anticipation and Imagery," in *The Potential of Fantasy and Imagination*, ed. by Anees A. Sheikh and John T. Shaffer (New York: Brandon House, Inc., *circa* 1979), pp. 11-17.

⁵ Winson, *Brain, pp. 209-47.*

⁶ Desoille, *Daydream*, pp. 30, 31.

⁷ Alfred North Whitehead, *Religion in the Making* (New York: New American Library, 1926), p. 16.

⁸ Desoille, *Daydream*, pp. 13-17, 33.

⁹ Laurens van der Post and Jane Taylor, *Testament to the Bushmen* (New York: Viking Penquin, 1984), pp. 151-52.

¹⁰ Milton H. Erickson, *Life Reframing in Hypnosis*, ed. by E. L. Rossi and M. O. Ryan, Vol. II, 2 vols. (New York: Irvington, 1985), pp. 200, 201.

¹¹ Rossi, *Psychobiology, passim.*

¹² Winson, *Brain*, p. 241.

¹³ *Ibid., passim.*

¹⁴ Desoille, *Daydream*, p. 9.

¹⁵ Desoille, *Daydream*, pp. 30,31. See also, Robert E. Ornstein, and David Sorbel, *Healthy Pleasures* (New York: Adison-Wesley, 1989), *passim.*

¹⁶ *Dictionary of Pastoral Care*, p. 1053.

¹⁷ Alexander Lowen, *Bioenergetics* (New York: Coward, McCann and Geoghegan, Inc., 1975), pp. 124-33.

¹⁸ The final unlocking key of understanding came as I was reading a just

off the press copy of Joseph Wolpe's book, *The Practice of Behavior Therapy* (New York: Pergamon Press, 1969). After finishing it, the concept flashed upon me that powerful as images were, the *body* still needed to participate more in *some* (not all) psychotherapy. (That made the Doctrine of the Incarnation even more believable.) This insight led to getting *total* body involvement with the command to the client to "*STRESS!*" The response to that command also stressed the body as the psyche was already stressed by some trigger; thus we tended to get holistic involvement and a more complete resolution than with behavior or imagery therapy alone.

[19] Dr. John Eberhart held that we needed to talk thus (out loud or at least use the vocal chords quietly, in a near Hasidic way to God *or* our unconscious) if we really expected anything to happen. He had a mystical view of the power of *the word*.

[20] See also, Ornstein and Sobel, *Healing*, pp. 61-65. Also see, Ornstein, *Evolution*, pp. 79-101.

[21] Whitehead, *Religion*, pp. 14-16.

[22] After experiencing either Crisis Intervention Technique once or twice, the client will respond well to briefed-down uses of these Exercises.

[23] Martha Crampton, "Some Principles and Techniques of Energy Transformation at Psychological Levels," in transcript of *Psychosynthesis Seminar*, April 27, 1973 (New York: Psychosynthesis Research Foundation, 1973), pp. 10-12.

[24] Joseph Wolpe, *The Practice of Behavior Therapy* (New York: Pergamon Press, 1969), pp. 224-26.

[25] An example will be found in Chapter XIII, "The Client With 'Burn-out'".

[26] Assagioli, *Psychosynthesis*, pp. 106, 112-16.

[27] Carl Gustave Jung, *Psychology and Religion* (New Haven, CT: Yale University Press, 1938), pp. 44-53.

[28] Desoille, *Daydream*, pp. 23-31.

[29] Ornstein and Sobel, *Healing*, pp. 140-55.

[30] Claude M. Steiner, *Scripts People Live: Transactional Analysis of Life Scripts* (New York: Grove Press, 1974), pp. 22-24.

[31] Wolpe, *Behavior*, pp. 61, 62-68-70.

[32] Muriel James and Dorothy Jongeward, *Born to Win: Transactional Analysis with Gestalt Experiments* (Reading, MA: Addison-Wesley Publishing Co, 1973), pp. 263-66.

[33] C. G. Jung, "Forward," in *An Introduction to Zen Buddhism* by Daisetz Teitaro Suzuki (New York: Grove Press, Inc., 1964), pp. 22-24.

[34] Ervine Polster and Miriam Polster, *Gestalt Therapy Integrated: Contours of Theory and Practice* (New York: Vintage Books, 1974), pp. 265-69.

[35] Emma Jung, *Animus and Anima*, trans. by Carey F. Baynes (New

York: Spring Publications, 1957), pp. 1-11 ff.

[36] Assagioli, *Psychosynthesis*, pp. 74, 75. See also Ornstein, *Evolution*, pp. 141-42.

[37] *Ibid.*, p. 76. See also, Robert E. Ornstein, *Multimind* (New York: Doubleday, 1986), pp. 185-89.

[38] Robert Gerard, "Symbolic Visualization—A Method of Psychosynthesis" (Greenville, DE: Psychosynthesis Research Foundation, 1961), p. 2.

[39] *Ibid.*, p.3.

[40] *Ibid.*, p. 2.

[41] Some persons may have difficulty in their thinking with the concepts of The Sword of Masculinity and The Rose of Feminity, finding them to be stereotypical and culturally oppresive images better eliminated than considered archetypal. In all these years of practice I have not found it to be so, as therapeutically experienced by clients of both sexes but helpful instead. *Since one must be a man person or woman person,* it behoves us to strengthen sexual identity because God created us this way for species survival and continuance. The magnetic drawing power of woman (symbolized by the rose) is equal to the active thrusting power of man (symbolized by the sword) and need not be offensive to anyone. Also, one should keep in mind that Jung pointed out that *some cultural images* grew into powerful *archetypes* due to rich meaningful use and had the capacity to draw into themselves spiritual force, e.g.: the early "image" of the cross now having become the Christian "symbol" of the cross.

[42] This is one of those symbols Dr. Eberhart contributed of which I have no sure knowledge of origin. I can only point to such possibilities as poetry, the myth of Beauty and the Beast, Briar Rose, etc.

[43] Albert Pesso, *Movement in Psychotherapy: Psychomotor Techniques and Training* (New York: New York University Press, 1969), pp. 159-65, *passim.*

[44] Bernard S. Aaronson, "Psychosynthesis as System and Therapy," *The American Journal of Clinical Hypnosis*, Vol. X, No. 4 (April, 1968), pp. 332-33.

[45] Desolle. *Daydream*, pp. 31, 32.

[46] Dr. John Eberhart contended that all this symbolic work tended to lose its religious efficacy and its *deeper* meaning unless begun and ended in this manner with God. I am in total agreement.

[47] B. F. Skinner, *About Behaviorism* (New York: Alfred A. Knopf, 1974), p. 46.

[48] Pierre Teilhard de Chardin, *Human Energy*, Trans. by J. M. Cohen (New York: Harcourt Brace Javanovich, Inc., 1962), pp. 43-47.

[49] Desoille, *Daydream*, p. 17. See also, R. E. McMullin, *Handbook of Cognitive Therapy Techniques* (New York: W. W. Norton, 1985), p. 272.

[50] Orenstein and Sobel, *Healing*, pp. 107-9.

PART II

THE THEORY FRAMEWORK

This part of the text is presented in three chapters: "Theological Convictions," "Psychological Models," and "Convictions and Models Structurally Synthesized:...." "Theological Convictions" presents the spiritual development of the overall theory as it unfolded under the influence of certain specifically Christian beliefs as they also seemed to mesh with insights from the fields of psychiatry and psychology. The Chapter on "Psychological Models" presents a viable theory for this methodology which I hope will also make some contribution to the field of Psychology of Religion. Though much of the chapter's conceptual content is based on the work of Freud, Jung, and Assagioli, it has also been necessary to include psyche concepts from others. Additionally, Dr. Eberhart and I had to create some new constructs as the therapy's successful results demanded additional conceptualizations in its theory (in order to understand and explicate the psyche). The final chapter "Convictions and Models Structurally Synthesized: Faith Is the Psyche's Primary Operation" integrates the entire theory into a harmonious whole and adds new information to the former concepts. I will develop this synthesis by using the epistemological approach of structuralism. Also at appropriate points, I will offer diagrams which I hope will be helpful to the reader in more clearly conceptualizing the material.

Chapter V

THEOLOGICAL CONVICTIONS

In this chapter, I set forth a body of beliefs and understanding about God and His/Her relationship with humanity which provides the necessary element to make the endeavor of this therapy complete and more valuable.

The Therapy Origins: Based Upon Faith, Hope and Love

I must become somewhat *subjective and historical* in order to present the faith assumptions and more specifically religious aspects of this therapy's origin. This subjectivity is unavoidable because Christian religious convictions which worked to form this method grew out of personal efforts to minister to needs in local church situations. Further, the subjective approach seems to serve two ends: first the method's content appears less esoteric, providing a more realistic perspective on the origin; and second, it demonstrates that the Church is a living organism and caring faith community out of which special spiritual growth and sound therapeutic methods can arise. For example, John Eberhart, the psychiatrist who was friend, mentor, and co-laborer in originating this therapy, and I became acquainted through the Church. I also met Dr. Roger Birkman, personality psychologist and friend, through the Church. Birkman's test and its contents derived from the teachings of Christ, made available toward the latter part of the Therapy Method's most formative period, clarified and amplified all aspects of Faith Therapy.

Work on Faith Therapy began with the conviction that the Christian religious experience, which is subsumed under the interpretive category of The Holy, has the capacity to change people profoundly, to give them new, positive meaning and purpose.[1] Eberhart held that since healthy Christian religion can bring about change for "normal" persons, it could also do so for the deeply disturbed—and even more with religious, psychological, and medical cooperation. The Biblical basis for this belief is in the Gospels where Christ's manifold acts of healing both body and mind are recorded. It seemed evident that he accomplished these acts with a personal concern and *love or life-energy* expressed as Divine force, loving act, or will. Interestingly, Jesus often extended this healing energy in response to someone's longing and reaching out, an act of desire he called *faith*. Evidently, this attitude of faith was accompanied by and connected to another attitude, an anticipatory disposition which may be referred to as *hope*. Early church writings joined the two qualities together as in Hebrews 11:1 (RSV) "Now faith is the assurance of things hoped for,...." Perhaps assuming that hope was part of the necessary background of a fixed positive attitude, Jesus also used faith as if it were closely connected with *belief*. As he used faith, the term seemed to have an added dimension of highly perceptive emotional AND intellectual conviction. But Jesus's understanding and acts of faith and belief were much more than those of others. With him faith extended into *sympathy*, which added a profound compassion as he went about teaching and healing. His faith-belief was filled with effective, caring emotion or love-energy—to say nothing of his unparalleled intellect.

Yet confusingly to me, this greatness of love and understanding in Jesus at times seemed similar to the capriciousness of the Greek gods, since Christ would use it to meet some needs for healing, yet deliberately walk away from other needs at other times.[2] This dilemma was finally clarified by Dr. Eberhart's conviction that Jesus's love was so *personal* that it also seemed *impersonal*. He had to love and take care of himself too, if he were first to preach the Gospel. From my viewpoint this explanation satisfactorily answered the question, but my personal understanding of the teaching was much slower in arriving and had to do with clarifying the difference between sympathy and empathy.[3]

Jesus's use of the term *belief* seemed to suggest a more profound concept of one's capacity for *understanding*, and yet it fell short of the absolute certitude of *to know*. So it began to dawn that perhaps in his epistemology, exercising a more perfect type of perception, intelligence, and love-energy somehow could bring about a more complete and powerful knowledge. If "...God is love" (I John 4:8 RSV), Jesus's way of apprehending that love provided the key for the more adequate development of the other major psychic functions for fuller human living. So such a goal had to start with the attitude and energy of Universal Love and Intellect somehow willfully interacting and desiring wholeness, freedom, and feelings of ultimate safety for man in the totality of his existence. With this insight, the teaching that "...perfect love casts out fear" (1 John 4:18 RSV) made sense. Too much living in fear/anxiety (an active survival reflex or threat response) was obviously the source of much of the illness in our total being.[4]

This conglomeration of ideas appeared to be some sort of hodgepodge of profound related concepts with truth vested within them all but which lacked lucidity. Then the insight occurred to us: as confusing as the concept mixture had been to us, Paul, in his genius, had put it all together long ago in his great passage on love in I Corinthians 13. Here he summarized the attributes of this universal energy and its primary attitudinal predispositions with the accompanying perception and thinking. He had given the life-directions for more complete Christian living to all persons who would take this easy yoke (Matt. 11:30 RSV). For clarity's sake I would like to exercise a bit of artistic liberty and paraphrase what this teaching came to mean to us as a guiding intuition in development of the therapy. In effect it seemed Paul said:

As emotion and attitude, love is unending transforming power, but all our depth envisioning, eloquent speaking with released certitude and what seems like self-evident intelligent conviction is only a passing process of incompleteness. Our epistemology and imaging of the future is not whole, but when wholeness is achieved, it will transform the incompleteness. For example, in my childhood I had all the child qualities, but when adulthood came I allowed my child nature to be transformed into my adult nature.

For now our perception is very unclear but then (when our love is unified in Christ), we will perceive exactly as all reality truly is. At present my knowing ability is very limited; then my intellectual, perceptual and emotional cognition will be complete, just as God now with total understanding apprehends me. [The sure way to proceed to that goal is as follows:]

This is how the life-fulfilling process operates: there are three attitudes, or emotional predispositions, which are lifelong and eternal personal strengths; they are FAITH, HOPE AND LOVE* but the most important of these is *creating and keeping* the fulfilling, life-giving emotion charge, also called LOVE-[for it is the essential, positive, energy-flow—the FORCE of the Universe].

* "Love [as an attitude] is irreversible good will."[5]

Now lest the reader mistakenly think that the above paraphrased understanding of Paul's words came back at that time with a revelatory flash of insight, let me hasten to state that it was in the beginning only a dimly perceived, guiding truth, more vaguely and intuitively grasped. In our striving for a growth oriented psychotherapeutic ministry for Christ, we had no vision of such structured clarity as I hope ultimately will be evident in the material of Chapter VII. The structural understanding has been of much more recent origin, and even then it first came only as a dim suspicion. It was a later, slow realization to me that this teaching of Paul's appeared to be a structured whole.[6] However, at that earlier time it seemed to us that Paul had grasped an association between concepts which had strong bonds and gave direction as to which ideas should be given priority in developing a healthy nature through Christian love and understanding.

In Search of an Affect Enhancing Procedure

From the beginning Eberhart and I guarded against manipulating people and yet wished to help them find how to regain personally the power of Christ's example of living. Our concern was to help them discover how they individually could open themselves to experience more fully God's transforming love as it was made concrete and real in *person* form in Jesus as a special evolutionary creation. To us it seemed that Jesus had appeared on the stage of history at the exact time in order to help persons psychologically and spiritually cope better with their rapidly changing world. It also seemed that in recorded history, Christ came at an unprecedented time of confusion and upheaval. With the evident rapid rise in mental health problems, it appeared we were entering that sort of mind-rocking world again.

The immediate problem was how could a concerned pastor and a caring Christian psychiatrist, who desired to minister to profound needs of Christians, most effectively apply Paul's affectively-charged insight for others' help (as well as for themselves). After a lifetime of practicing medicine, Eberhart's position was (even after the advent of psychotropic drugs) that ultimately one has only one means by which to help people with psyche problems get well, to minister through one's own personality and ability to love. Using this concept of loving relating and interacting, the counseling technique (presented in Chapter II, "Dialogical Counseling") part of the religious growth and psychotherapy method was proceeding in its development with a certain ease and effectiveness. But we felt a profound need to help people arrive at a more *affectively* rich religious faith experience. Some basic attitudinal and energetic change seemed to take place in people experiencing a conversion or growth in grace experience. We believed the key to this change probably lay primarily in the unconscious or affective domain.

However, it appeared that somehow much of the spiritual knowledge of how to make these changes had been consciously cognitively lost with the passage of time. Yet there was a thread of this knowledge still remaining. For throughout the centuries there had been a small group of Christians, usually referred to as the saints of the Church, who appeared to live life with the sustaining power of a more intense experience of faith. Even their writings evidenced a greater than average affective awareness of God's undergirding daily strength. Readings from the devotional lives of these persons indicated that their secret had certain elements in common: solitude, meditation, contemplation, prayer, varying symbolic disciplines or rituals, looking inward in search of Christ within, and a deliberate quietening of body and mind. The physician also pointed out that Jesus, too, went off alone for rest and solitude, to pray and to know himself spiritually. A closer analysis also revealed that most saints had some common profound spiritual qualities evidenced in their practices. These qualities were a committed BELIEF or intellectual conviction, a dedicated expectation or stance of HOPE, a steady focusing inward with an emotional reaching or amplification of FAITH, which had connected to it a longing, and magnetic power which was somehow also attached to LOVE. All of these qualities seemed interrelated and oriented around a hunger to KNOW God.[7]

Another item often noted was the presence and use of numinous images and symbols, a spiritual emphasizing of the imaging abilities of the mind. In analyzing these mystical practices Eberhart noted especially that images and symbols frequently occupied a central position. He noted also another practice: the use of some sort of auto-suggestion to quiet the person and center the entire psyche upon the central object of desire.

From studying some of the religious practices of the Orient, we gained further insight. We learned that depth meditation and prayer practices were very akin the world over, no matter how God was called or conceptualized. Basically we also found the repeated patterns of committed belief, longing for unity with the source of the world-energy, anticipation, disciplines and rituals, aloneness, quietness, focusing upon the inner world, strange and numinous symbols (yet not so strange, many of them somewhat akin to those of our Judeo-Christian symbols) and, again, auto-suggestion. It now occurred to us that suggestion was a universal mental capacity through which one could gain access to a special religious space in the psyche. We believed that through this capacity one could elicit a stronger faith experience.

The Therapy Nucleus Forms

We also saw (from a psychoanalytical viewpoint) that in order to survive, man has unconsciously always learned the most, most quickly, prior to the age of five or six, even if what he learned in fact and feeling contained much error. This time period was the age of greatest suggestibility, as well as the age in which one learned the *largely unconscious* distrust and fear of the environment, guilt attitudes and feelings, shame, self-doubt, and inferiority. With these withdrawal feelings also went their assertive complement, anger, or even rage.

For some, the base of all this difficulty was the mother's fear, perhaps even terror of living. Medical evidence seemed to indicate that sometimes the infant in the mother's womb even vaguely sensed her body tensions.[8] Eberhart was convinced that some new mothers, particularly in our confused present age, at times felt an unconscious resentment toward their new baby. An additional child increasingly became a liability rather than an asset because he/she was not greatly needed in the house, in the field, or in the family trade as in earlier times. Also, the mother felt hostility because of unconscious envy of the attentions the baby required, attentions the mother as an infant often did not receive and unconsciously still needed. Further, there was less opportunity for learning to mother because of smaller families and fewer siblings. Some mothers even resented their body's sexuality and its urges (a baby was living proof of these needs) and felt hostility at being a woman.

But mother was not culpable alone. Father was often as guilty, perhaps guiltier, though usually more indirectly so. For he, too, had resentments at his new heavier responsibilities. These came out in hostility directed at both mother and infant. Also, many fathers felt their attention needs were now not being met because of the baby, so the jealous father tormented the mother's life.[9]

These phenomena are examples of negative elements which possibly surrounded many infants (some even before birth). They suffice to point up the realizations which Dr. Eberhart and I began to confront in our hypothesizing. Because our minds and bodies seem to sense and try to adjust to the ambient feelings of stress, positive or negative, we needed to consider seriously the lifelong affects unconsciously learned in this highly suggestible period. In the first year or two of life—and perhaps even prior to birth—the entire social milieu, especially the mothering figure, was *god*. Obviously, fathers contributed heavily to the whole matrix, whether admittedly or not. They directly affected the mother's peace in her role fulfillment. Mother's role called for her to affirm the baby's BEING as *worthy, without requirement*. It appeared obvious that for the baby's early life mother seemed the origin of all subsequent out-of-awareness feelings of safety and pleasure of existence. *We hypothesized that the origin of later negative perceptions and concepts of God could be found in this early experience.*[10]

The problem now facing us was how to help people unlearn the sick love lessons that were unconsciously and unintentionally taught. Next, the problem was how to help people find the higher love experience with God, who had the power to correct early parental, negative love experiences and re-form life toward fulfillment. We were convinced of the phenomenal potential of intense Christian faith. But we believed the faith experience to be different, of a higher level of awareness than our usual conscious state. Nor was this special experience based on illusion. Rather, when attuned to the inner world through imagination and symbol, it provided healthy psychic transformation. Paul himself had alluded to it as another *growing up* point to be compared to the transformation of the whole person from childhood to adulthood (I Cor. 12:11 RSV). Even more important, Jesus told Nicodemus that one must be born again, transformed to a higher level of psychic functioning (John 3:1-15 RSV). It seemed to both of us that the onset of severe mental problems was akin to this type of chrysalis *but* had somehow gone astray due to an unknown and previously undetected psychic malfunction. We were convinced that inability to believe and experience God's love lay at the base of many psychological troubles. Notably, recent indications of the power of such central belief systems, religious and otherwise, to effect all health positively have further validated this early hypothesis. The core assumptions about all existence became the central belief from which all other life assumptions and beliefs hung in a balanced way, giving real viability to the whole of life.[11]

We adopted the positive attitude of Jesus who when confronted with illness, focused on the *potential* for good rather than the actuality of evil. He recognized the beauty of the as yet incomplete whole which God intended. He then proceeded to realize that potential. For example, when questioned about whose sin was responsible for the man born blind, Jesus answered that the blindness was for evidencing fulfillment of the will of God, not punishment for some wrongdoing by parent or child. Then he immediately created in the man sight—for the first time (John 9:1-12 RSV). As a friend once put it, Jesus never did anything silly, mean, cruel or stupid.[12] God must have had an ultimate good intention or will for this concrete world in which He/She worked and continues to work because it seemed God was still involved in a process of improvement in His/Her world-creating. Jesus further validated this concept when he healed a man on the sabbath and then answered his critics with the remark that his Father was still working, so he was also working [healing, perfecting] (John 5:9-19 RSV). Also, when Jesus later said that his followers would do even greater things than he had done (John 14:12 RSV), it seemed an injunction and commitment to DO good things for others. This fit in with Jesus's role as physician and pastor: to help and do for others if one could assist people to accomplish the good they wished for but could not accomplish alone. In other words, Jesus seemed to say, "Don't meddle with people's autonomy, but if they wish good and you can help that good to be, DO IT—IN MY NAME!"

An Organizing Concept: "The Creative Wedge of Faith"

About that time we were inspired to work further on creating this intensified religious faith method by the writing and teaching ministry of another person who also became a friend. Her premise about living the fullness of Christian life was that an object of faith had to be represented in one's mind as an image, a *pattern*. One held this pattern up to God in prayer for assistance to create life accordingly. (If one did not create, envision the needed form, how could God help one fill it with content?) Her faith convictions were so important to the beginning faith assumptions of this therapy that we can best present them in her own words:

> Prayer is only one of the many methods by which the energy of faith is released. Faith is a law unto itself and always carries its reward at the level on which it is expressed. Faith is the greatest energy in the universe. By its use and misuse all things that man has ever planned or invented or done, have been achieved. Power is the ability to use energy and the fruit of faith is good or worthless according to the nature and motives of the person using it. Faith is impersonal energy at the disposal of persons.[13]

In order to illustrate this concept of faith she recorded the true story of a man who apparently was an atheist or agnostic. He had only one major goal for his life: to live it entirely without illness. Superstitiously, he placed his faith in the healing abilities of a buckeye (an acorn) which he carried at all times, a practice presumed to ward off illness. She further pointed out that he lived to the age of eighty-seven and died, apparently of natural causes, in his sleep. In relating this to faith she said:

> Our circumstances are largely the result of our own and other people's use of faith and the choice of objects in which it is vested.... As no belief has the dynamic of faith unless it is patterned in a

concrete design of aim and action, this aim of his engaged the
energy of faith in a specific pattern upon which he acted faithfully,
constantly and consistently. This gave to his faith, the dynamics of
the mustard seed which we have seen are three-fold: PURPOSE,
PATTERN and POWER. "According to your faith be it unto you"
(Matt. 9:29).[14]

To the above faith concept, other convictions, and observations
from research, Dr. Eberhart and I then added the primary
conviction that the soul's center was the real spiritual center of
transforming power, the *imago Dei*, the Transcendent Self, the
Spark of God within persons. If properly attuned to God as the
Universal Presence and Love-energy Source, it seemed the Self
could and would help one through his/her ego to activate better the
positive growth aim or good will God already intended for each
personal life.[15]

At that intermediate point we envisioned the affective
interaction of these concepts, forming what we had construed as
the "Creative Wedge of Faith," with their capacity to vitalize the
love-energy of the person and to work religiously. I have
diagrammed it as Figure Number Two. Surprisingly enough, the
wedge image did not seem too removed from an ancient archetypal
pattern seen in the sky, that of wild geese going south for the
winter, guided by perhaps animal faith? Was this too a similar sort
of longing which we are in this theory now calling cosmic intuition
and which in a higher form was seen in the faithful reaching of
persons toward Jesus? It seemed so.[16]

Clarifying the Theology Behind the Concept

Now convinced the Self was the original center which drew into
existence the lesser center of the ego, it seemed biblically right to
postulate that the Self was the image of God in man. One could
infer this from the Genesis story in which God breathed into man
the "breath of life" and man became a "*living* being" (Gen. 2:7
RSV) (Italics mine). We conceived of *man's life* as different from
that of other beings. Divine and everlasting, it also had unique self-
awareness and introspective consciousness. The same sort of
inference can be drawn from Jesus's saying that the Jewish scripture
called the people "gods" (John 10:34 RSV).

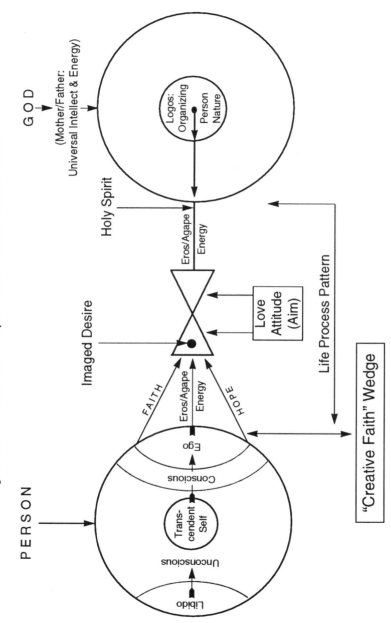

Figure No. 2   The Faith—Hope—Love Pattern of Life-Process

We hypothesized a person's life mainly as having two aspects, one which unfolded in time and the other eternal. The Self was conceived of as a unit of pure spirit (not just soul, animating principal only) originating with and in Adam and designed by God to create the ego as a spatio-temporal center and as a focus for human personality and character development. The ego was created evolutionarily to teach humanity certain necessary eternal qualities: the capacity for good reasoning; the ability to order by thinking logically and reflectively; and also, the capacity to place the correct weight of importance upon the feelings. It appeared to us that mankind's current life on this earth was training for his ultimate existence. We speculated that perhaps God was teaching mankind some lesson here which would enable him/her to be a better co-creator with Him/Her beyond this existence.

Thus the inner Self as a pure spirit center came to be called the Self or "God-spark." This *imaging nomenclature* was chosen from philosophical thinking of the past, spiritual experiences of some of the great Christian mystics, readings in Jungian psychotherapy techniques, and from certain mystical experiences of Christians who were in psychotherapy with us. But perhaps Leibniz's description of the human monad as fulgurated, flashed, or struck off (sparked) by and from the Divine Monad, God, ultimately gives the most easily grasped rationale for the founding concept of the term "God-spark" or Self.[17]

As promised, we will now deal more clearly with our use of the term "God-spark" instead of "Self" only. The former is more descriptive and has more helpful imaging, right brain amplification of the concept. Some have had difficulty with "God-spark" as seeming to allude to Gnostic precepts, and others have sensed the term as having some "god-reduced-to-me" implications. In order to help allay these concerns, let me propose an explanation offered to clients seeking to understand the symbolism of the Inner or Transforming Self. Soul, or the animating principle, belongs to all animal life; elemental life-forms, higher animals like frogs, pigs, and primates and humans also have soul but in an ascending order of conscious awareness. However, in humanity our existence is often experienced as beyond our usual center of activating power alone and also has self-aware awareness. This awareness additionally seems to possess a higher, cosmic, or God-like participatory power somehow related or connected to God Him/Herself. This experienced Inner Self, "God-spark", or Soul-center may be likened to the paradoxical reality of a spark sprung from a fire, still being a part of that same fire, though now strangely totally separate. In our hypothesis this God-spark is the *imago Dei* or humanity's *"living* being" plus the animating principle, or soul, which lifts us above other animal "beings" through our reflective self awareness and everlastingness. At times it is also helpful to remind clients that as humanity evolved, the ancients often conceived of the stars as being the visible evidence of the eternal aspect of the souls of the dead. Over the ages such thinking probably gave rise to the collective unconscious archetype of a God-like eternal self-image which clients sometimes tend to experience in Faith Therapy Meditations. As counseling proceeds the client begins to understand God as spatio-temporally manifesting Him/Herself as both Primordial and Consequential. The "God-spark" *imago Dei* concept of one's Inner Self experience in some of this therapy's experiences helps him/her understand the experience of feeling both *unity and separateness* with God as well as in some measure possessing some of these attributes of divinity within him/herself.

Now let us return to the flow of our story of the development of the Therapy's Theological Convictions. Speculatively striving to synthesize theology and science, we construed the Self as having had its beginning with Adam, the spiritual first in the species *man*. But since the creatively advanced and completely successful, prototypal life of Jesus Christ, we posited the Self as now evolutionarily bearing from God a new design, a Christ-like potential. As Paul said, it started with "'The first man Adam;...'" but climaxed with Christ as "...the last Adam...." (I Cor. 15:45 RSV). From thenceforth the Self had received from God an imprint or additional, evolutionary overlay which is the *mark of the Christ* present in all mankind as a possibility for a more satisfying life regardless of any particular type of formal religious faith or even the apparent lack of it. This concept caused us to consider that perhaps all men now even have a *spiritual body* such as Paul spoke of (I Cor. 15:42-50 RSV). And we speculated such a body was being currently built up at the direction of the Self by the soul, the human monad's animating force field, from relational awareness and energy originating in the physical body. This building up gave rise to the combinations of higher vibrational levels of energy and greater capacities of thought we generally meant by the term spiritual dimension. We also considered that the Self and this transformed body, with its ego-learned experience, survived death as an experiencing subject. Our position bore a close resemblance to that of Teilhard, when finally his work was published, that an organism like God, which was growing, did not do so by destroying its component cells but rather by building them into stronger units.[18]

As an important aside: the above concept provides a sensible explanation for persons undergoing a self-validating experience as is sometimes attained with intensified faith in this method. For example, see the verbatim transcript in Chapter XII in which Speck experiences God as "Core of Light and Father of Love, Forgiveness," and is aware of his "inner (spiritual?) body." However such an explanation is offered, not imposed. In this method this sort of answering attempts to give an understanding of this type of experienced religious reality, as a caring parent would answer the questions arising from the confusing subjective experiences of a three to six-year old.

We also postulated that in earthly life the ego made contact with the Self in a powerful burst from which issued forth personal religious feelings of being saved—an experience possibly similar to the primal love-flow felt by the infant first finding the breast. But on a higher level such a profound ego-Self contact, producing a feeling of unity, would then be perceived as the safe-secure affect, a transforming, religious experience leading to spiritual growth. Continuing this thinking, we considered that this higher unitive feeling was caused by the Self's constant close contact with God as a Presence, the Logos. Paradoxically, this Self was experienced as in unity with God, yet at the same time set completely free to do as it might with its own time-constructed existence. As Whitehead contended, it seemed God was more interested in manifesting His own nature as Savior than anything else.[19]

An interesting inference was derived from the above understandings; since we postulated the "God-spark" now bore the Christ imprint, it seemed possible that many people could evidence the nature of Christ alive within them without ever having formally, officially claimed the name of Christian. Frankly, this insight-question arose primarily from past military experience. During World War II, in the South Pacific Theatre, both of us had noticed more of what seemed to be the mark of Christ in believers of other Faiths than was observable in many "formal" Christians. Also we had separately experienced this phenomenon as an almost numinous insight which had to wait a while to be more fully conceptualized. This broad position may have been what Christ meant when he said he had many other sheep who were not of "this fold" and that these sheep were also to be brought *by him* into the fold (John 10:16 RSV). This viewpoint represented the magnanimous and all-embracing love of God for all mankind who were filled with true loving natures. Christ himself appeared to embody such saving concern in his relations with the Gentiles and Samaritans who evidenced his kind of loving faith. (Could this also be what the Roman Catholic thinkers are moving toward in Vatican II's "Implicit recognition of 'anonymous Christianity'"?[20])

When and where was this gathering to take place? Was it to be in heaven (a pure spirit, non-spacio-temporal, existence beyond death?) where everyone would finally have a fair chance to perceive clearly? Here could be a real opportunity to learn of God as a Person, Presence, a special essence of I-Am-ness. This human parental type of love was only to be known through the I am-ness of Jesus. And he stated he would create a room (special spiritual space) in the Father's house (heaven) for those who could ultimately relate to God as person-like I-Am-ness or Presence-center. This quality was especially revealed in Jesus in whom God Him/Herself could most intimately be known as Person. And was it not powerful and wonderful that Jesus could so intimately relate in some entirely new, creative, and perceptive way to life's Ultimate Mystery. Many others only seemed to experience there the Void. Yet Jesus found that there he could call this Mystery, Father, or *Abba. Abba*, or Papa, was a warm, familiar name. For Jesus to create such a space in heaven for those who wished a *personal* relation to God was a powerful inspiration to faith and hope (John 14:1-11 RSV). It meant one could be purposefully optimistic in all life, even through suffering and the ultimate threat, death.

It is interesting to note that the above speculations about life after death seem to fit comfortably with the findings of more recent investigations of near death experiences (or beyond clinical death experiences) investigated and reported by Raymond Moody, M.D.,

Kenneth Ring, Ph.D., and other empirically oriented researchers. The investigations indicate after having such experiences many people find new meaning for life and are oriented toward a higher, more loving and moral existence. The experiences are transforming and while largely personally symbolic, they present a common thread of truth. Such experiences seem to give persons greater hope and stronger faith, and a desire to live life more lovingly. Thus, speculatively, such an experience is similar to this therapy's purpose, and great good may be experienced personally through the therapy's production of fuller religious lives.[21]

The above earlier speculative theological views allowed a Christian ministering approach to spiritual growth and psychotherapy which was both optimistic in basic premise and did not violate the autonomy and integrity of either therapist or acceding patient-parishioner. This gave an ambient sacred respect to all, regardless of faith, atheism, agnosticism, or varying denominations of Christianity. This openness of theological position was not meant as an umbrella of compromise; it arose as the honest conviction of both therapists.

Crystallizing the Guided Meditation Construct

The major motifs of the counseling part of the method had by now largely fallen in place, and the particular technique was later to assume the form presented herein as Dialogical Counseling. But even with this interactional approach to therapy we were still unable to get to the deepest affective roots of problems. Obviously the conscious cognitive approach needed something more than just the *mild* affective aid brought by the addition of fantasy and imagery therapy techniques.[22] These mild meditative additions had flowed into the counseling method as a result of using Jung's Active Imagination approach where the imagination moves itself much as in dreams.[23] The missing necessary dimension seemed to lie further in the general direction of depth affective prayer, contemplation, and meditation.

We started with the insights from previously cited psychological disciplines and the common elements observed in mysticism. Dr. Eberhart was especially impressed by the central element of auto-suggestion in most cases of mystical experience, and he kept us oriented toward finding a solution along these lines. But in the West, since most people with problems could scarcely calm their anxiety (tranquilizers were not in existence then) much less let it go in order to achieve a deep meditative or prayerful mood, to us it seemed ethical and necessary to use suggestion and a ministry of Christian shepherding, to help needy persons gain this mood. Evidently, achieving this mood was an emotional prerequisite to becoming intensely aware of God's love and to doing better problem solving. Therefore, we decided to begin by using a religious, instead of clinical, approach to hypnotherapy. Starting with body relaxation techniques, we first helped persons become calm. To this state we then added prayer, contemplation and some Christian symbolism therapy techniques. The use of such powerful symbols suggested itself to us through our recent use of Initiated Symbol Projection material.[24] All imagery use had amplified our techniques prior to any hypnotherapy use; these tools could possibly further enhance our developing methodology to be used in the service of the Church.

As we utilized this religious approach in addition to some symbolism concepts gained from knowledge of Jungian dream interpretation, we gained significant insight. *We learned of slight shifts in mood type and intensity, greater independence and power of the will's functioning, a lessening of unquestioning compliance with some seemingly innocent suggestion and, of great importance—a tremendous upsurge of numinous emotion.*[25] We viewed these factors as evidence that the person was indeed having something of an intense religious experience. The experience went beyond anything the therapist could suggest and evoke symbolically in a subject and have it later remain real to him/her. Observations of positive results began to convince us that we truly were somehow helping people to gain better access to special mental-emotional-spiritual areas which were not easily or often tapped. From that higher psyche space people also appeared to gain greater access to some deeply repressed subconscious material, something often extremely hard to reach with hypnosis, even with a somnambulistic trance.

At first we both were convinced by the efficacy of the new approach that we were only helping enable people, *by their faith* and use of religious symbols, contemplation, prayer and a guided hypnoidal state, to gain for themselves greater contact with God's love in Christ. However, out of his professional knowledge of hypnotherapy, Dr. Eberhart concluded that since what was happening seemed so different from typical hypnotic material, the new method should be called Meditation Therapy, in order to delineate more clearly the goal and type of suggestion used in the process and more clearly define it as a *ministry*. It seems significant at this point, in view of Eberhart's somewhat intuitively calling the mind mood "meditation," to take note that it was several years later before the related revealing experiments were done by the Japanese researchers, Kasmatsu, Shimazono, and Hirae. Their scientific research clearly indicated the EEG brain wave patterns in meditation to be significantly different from those found in hypnosis. Also their studies found the unconscious to be more as it was conceptualized by Jung.[26]

A related statement will be found at the close of the Chapter in Note 27.

Our central working hypothesis was that no human love could be as pure or powerful as that experienced from God. The clients' reports now convinced us that this greater love, or life-energy flow, indeed many times could override negative parental conditioning, thus opening up formerly superego-blocked channels into the unconscious. Evidently this feeling of being loved was able to recondition the false negatives of the conscience function and free one's whole life to gain greater satisfaction through directly experiencing God's love. We believed this to be the actual dynamic of the Christian conversion or intense religious growth experience with its resultant saved (safe-secure) feelings. It then seemed feasible that this dynamic could be the same as that which worked in the enhanced faith-hope-love experience of Meditation Therapy.

Although to us this was not far fetched, we made serious efforts to keep close watch on our belief systems. We granted the possibility as Freud had believed, that the oceanic feelings of unity found in religious experience were to be attributed to the earlier experience of the pleasantness of womb existence and/or the first months of life. This position construed such religious feelings as regressive, delusional, and even in some circumstances, very dangerous.[28] However, the Meditation Therapy experience did not indicate such distortion but rather evidenced greater faith growth, a higher level of personality integration, improved self-image, heightened positive affect, increased awareness and rationality, as well as improved capacity to cope with outer and inner world reality. But the greatest joy of all was the spiritual growth of people deepening their awareness of God's love and expansion of their concept of His/Her nature. It was a joy of fulfillment of the Christian healing ministry. And, we also noted that people seemed closer to the positive affects which Jung spoke of as originating within the Self and objective psyche in the individuation process in order to promote spiritual growth in the personality and bring unconscious and conscious balance.[29]

At about this time we began to shape a more helpful mental construct of the psyche. Our contact with the Psychosynthesis Research Foundation began to lead us more deeply into the thinking of Roberto Assagioli, an Italian psychiatrist and contemporary of Freud, Jung, and others who were early workers in the field. In an early publication Assagioli outlined a new and synthetic construct of the psyche. The basics of this construct are still to be found in our current paradigm, which conceived the unconscious as having an upper part oriented around specifically altruistic drives and home of the Higher Self [Self] center as a phenomenologically palpable spiritual reality. He indicated the task of therapy was to produce a synthesis and harmony of all psyche structures and functions—particularly between the "I" (conscious self) [ego] and the "Higher Self."[30] Then Assagioli produced another significant work in which he dealt with the crises of spiritual awakening. The booklet gave identifying characteristics of such a crisis, held it to be a normal part of intensive spiritual growth (they seemed very akin to those accompanying Jung's process of individuation) and offered suggestions for treatment of these crises.[31] All his work fit well into our observations and gave us some broadened and better defined constructs with which to build.

With these new insights in mind and upon further close scrutiny of our method's dynamics, it also seemed that in the meditations the ego was so accented in its structure and functioning that it was going back to recapture something of the infant's unconditionally loved feelings in order to build upon them a higher level of ego stability and growth. This understanding also fit with the concepts of rebirth found in religious conversion and transformation. It was at this time that the insight burst that these experiences apparently occurred WITH THE ADULT EGO IN SERVICE TO THE SELF. If so, the entire process could not be pathologically regressive in normal people, for that would imply that the infantile personality or more primitive ego should be regressively present. And this was not the case. Lack of evidence of a regressive ego's presence also offered the possibility that some prior situations of highly lucid hypnotic experiences may even have been *unrecognized* meditative experiences. It seemed the meditation experience with its enhanced ego functioning must be a transformation into a higher level of consciousness which reached the whole person and allowed him/her, as a genuine intense religious experience usually had, a brief experiential, inspiring glimpse into larger patterns of existence.

The Development of the Intensified Faith Schema

The new insights led us to consider Desoille's findings about the archetypal significance of height and depth and to postulate applying these principles to the formerly named Trance Induction Techniques.[32] Our notion was that the psyche's prayer-meditation mood, wherein one appeared to experience God's love more fully and articulately, could perhaps be intensified by use of this special archetypal direction. We hoped that the love-suffused ego would thereby carry conscious awareness to higher levels of functioning.

We then asked how we could apply the concept of consciousness raising and the further intensification of the safe-secure affect in such a manner as to reorganize more thoroughly and effectively the unconditionally loved feelings around God rather than human mothers and fathers. One thing seemed sure; the experience of being loved was usually first centered upon mother, so it appeared that the therapy method indeed must have been operating by reconditioning these early emotions around Jesus Christ as the supreme, perfect loving person. If so, the experience needed to stay in the framework of a PERSON-CENTER in order to avoid psychic diffusion and possible pathological experiences. For if what was being dealt with were indeed the transforming key to Christian experience of The Holy, and if the resultant *abiding* in that psyche space were to be used as a temporary mind state in which therapy work could be done without prohibitive levels of fear/anxiety, then we needed to find some more organized and reasonably certain way (or steps) by which to arrive at this religious mind mood.

How was it to be done? We first realized that the method should continue to embody the prior concept of the constantly interacting Christian virtues of faith-hope-love, as the attitudes which could lead the love-energy upward in increasingly powerful steps. The effectiveness of this dynamic relating had already been established. But how had this emotion state been amplified? Obviously the answer was imagery expressed in archetypal symbolism. But such symbolism did not necessarily stay centered and moving toward a faith goal without the longing which belonged to faith and committed belief as *aimed rationality*. God seemed rational as He/She was revealed in Christ, and we held this position to be basic to a deeper understanding of God. Therefore we postulated that emotion as love-energy, aimed by faith's reaching, backed up by hope's stance, and oriented by love's attitude, with unconscious or primary mentation, should be further led by the evolutionarily more advanced secondary mentation as belief, with its increasingly reflective thought processes. And if one took into consideration Jung's and Desoille's positions on archetypal imagery's power, it seemed the immediate envisioned destination should be a mountaintop scene, an image already strongly suggested by descriptions of feelings in Christian and other religious experiences and found effective in psychotherapeutic imaging.[33]

The query naturally following was from where should such a psychic journey of religious amplification archetypally start? Since the unconscious was frequently depicted in dreams as the sea, the mother of us all, for most people the seemingly obvious place to start would be a relaxing, peaceful seashore scene, an image also conducive to the body relaxing techniques. Inasmuch as our deliberate aim was the inclusion in consciousness of unconscious content, in our research we avoided starting with an *into the sea* image. We felt that such symbols should only be approached after consciousness' safety and security were first elevated and firmly established.

As previously stated we were already using Jung's concept of active imagination, one of the functions of the symbolizing capacity. Now in the meditation part of the therapy we were finding this Jungian construct to reveal unsuspected qualities. For active imagination even seemed to have the ability to intensify the efficacy of the symbols as well as give positive direction in psychic movement. Apparently the faculty had its own uncanny inner guidance system.

At this point we became influenced by a relevant book written by Raynor C. Johnson, an Australian physicist. Johnson set forth the metaphysical hypothesis that God and all the universe worked primarily by the essential psychic function of the imagination. He asserted that all creativity was based upon the working of the imaginal dynamic. Imaginals, from his view, could be compared to Whitehead's eternal objects.[34] While we did not agree with all points of the hypothesis, we saw that imagination, properly used, was perhaps a more creative force than we had conceived thus far. The concept of such a force working through imagined archetypal symbols helped us comprehend the efficacy of the then named Meditation *Elevation* Exercise, later to be re-conceptualized as the Intensified Faith Schema Exercise.

Johnson also provided us with further conceptualization of the term cosmic intuition. He called this psychic construct the "Intuitive Self," a level of the Self, functioning imaginally, to perceive beyond the "highest reaches of the intellectual mind."[35] It was an extraordinary and omniscient psychic faculty belonging to all people whether consciously used and cultivated or not. Since hypothesizing and using this faculty seemed to enhance the therapy's effectiveness in imaging or symbolizing, we further construed this drawing ability of the imaginal function as a part of that unitive perception which seemed to operate in a psychoid world, one in which mind and matter unitively interacted constantly. It tended to lead love's energy toward its inwardly sensed goal. Also, this line of thought appeared to be akin to Jung's construct of the Self as the religious or unitive and dynamic function of the psyche.[36] Combined, these concepts gave the name Imaginal Intuition (later to become cosmic intuition) to that basic psychic function which was next conceived of as the drawing power contained in love's *aim*, faith's *reaching*, and hope's *expectancy*. Imaginal intuition, then, could be depended upon to keep the archetypal images and symbols moving the love process steadily upward toward an intensified, unitive experience in the meditation elevation's organizing pattern.

The present structure of the Intensified Faith Schema Exercise basically reveals the pattern's final form. These levels and steps—now evident as stages and sub-stages—were first conceived of as mind mood or affect elevating *scenes* with amplifying and intensifying steps between them. They were thought of simply as a form of spiritual dynamic, operative in the psyche, which naturally led a person's ego through an evolutional pattern toward the Self—an ordered procedure rhythmically spiraling upward within each step and scene. (Obviously, such *imaged* stages and sub-stages amplified right brain functioning and made the meditation more effective, but to our knowledge at that time brain research had not revealed the effect of that hemisphere's functioning.) We found the results of the method's use, with its enhanced numinous emotion and unitive love experience, more gratifying as a ministry with each new development.

When we had developed the meditation elevation journey to the conclusion of the Mountaintop Scene, which included the concept of contemplation of the paradox, we discovered the next sequence of mood elevation development through intuition aided by notions gained from our prior therapy work observations, Christian convictions, and implications from psychosynthesis.[37] It was called the Unitive or Heavenward Level with its Steps. We conceived this part as a refining movement involving accumulation and abstraction of certain Christian beliefs as well as transformations of feeling into a more transcendent functioning of the psyche. The principle aims in it were to elevate the affect to its highest spiritual capacity for Christian love, to remove the *Not I*, or object elements, in the ego, thus allowing it to activate the individual's greatest capacity for functional conjunction of ego and Self in the upper unconscious. Ultimately, one would arrive at a focal point of LIVING BEING in order to make a final Christian faith affirmation. This final center was conceived of as one's ultimate identity and in constant connection/relation to or with God.[38] The committing prayer was a meaningful part, from the beginning, of all the meditation methods attempted, not just the elevation itself. Our aim was to keep the experiences in a psychic framework of specifically Christian belief and experience.

To put the matter succinctly, the method worked. Apparently people were able to give themselves over to this Christian religious growth or therapeutic experience with varying degrees of effectiveness according to differing inner given or developed spiritual abilities. At any rate, most could reach enough mind mood elevation that use of the Meditation Therapy Procedures were effective for them. Dr. Eberhart and I continued to work at simplifying, refining and amplifying this method as a special expression of Christ's healing ministry. Eberhart's death in 1970 closed that part of the conjoint work. Since that time I have continued in the tradition in which we began: answering the *call* to be a pastor, servant, healer, and herald of the Lord's message of salvation.

A Vital Contribution

I would be remiss at this point if I did not note the immeasurable overall contribution to Faith Therapy which has been made by Dr. Roger W. Birkman. This outstanding psychologist is also a committed Christian. His personality inventory was (and still is) highly successful as used in industry, and he hoped it would be of even greater use to the Church in deepening experiential awareness of God's grace within local faith communities. The test contained the major, current, and comprehensive psychological truths, but it was also firmly anchored in the teachings of Jesus Christ. The combination revealed a depth of insight into the human psyche that was of untold help in pastoral counseling and psychotherapy on a one-to-one basis but also *especially* in church sponsored growth-groups.

Most of the basic theorizing work on The Intensified Faith Schema and Guided Meditation Therapy Procedures was already completed when I met this Christian psychologist who had made his information available for Church use over thirty years ago. His insights have further informed the theoretical element of the therapy, especially the Guided Meditation dimension. However, the test results and other information have also contributed to the Dialogical Counseling. In groups, the test puts all on common ground, including the ministering leader, and as results are shared, God's grace is an experienced reality. And in one-to-one work, using the test data helps in defusing many resistances and defenses, enabling the therapist to work more easily through the interpersonal problems. This conscious and unconscious personality component testing instrument provides a positive meeting ground for both science and religion where problems of the human psyche can be healed.

With the Early Church

As Paul said to the infant Church, life's abiding attitudes are faith, hope, and love—guiding and amplifying the love-energy. Love's first movement is an *act* called faith. This Christian view of the life process as activated and sustained by faith does lead one to more accurate perception and higher transformations of thought and feeling. Faith's activation of Christ-like love can bring an ultimate, unifying wholeness of understanding.

Faith Therapy is also an expression of liberation theology.[39] Liberation exists along a continuum of freedom, one end resting inside oneself, with all the distressing negative forces of the unconscious; and the other end resting in the world outside in which one's fellow human beings (and also oneself) may well exist in the hopelessness of outer imposed bondage. Christ came to set free, and much liberation theology thinking has rightfully oriented itself around such issues as racial, sexual, or political freedom and justice. Primarily, our lives are oriented around the outer world issues of spatio-temporal reality since life's basic body survival needs must be met.

We should remember, however, that this outer life arises from a subjective sense of selfhood. If one is not aware of one's inner liberation from the "damming power of The Law," (as it is frequently experienced because of a sick conscience) through experiencing the transforming power of Christ's grace, one may still be in an inner spiritual dungeon and, consequently, suffer self-hate to the point of projection upon others to enslave them. In order to make outer world transformation possible, one must be capable of loving oneself enough in Christ to love one's neighbor (the world over) equally; then the inwardly liberated person can wholeheartedly desire and work for justice and liberation for his/her neighbor. Consciously, a person must perceive him/herself as lovable and acceptable, absolved of sin and weakness through grace, before the person can have enough self-esteem to love others enthusiastically enough to want them liberated *inwardly and outwardly* also.[40] In the movement of inner and outer liberation neither emphasis should take precedence if the outer is to be lasting, for both are equally vital in freeing humanity in a holistic way. Faith Therapy addresses itself primarily to the inner, unconscious dimension, to liberate the individual to relate wholesomely to all his/her unconscious nature, thereby making possible a sincere desire for *outer* freedom for all.

NOTES

[1] Otto, *Holy*, pp. 5-7.

[2] For example, Christ's leaving the waiting multitude at Peter's house the next morning after healing Peter's mother-in-law and many others the preceding day. (Mark 1:29-39).

[3] *Sympathy* emotionally participates completely with the feelings of another. *Empathy* emotionally participates only partially, but with depth perception, and then it goes the remainder of the distance to another's feeling with intellect (e.g., without this capacity, at a funeral the caring pastor could weep uncontrollably with the mourners at the graveside and be unable to do the loving thing—bury the body).

[4] Dr. John Eberhart maintained from the first that the realization of the awareness of God's love as shown in Christ was the ultimate healing force because it was the only thing which ultimately could make persons unafraid—even in the face of death.

[5] James Carlyon, Perkins School of Theology, Southern Methodist University, was a beloved, early, theological professor of mine. This statement of his made such sense that I committed it to memory.

[6] R. Droz and M. Rahmy, *Understanding Piaget*, trans. by Joyce Diamant (New York: International Universities Press, Inc., 1976), pp. 36, 37.

[7] See also Thomas S. Kepler, ed. *Fellowship of the Saints* (Nashville, Tenn.: Abingdon-Cokesbury, 1948).

[8] See also Camilla M. Anderson, *Beyond Freud* (New York: Harper and Brothers, 1957), pp. 25, 26. See also Jonathan Winson, *Brain And Psyche* (N.Y.: Vintage, , 1985), *Passim*.

[9] See also Alexander Lowen, *The Language of the Body* (New York: Collier, 1971), pp. 23, 24, 107-09, 379-84.

[10] The term "we hypothesized" is somewhat overstated, for while I agreed with it Eberhart first developed the concept in our conjoint work. See also Ana-Maria Rizzuto, *The Birth of the Living God: A Psychoanalytic Study* (Chicago: University of Chicago Press, 1979), pp. 180-216.

[11] Ornstein and Sobel, *Healing*, pp. 57-59, 97-99, 105-116.

[12] This was a position taught by Agnes Sanford, an outstanding teacher in Christian spiritual healing in her lectures on such healing at a retreat for that purpose, which John Eberhart and I attended.

[13] Mary Welch, *What Wilt Thou?* (Henderson, Texas: Park Printing Co., 1952), p. 46.

[14] *Ibid.*, pp. 46, 47.

[15] Outler, *Psychotherapy*, pp. 82-98. See also, Martin Buber, *The Way of Man: According to the Teaching of Hasidim* (Seracus, N.J.: Citadel, 1966), pp. 5, 6, 23, 30.

[16] It is interesting to note that the *triadic symbol* has been noted more recently by analytical psychologists as an apparent indication of religious change. See Edward F. Edinger, *Ego and Archetype* (Baltimore: Penguin, 1974), pp. 69-76.

[17] B. A. G. Fuller, "Leibniz," in *History of Philosophy*, Vol. II (2 Vols.), 2nd ed. (New York: Henry Holt and Co., 1945), pp. 105-19. See also, Frances G. Wicks, *The Inner World of Choice* (New York: Harper and Row, 1963), pp. 40-42.

[18] de Chardin, *How I Believe*, pp. 47-59.

[19] A. N. Whitehead, *Process and Reality* (New York: The Free Press, 1929), pp. 407-08.

[20] Karl Rahner, *I Remember*, trans. by Harvey D. Egan (New York: Crossroads, 1985), pp. 3, 77-78.

[21] Pythia Pey, "The Changing Face of Death, "*Common Boundary*, Vol. 9, No. 1 (January/February, 1991), pp. 14-20.

[22] Kretschmer "Meditative Techniques," in *Zeitschrift Für Psychotherapie*, pp. 1-8.

[23] Jung, *Analytical*, 19 ff.

[24] Leuner and Kornadt, "Initiated Symbol Projection," pp. 1-11.

[25] Otto. *Holy*, pp. 60, 61.

[26] Kamasatsu and Hirae, "An Electroencephalographic Study on the Zen Meditation (Zazen)," in *Altered States of Consciousness*, ed. by Charles T. Tart (New York: John Wiley and Sons, 1969), pp. 489-501.

[27] It seems appropriate to me at this point that I make a somewhat embarrassing confession. Though Eberhart had appropriately correctly named the technique Meditation Therapy, because of the then generally negative reaction by the public toward the Eastern types of *meditation*, I compromised. In my pastoral counseling as a parish minister who did not want to seem too eccentric, I primarily continued to refer to the meditation as *religious hypnotherapy*. Both techniques used suggestion, and the term hypnosis seemed less threateningly esoteric to my parishioners. Seven or eight years passed before I was fearless enough openly to call the technique by the name Eberhart gave it.

[28] Sigmund Freud, *Civilization and Its Discontents*, trans. and ed. by James Starchey (New York: W. W. Norton, 1962), pp. 11-32.

[29] Jung, *Modern Man*, pp. 175-95, 214-20.

[30] Assagioli, "Dynamic Psychology," pp. 1-20.

[31] Assagioli, "Self-realization," pp. 1-22.

[32] Gerard, "Symbolic Visualization", p. 4.

[33] Kretschmer, "Meditative Techniques," p. 3.

[34] Raynor C. Johnson, *Nurslings of Immortality* (New York: Harper and Brothers, 1957), pp. 23-81.

[35] *Ibid.*, pp. 96, 97.

[36] Fordham, *Introduction*, pp. 69-83.

[37] Psychosynthesis Research Foundation, "Introduction to the Techniques," 4 pages.

[38] *Ibid., passim.*

[39] An excellent overview of this more recently conceptualized but vitally important movement in theology may be obtained by reading Robert McAfee Brown's *Theology in a New Key* (Philadelphia: Westminister Press, 1978).

[40] Stanley C. Russell, M.D. "Coping with Stress—Christ's Way," *The Christian Counselor*, (Spring, 1986), pp. 1-3.

Chapter VI

◌

PSYCHOLOGICAL
MODELS

In this chapter we will establish that the complex human psyche
forms the foundation on which this spiritual growth therapy
method stands. As we examine the following psyche components, it
must be kept in mind that this understanding of the mind is *a construct*, largely composed by observation of mental functioning. It is,
however, increasingly verified by relevant neurological evidence.
The biological facts of neural mechanisms, circuitry, and functions
establish the existence of the conscious, preconscious, and unconscious. Scientific study indicates that all these mechanisms produce
behavior patterns and strategies enhancing individual and species
survival.[1] They are actively evidenced in faith's beliefs which orient
the human organism toward a life of personal safety and satisfaction.[2] However, we must remember that the individual psyche is
tied to relating positively to others within a given social matrix for
society's survival.[3] One's brain and neurological system even effects
the positive functioning of his/her healing and regulating system
through messenger molecules and their cellular receptors, thus
determining the nature of the interactions of all the psyche's components.[4] At no point should Cartesian dualism come into consideration. Herein a human is viewed biblically as a unity, *a living
being*, but humans interact through more observable parts, mind
and body.[5]

Concepts of the Term Self

In the construct we are proposing for understanding this religious psychotherapy method, the *Self* or "God-spark" [God as
immanent in humanity (the *imago Dei*)] is conceived as being pre-

sent in the human organism at some point prior to birth, although the exact point would be hard to establish. This Self or Soul-center is the individual's basic center of spiritual beingness, awareness, or I Am-ness (note the capital "A"), the Thou sense of being out of which further selfhood grows. In my estimation, neurological findings infer that the Self's primary physiological location may be somewhere within the human brain. If the Self is indeed the *imago Dei*, evolutionarily it would seem to be God's special gift of life to humanity and effectively located in that area. (It is interesting that some few clients undergoing intense regression work in guided meditation have reported they seemed to be in their mother's womb and were aware of her pre-natal feelings toward them. Of course, there is no valid way of checking on such awareness, and therapeutically in such events, all that was needed was some such strongly symbolized concept which allowed the client to release the traumatized affect.) While it is the center of the psyche, this Self is operative in all areas of the person. The Self is a holistic, *reasoning*, (a later capacity made more available through ego experience interacting with spatio-temporal existence), structuring, synthesizing, and transforming spiritual or transpersonal center. As experienced in this therapy, this focal point of awareness is also at least partly beyond spatio-temporal bounds. This center operates through its spirit force-field, the soul, and has the ability to take the physical energy of matter as feeling (sensation and emotion) and meaningfully combine it with thought, the ordering, conceptualizing, and reflective capacity of the mind, by using archetypal symbols to effect the process. As the psyche's innermost core, the Self or Soul-center is the ultimate balancing principle in all the person's equilibration needs whether they be of body, emotion, thought or spirit.[6]

This primary sense of Self is also the larger, UNCONSCIOUS *center* of the psyche and is usually out of awareness except as manifest in meta-peak, mystical, or intense religious experience. The entire unconscious is conceptualized as more oriented around deeper emotion or feeling and primary process mentation (Freud's concept).[7] The CONSCIOUS *center* of the mind is the lesser center, largely manifested in daily and usual awareness. This center is also a focal point of usual being, awareness, or I am-ness. (Note the small "a")[8] As a personal center, it is not evident as a clearly defined self-aware *subject* until about age three when the symbiotic tie with the mother is broken; then it generally remains in a state of continuing development until senescence or death. This point of usual awareness is referred to in this paradigm as the *ego* or ego complex and is the primary origin of conscious reasoning or secondary mentation (Freud's concept).[9] We will also recognize another usage of the term self. In much writing this term is used to indicate what is generally meant by person, human, or the total being of the individual. The word also alludes to a person's potentialities as well as actualities, so this inclusive use of the concept will be referred to as the *total self* when a highly discriminating clarification is needed.[10]

Psyche Topography, Structure, Relations and Operations

Having now clarified our use of Self, ego, and total self, in this section let us indicate their further interrelations and operations as well as the psyche's other chief aspects—as work with this therapy has led to its conceptualization. In general, the material presented below closely approximates the conceptualization of the psyche by the field of Psychosynthesis.[11] But the differences will be clarified by reference to the accompanying diagram. Help in understanding these constructs will be found in the illustration, Figure Number Three.

Self (Agape Source) and Upper Unconscious

The Self is visualized as located at the top of the Upper Unconscious. It is partly outside the total self and in constant contact with the Collective Unconscious, God, and the Cosmos. This Self is also conceived as having a chemical-like spiritual valence and transforming power which is capable of changing eros into agape when Self-ego interaction is strong. The *Upper Unconscious* is envisioned as the source area of the more highly creative, meta-peak, heroic, altruistic, and spiritual experiences. This area is the location of the higher, affect-laden cognitive structures of spiritual development. Jung referred to these structures as the transforming and transcending archetypes of individuation.[12] The section is also the reservoir of the more subliminal and repressed spiritual memories and matter of the personal unconscious.

Figure No. 3 Basic Psyche Diagram

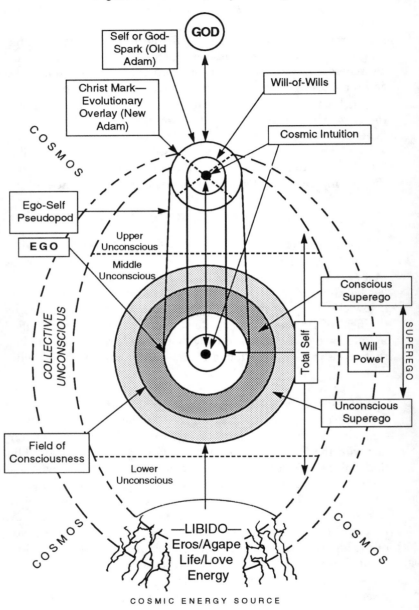

Please observe that most of the dividing lines in the diagram are dashes. This is to indicate their porous nature so that there is a relatively free flow of material from one area to another. Also, note that the Ego-Self pseudopod is drawn somewhat in reverse order size. This is simply done for the sake of showing superego dimensions which require more space.

Ego, Field of Consciousness andMiddle Unconscious

The ego (or ego complex) is located at the center of the *Field of Consciousness*, our usual area of awareness. The conceptualized location of this field is in the *Middle Unconscious*, the more *pre-conscious* (Freud's concept) and humanistically oriented part of the psyche.[13] In this sense the Middle Unconscious is the location of the usual cognitive structures (Piaget's concept) which produce intellect for consciousness.[14] Also, this area of the unconscious has access to much readily available and non-threatening experiences of the *Personal Unconscious* or that part of the psyche which is presumed to contain most memory matter from the personal past. For all practical purposes the predominance of the material in the Personal Unconscious (except for the cognitive structures themselves) could easily be conscious, but being so would clutter awareness.[15] Also, the ego most usually is the source for the brain's executive function but may be replaced by alter egos or personality fragments under unusual or negative stress conditions.

Libido (Eros Source) and Lower Unconscious

The *Lower Unconscious* is envisioned as the primary psychic location of human physical action material, life rhythms, basic instincts, more primitive affect-laden cognitive structures, and animal energy. At its lower end is the infusion of the basic cosmic life-energy (bubble shaped on the diagram) or energetic life force often called Eros type of love or *Libido* whose operation is largely instinctual and oriented to pleasure attainment and avoidance of the unpleasant.[16] This life force filters through the impact of the collective unconscious which directly adds its own energetic shaping influence and power. As the human organism grows, the libido supplies all needed energy for subsequent transformations of emotion, thought, and spirit through its bio-chemical action. But this lower unconscious area of the psyche also contains the more noxious parts of the personal unconscious and its deeper, subliminal (as well as repressed) usual (without spiritual content) memories and perceptions.[17] Also, this area is highly akin to the Freudian concept of the Id and the source of much mental-emotional illness.[18] In our construct this area corresponds to the general concept of the *Subconscious*.

Total Self and Collective Unconscious
The three unconscious areas of the personal psyche may be thought of as encompassed by the *total self*. (Interestingly, Jung conceived of the Self as *both ultimate center and circumference* of the psyche.)[19] In turn the total self is conceived of as nearly enclosed, except for a part of the Self and libido, by the *Collective Unconscious or Objective Psyche*. It is so called because at vital times it tends to send into the psyche *equilibrating* spiritual impulses as archetypal symbols, coming from nature's own needs, eliciting behavior and attitude changes which help preserve life *impartially*. This objective psyche is thus understood as the genetically programmed, psychic storehouse for the cumulative and hereditary past experience of mankind.[20]

Superego: Perception by Sensation, Usual Intuition and Cosmic Intuition—Will and Imagination
The term *Superego* is roughly akin to the concept of "conscience."[21] However, here the superego (as an aspect of its guilt feelings) is understood as containing the *conscious and unconscious* critical, judgment, or valuing factors (attitudes) of the perceptive faculties. These factors in turn are considered, as in the Jungian construct of perception, to be *Sensation* which relates us to the outer world of reality, and *Normal or Usual Intuition* which relates us to much of the inner world of reality and seems to perceive subliminally via some unconscious route.[22]

We conceive *Cosmic or Unitive Intuition* type of perception as relating people to all unitive needs for life fulfillment with Ultimate Reality by using a sense of lure, valence, or meaning. This type of intuition as well as the *Will* has a different location on the diagram. The reader may note there is also no designated location for *Imagination* or *Imaginal Function*; this lack of designation is because the functions are operative throughout the entire psyche, although imagination may in special needs be focused and used by the Self— utilizing cosmic intuition—to produce archetypal images.[23]

The next concept may be better clarified by using an analogy. As a newborn infant interacts with the environment, he/she begins with the unconscious life-energy thrust to build a coping mechanism between him/herself and the outer world in order to protect safely his/her own inner world while fulfilling outer world needs.

This mechanism is first seen as a dim or diffused field of consciousness with a rudimentary, primal ego, both of which continue to develop slowly as they undergo certain transformations of the body, perceptions, feelings, and thought.[24] Faith Therapy theory holds that concomitantly there is a drawing-up or valence-like *pull energy* caused by cosmic intuition coming from the Self. This force works in conjunction with the libido's *thrust energy* to produce the ego. The Self may be envisioned as forming a pseudopod-like extension of itself in the form of the growing ego.

Will and Total Will

By amplifying the above analogy we may further clarify, enlarge upon, and diagram the concept just presented. If we envision the Self as an amoeba, a unicellular animal living in fresh water, we can observe that in order to get food it extends into the water a pseudopod to capture and consume by osmosis a piece of algae floating by. The pseudopod, containing the food, is then drawn back into the usual, non-extended shape of the organism so that the needed food may be assimilated into its total structure.

Let the amoeba's nucleus represent the entire *Will*, *Total Will*, and the genes in the nucleus be pictured as grouped together into a central ball within. This ball will represent cosmic intuition, or unitive perception. Now as we envision the pseudopod being extended downward, instead of the nucleus being unextended, let us conceive of the organism looking as though it were about to cell-divide. In this manner, the nucleus and ball of genes are also stretched to a very thin band of connecting elasticity, and the cell wall at the lower end begins to form a smaller, bulbous shape similar to the original amoeba. Now, except for the thin connecting band of cell wall and cytoplasm, nucleus and gene matter, we all but have a parent (Self) and child (ego) amoeba, and yet it remains connected until the food gathering is done and the pseudopod withdrawn. For persons, however, the extended shape would last a lifetime.

Will and Ultimate Will (Will-of-Wills)

Now let us look more closely at the Self with its extended bulb of the ego so that we may clarify the two meanings of will. The *Total Will* is defined as the psychic function of intentionality, choice, and decision. That part of the total will remaining at the center of the Self is herein referred to as the *Ultimate Will* or *Will-of-Wills*. It is also understood as a *good will*, for it unitively desires the best equitable good for God, oneself, and everyone else. Therefore, it is conceived of as the center which originates the structuring of all later *social cooperation needs*.

Will, Will Power, Will-to-power and Negative Superego

That part of the total will which is at the center of the ego is conceived of as what we usually mean by the term *Will Power*. However, since will power is construed as operating primarily on the ego level, it is highly subject to erroneous, deterministic and conditioned-into *excess* guilt feelings. Careful observations indicate that in such an event will power is apt to become overly oriented toward becoming an overactive *Will-to-power* and result in severe neurosis or psychosis.[25] However, these same deterministic and conditioned-into guilt feelings may also be so few and yet so severely traumatized by early life's negativity and accompanying ego development that they may lead to anti-social or sociopathic behavior. Such problematical guilt feeling problems seem to be caused by too great a difference in ratio between the conscious and unconscious expressions of one's critical factors, judgment factors, valuing factors, or guilt attitudes (all seem to be merely different names for perception) on these two levels of the superego.[26] These problems are further compounded by the fact that the power of a negatively inclined superego's guilt feelings may be so great as to powerfully clamp down upon (figuratively) the thin psychic band connecting ego to Self, almost cutting off the power-flow between the two centers. Thus, this negative superego power may shut away upper unconscious religious or altruistic growth impulses and experiences.[27] One of the great advantages of this therapy method is its ability to often bypass the resistances and negativities of the super-ego. This power seems to originate from the safe-secure feeling caused by the use of the Intensified Faith Schema. Experiencing this primacy of God's personal valuing enables the individual to become aware of the unconditional Universal Love needed to accept many painful insights.[28]

Total Will and Cosmic Intuition

Let us next consider the two dimensions of expression of cosmic intuition. (Keep in mind that its chief operative tool is the imaginal function—a point elaborated upon later.) That part of cosmic intuition which remains at the center of the will-of-wills, in the Self, is construed as that sensitivity which is always keeping this upper dimension of the total will, and thereby the Self, oriented toward unitive relation/connection to God. That part of cosmic intuition which is centered in the ego and will power is hypothesized to be an agent which aids in constructing consciousness itself. Its drawing power (originating from its Self source) structures as it pulls the life-energy up into the middle unconscious where the ego is manifest and can best equilibrate itself in usual, daily functioning with the outer and inner worlds. It is this same consciousness-oriented part of cosmic intuition which is more activated by Guided Meditation and the Intensified Faith Schema and therefore leads the love-energy upward toward increased, powerful functioning in the upper unconscious. As this entire energetic process moves upward, it naturally also draws with it the ego and its major accoutrements (the field of consciousness, secondary mentation, eros and will power) while simultaneously lessening superego negativity. The closer these elements are drawn toward the Self with its components (expanded awareness, will-of-wills, agape and greater unitive perception capacities) the more clarified, amplified, and discriminating all psyche functioning becomes. (Figuratively, the bulb and pseudopod would be almost withdrawn from the extended state and more nearly conjoined.) As a result of centering in or near the upper unconscious, a person opens up to all reality, both inner and outer. If well attained, this transcending state of consciousness usually leads to greater sensitivity and awareness and makes more cosmic, objective rationality possible.

The Numinous

If the above transcendent experience takes place, it may open one to a *numinous* experience or awareness of The Holy. However, this happening is also at times a part of our usual level of consciousness. In Faith Therapy this awareness of the *Mysterium Tremendum et Facinans* is caused by a more complete simultaneous activation of both ego and Self expressions of cosmic intuition. When one is highly sensitive to the presence of Cosmic Force, the fullness of his/her entire emotional power is experienced as it becomes polarized toward God. As the needle of a compass shudders in first lining up with the north pole, often there is a shuddering in nearing God's presence, and *all psychic functioning* is specially experienced as numinous.[29]

A. N. Whitehead has rightfully made the point that there is no special religious emotion; however, he does contend that there are special moods or states of mind more conducive to religious experience and contemplation.[30] Such a mood is provided in Faith Therapy as the psyche undergoes a numinous experience.

Two Centers of Volition, Affection, and Cognition: Implications They Exist

Psychological Measurement

There is now evidence from the field of psychological testing which strongly suggests that there are two distinct but connected centers of volition, affection, and cognition.[31] The Birkman Method—Birkman Personality Inventory—a currently available testing method designed for normal people, lends new impact to this position. The Birkman test is especially good for growth therapy use because its validity rating for accurate description of a personality is at the ninetieth percentile.

In addition to indicating the existence of two distinct yet interconnected centers of selfhood, this test discloses the existence of two entirely different groupings of attitudes and emotions accompanying the centers. The smaller, less powerful center is totally conscious and concerns the ego, usual I am-ness. The other center is larger and unconscious or out-of- awareness. In stress, it is quick to take charge. This center is the seat of the more emergency function center of personality. When a person is under *threatening stress,* this center *tends to take over negatively.* The person may not even realize that a shift of the center of personality vantage point of relating has taken place, although others around may make such remarks as, "He/she isn't him/herself." Therefore, it seems evident this unconscious center of I Am-ness is also a more powerful center of volition, affect, and cognition.

In general this unconscious, larger center meets the qualifications of being the Self—but is currently (with life's present level of experience) located at a particular scientifically graphable "stress function" point. Its location may change with a religious conversion, psychotherapy, and *possibly* more slowly, with natural growth. However, this center of being not only has negative personality aspects, it also has equally positive and balancing traits. When the person is not under any stress, the power underlying the unconscious positive aspects produces the energy to enable the conscious or ego center personality to function. At other *positive* stress times (eustress);(such as skiing or running a race) the unconscious positive traits can break through on their own with great power, sometimes with no consciously apparent modification of circumstances. The person has spontaneously met some powerful unconscious need—perhaps even a transpersonal or meta-need. Others are apt to say something such as, "He/she acts like a new person." Also, at such times the individual him/herself is likely to say, "I feel like a new person!" Obviously, the individual seems to have made some new, central and equilibrating growth break-through. The brain's need for personal survival seemingly has called forth other "multi-minds," alter egos, or personality fragments subjectively seeming more able to fill the current need and the will-to-power gives the subject the *feeling* of having used one's executive function.

At this point one may be inclined to ask why one does not have transcendent experiences when the executive function shifts from ego to Self center. The reply is twofold: first, we cannot be sure this does not happen in profound worship experiences or other meta-peak life experiences; second, in negative stress it may be that the ego only shifts to the Self's location, defensively carrying the ego's limited awareness focus and its incomplete logic capacities, but does not cause real affective union with the Self and thereby claim its expanded unitive level awareness' benefits and strengths.[32]

The Birkman test also tends to rectify the erroneous, more pessimistic concept of an Id only. These test findings indicate a more expansive unconscious which contains equal portions of good or strong personality traits to balance those which are bad or weak. Therefore it appears that the upper and lower unconscious construct is viable. The test also provides evidence of free will as it points out what psychological needs a person must keep filled by courageous choice and growth. These needs must be met if one is to use his/her positive personality characteristics. These findings, therefore, seem to point toward *some* personal responsibility in self-creation: it is true that we are obviously somewhat determined by our past, but we may now choose to use modern psychological devices in order to increase personal awareness. Thus we can realistically know our needs from the unconscious and with greater accountability meet them by conscious will and choice.[33]

This test further indicates the probable existence of a modified concept of the superego in the form of both conscious and unconscious guilt or valuing attitudes or critical and judgment factors. (Also please note that nothing is said of introjecting the parents; nevertheless, through their attitudes and behavior they were very powerful in early, unconscious shaping of the child's safety standards.) These two separate groups of judgment, critical, valuing and/or perceptual factors seem to be the main reason for the conscious and unconscious divisions between the person centers. These groups also appear necessary for adequate psychic defense of the Self by the ego and the roles one plays in life when not under stress. However, when existence is threatened or challenged, the Self with its needed positive or negative traits and greater power (as subjectively perceived from prior life crises) takes over with different personality traits to strive for survival or on favorable occasions to secure greater pleasure. In such challenging situations these two interchangeable centers also offer the element of surprise to the source of threat.[34]

Complementarity of Awareness

The following data sheds some light upon a unique phenomenon in the Guided Meditation and Intensified Faith part of the therapy. While one is in this intensified faith and meditative mind state, he/she is able to be at the same time fully aware on two levels of consciousness, concomitantly more subtly aware of one and then the other, but able to choose to focus on either. Two jointly existing awareness centers in the human psyche could be explained as simply being illusory and caused by a "will to believe" or the nature of the ego's shifting focus of awareness were it not for apparent suggestions to the contrary. However, evidence comes from the work of Wilder Penfield, the prominent Montreal brain surgeon, who discovered in brain operations that he could touch a small area of the cortex, and the patient would psychically relive *what seemed to be* exact happenings from formerly unrecalled life, even childhood. This information implies that everything which has happened to one is available to memory through the brain cells in some form (perhaps even restructured, reinterpreted, or symbolized). (Another indication comes from the battle flashbacks common to Vietnam war veterans.) In turn, this phenomenon suggests that the energy and thought structures of many former traumatic events, even though synthesized and reconstructed, should still be available in some manner for abreaction and relief. Certainly, in theory these events should be more available to the Self, as a more totally aware and unconscious center. Indeed, these memories or constructions of memories frequently do seem to have this availability in the use of this meditative part of the therapy, with its accented Self plus ego functioning. Interestingly, Penfield's patients were still awake in the surgery and were aware on one level of the surgery room and operation itself—they were even talking to the surgeons. But according to their simultaneously given reports, they also were currently reliving the restructured and synthesized experiences. That is, they were apparently re-experiencing what seemed to be an original incident.[35] This occurrence implies there could have been another center of awareness reproducing the former experience in seemingly complete continuity *but apparently not mixed* with broken and jumbled awareness from single focus upon the current experience. This implication of two clear-cut awareness centers, which can both be active at the same time without contaminating each other, bears likeness to the complementarity theory of light which is *both* particles or waves according to the assumptions of the viewer.[36] In the intensified faith mood of this religious therapy, this same complementarity of awareness is seemingly experienced by clients. They know they are in the reclining chair in the therapist's office and are undergoing a current guided meditation experience. Yet at the same time in regression they are also aware, without major confusion, that they seem to be fully experiencing some traumatic memory and are able to talk rationally and coherently about it to the therapist. He/she can then guide them safely through abreaction or transformation of many seeming unresolved conflicts from the past or present.

For this therapy's effectiveness, it is not important that what seems to be memories of details are not exactly so. Ornstein (as well as Piaget) has indicated that many memories are later groupings or structures of semblances into a pre-existing mental schema into which we fit our experiences using current interpretation through our suppositions concerning the meaning of a particular event. Therefore much recall is only a partial representation. In using this therapy method, it is only necessary that the memory event be adequately symbolized and contain *subjectively* correct emotion.[37]

A Therapy Centered in Affective Tone and the Safe-secure Affect

The experiences the surgeon elicited would appear to be of such insignificant engram charge as to require a mild instrumental touch type of shock from an external source to bring them to consciousness. However, these energetically charged memory structures seemed coherent and clear enough to indicate the probable existence of other more powerfully charged and out-of-awareness structures which could effect the amount of energy available to consciousness and the ego from the unconscious source. Such phenomena have been described in psychoanalytic terms as complexes, highly emotionally charged or toned "agglomerations of associations" which sometimes threaten consciousness and healthy ego functioning with memory blocks and may result in poor or bad psychic adjustment. It is good to remember that even the ego is a "complex." This grouping of conscious personality traits probably came to be the usual center of consciousness because it was the most successful way to meet usual life-challenges satisfactorily. Each complex seems to have a will of its own and evolved or developed to meet specific psychobiological needs.

In use of Therapy Procedures, it is helpful to remember that a complex, an intensely affectively charged structure, is similar to the experience Penfield was able to produce in that it seemed a totally forgotten but stored up memory. Such a grouping of consciously forgotten, emotionally unrelieved experiences may become conjoined by their mutual affective tone relations or common psychic valence, as though held together by magnetic charges. These complexes sometimes energetically have such power of emotional kinship that under certain strong negative stress conditions they can become traumatically explosive even to the point of replacing or destroying the conscious personality. If less intense, these complexes may form strongly unified unconscious personality fragments, "multiminds," or alter egos, which threaten consciousness' unity and the ego's current reality awareness and functioning.[38] Primarily it is the blocking affective tones (feeling related)—not ideational, consciously logical associations—of the negative energetic parts of the cognitive structures which this therapy follows. The therapy relieves these negativities by first inducing the intensified faith mood with its feelings of God's ambient love and safety. By also using regression techniques, the therapy searches for, follows, and identifies these structures made up of encapsulated and unassimilated traumatic material, hidden within otherwise healthy related structures. Then by therapeutically dealing with them, the energy is released to be restructured in a more growth oriented manner, realistically equilibrated, and made conscious. Such an affect oriented search is made possible by Ultimate and Unconditional Love, a part of Christian religion's SAFE-SECURE AFFECT (the feeling of being saved caused by heightened ego/Self interaction) to search fearlessly for and resolve the traumatic material.

Communication by Life-logic and Feeling-thought

The term *logic* is used here in the manner of many mental health professionals to represent any mental organization, other than perceptions or other given mental phenomena, which leads one to an accurate understanding. There are different types of knowing or cognitive processes, a fact which needs to be kept in mind in Faith Therapy, but the principle of consensual validation remains the measure used for the concept of accurate understanding.[39] Life-logic expressed verbally as feelings and thought in social interaction (also identified here as well equilibrated assimilation and accommodation of patterned psychic energy) is one of the major components of this entire therapy method. This communication mode is subtly present in Dialogical Counseling but is more obvious in the Guided Meditation dimensions of the therapeutic processes. The vocal mode of expression of life-logic's feeling-thought is poignantly observable in therapist-client interaction when using the Guided Meditation Therapy Procedures, but it is especially highly emphasized in use of the Intensified Faith Schema. In the Schema life-logic and feeling-thought's functioning is greatly enhanced by the therapist's use of suggestion expressed through archetypal symbols and religious belief statements (particularly Christian)—much as one might intensify the sun's power by using a magnifying glass and focusing it to a burning point. Such image-oriented thinking and feeling is a living process of experiencing psychic wholeness of existence, of the interpersonal relating movement of life.[40] This psychic action leads the way, wedge-like, just behind the images of the cosmic intuition function on any level as it draws us through life toward home with God.

Herein *life-logic*—itself not necessarily verbalized—may be conceived of also as a living process, leading or preceding experiences of Aristotelian logic. While Aristotelian logic *is* "the art of true thinking," it has little immediate and spontaneous voice in "the art of living." Life-logic may also be said to be a dialectical and creative attitude process of the logic of daily existing which arises from a person's inner experience of life in social and biological or humanity-nature conflict. Its deepest foundation is *the act*. Life logic is characterized more by affective tone and cosmic intuition in the spontaneity of life than it is by rational or empirical concentration and evaluation. Life logic is also more oriented around the process of growth and rebirth which arises out of one's moment-by-moment sensitivity to his/her existential anxiety and difficulties. Consequently it is plausible to speculate that it came into being evolutionarily as a psychological stimulus which encouraged healthy personality development. Existential anxiety became a psychic energy which was in search of life's final rebirth, a *final integration*. Life-logic, therefore, appears to be a cosmic, structuring process of life-energy and intuition in search of an ultimate answer! Thus, to deny awareness of the existence of this anxiety would be to deny the essential value of the Ultimate Object for which it searches as well as the reality of the searcher's own state of perceived inadequacy. While this type of active aliveness is characterized by fear, as existential anxiety, it is also filled with an overriding faith, hope and love and thus may be classified as a visionary experience.[41]

The function of rational and empirical thought in daily living is to guide and stand by supportively while life-logic (at times expressed in vocalized feeling-thought) safely and securely presses forward through the middle of much of daily life toward new and higher levels of creative experience. The purpose of Aristotelian logic is to help us to understand reflectively the development of our life and to claim more of the total psyche for human consciousness—not just express life in dangerous hyper-intellectualism.

The Power and Types of Symbols

Much of the content of this therapy involves thinking and feeling in universal or archetypal symbols. However, this is not to exclude the power of private or personal symbols. This latter type of symbolization, belonging to what Piaget calls the semiotic function, originates in the experiential material of every private life and its connection with a particular cultural milieu. We tend to derive most of our common signs and symbols through environmental interaction and growth by assimilation, accommodation, and intellectual equilibration. And as these symbols are learned, they are stored in what we have designated as the personal unconscious.[42]

According to the paradigm of this work, archetypal symbols exist deeper (or higher) in the unconscious than these private symbols. Experience indicates that archetypes have their origin in the collective unconscious. Archetypes are feeling-thought pictures or universal axial systems such as those of a snowflake. They are imaged, sometimes only geometrically, spiritual structuring units which are also bipolar in psychic manifestation. When archetypes appear, their objective seems to be to bring equilibrium to the whole person. As the objective psyche's generic symbols of man's instinctive nature, archetypes contain a nucleus of meaning, but it is in abstract principle only not concrete. The clarity of their image crystallizes around the experienced concreteness of human life, both past and present.[43]

As conceptualized here, an archetype, as a universal axial system, is energized in the personal unconscious part of the upper or lower unconscious section of an individual psyche. It is summoned into presence there from the collective unconscious by the Self which does so by using cosmic intuition with its spiritual valence and imaging power. From there this primeval image is drawn into the personal unconscious containing the preconscious material and the higher and pre-conscious cognitive structures, and then finally into the field of consciousness.

Thus the individually experienced psychic universal axial system seems to clothe itself as much as possible with the content of the person's private experience. And with ever-increasing energy and clarity of symbol the archetype makes its way into consciousness in order to equilibrate (cognitively and affectively) the entire psyche of the person. (We might also note that archetypes tend to express themselves in religious, metaphorical and/or mythological ways.)[44] Viewed from the above understanding, it would appear that archetypes in axial form must have an *a priori* nature inasmuch as they arrive in the personal unconscious to be arrayed with privately experienced concreteness even when people may yet be in the ritual or primitive stage of evolution. Interestingly, archetypes are still found today, sometimes even as primitive content in the dreams and fantasies of modern, civilized persons.

The Psychoid Archetype

Certain evidence and reliable speculative thought indicates that archetypes may need to be taken into account in another way, other than just as individual psyche symbols and images, for they also seem to have a transcendental psychoid base. They may have a metaphysical reality which is manifested in two ways: as psychic energy *or* purely physical energy. In this psychoid quality the archetype is hypothesized to be the arranger of synchronistic events, meaningfully related but acausal occurrences within the world of causality, which at the same time make up that reality beyond space-time which accounts for these acausal events. This "archetype per se" is conceived of as a transcendent causal power and represents the ultimate reality behind psychophysical parallelism. This power probably accounts for seemingly related spatio-temporal events which have no causal explanation; such as, the stopping of clocks or falling of a picture belonging to the owner at the time of his/her death.

This hypothesis relates with Oriental or Taoist systems of thought which generally assert: "Certain things tend to happen together without cause but have a distinct relational meaning or purpose." This transcendental nature of the archetype is envisioned as the common bond of meaning between the realms of physics and that of psychology. And it is also in this bond that we once again may have a "wholeness understanding of the world," which if ultimately proven philosophically viable, can give new unity and meaning to human life.[45] This concept of *synthesizing spirit* reasonably explains Faith Therapy's effectiveness. The universal archetypal symbol, pictorial feeling-thought as imaged by the psyche, gives man a language of emotions as well as thoughts expressing transcendent truths having both an *outer*, cosmic order meaning, and also an *inner*, spiritual, moral meaning. The archetype also appears to have the ability to express simultaneously the thesis and antithesis of the ideas it represents. Even further, this type of symbolizing seems to occur spontaneously at the exact time when a state of organic tension is present due to the polar extremities of the psyche—tensions of polar opposites which consciousness and ego alone apparently cannot resolve. These images seem to bring the affective power, ideas, and the equilibrating capacity the person desperately needs. Many Orientals and other thinkers have for a long time based their understanding of this type of symbolism upon the equation macrocosm = microcosm. Perhaps this understanding derives from their concept of the archetype as having a psychoid base which ties inner and outer worlds together. With this understanding we may also conceive of universal symbols as central to the art of thinking in pictures or images—"an art which some claim was lost with Descartes and the Enlightenment."[46]

The role of archetypal symbols used with the imagination in Faith Therapy's meditative symbolic work lends credence to the notion of *force* in the archetypal images used with feeling-thought and life-logic. This type of use of these images seems to have the power to elevate psychic functioning and consciousness to transcend to the upper unconscious by way of the Intensified Faith Schema with its accompanying elevated, meditative mind mood. Further, this concept helps explain what seemingly often takes place within this transpersonal psyche space with its observed positive results brought on by use of Therapy Procedures. In this inner area our Self reaches its point of most powerful connection to God or whatever one envisions as Ultimate Reality because a psychoid archetype, as an activating spiritual unit, would have its greatest power with the Self and in the Upper Unconscious.

The Unifying Symbol

Both the Schema and Procedures reveal the need for centering upon the most dynamic archetypal symbols which can activate the healing, growing and unifying powers of a person. In the realm of consciousness and intelligent thought or secondary mentation, we may find a reference to the structural formation of conscious knowledge symbolized as a circle or constantly increasing, spiral shape of wholeness, transformation and self-regulation. This representation is based upon the understanding of similarities between logico-mathematical and organic structures. It is within such a construct that some consciousness centered type of cognitive theorizing situates the "problems of relation between life and thought."[47] The circle or spiral image is found in many dreams and transforming experiences within this religious therapy and could indicate a many-faceted and universal symbol of symbols. In the unconscious part of the psyche, where orientation around emotion far overrides thought, we find other powerful symbols of structuralizing force which also tend to equilibrate the entire psyche (not just conscious intellect) in a holistic, self-creating and self-regulating manner. The field of Analytical Psychology has affirmed the circle and spiral and has added to the list of symbols of wholeness the god image, square (or squared circle), pyramid, triangle, and multiples of four, all of which are symbols of the Self.[48]

Another symbol which bears close examination is the mandala-like sun wheel. It first appeared in consciousness as indicated in the Rhodesian cave drawings done during the Paleolithic Age. This fact dates the symbol's origin as prior to any invention of the wheel and, therefore, says something highly significant about the dawning and centering of man's consciousness. The sun wheel symbol is a circle with a center and eight evenly divided radii running between the middle and the rim.[49] We still find the same axial system expressed in symbols, rituals, and play in primitive man today, and we also find the circle with a center part of the pattern in the energizing play of higher primates.[50] However, it is interesting to note that *humanity's* circle and center symbol has a meaningful addition, the evenly divided radii. These lead the eye always back to the center as an important focal point as though the symbol were trying to tell us that both we and the cosmos have a vital center.[51] Significantly, this particular symbol is also manifest the world over, with patterned development, in the drawings of children between ages two and three—the exact time in which a clearly observable ego is forming.[52] Such universal symbolizing in this age group indicates the formation and equilibration of the ego and its healthy enclosure in conscious *and* unconscious wholeness by the power of archetypal symbolism. Many times even today in a person's dreams and imagery the appearance of this symbol is accompanied by intense, numinous emotion.

Psychological and Theological Meshing
In This Therapy's Symbolism

The synthesizing spirit aspect of the psychoid archetype indicates much about this therapy's effectiveness. The synthesizing spirit viewpoint was also expressed by C. G. Jung who believed that metaphysically this Ultimate Unity can most reasonably be called Eros or Love—ultimately God.[53] This position seems the most coherent and adequate explanation of this religious growth therapy's experience of wholeness. Some persons' experience in the transcendent psyche space includes awareness of universal unity and multiplicity, as well as an awareness of proper grades of relevance and valuation.[54]

Taking into consideration this metaphysical position and observations made during the practice of this method, it may be asserted that the Self is a psychoid archetype. The Self is a spiritual center which uses lesser archetypal symbols to structure persons. This center may also present itself archetypally as a symbol of the Self and/or of God Him/Herself working within the individual psyche to structure, transform, and equilibrate the total person.[55] We envision this Self to be the *imago Dei*, what the Quakers call "that of God in every man."

The Christicised Self-symbol

If we also hypothesize that the image of Christ as spiritual person or new humanity has now been evolutionaarily stamped like an overlay imprint upon the old humanity Self, then the experience of the Self as this powerfully unifying archetypal symbol may never have been needed more than now, especially in the Occident. Jung himself believed that the West's unconsciously threatening gap between *faith* and *knowledge* could only be closed by such a powerfully numinous personal religious experience.[56] The guided meditation and intensified faith part of this therapy makes this unifying experience available to many. Its force is centered upon raising consciousness and experiencing the balancing power of the unconscious through love energy interacting with the Self—oriented around God as the Christ Symbol.[57] The intensified faith experience helps the irrational human being to understand consciously the deep underlying rational, structuring meaning of his/her formerly seemingly non-rational or unconscious material. While this reasoning process takes place in the transcending state, it is more lastingly effective when the client returns to his/her usual world of reality or frame of reference where he/she can share symbol analysis with the therapist. If the client is receptive to him, Christ provides the needed unifying Symbol of the Western World.

Moving Toward Meshing with Theological Convictions

The key to allowing the Christ symbol to work effectively in this manner is trust in God—known as a person—as Christ presented Him/Her to us and especially as He/She was experienced in the early Church's faith structure.[58] In the Schema Exercise, life's first year trust crisis is transformed and restructured with unconditional love, Christian concepts, and graceful valuing received from God as experienced in Christ under the aspect of the eternal now.[59] Naturally, if the client is incapable of much trust, some degree of adequate trust in the ministering therapist must first be established as a vital part of the new transformational process. (A description of how this is accomplished is found in Part III "How to Practice This Method," Chapters VIII and IX.)

In actually doing the Intensified Faith Schema Exercise, the client is encouraged to accept his/her feelings of near total dependency similar to those in childhood. *But this dependency is now oriented around God in Christ.*[60] In this way, life at its emotional base, even in the present, can be more healthfully and fulfillingly structured anew in faith. A major difference from childhood is that this present experience of learning faith is accomplished with the ego acting in service to the Self, so that the client now possesses his/her complete adult ego and can accomplish this building of trust in God by willful choice. The life- restructuring efficacy of the Christ symbol is allowed to release and keep the unitive drawing force, cosmic intuition, strongly flowing from the Self (with its Christ-imprint) to the ego.[61]

Additional powerful symbols and archetypes relate well to this discussion. Many times God is symbolized by a special beam of light coming from a hidden source.[62] This same depiction recurs throughout the Bible, mythology, artistic painting and religious rituals the world over. Further, the symbolic movements of ascent and descent are also powerful religious archetypes of the directions of the human psyche.[63] This particular type of imaging is especially helpful to clients in realizing the effectiveness of the Christ symbol. However, a word of caution needs to be added, for sometimes the light becomes black light or even quanta of blackness as a part of the light beam. Further, the movements of descent may become very threatening, while those of ascent may become too exhilarating and the light too intellectually abstract. Observations thus far indicate that while blackness is usually present simply as contrast to the light, it may be that sometimes black suggests the person is in need of facing the earthier parts of life more realistically. The same need for further conscious clarity tends to apply also in cases of overreaction to ascent and descent movements. All this seems to indicate that the client has not taken the Doctrine of the Incarnation seriously and first needs further counseling.

The Importance of Personal Symbols

It is necessary that we give some additional consideration to personal symbolism because of its effect throughout this therapy. In the process of growing up, and indeed throughout life, the symbol creating functions of the individual are active. But from approximately ages one and one-half or two through five or six the representational function appears to be at its most intense. Cognitive symbols forming at that point apparently almost immediately become a part of the child's unconscious wherein they have great lifelong affective power. These symbols are directly related to the individual's development of intelligence, acquisition of language, and assumption of a functional role in a particular family and cultural milieu.[64] The *undifferentiated period* is that time before age one and a half or two when the baby seems to be in a generally highly unitive state with very little subject-object clarity. However, it appears that in this period even more powerful symbols, which are usually never conscious, outside of depth psychotherapeutic work, are being formed. These symbols remain highly affectively charged and, in the psychoanalytic concept, are much of the basis for primary mentation. Because of their highly emotional nature and primitive power these symbols demand close scrutiny by the therapist.

Neurological research further validates this time frame as being the critical period in brain formation in which basic behavior patterns for survival are established.[65]

Observations concerning symbol formation in this therapy work indicate that these private symbols are stored in one's personal unconscious. And, if the nature of these personal images is sufficiently strong enough to identify them with the universal archetypes, the two symbol sources, archetypal and personal, will need to be carefully differentiated in the counseling part of the therapy. This sorting out determines the correct identity and symbolic meaning of the experienced material. For this reason, it seems advisable to utilize Jung's Analytical Psychology approach of amplification for symbol interpretation. It is chiefly used in dream analysis but also applies to uncovering the meaning of symbols in this therapy.[66] Certainly, Freud's method of free association and dream interpretation should be added.[67] Anything which will promote comprehension of any symbol is appropriate. Any misunderstanding of doctrine or symbol between client and therapist when using the Faith Schema or Therapy Procedures should be attended to immediately. The client is free to do so at any time. Consideration of such possible therapist-client symbolic representation differences leads us rather naturally into the next chapter, "Convictions and Models Structurally synthesized: Faith Is the Psyche's Primary Operation," where Christianity and psychology are joined.

NOTES

[1] Winson, *Brain*, pp. 202-33.

[2] Ornstein and Sobel, *Healing*, pp. 88-97.

[3] Ornstein, *Evolution*, pp. 32-37.

[4] Rossi, *Psychobiology*, pp. 99-207.

[5] May, *Addiction*, pp. 64, 65.

[6] C. G. Jung, *Memories, Dreams, Reflections*, ed. by Anelia Jaffe, trans. by Richard and Clara Winston, revised ed. (New York: Random House, 1961), pp. 35-54. See also, Winson, *Brain*, pp. 228-29, 244.

[7] Calvin S. Hall, *A Primer of Freudian Psychology* (New York: World Publishing, 1954), pp. 22-27.

[8] C. G. Jung, *Analytical Psychology* (New York: Random House, 1968), pp. 10-11.

[9] Hall, *Freudian*, pp. 27-31. See also, Winson, *Brain*, pp. 150,151.

[10] Fordham, *Introduction*, p. 64.

[11] Assagioli, *Psychosynthesis*, pp. 17-19.

[12] Jacobi, *Psychology*, pp. 102-40.

[13] Sigmund Freud, "The Interpretation of Dreams," in *The Basic Writings of Sigmund Freud*, trans. and ed. by A. A. Brill (New York: Random House, 1938), pp. 491-93, *passim*.

[14] Jean Piaget, *The Child and Reality*, trans. by Arnold Resin (New York: Grossman, 1973), pp. 32-48. See also, Winson, *Brain*, pp. 58, 59.

[15] Fordham. *Introduction*, pp. 21-23.

[16] Lewis R. Wolberg, *The Technique of Psychotherapy*, Vol. 1, 2 vols., 2nd ed. (New York: Grune and Stratton, 1967), pp. 177-82.

[17] Jung, *Analytical*, pp. 22-25.

[18] Sigmund Freud, *An Outline of Psychoanalysis*, trans. by James Strachy (New York: W. W. Norton, 1949), pp. 13-24

[19] Fordham, *Introduction*, p. 64.

[20] Jacobi, *Psychology*, pp. 35-49. See also, Ornstein and Sobel, *Healing*, pp. 131-137.

[21] A. A. Brill, "Introduction," *The Basic Writing of Sigmund Freud* (New York: Random House, 1938), pp. 12, 13.

[22] Evans, *Jung*, pp. 99-107, 140.

[23] Jung, *Memories*, pp. 335, 336.

[24] Charles Brenner, *An Elementary Textbook of Psychoanalysis*, 2nd ed. (Garden City, N. Y.: Anchor/Doubleday, 1974), pp. 35-45.

[25] Wolberg, *The Technique*, pp. 212-14. Also, it should be noted that Faith Therapy's concept of will-to-power differs somewhat from Adler's inasmuch as the distressing inferiority feelings are considered as first being initiated by guilt *attitudes* caused by the perceptual functions of the super-ego.

[26] Roger W. Birkman, The Birkman Method: *Manuals of Description and Instruction*, 3 vols., (Houston, Texas: Birkman and Associates, Inc., 1952, 1967 and 1970), *passim*. (The author has worked in conjunction with Dr. Birkman and used his psychological personality inventory in church growth-groups and private pastoral psychotherapy for over thirty years. Some vital insights have come from this personal association and practical use of the inventory's findings through the period, and many of them are presented in this manuscript. It is important to affirm that the above information is documented by the content of the manuals; however, these are without page numbers, and it is necessary to footnote the information as above.)

(If needed, the current address is Birkman and Associates, Inc., Suite 1425, 3040 Post Oak Blvd., Houston, Texas 77057.)

[27] Frank Haronian, *The Repression of the Sublime* (New York:

Psychosynthesis Research Foundation, 1972), pp. 1-11.

[28] This is an evaluation given by Dr. Stanley C. Russell, a medical school professor of psychiatry, close friend, and sometimes personal teacher, when once asked what was Faith Therapy's strongest contribution to the psychotherapy field. It seemed an apt observation and especially fitting at this point in this explication.

[29] Otto, *Holy*, pp. 15, 23-40.

[30] Whitehead, *Religion*, pp. 119-22.

[31] Some postulate these centers to have a recognizable physiological base in brain functioning. For them the experiential origins seem to be due to cortical and subcortical activity. Perhaps future research will further clarify this postulate and the concept of two centers of awareness.

[32] Birkman, *Manuals, passim*.

[33] Roger W. Birkman, "Evangelism Through Small Groups," *Pastoral Psychology* (June, 1968), pp. 42-48.

[34] Birkman, *Manuals, passim*. See also, Winson, *Brain*, pp. 136, 245

[35] Maxwell Maltz, *Psycho-cybernetics* (Englewood Cliffs, N.J.: Prentice Hall, 1960), p. 20.

[36] Thomas R. Blackburn, "Sensuous-Intellectual Complimentarity in Science," in *The Nature of Human Consciousness*, ed. by Robert E. Ornstein (San Francisco: W. H. Freeman, 1973), pp. 29-31.

[37] Ornstein, Evolution, pp. 182-191. See also, Piaget, *The Child*, p. 32.

[38] Jung, *Analytical*, pp. 79-82, ff. See also, Ornstein, *Multimind*, pp. 21-23, 39-46, 73-77, 81-104, 120-121, 185-189.

[39] Silvano Arieti, *Interpretation of Schizophrenia*, 2nd ed. (New York: Basic Books, 1974), pp. 126, 215, 229, 230, 237, 238.

[40] Donald P. Spence, *Narrative Truth and Historical Truth; Meaning and Interpretation in Psychoanalysis* (New York: W. W. Norton and Co., 1982), pp. 52-54.

[41] Arasteh, "Final Integration," pp. 19-35.

[42] Jean Piaget, *Play, Dreams and Imitation in Childhood*, trans. by C. Gattegno and F. M. Hodgson (New York: W. W. Norton, 1962), pp. 1-4 *passim*.

[43] Jacobi, *Psychology*, pp. 39-50.

[44] *Ibid.*, p. 49.

[45] Anelia Jaffe, *From the Life and Work of C. G. Jung*, trans. by R. F. C. Hull (New York: Harper and Row, 1971), pp. 34-45.

[46] J. E. Cirlot, *A Dictionary of Symbols*, trans. by Jack Sage (New York: Philosophical Library, 1962), pp. xxx-xxxi.

[47] Jean Piaget, *Structuralism*, trans. and ed. by Chaninah Maschler (New York: Harper and Row, 1970) pp. 3-6; *The Child*, p. 105, 172.

[48] C. G. Jung, *Mandala Symbolism*, trans. by R. F. C. Hull (Princeton: Princeton University Press, 1972), pp. 3-5. 36, 38.

⁴⁹ Jung, *Analytical*, pp. 41-45.

⁵⁰ Joseph Campbell, *The Masks of God: Primitive Mythology*, Vol. 1, 3 vols. (New York: Viking, 1969), p. 358.

⁵¹ Pierre Teilhard de Chardin, *How I Believe*, trans. by Rene Haque (New York: Harper and Row, 1969), pp. 24-26.

⁵² Ronda Kellogg and Scott O'Dell, *The Psychology of Children's Art* (New York: CRM-Random House, 1967), pp. 13-27.

⁵³ Jung, *Memories*, pp. 350-354.

⁵⁴ John B. Cobb, Jr., "Alfred North Whitehead," in *Twelve Makers of Modern Protestant Thought*, ed. by George L. Hunt (New York: Association Press, 1971), pp. 131-139.

⁵⁵ Jacobi, *Psychology*, pp. 123-28.

⁵⁶ Jung, *The Undiscovered*, pp. 83-100.

⁵⁷ C. G. Jung, *Aion*, trans. by R. F. C. Hull, Bollengen Series XX, 2nd ed. (Princeton, N. J.: Princeton University Press, 1959), pp. 32-43.

⁵⁸ James C. Livingston, "Rudolph Bultman," in *Modern Christian Thought* (New York: McMillan, 1971), pp. 370-74.

⁵⁹ Tillich, *The Shaking*, pp. 34-37.

⁶⁰ Schleiermacher, *op.cit.*

⁶¹ Anton T. Boison, *The Exploration of the Inner World* (Philadelphia, Pa: University of Pennsylvania Press, 1936), p. 82, *passim*.

⁶² Gerard, "Symbolic Visualization," p. 6.

⁶³ Kretschmer, "Meditative Techniques," pp. 4, 5.

⁶⁴ Leroy T. Howe, "Jean Piaget's Theory of Cognitive Development: An Overview and Appraisal," *Perkins Journal*, Vol. XXXI, No. 1 (Fall, 1977), pp. 45-47.

⁶⁵ Brenner, *Elementary*, pp. 48-55. See also, Winson, *Brain*, pp. 162-179.

⁶⁶ Jung, *Analytical*, p. 52 ff, *passim*.

⁶⁷ Brenner, *Elementary*, pp. 7, 8, 127-70.

Chapter VII

CONVICTIONS AND MODELS STRUCTURALLY SYNTHESIZED
Faith is the Psyche's Primary Operation

An Exploration of Faith

Inasmuch as *faith* forms the core of religious convictions, we first need to view faith from its many facets. What follows is a discussion of the innate nature of faith. While these are certainly not all the facets of faith, I believe these are those with the greatest immediate relevance to this subject matter.

Let me begin by pointing out that the term "faithing" is used here as a progressive verb form of the noun "faith." The term indicates a more dynamic than static meaning and conveys a participational or "knowing" quality.[1] Actually, faith precedes knowledge *per se*. Knowledge in a rational way comes only when faith with its epistemological interpreting organizes our sense input.[2] As an active ongoing process, faith is a specifically religious mental habit, the attitude with which we approach things as a whole.[3]

Further, faith and reason are *intimately* bound together. Faith manifests itself through reason. Scientific ventures and experiments are concrete expressions of faith.[4] Reason cannot exist without faith because reason derives its presuppositions from faith. These presuppositions lead scientists to investigate our spatio-temporal universe.[5] Faith is thus ultimately fact-oriented. The essence of reason-related faith may be called "intuitive immediacy" (a synonymous clarifying term for what has already been designated cosmic intuition).[6]

The difference between faith and belief is difficult to define as the two processes are also inextricably interrelated and recursive. However, the term belief, as used today, generally indicates the more consciously cognitive and intellectually emphasized ordering function of faith as things are more distinctly comprehended by the understanding. Belief, in this sense also participates as faith does, as a part of *will*, in the forms of decision and choice.[7] Generally, however, belief stops short of the experience of certitude that people today call knowledge.

Although faith is fact-oriented, faith's knowing and fact's knowing are not necessarily the same experience. Nowhere does this differentiation apply more than in the field of religion where the proven existence or non-existence of God is an entirely subjective judgment and can never (so far as we currently know) be scientifically evidenced.[8] But the numinous feeling of certitude about "The Holy's" existence—if it is not of psychotic or irrational nature—certainly makes up a human universal.

Today there appears a crucial need for a viable method of bringing together into an experienced whole the many varied expressions of theistic faith. This method would then allow those who so choose to check the validity of their subjective personal experiences as may be done with the beautiful and the good. For the certitude feeling is much the same in both faith and fact types of knowing. One can easily see how this feeling can be confusing concerning the experiencing of God in faith-knowing. Hence, individual and collective experiences concerning this delicate matter of ways of "knowing" God leave much to be explored and illuminated.

A great problem often results from the intensity of human faith, an inner compulsion to project a god image upon almost anything outside us, a god who may claim our highest loyalty and interest. We may also even make a god of our own ego in a narcissistic way. Submission of faith to these gods is problematic, however, because frustration arises since none of them are able to give content and universal meaning to life.[9]

Faith in the God who is the One involves an unending and profound revision of a person's morality. Once a person experiences faith, he or she changes in that afterwards all being is valued. All restrictions are removed from a person's thinking so that his or her understanding is opened and freed. This liberating force of faith is a gift from God.[10]

Another significant yet mysterious aspect of human faith is its adequacy for resolving the threat that humans experience in their search for orientation in this world of ambient powers and pressures. Fully activated, faith can be as powerful as the disconcerting forces of this modern environment. Viewed in this way, faith may be envisioned as an "ascendent energy in the world."[11]

Faith must be accepted as an affect. (This idea is foundational to the concept that the faith operation begins the life process.) It saturates a person's whole existence and gives him or her an emotional tone or disposition toward the world as well as towards the self. In this manner faith energetically permeates a person's whole being and has a profound interpreting effect upon all perceiving, acting, willing, thinking, and feeling which unifies and integrates one's entire existence. Thus faith enables people to find meaning in everyday living, which otherwise would probably remain a perplexing but unquestioned routine.[12]

Christian faith, specifically, originates *consciously* in the midst of stressful life-conflicts. A person finds him/herself caught between the growing, confusing forces of this world and any individual, personal suffering. In this duality of existence, God exists as the connecting force between the two sources of distress. And this connection appears as a solution to the conflict. He/She comes as the God-shaped man—the Jesus of the New Testament Church who is the synthesizing spirit. As Paul pointed out to persons who search for the Christian answer, Jesus is the "pioneer of faith." He is the new evolutionary symbol of the man of faith who outwardly and inwardly evidences God's way out of life's hopelessness to new joy.

After one accepts God's way, his/her life outwardly becomes an expression of "God-Ruling," while inwardly, life is a witness of "God-Intending." This type of faith in Christ orients a person's whole existence towards desiring to live *now* in the Kingdom of God. But the desire for such living is not of an argumentative or offensive nature; rather, it is demonstrative of a true motivation by the quest for "the divine good-pleasure."[13]

Faith also partakes of imagination, and as it does it becomes an "active mode of knowing." Faith has the ability to compose an image of the ultimate existence. This function of faith then empowers one to interpret and conduct his/her life in relation to this ideal standard. Further, this world-view image may change its visage as one undergoes major, life-shaking crises, for only when the old image dies "can a new and more adequate one rise."[14] (Faith Therapy finds its natural home in this use of the imaginal function.)

Further, faith has an affective and volitional component which gives it a participatory logic structure which may be called "the logic of conviction." The logic of faith does not, however, negate Aristotelian logic which may be called "the logic of rational certainty." The two types of logic work together, but "the former, being more inclusive, does contextualize, qualify, and anchor the latter."[15] In other words, the logic of faith forms the foundation and surrounding structure of the logic of reason. This "logic of conviction" helps propel faith's movement toward its goal. With its affective and volitional emphasis this logic appears to participate in the aforementioned life-logic, directing the process of freely expressed daily living.

For a person to have the satisfaction of the ultimate unconditionally loved experience available to those of faith, the following conditions must exist: cosmic intuition is fully open; love-attitude is positively polarizing love-energy; love-energy is providing full power; faith is reaching in all desire; hope is taking a firm and positive supportive position; belief is willing for new and different intellectual conviction, and one is entering into personal awareness of God's response through His/Her grace. For most people this series of circumstances brings into consciousness the feeling of certitude caused by mystically experiencing the presence of God. Even then in order to be worthy of following, this faith-insight should point strongly in the same direction as objective truth. Certainly the insight should not deviate too far afield from the conclusions of the best objective minds of the larger faith community. As a standard of measure, it should agree with the empirically gathered information of others who have experienced the same state of consciousness in the same intensified faith, religious psyche space.

Also, the experience of certitude should indicate awareness of the highest of moral intuitions. This moral grounding provides checks against the possibility of *false* feelings of certitude, breeding places for arrogance, intolerance, and potential atrocities committed against others. Such erroneous conviction has often caused great evil in religion, even today. Religion, while being capable of producing the greatest good of the whole human condition, has as its opposite pole the capacity for enormous evil. Ultimately the transcendent quality of a faith experience is the basic test of its legitimacy.[16]

The psychological-theological testing conducted in the relatively recent past by James Fowler has presented a number of important additional insights into faith as a human function. Fowler's research found that faith forms in cognitive, conceptual, and developmental structural stages. There are six such stages which are sequential, hierarchical "patterned processes" of structured wholes similar to the cognitive stage development theories of Jean Piaget and the moral stage development of Lawrence Kohlberg.[17] (Fowler's Stage 6 Universalizers, the highest, would be made up of the "living saints;" such as Mother Teresa.) "Life as lived" gives an individual the concreteness needed to grow in faith stages through opportunities, challenges, and cognitive abilities drawn into one's life process. Faith is a means of optimistically moving forward with purpose by (attitudinally) leaning into the ongoingness of life.[18] Faith thus gives humanity its purpose, meaning, and order for existence.[19] It should therefore be viewed as a more specifically religious operation, for it tends to communicate or express itself by using religious symbols, rituals, or similar constructs.[20] Faith is also a "mode-of-being-in-relation" with others, establishing a consensual core which shapes morality and forms a common value center which gives coherence to the participants' lives. This understanding of the triadic relation between people and values is diagrammed below:[21]

Figure No. 4   The Self/Other Value Core of Trust

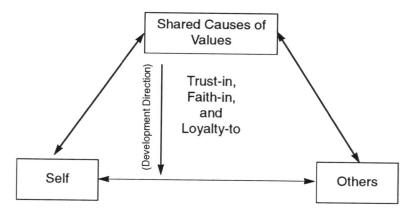

The relational expression of faith's operation in an *outer* manner gives an orientation toward world maintenance.[22] For example, (for Christians and Jews) the concept of the coming of The Kingdom of God may be expressed as a conjoint idea.[23] Also, faith in its outer relation with others becomes the primary creator of character.[24] In its social expression faith is the transcendent which gives direction to all who are involved.[25] Faith also has an *inner* expression which is bi-polar and relates to something transcendent for the person. Karl Marx's belief in communism illustrates this expression. When this inner expression relates to God, however, it would be to the Transcendent.[26] Such is the faith A. N. Whitehead refers to as *being* one's religious self in one's solitary existence.[27]

At this point Faith Therapy dovetails with Fowler's concept of conscious cognitive faith development stages by dealing with one's preconceptual affective (energetic) supply origin: namely one's experience.[28] The experiential Therapy may contribute to development of faith in God as it proceeds through each conscious cognitive stage. The Therapy Method helps feed energy to the unconscious' predominantly affectively-charged structures which will in turn activate the consciously expressed conceptual structures.[29] (See Figure No. 5.)

In this inner relating to God, faith allows one to envision the possible good propelling action toward God's desires for humanity. The results of this impetus are the concrete "Fruits of Faith." I believe this action to be the origin of works of supererogation, duties of second-order obligation. Such an inner expression of faith also is a transitional mode of coming to know God, as Whitehead has pointed out, first as Void, then as Enemy, and finally as Companion.[30] From Faith Therapy's evidence, however, I have come to believe that in the transcendent psyche space the deeper experienced image of Companion is Friend.

Another important factor in understanding faith as it relates to the religious understanding is that humanity's approach to reality exercises more than only the interpretation of existence. Faith's evolutionary drive upward indicates it to be a "second-order conceptualization ability." This ability works to idealize understanding and thereby offers humanity alternate suggestions for a better reconstructing of realistic life-options.[31]

Fowler's concepts of faith-knowing in human existence have also directed Christianity's understanding toward faith's unconscious components. Influenced by the concepts of C. G. Jung and Eric Erickson, Fowler considers the dynamic components of faith to contribute to its essential nature.[32]

The understanding of the many components forming the nature of faith as a method of dealing with our existence contributes to our Method. Faith Therapy provides immediate experiential knowledge of God; this immediate experience then becomes a part of energizing the transition from one cognitive faith stage to the next. Repeated experiences with the Therapy Method build upon one another to advance one through the conscious cognitive faith stages. The reader is referred to Figure No. 5 for a comparison of faith-knowing by immediate experience with faith-knowing as a series of developmental stages.

The Mother-infant Bonding Pattern:
The Initial Experience of The Faith Operation

If the ongoing life process is generationally carried out correctly from the human mother to her infant, all early forming of the baby's affect is positive and good phychic structuring is established for life. When a mother gives birth, God infuses her with His/Her unconditional love. A new mother feels a never-before-experienced burst of love as the valence-like lure of cosmic intuition, and the species-specific human bonding pattern starts operating. As the mother gazes at the baby's face with hers at the same angle as the infant's, a specific touch order takes place, and the mother speaks to the newborn in soft, tender, high pitched tones to which a baby's ears are especially attuned. This experience is now commonly known as bonding. For the first few hours the infant is very alert, actually producing a special burst of alpha brain waves. The baby is responding to an archetypal pattern of the human face with emphasis upon the eyes. As the bonding process continues, the mother spontaneously wants to nurse the baby; and the newborn instinctively recognizes and responds to the nipple, apparently an archetypal and *a priori* image.[33] The mother is exhibiting love for her infant induced by her own cosmic intuition of God's grace and unconditional love. The baby's response also exhibits cosmic intuition as the infant's Self is drawn to the influence of God in the

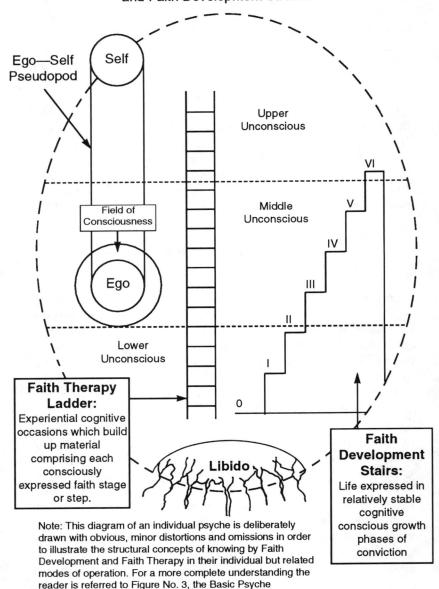

Figure No. 5   The Psyche Showing Faith Therapy and Faith Development Structures

Ego—Self Pseudopod

Self

Upper Unconscious

VI

Middle Unconscious

V

IV

Field of Consciousness

III

Ego

II

I

Lower Unconscious

0

Faith Therapy Ladder:
Experiential cognitive occasions which build up material comprising each consciously expressed faith stage or step.

Libido

Faith Development Stairs:
Life expressed in relatively stable cognitive conscious growth phases of conviction

Note: This diagram of an individual psyche is deliberately drawn with obvious, minor distortions and omissions in order to illustrate the structural concepts of knowing by Faith Development and Faith Therapy in their individual but related modes of operation. For a more complete understanding the reader is referred to Figure No. 3, the Basic Psyche Diagram.

actions of the mother. This total process reveals a unitive force of perception and intuition. It is a triadic process of faith, hope, and love (as attitude and energy): it is initiated by the reaching of faith and repeated by the anticipatory action of hope that the life-giving, life-sustaining love energy will continue to flow. We refer to this holistic function as the *faith operation*: the psyche's first and primary operation, where fundamental unconscious cognitive structuring begins.

This is a slightly modified structural pattern, for we consider the faith operation to be lured into existence through God's and mother's cosmic intuition *pulling* valance. This is not to say, however, that the responsive cosmic intuition does not cooperatively *push* the infant into the faith operation as the child organismically and independently reaches for the mother's breast and warmth. At the same time, the infant unconsciously learns grace *passively* through the mother's freely given love. The whole graceful and interactive faith operation arises from God's first gracefully giving the gift of life. Grace's interrelational nature (action and response) thereafter becomes the basis for shaping the growing infant for moral development. This shaping prepares the child to respond and interrelate appropriately throughout life.[34] Let us again note that the first outer world experience of life is totally oriented around a person, namely mother. Her grace-filled responsibility to her infant draws life into being by faith and becomes life's original affective structuring providing the core of energy for life's further structuring.

Cognition (Knowing) by Structural Development

Jean Piaget's basic concepts of structural development are helpful to understanding cognition. Piaget indicates that human life begins (beyond basic rhythms, etc.) as the infant interacts with its environment using behaviors which take in its surroundings through interaction. He calls this *assimilation*, for it seeks organic satisfaction. The infant then forms a reenforcing and self-limiting feedback behavior. Piaget calls this *accommodation* because it places a biological closure upon environmental intake. Between these two limiting poles then forms a balancing factor which Piaget calls *equilibrium*. Equilibrium becomes oriented around finding the best means of meeting both internal and external needs and adapting to them. This type of organizing behavior thereby becomes *intelligence*, which then also begins to participate in the holistic life process. The whole triadic operation moves life forward in self-sufficiency and closure, using genetically pre-determined abilities and safe limits. In effect, the organism both pushes and pulls itself forward by an interplay of anticipation and correction. At certain points in development (if the advance is successful in bettering life) the organism's own innate laws cause the process to transform itself. The transformation represents growth; the human infant does not forsake its old elements; rather it includes, expands, and combines them into a new nature as a child. The transformations continue to adolescence, and then to adulthood displaying age-appropriate cognition all the way. These periods are called cognitive structural stages and are developed in invariant, sequential, and hierarchical order, which later develop decentered true reasoning ability for the adult person.[35]

In his studies Piaget paid close attention to conscious cognition, which was largely oriented around the formation of reason through Aristotelian logic. He deliberately, however, avoided focusing on the functions of the energetic domain of the unconscious. He once confessed to an interviewer that he disliked the "tricks of the unconscious," an aversion stemming from childhood fears caused by his mother's mental illness.[36] To Piaget's credit, in later years he urged that work in the conscious cognitive realm be joined by the work of psychoanalytic findings of unconscious affective cognitions in order to produce a more complete understanding of the psyche and cognition, knowing.[37]

Unconscious Cognition

All animal knowing, as demonstrated in the mother-infant bonding experience, is first oriented affectively (largely unconsciously) around the mother. She assists the infant in its adaptation to its environment by correct assimilation, accommodation, and equilibration, the elements that make up growing intelligence. Thus even before consciousness has developed, affective cognition, knowing, has formed through interacting with the mother and her environment in order to meet life's demands. Neurological research has indicated that in life's first two years the foundational patterns of the incomplete but growing brain are being firmed up. And while completion of the formation of the neural pathways governing behavior structures does not occur until puberty, the basic unconscious behavior patterns used throughout life are being solidly formed during these first two years. These *critical period* structures primarily remain unconscious causal agents powerfully participating in life's basic behavior. This period is central in formation of the area of the brain by which the psyche operates without the person's awareness of the circumstances which shaped his/her underlying attitudes and life-energy directional flow. It is the deep, mostly unconsciously unavailable part of the psyche.[38]

The cognitive patterns developed in this period later have an impact on all affective structures operating throughout life as the attitudes of faith, hope, and love. These attitudes in turn shape the love-energy leading to one's life behavior. During that two year period in infancy, the undeveloped neuronal dendrites and axions of the brain's perfrontal lobe and neocortex are predominantly completed, and interneuronal connections are made which will allow the person to survive in a particular environment. Usually these earliest affective patterns serve the person reasonably well as an emotional foundation for all of life.[39]

But like a poorly constructed house foundation, which later gives way and sets the building askew or destroys it, early maladaptive patterning caused by poor or erroneous bonding and the accompanying formation of inadequate critical period neural circuits may become the foundation for a subsequent poor life style. The person's perception, feeling, and thought, as intelligence, are not functioning with true rationality. Much cognitive and rational-emotive type therapeutic effort is expended in the hope of bringing about correct rationality in relating to the inner and outer world. This therapy would be more effective, however, if it began by adequately addressing and remedying the unconscious primary mentation. Conscious cognitive error correction can be useful in therapy only if unconscious cognition's misinterpretations also are corrected. The needed intelligence cannot be truly rational otherwise.

Faith Therapy is a process of uncovering the formerly *ir*rational or *non*rational basic structuring of memory and finding the deeper but erroneously perceived flaws from former life and rightly restructuring them. In this way, Faith Therapy can make a valuable contribution by bringing more rationality to one's intelligence as the person's unconscious affective primary mentation perceives with true accuracy. Life's first but incorrect structuring of the energetic faith, hope, love, and love energy's triadic process flow (libido) can be changed. If poor structuring happened under Mother's inadequate patterning (that of Father and other parenting figures also), still the initial affective experiencing can be positively altered. This alteration is accomplished by using the Faith Intensification Schema and Guided Meditations with their current, experienced unconditional love from God in order to override, correct, and restructure poor basic life-flow patterns. In God's unconditional love the safe-secure affect of Faith Therapy's transcendent psyche space, true rational intelligence (containing positive affect) can correctly understand life's past traumatizing experiences and produce better total health for the future.

But intelligence properly structured into rationality presents us with the problem. of "what is *reason*?" A. N. Whitehead has given a good explication of reason: reduction to basic organismic process and initial aim.[40] If this is the most intensive point where the Self monad combines energy's rightly valued physical feelings with conceptualizing's patterning into meaningful relation within a living body, here is life's beginning point. It is at this point that Piaget's insights are pertinent:

> Assimilation is the operation of integration of which the scheme is the result. Moreover it is worth stating that in any action the driving force or energy is naturally of an affective nature (need and satisfaction) whereas the structure is of a cognitive nature (the scheme is sensorimotor organization). To assimilate an object to the scheme is therefore simultaneously to tend to satisfy a need and to confer action on a cognitive structure.[41]

If we consider Piaget's "assimilation" the same as Christianity's concept of active faith, take his use of "accommodation" as the opposite closure pole as Christian hope, and "equilibration" as the intelligent cognitive structuring of affect into the initial aim of love, we then have a truly rational and safe structuring of life's initial affective movement. It will later become the core experience which thereafter shapes and influences one's disposition and interpretation in all life's experience and its subjective rationality.[42] In human infants assimilation is akin to Santayana's "animal faith," as is evidenced by human and chimpanzee babies being alike until age two.[43] At the point of infancy until consciousness forms with a rudimentary ego appearing later, all cognitive structuring of the psyche is caught up into conditioned bodily and genetically programmed action. All experience and intelligence (even erroneous) is present in the infant's bodily action on an unconscious awareness level as meaningful perceptions, for as yet the action has not been abstracted into conscious thought. As this triadic love-energy core proceeds through life, it will be manifest foundationally in all basic cognitive, interpretative transformations into adulthood. If early conditional love experiences distort the person's intelligence, responsiveness (morality's origin), social relating, and reasoning ability, it may even lead one into maladjusted, criminal, or psychotic behavior.

The Safe-secure Affect Core Structuring in The Trust Crisis

As life advances, the infant's faith core affect structures itself into the growing child's first year prime conditioning "Trust Identity Crisis." The first six months of a baby's life involve what is often called the lifetime existential position. If good parenting is present, the core affect will become the feeling of being safe in this life. These positive feelings extend to an awareness that being is not only a safe but also a secure existence. These feelings develop in the next twelve months as the baby learns it has a right to reasonable control of its own body and its functions. As the baby crawls and toddles, explores its surroundings and exercises its curiosity, it develops its freedom within good (safe) limits. At this time, the house needs to be baby-proofed so that no harm can come to the child. For example, if a bookcase were to fall on the baby as it tried to climb on top to get a toy, the baby would inwardly experience the hurt as inflicted by the parent. Subjectively, free will would now seem to be dangerous for the child to use. The baby is still largely in an undifferentiated state and perceives the outside world as part of the parent's area of extended being.[44]

It appears that safety experienced in the first six months of life extends into the next six months where it becomes feelings of security. As medical psychology has discovered, this general period of first year feeling orientation becomes the "basic trust set"—with the prime resultant life-long attitudes being hope and faith (or drive)—which thereafter saturates and effects all subsequent interpreting of life as trustworthy or untrustworthy.[45] This period seems further validated as we consider the fact of neuronal development in the critical period of earliest existence. The basic trust set or feeling flow as conditioned by parental caretaking becomes the way one trusts life in general.

If the nature of this trust core is weak, the child mistrusts the outer world; much of life then becomes threatening to the child. All this early conditioning is centered upon a person, mother or other significant parenting figures. We hypothesize that later in life God is unconsciously experienced as "the parent of all parents" who controls the ultimate environment of life. The growing child will develop a view of God as being of the same underlying nature as his/her parents.[46] This faith/trust structuring of affect needs to be corrected by using Faith Therapy's Intensified Faith Schema and Guided Meditations in order to effect transformations and correct errors within one's underlying emotion set. We hold that no parent (since all are imperfect) can provide the perfect safety available only from God. Many times this Method can help a person to change positively; the therapist leads a client's consciousness into the formerly unconscious psyche space where he/she may directly experience the unconditional and confirming love of God made truly real through Jesus Christ. If the person can receive this love, the experience elevates consciousness and makes available the love-energy needed for higher transformations and a right understanding of reality.

Other Early Human Qualities Factored into the Trust Core's Safe-secure Affect, Preexisting in Future Transformations[47]

The recursive ambient experiences of life's first year impel us to examine closely some of the formative components of object relations shaped by the faith operation in the trust crisis.[48] These experiences are all included in later formation of the ego complex or self.

Feelings
All feelings, both sensation and emotion, will increasingly be affected by blocking and repression if they are characteristic pat-

terns of mother and other parenting persons who misinterpret the nature of rudimentary feelings. In its sensitivity to the first year's social milieu, the baby will simply internalize the feelings of those who surround it. As this trust core increasingly differentiates in the future, the early misinterpretations of the feelings will negatively influence the person's world comprehension. Perhaps the most serious problem possible in the formative period of environmental adjustment is that the primary affective predisposition may become the person's feelings projected toward all life.[49]

Morals

One facet of faith is its profound effect upon a person's morality. At the same time the faith operation is being formed with the infant and mother learning responsibility (response ability) in relating to each other, the base experience providing for later moral transformations is established.[50] While the mother responds to the infant's true needs (i.e. giving her breast to satisfy its hunger), in equitable return the baby behaves in a way acceptable to the mother (i.e. not biting the nipple). Thus the initial core experience of harmonious responsibility forms. This may seem simplistic but as Whitehead has pointed out, all the varying moral codes witness to the perfection and harmony of things. Further, he said that this concept of harmonious interrelating is not just wishful thinking: "it is a fact of Nature."[51]

Perception

In the period of early faith operation formation, the essential judgment factors patterning life's safety standards are assimilated through interaction with mother, father, and other parenting figures (this capacity apparently later gives rise to the superego or conscience). The baby senses and internalizes the parents' ways of interpreting events. To the baby, these perceptions appear to be the correct relation to assume toward the whole environment.[52] If the baby is surrounded by positive, attractive energy, all life is felt as good. The baby acts and reacts to life's surroundings with positive feelings and experiences itself as happy and satisfied. These positive affections are caused by feelings of love which pre-affect perception's interpretive components. Thus perception by love is an important part of the trust crisis of early existence with mother and family milieu.[53]

Will

In the paradigm of the Faith Therapy construct we have the concept of two dimensions of *will*: will power or will-to-power, which serves the self or ego; and the will-of-wills which serves the High Self. We are considering here only the ego self's development of will power. Will power is that dimension profoundly influenced during the trust crisis as a part of *rudimentary* consciousness and ego.

As the baby starts crawling and toddling, it becomes unconsciously aware of the fundamental right to its own body and its functions. Some vague *early* feelings of autonomy begin to form. Self-directed choice—intending toward action—is now evident as an indistinct feeling orientation. It will not become more evident until between ages two and three. The early executive function of the brain, with its behavior schemes, is being constructed in the pre-frontal lobe where the capacity to choose one's best action patterns by which to direct one's life develops.[54] This faculty, then becomes fundamentally available for additional transformations included in life's further autonomous vectoring.

Personal and Social Relations

Through interaction, first with mother, then with other parenting figures, the baby begins unconsciously to assume a "world view" of interrelationships as safe or unsafe. This view will be transformed further into an approach to all persons later in life. It will manifest itself especially under negative stress in close relations such as with a spouse and one's own children. Most problems in close interpersonal relations have their origin here in the trust crisis period, and if the early negative social matrix were severe enough, these personal social situations will also evidence themselves throughout life.[55] This type of early interpersonal knowing lies at the base of all later personal relationships. If God is conceived of as a Person, one's affective relationship with God will be strongly influenced by this early socializing experience.

Reason, Intelligence, and Belief

(*Reason* was earlier presented as part of Dialogical Counseling in Chapter II. Herein, we deal with reason at its core formation as offering greater help for the client and therapist.)

The first year trust crisis receives its life energy from the faith operation, which is chiefly drawn into existence by the action of the Self monad. Coming from God, cosmic intuition's spiritual valence exerts itself upon the mother's Self and her cosmic intuition, then exerts its pull upon the infant's Self. The infant's Self, then, using the archetype of *reason*, starts independent life by the faith operation.

Reason first energetically manifests itself by unconsciously cognitively structuring itself into the faith operation. According to Whitehead's metaphysical concepts we conclude the initial aim of reason is the cosmic intuition found in the love attitude; this then orients the action of the faith attitude; faith in turn gets feedback from the hope attitude. These produce equilibration in the form of intelligence as growing problem-solving ability for the infant. In its rudimentary form we see this problem-solving as the baby adjusts for optimum functioning to environmental demands. What we have is "practical reason" which serves the infant's animal nature in the quest for survival.

The surrounding human matrix, as it works, represses, or allows freedom of safe expression for the infant, will have a profound impact on reason's capacity to express itself fully as intelligence. The influence extends to later in life when practical reason transforms into "speculative reason." One's reasoning capacity determines later combined ability for critical thinking and imagination; these qualities provide the growing understanding with a framework upon which to project, evaluate, and analyze reality.[56]

A problem in dealing with reason is a common tendency to consider intelligence as the natural abstracted thought patterns of action. This assumption leads to gross inaccuracy because the necessary introduction of feeling as attraction or aversion is really reason's first impetus leading to further understanding of cognition by thought.[57] Emotions have a separate system of neural paths. They *first* go through the limbic system and *then* to the cortex, and this path allows many emotions to avoid conscious control. This avoidance of conscious control was necessary evolutionarily as a "first alert" signal system for early humanity and still is for infants. Emotions serve survival needs first. Ornstein has said, "(Emotions) organize the mind....For many purposes they are the mind....They underlie most strong feelings; such as anger, fear, and joy." As we go up the phylogenetic scale such items as fear may even appear as anxiety, the anticipation of harm. Emotions first set our psyche's agenda and guide our lives.[58]

In the human infant's first year, emotion sets the life direction. As there is little consciousness, emotion and the limbic system are in control. Early engrams are established from stimuli received, which copy the family milieu emotion tone. No conscious cognitive assessment of these stimuli is made. Further, these engrams will remain as a part of the emotion flow core "set" for all of life. This type of energy later feeds thought and ultimately becomes a part of faith as belief.

I have deliberately emphasized the Self's archetype of reason in therapy because many times that which has been labeled as *non*rational or *ir*rational simply is not. When regarded as the psyche's first alert response, seemingly irrational or nonrational behavior can be understood as the result of early primary type thought and reasoning and, therefore, of great importance and significance to a person. Emotion as yet may not have had thought as secondary mentation accurately applied to it, and it may not seem logical, but it is logical when the perceived needs for immediate survival are taken into consideration. From this viewpoint the emotional response is rational, and it should be therapeutically sought for and understood. Faith Therapy searches for inaccuracies in the trust crisis caused by distortions fed into the faith operation. For real wholeness through reason the Self and ego must combine proper valuing of feeling (weight of importance) with right cognition (correct ordering). An outcome of this ingression into the life process results in the personality's leaning toward either a conceptual or feeling pole.

To further clarify the concept, "Faith Is the Psyche's Primary Operation," please consult Figure No. 6, which immediately follows this chapter.

Figure No. 6   The Faith Operation in the Human Infant

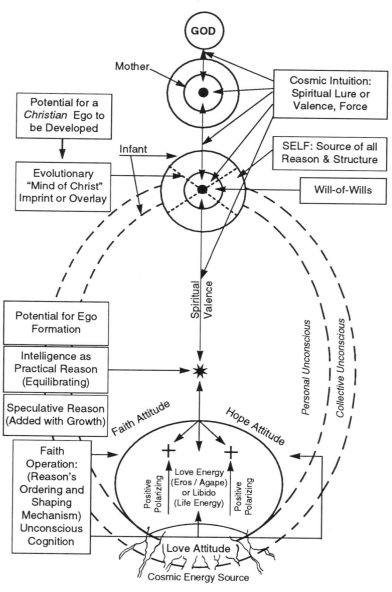

Note: Since this is a construct of a new infant's psyche, the unconscious is shown with no differentiated consciousness, ego, superego, etc. These will be structured later with growth. However the *basic* structuring of the life energy into the "libido bubble" by the faith operation remains as the necessary energy's lifelong affective core.

NOTES

[1] James W. Fowler, "Stages in Faith: The Structural-Developmental Approach," *Values and Moral Development*, ed. by Thomas C. Hennessy, S.J., (New York: Paulist Press, 1976), pp. 174-75.

[2] David Elton Trueblood, *The Logic of Belief* (New York: Harper and Brothers, 1942), p. 58.

[3] R. G. Collingwood, "Faith and Reason," in *Faith and Reason*, ed. by Lionel Robinoff (Chicago: Quadrangle Books, 1968), pp. 140, 141.

[4] Ibid., p. 143.

[5] Ibid., p. 144.

[6] *Ibid.*, p. 121.

[7] Elizabeth MacLaurin, *The Nature of Belief* (New York: Hawthorn Brooks, 1976), pp. 78-88.

[8] Paul F. Smidt, "Factual Knowledge and Religious Claims," in *Religious Language and the Problem of Religious Knowledge*, ed. by Ronald E. Santon, (Bloomington, Ind.: Indiana University Press, 1968), pp. 213-24.

[9] H. Richard Neibuhr, *Radical Monotheism and Western Culture* (New York: Harper and Row, 1960), pp. 114-22.

[10] *Ibid.*, pp. 125, 126.

[11] Richard R. Neibuhr, *Experiential Religion* (New York: Harper and Row, 1971), pp. 35, 36.

[12] Ibid., pp. 41-48.

[13] Ibid., pp. 107-37.

[14] James W. Fowler, *Stages of Faith: The Psychology of Human Development and the Quest for Meaning* (New York: Harper and Row, 1981), pp. 24-31.

[15] *Ibid.*, pp. 98-105.

[16] Whitehead, *Religion*, p. 17.

[17] Fowler, "Stages in Faith," pp. 173-75.

[18] James Fowler, III, "Toward a Developmental Perspective on Faith," *Religious Education*, LXIX, No. 207 (March/April, 1974), pp. 214-18.

[19] Fowler, *Stages of Faith*, pp. 3,4.

[20] "James Fowler Constructing Stage Theory of Faith Development," *Harvard Divinity Bulletin*, Vol. IV, No. 5 (February, 1974), pp. 1, 4.

[21] Jim Fowler, "Life/Faith Patterns: Structures of Trust and Loyalty," in *Life Maps: Conversations on the Journey of Faith*, by Jim Fowler and Sam Keen, ed. by Jerome Berryman (Waco, Texas: Word Press, Inc., 1978), pp. 17-21.

[22] Fowler, "Stages in Faith," pp. 176, 177.

[23] Jim Fowler, "Life/Faith," p. 24.

[24] *Ibid.*, p. 25.

[25] Fowler, "Stages in Faith," pp. 176, 177.

[26] *Ibid.*, pp. 177-79.

[27] A. N. Whitehead, *Religion In The Making* (New York: American Library, 1926), pp. 14-16.

[28] Alfred McBride, "Reaction to Fowler," in *Values and Moral Development*, ed. by Thomas C. Hennessey, S. J. (New York: Paulist Press, 1976), pp. 217, 218.

[29] This particular theory of the relation between the two uses of knowing by faith was worked out by Dr. Fowler and me at the times of several of his special lecture occasions I was fortunate enough to attend, his listening to tapes of therapy sessions over a number of years, and his having read and critiqued this manuscript in several prior forms.

[30] Fowler, "Towards a Developmental Perspective," pp. 210, 211.

[31] Howe, "Piaget's Theory," Manuscript pp. 8-17.

[32] Fowler, "Towards a Developmental Perspective," pp. 210, 211.

[33] Marshal H. Klaus and John H. Kennell, *Maternal-Infant Bonding,* (St. Louis, MO.: C. V. Mosby Co., 1976), pp. 1-98.

[34] Frederick S. Carney, "On Frankena and Religious Ethics," *The Journal of Religious Ethics*, 3, 1 (Spring, 1975), pp. 17-23.

[35] Jean Piaget and Barbel Inhelder, *Memory and Intelligence,* (New York: Basic Books, 1973), *passim.*; *The Psychology of the Child*, trans. by Helen Weaver (New York: Basic Books, 1969), pp. 3-8, 10-25, 71. See also, Richard I. Evans, *Jean Piaget: The Man and His Ideas* (New York: E. P. Dutton and Co., 1973), pp. 77-79. See also, Jean Piaget, *Structuralism*, trans. and ed. by Chaninah Maschler (New York: Harper and Row, 1970) pp. 6-16; *The Child and Reality*, trans. by Arnold Rosen (New York: Grossman, 1973), pp. 6-16, See also, R. Droz and M. Rahmy, *Understanding Piaget*, trans. by Joyce Diamont (New York: International Universities Press, 1975), pp. 85-99.

[36] Elizabeth Hall, "A Conversation with Jean Piaget and Barbel Inhelder," *Psychology Today*, Vol. III, No. 12 (May, 1970), p. 27.

[37] Piaget, *The Child*, pp. 47, 48.

[38] Winson, *Brain*, pp. 209, 239, 246. See also, Stephen M. Johnson, *The Symbiotic Character* (New York: W. W. Norton, 1991) pp. 28-41.

[39] *Ibid.*, pp. 162-79, 245-46.

[40] A. N. Whitehead, *Process and Reality* (New York: Free Press, 1929). pp. 405, 406, 410.

[41] Piaget, *The Child*, p. 71.

[42] Jean Dalby Clift, *Core Images: A Symbolic Approach to Healing And Wholeness*, Three lectures given to the annual meeting of the Southeastern Conference of the American Association of Pastoral Counselors (Episcopal Conference Center, Hendersonville, NC: October 18 and 19, 1991).

[43] Fuller, "Santayana," *History*, pp. 499, 500.

[44] This information was largely first learned by the author in a weeklong

workshop on "O. K. Childing and Parenting" conducted by Jean Maxwell and Linda Dietrich, who are Training Members in Transactional Analysis. However, most of the same information is contained in *Cathexis Reader* by Jacqui Lee Schiff, *et. al.*, (New York: Harper and Row, 1975), pp. 32-41.

[45] Arieti, *Schizophrenia*, pp. 82-84.

[46] Richard I. Evans, *Dialogue with Eric Erickson* (New York: Harper and Row, 1967), pp. 12-18.

[47] Althea J. Horner, *The Primacy of Structure: Psychotherapy of Underlying Character Disorder* (Northvale, NJ: Jason Aaronson, 1990), pp. 3-8.

[48] *Dictionary of Pastoral Care*, pp. 796-98.

[49] See also, Frank, *Persuasion*, pp. 25-26, 31-32.

[50] Carney, "Frankena," p. 17.

[51] Alfred North Whitehead, *Adventures in Ideas* (New York: The Free Press, 1961), p. 591.

[52] Howe, "Piaget's Theory," pp. 36-42. See also, Jean Piaget, *The Moral Judgment of the Child*, trans. by Marjorie Gabin (New York: MacMillan, 1965), pp. 13-108.

[53] Roger W. Birkman, "Perception as a Unifying Theory, An Approach to Mental Health and Spiritual Growth" (Manuscript, Houston, TX: Birkman and Associates, Inc., 1962) no page numbers—information on second and third pages.

[54] Schiff, *Cathexis Reader, passim*.

[55] Frank, *Persuasion*, pp. 30-34.

[56] A. N. Whitehead, *The Function of Reason*, (Boston: Beacon Press, 1929), pp. 4-8, 26-29, 37-43, 65-89.

[57] M. B. Arnold and J. A. Gasson, S. J., "Feelings and Emotions as Dynamic Factors in Personality Integration," in *The Nature of Emotion*, ed. by Magda B. Arnold (Baltimore, MD: Penguin Books, 1968), pp. 206-09.

[58] Ornstein, *Evolution*, pp. 80, 89-91, 96.

PART III

HOW TO PRACTICE
THIS METHOD

Putting into actual use any methodology always presents problems. Faith Therapy is no exception. This section will attempt to make the task a bit easier. The material in this section has been drawn from over thirty years of this therapy method's growing successful use and will try to pass on that experience briefly and simply.

Chapter VIII

ᐁ

PRE-PROCESS INSTRUCTIONS FOR THE THERAPIST

Prior to the first time the Guided Meditation part of Faith Therapy is used, the therapist should become familiar with the following instructions and be prepared to share them with the client to whatever degree necessary in order to lower anxiety and secure his/her maximum cooperation.

1. The client should be made aware that the intensified faith and meditative psyche state is also an elevated and Christian religious experience state specific state of consciousness which is closely akin to alpha-theta brainwave states produced with biofeedback devices. The mind mood is also somewhat akin to the Zen meditative state of *Zazen* in Buddhism and the *Samadhi* meditative state of Hinduism but is much lighter and milder. However, this state is set apart because it is oriented around Western thought and generally accepted Christian belief concepts and statements. The mood seems more akin to the mystical states indicated by the special religious experiences of some Christian saints. Also, when combined with archetypal symbols of Christian origin or adaptation, such mentation elicits powerful feelings and thoughts as do some dream figures. The prayerful, contemplative, and dedicated use of the Faith Schema tends to lift one structurally to an elevated meditative psyche state. This is a state of consciousness which elicits a condition of heightened awareness, intensified unitive perceptive function of the psyche often called mystical, transcendent, or visionary. How intense or rewarding one's experience may be depends upon individual faith development, gifts, abilities, or aptitudes.

2. This special faith state is entered by using a trained guide (one aware of his/her role as *minister*). For the most part, it is a different psyche mood of depth, relaxation, peace, and passive, not active, concentration. It is somewhat like the experience of a child lying in the grass, daydreaming, and watching the clouds make pictures. The person's Total Will is not disturbed, and actually he/she is fully in charge of him/herself and the entire meditative mood and faith intensification process, but is even more willful than usual. However, he/she should be told that he/she will probably trust and cooperate with the therapist in order to carry out the therapy. He/she should be further informed that concern about personally being in charge will be checked out to total satisfaction after the prayer at the end of the faith intensification exercise. After the check out there will be no problem of this sort unless resistance is met or client autonomy is mistakenly threatened. The result upon the therapist is that he/she must be *trustworthy*, otherwise the client will end the session immediately.

3. Since the brain's alpha wave activity is usually produced more easily with the eyes closed and in a relaxed body position, the client is asked throughout the entire meditation session to keep his/her eyes closed and remain in as deeply relaxed a body state as possible. One is instructed not to cross or cover any parts of one's body as doing so is a false and unnecessary means of self-protection. Usually, the person is also asked to refrain from talking back to the therapist (if comfortable in doing so) until the intensified faith state is established and the therapist requests the client to carry on a conversation with him/her while doing the therapeutic work.

4. Some persons may benefit greatly from the knowledge that the therapist will cooperate with the client so that he/she may go at his/her own pace in proceeding through the Intensified Faith Schema. This allows the client to explore at his/her own discretion each new psychic faith space at each new Level (or even Stage if he/she prefers a slower pace) entered and receive optimum benefit of affect and insight from awareness of his/her own (rather than the therapist's) direction of the Schema Exercise. This can be an excellent worship experience. (Making a tape of the client's remarks at each level, so that he/she can copy it for playback when desired, is a way of helping to strengthen the Self-ego axis and is strongly recommended.) But if the experience is perceived as somewhat threatening, the therapist may offer the client the option (for whatever reason) of stopping the process in order to explore the current inner space more thoroughly; if the client feels this is necessary, he/she is to tell the therapist immediately. The therapist will then

wait to resume the exercise until the client again informs him/her to start. However, if enough mutual trust is present, this procedure will not be needed for therapy itself (though it may be for a worship use), nor is this approach necessarily the most helpful to the client. Great faith intensification benefit accrues to one in the uninterrupted flow of following the Schema and especially by talking very little while elevating the psyche state through the Exercise's process. Questioning while in Schema use tends to inject beta brain wave interruption of the alpha/theta flow and its needed amplification.

But it is equally important that the client perceive ultimate control of the process is in his/her hands. While perhaps slower, the approach of stopping and/or questioning *can* even make the experience of the Faith Schema itself therapeutically or worshipfully beneficial. In some cases this slow-down technique has been helpful. If a client is primarily interested in experiencing a profound worship, transcendent, or mystic experience or in exploring, deepening, or enriching his/her perception of personal religious faith, this procedure may be preferred. In such cases, problems needing therapy Procedures are often negligible. If not, such need will tend to become self-evident to the client him/herself as the entire Therapy process moves along.

5. Additionally, the client should be advised the mental mechanism of suggestion will be used, but simply as one of the normal methods of communication though focused as a magnifying glass does to the sun's power. The suggestion will be done with symbols and Christian belief statements in order to facilitate amplification and intensification of the total power of one's faith operation and get into the transcendent psyche space. But again the client is reassured he/she will be in charge of the entire experience at all times. Reinforcing this self-assurance should be carried out *immediately*; before the Schema is used, and alsobefore doing any therapy work, following the PRAYER OF COMMITMENT, and as a part of the PRE-THERAPY WORK CHECK-OUT.

6. The client should be informed that he/she will be using both imagery and contemplation of generally accepted Christian concepts to relax the body and concomitantly move consciousness toward a state of more elevated and unified awareness. There the ego, which is his/her lesser I-am-ness, logic-center and usual awareness level is in closer connection with the Self, which is one's larger and expanded awareness core, Soul-center, High Self, or center of one's larger I-Am-ness. Any of these terms may be helpful. The main concern is to give the client some comprehensible idea of the parts of him/herself involved in what is expected to take place. To fail to give some explanation will defeat the purpose of the experience. The ministering therapist should stress the fact that the special psyche state is an elevated, transcendent, or intensely worshipful spiritual state which is *normal* for all but is most often only occasionally and temporarily experienced in private.

7. Emphasis should be placed upon the fact that this is a transpersonal type of therapy which is an expression of the Church and its ministering; it is, therefore, a specifically religious and God-centered, Christian growth or psychotherapeutic instrument. Faith Therapy's Guided Meditation and Intensified Faith expressions emphasize and use the more religious operational capacities, realms, and spaces of the psyche, as approached and interpreted from the Christian perspective. This method often helps gain a more satisfying problem resolution or meaningful developmental stimulation through the function of transformation of psychic energy for growth, rather than sublimation only. The latter tends to aim more at simply adjusting to the problem, which is often a personally less satisfying and acceptable solution.

8. All the foregoing is to allay the threatened feeling many people have as they approach an unknown psychic process such as the Guided Meditation part of Faith Therapy. This threat is experienced especially if the client is already under profound stress and is experiencing fears of being controlled by another or coerced into an undesired solution. In such event, the therapist should use as gentle an approach as possible for maximum reduction of the anxiety *prior to beginning* this part of the methodology. Thereafter, the therapist should proceed at the pace needed which will best enable the client to enter the intensified faith psyche state trustfully. Perhaps he/she will only choose to enter one new Level or Stage at a specific session until familiar enough with the space to be largely anxiety-free within it or when he/she feels he/she has explored the new spot with satisfaction and fulfillment.

9. When indicated, the entire Schema may be used at the time of the first session if the client desires it and has sufficient sense of selfhood. Such instances are rare. However, with all first time use of the entire Exercise or ANY Schema variation much emphasis

should be placed upon such phrases as "now, *let* yourself...," or "now, using your imagination *let* yourself...."

10. Some people, in their first or second Schema Exercise, will open their eyes from time to time and ask questions. Observations indicate this is done by the client from beyond his/her immediate awareness so that he/she may check whether or not he/she or the therapist is in control of one's will. The therapist should go along with such testing procedure as far as possible in order to reassure the client. A simple reminder that "Alpha waves necessary to the effective functioning of the Faith Schema largely can only be produced with closed eyes" is usually sufficient to gain the client's cooperation again.

11. As a general rule, first time use of the entire Faith Schema with the aim of reaching Level III, Stage 9 should be thought of primarily as a training exercise because of its greater length and the need to keep anxiety at a minimum during the process. Preferably, this more complete structuring should not be used until the client has become comfortable enough with the entire process that through use of lesser or modified levels he/she feels ready to move toward higher experiences by using the full Schema. Strangely enough, some clients may learn to produce some dimension of transcendent mood almost completely on their own. Usually this is done *only* in the therapist's presence. Apparently, this is accomplished through conditioned learning of autonomic process control as demonstrated by biofeedback experience. However, some few clients will be able to produce some type of transcendent mood totally on their own and anywhere. This is not recommended (except in rare cases) because certain psyche spaces can elicit frightening symbolic experiences which are best dealt with using the outer world reality orientation which the guide's presence provides.

12. At the point of complete client comfort with experiencing the entire Schema or variation of it when fear of being controlled has been lost, such phrases as "*let*...," and "using your imagination, *let*...," may be dropped because the client will no longer be in any doubt of being ultimately in charge in the Guided Meditation process. As the therapist increasingly proves trustworthy—particularly in the use of word meanings—the depth of comraderie, especially spiritually, will deepen. Faith, hope, and love as the triadic faith operation process will increasingly manifest itself in the mutual responsiveness in the therapy situation and will point beyond, toward the ideal depth of fellowship in the larger faith community.

13. Note should be taken that for the average person, after having undergone several faith intensification experiences, only a period of approximately ten to fifteen minutes of uninterrupted flow of the Schema's feeling-thought charged faith process is needed to establish adequate intensity of the psyche's transcendent mood. Usually it appears the client cannot enter the intensified faith state without some Schema use. However, after enough use some persons seem to accomplish use of the Crisis Intervention Techniques with fair results by only using Schema Level 0, Imagination Only, or Level I, Stage 1, with its body relaxation and breathing exercises only. Experience is the best indicator for the therapist here.

14. If possible, at no point in use of either the Schema Exercise or the transcendent psyche space itself should the therapist allow the client to terminate his current psyche mood without using the proper suggested procedure for returning from the mood into the usual and everyday psyche state of attunement to outer world reality. The purpose in this deschematization procedure is to avoid leaving any confusion of affect or thought processes. A too abrupt ending to the transcendent mind mood will further intensify the client's anxiety which may already be present due to fear which possibly became aroused while using the Schema. Basically, such anxiety seems due to an extreme fear of loss of any control whatsoever. It is possible but rare for a client to experience such intense new levels of fearful affect in these processes, even though he/she consciously may be most cooperative concerning the therapist and methodology, that he/she requests an immediate end to the entire experience. Usually the fear may be removed by immediate use of the Desensitization Technique or quick use of the Switch Technique for transforming the fear's energy. Or the therapist may give assurance that staying with (enduring) his/her feeling will allay and identify it because it is his/her feeling, and needs to be experienced through and dealt with. Also a reminder may be given that the therapist is right there to help, particularly to aid in understanding the feeling's message. However, if the client is still adamant, the therapist should immediately assure him/her that the mood will be ended immediately, but that his/her cooperation is needed to alleviate any mental fuzziness which might ensue unless the proper procedure is followed in returning to the everyday psyche state. Thereupon, as quickly as possible the client should be led down from the new space by the use of the Five Spiritually Significant Stairstep Words, OR by the request to fly, as though by magic, back to the beach—where he/she becomes aware that he/she has lain there long enough, that feeling rested, renewed, alert, refreshed—and with no bad aftereffects, he/she is to open his or her eyes and sit up. For some, even the briefer Deschematizing Exercise is adequate. Here the client simply imagines returning to the beach and focuses his/her imagination on the fact he/she has lain there long enough...(complete as with the pattern above). Then the entire strong fear reaction of the client should be immediately analyzed, reasoned through and resolved so that no inappropriate anxiety will remain after his/her leaving the session.

15. Dependent upon the intensity of anxiety present, it may be necessary to explain to the client why the anxiety level tends to rise as he/she leans far back in the reclining chair. The therapist gives the following clinical, direct explanation: "Do not be embarrassed by this sort of nervousness, for most men and women, whether consciously aware of it or not, develop anxiety when they recline in the presence of another relatively unknown person. The apparent reason for this is simple, for we all feel more vulnerable in such a physical position of openness. The anxiety is coming from the deep (and possibly) collective levels of our minds. For example, a woman reclining in a man's presence may be unconsciously a bit defensive because this is an often used position in which a man may be received for sexual intercourse. And, a man may experience the same sort of anxiety as he reclines in the presence of another man due to the primitive fear of being defenselessly pounced upon by an unknown enemy or adversary who could possibly deliver the "kill" blow. Usually, confronting such feelings together, directly, in a straightforward and unemotional manner will allay most anxiety present.

16. Insight into God's particular spiritual pole (conceptual or physical, in the process theology paradigm) from which the client is largely operating when in the intensified faith psyche space may be quickly and unobtrusively noted. As soon as the client's self control has been reassured in the PRE-THERAPY WORK CHECK-OUT, the therapist may then ask the client how he/she now feels about where he/she is in his/her own psyche. With attention, the therapist may discover that the client is relating to God in a distinct polar manner. If the client is operating more from his/her mental pole (it would appear God is free to interact from either of His/Hers), the client is apt to be caught up into ideation, tending to have Void-like or cosmic images and feelings, abstractions, color displays, and this may be randomly interspersed with forms or shapes. If some conceptual abstraction giving rise to anxiety is present, it is wise to use very soon the Plus-mark Guided Therapy Procedure in order to clarify the confusion and begin to unify the client's sense of being a person. If on the other hand, the client begins to talk of lifelike, connected or related symbolic entities or highly personalized experiences of his/her immediate awareness of God's presence as a Person, the therapist may reasonably assume the client is operating from his/her physical pole. In therapy work the particular nature of the creative symbolization material has a tendency to shift the polar emphasis according to the contents of the work. Much is yet to be learned in this polar experience area.

17. Many clients will repeatedly need assistance in clarifying for themselves the difference between *feelings, emotions, intuitions, and sensations.* In English these words are often used so vaguely and interchangeably that it is not surprising to find that much of the client's trouble is caused by a lack of early childhood clarity in understanding the denotation and/or connotation of the words. This lack of clarity presents a grave problem for the client in understanding him/herself and a need for semantic clarity in *all* verbal relations between client and therapist, both in Dialogical Counseling and Guided Meditation. Sometimes it is amazing how confused these concepts can be for the client when he/she is in the transcendent mind mood and as unconscious structures and associations are probed. One of the necessities of therapy is to come to a right understanding of what our feelings are so that we can combine them correctly with right thinking and deal with all life better. I have found that using the word *hunch* to clarify intuition is very helpful. Nearly everyone knows what the five senses are, so sensation presents no major difficulty.[1] That term giving the most trouble will be feelings which additionally are often viewed as synonymous with emotions. Clarifying these by using the concept of five basic or body-based feelings (emotions) of sad, mad, glad, scared, or excited can be very helpful. Scared and excited are explained as feeling alike, a tickling feeling in the belly, but with scared one wants to flee while when excited one wants to approach. Glad is explained as equilibrium; "things are going O.K." Mad is anger.

Sad, or crying, is indicated as anger which has given up because it cannot get its goal; therefore, the frustrated energy is physically released in this manner. Ideally the knowledge of how to distinguish between these basic emotion tones needs to be taught the child in the age period ranging from three to six by significant adults. Other emotions are more consciously cognitive and have been given many different names in varying cultures. Clients may need to have it pointed out that these five emotion-type feelings are the first universal branchings of the emotion or feeling tree whose trunk is made up of primitive, undifferentiated, varying intensities of infantile feelings of contentment, excitement, or fear/anger.[2] Use of these differentiations in therapeutically searching for affective tone origins is helpful. (Of course, such adult feelings as ecstasy or rapture are like blowing the emotional gaskets, in a positive way.)

18. It may even be necessary in Guided Meditation to help the person understand what either feeling or thought is. In these states of intensified faith and expanded awareness, the therapist may learn how little even a brilliant client may understand of his/her own psychic processes. Since generically, awareness of feeling of some sort arrives in consciousness before thought does, feeling gives energy to the primary thought process as an identifiable (primitive) feeling tone. Identification of the feeling tone then often can get the process of thinking (identifying the right organizational relation) in more differentiated, rational terms started. For the client it may be defined as a type of Therapy Procedure named "The Feeling Which Gives Rise to the Thought." This is further clarified as being like a waterlily. It starts growing from down deep in the unconscious as a vague energy-affect (as though from roots in the mud and muck of a pond); then it forms into a feeling tone (as though it were a stem coming up through the murky water), reaches the field of consciousness as a notion, an insight, a memory, or a perception (as though having broken the water's surface and formed its pad).

Then we become aware of the feeling and make some judgement about it (like the lily which forms and blossoms into a flower); finally we may focus our awareness and insight upon what the judgment ultimately means, think about our thinking itself, reflecting upon it. This last part of the process may be likened to examining further the innermost part of the lily (we are looking for the wisdom represented in the Orient as the "jewel of the lotus," that is, contemplation of the stamen and pistil). All this may need repeating several times, but again the thinking and feeling in pictures of life-logic expressed in feeling-thought will most likely slowly clarify the issue, and the client will see that the place at which feeling and thought merge into conceptual awareness is the dynamic evolutionary point in his own growth.

19. Any time the client seems unable to clarify needed imagery, the therapist may snap his/her fingers or clap the hands. The explanation, given the client, is that this is a means of breaking his/her tendency toward over-concentration which actually discourages symbol formation. When the therapist does this, it is to break momentarily the Aristotelian logic's hard thought flow. This procedure will allow for a more spontaneous appearance of the image or intuitive insight so that the client will not force some symbol or idea. This procedure may need also to be repeated.

20. Also it will be helpful to explain that at given points of the Schema the therapist may use the term "I" instead of "YOU." This should be explained in this manner: it is strictly using the I in an editorial manner or that the therapist considers him/herself socially accompanying the client and offering his/her own observations. However, if it is at all confusing to the client, the therapist should be glad to discontinue using it. Interestingly, most clients find this sense of company in such situations to be helpful and pleasing.

21. Prior to starting use of the Schema Exercise, it is wise for the therapist to explain his/her use of the timer bell, which is set to ring approximately ten to fifteen minutes before the client is supposed to end his/her therapy session. At the sound of the bell the client is to move his/her imaging toward a spot of reasonably comfortable closure for this particular Guided Meditation. Due to the time-distortion factor in this special psyche state, the bell is used as a signal for the client to begin to get him/herself to a psyche space of comfort and safe feeling prior to ending this particular part of the session.

At times the therapist may still have to draw the client's attention to the fact that the time is up. However, there will be other times when the therapist needs to be sure for his/her own sake that the client is in a safe place for a sense of closure. Therefore, the therapist may choose to disregard the bell and should tell the client to do likewise until he/she is instructed to find a safe feeling or place. Time in this therapy method has to be a bit more flexible than in many others. One of the chief reasons for this need is that the therapist must take care of him/herself also, he/she does not need an overly disturbed client getting more anxious between sessions.

22. After a Guided Meditation session containing strange or highly unusual symbolism, it is wise in the POST-THERAPY WORK CHECK-OUT to be sure of the client's psychic condition before he/she leaves. One needs to be in one's usual consciousness state. If the therapist has any doubt about later confusion arising, he/she should request the client call him/her at either office or home (but using discretion) if any intensely disturbing feelings or insights suddenly burst into awareness. This happens infrequently, but the client needs adequate reassurance that in such an event he/she will not be left in distress with no support or opportunity to communicate with the therapist until the next scheduled session.

23. A strange experience is that of Spinning or Spiraling. In the transcendent space some clients will spontaneously tell the therapist they are having this experience. The rapidity of the inner circular movement feeling is so disturbing to some clients that sometimes the Faith Schema or therapy work cannot be carried forward until the phenomenon is dealt with. There are three methods to do so: use of either Crisis Intervention Technique; Desensitizing which is probably the most effective, but the Switch is often effective and also quicker; the other is simply reassuring the client and asking him/her to stay with the feelings until they stop. Frequently the latter will work well with the assurance, "It cannot hurt you. After all, they are your feelings." Interestingly enough, after having had this experience a number of times and waiting it through, some clients have perceived the experience as an inflow of spiritual force, energizing them.

This spiraling experience most frequently seems to take place in the Void or in "outer space." However, other clients still more attuned to their outer world reality may report that their chair is doing the movement even though they know it is not so. The location does not matter, for the experience is dealt with in the same manner.

I have no explanation for this phenomenon, even after all these years. The most that I have to offer toward understanding it is a notion that the experience may be a subjective, Self or Soul-center awareness of space-time involvement in Life and Motion (process).

24. The therapist may have a legitimate question about the credibility of this method because of its dealing with subjective, inner world realities, fearing such experiences could be delusional or hallucinatory. He/she need have no such qualms, for interestingly this therapy method's results will bear the same test as healthy religious or visionary experiences always have. The test is that after the Deschematizing Exercise is completed the client should have this awareness and perception about any transcendent experience: the feeling of certitude about Ultimate Reality in this experience causes the reality of the everyday, outer world to become construed as more real in spite of what was experienced as a greater reality. This attitude (paradoxical as it may at first sound) may be contrasted to that of delusional or hallucinatory persons who want to live immediately in their unreal dream world in an escapist manner. The client having a mystical, revelatory, or visionary experience (experienced spiritual reality) does not desire to remain in the transcendent psyche space but will let it wait. He/she wishes to return to his/her usual life and duty for as long as it shall last. This attitude is in keeping with Jesus's approach when, after the transcendent experience on the Mount of Transfiguration, he insisted that Peter, James, and John return to the valley and daily work with him (Matt. 17:1-18 RSV).

25. The important use of imagery in this therapy method may need to be illustrated or explained as follows: we think and feel in pictures as the primary way we represent outer reality to ourselves from the time we first open our eyes. The baby first feels good because he/she sees mother. Later the baby becomes aware of the relations present as thought; "I feel good because I am hungry and mother is present with a bottle." These and other such pictures (some collective in origin) are stored in one's pre-conscious but usually come to consciousness with little feeling and largely as thought; however, most people remember at times dreaming lucid dreams with images of such powerful thought and feeling that they awake trying to run. Often then, if we change the preconscious image with its negative modulation to one of neutral or positive modulation, the conscious cognitive thought and feeling received from the preconscious will be more rational and realistic.

26. It is good to mention to the client, frequently but discreetly, that Faith Therapy is at its root a growth therapy. Its true, larger emphasis is either upon removing blocks to psychic growth or upon archetypally awakening stymied psychic growth structures so that life may be more inviting and free, as God intended it.

27. There will be times a client will confront the therapist about the "right thing" to do. There have never been enough laws to cover all possible human conditions. Some sort of situation ethic or moral principle is needed for guidance, and the client will ask the therapist for help. Christ's Supreme Commandment is the best example to follow. As Christians we hold this to be *his* instructions. When asked what was the first and greatest commandment, Jesus said that one should *love* God first and (equally) one's neighbor as oneself, "like unto" God (Matt. 22: 37-39 R.S.V.). According to the Lord (our authority) in relationships we have been directed to use the positive emotion of love which provides truer perception.

Of necessity we must closely examine what Jesus said. His instructions involved an equal triadic form of loving, but he equated loving one's self and neighbor with loving God. In this triangular relating, what "self" was Jesus speaking of? Perhaps he meant one's unconscious Self, because from the usual viewpoint of the ego the Self seems an object (when more intimately known it is recognized as a higher subject) and is always in connection with the total self and objective psyche. In that event his teaching could mean a human being (ego) the subject—is to love (positively, affectively relate to) the verb—him/herself (Self as unconscious center, total self, and one's part of the objective psyche) as the object. Then one is act lovingly toward neighbor and God. Spiritually and psychologically one tends often not to love his/her Self (from an ego-self viewpoint) with its access to unconscious content, because he/she fears it as ungodly. Unfortunately, under threat (as the Birkman Personality Inventory indicates) a person has an inclination to project onto others—and yes onto God also—one's own unconscious negative traits even while acting them out. This stems from the fact that pride makes it difficult to consciously face our unconscious negative stress traits. When one refuses to accept God's forgiving grace, as giver to his/her unconscious negativities, and tries to live by immediate awareness of consciousness only, one makes a great faith mistake, making a god of one's own ego. He/she will continue to scapegoat others and create for him/herself a continuing spiral of misery.

Christ pointed out the solution comes in learning from *ego-self* perspective to love God (as love's normative measure), oneself, and one's neighbor equally (in process manner). One's *Self* and neighbor are to be related to as objects of God's creation. In this manner one may come to be unafraid of the unconscious and quit projecting upon others one's out-of-awareness negative qualities. This understanding helps a client in negative stress to quit scapegoating others, view God with more accurate perception, and view one's total self and neighbor more objectively, thus gaining better overall humility and honesty. This forms a background for the client's immediate help and a willingness to change and adjust. It is of great assistance to the therapist to point out God's gracefulness to all involved.[3] For greater clarity of this concept of Christ's teaching the reader is referred to Figure No. 7, immediately following.

NOTES

[1] Jung, *Analytical*, pp. 11-15.

[2] Maxwell and Dietrich, "Passivity and Reparenting Workshop," *Op. cit.*

[3] Information from my personal counseling and therapy use of the Birkman Personality Inventory and its results (See prior relevant end notes).

Figure No. 7 The Perceptive Relating of Ego to God, Neighbor, Self

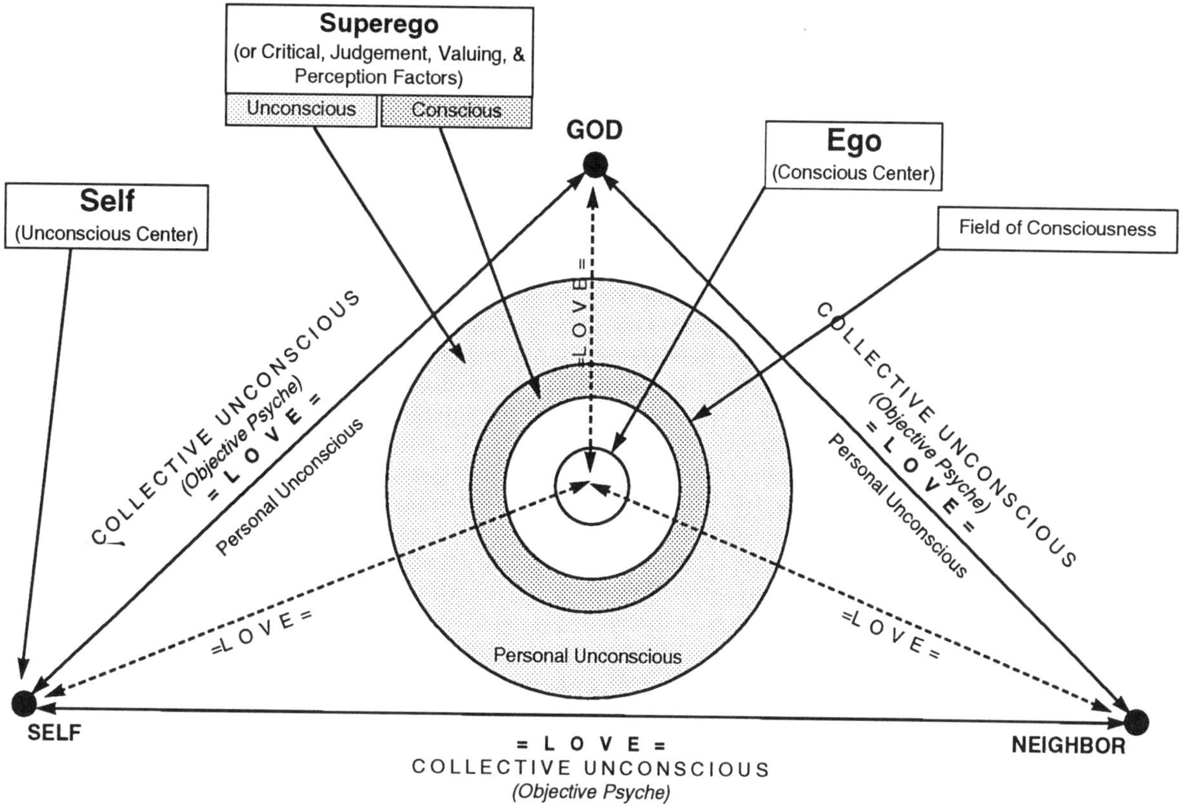

Chapter IX

~

SPECIAL CAUTIONS FOR THERAPIST CONSIDERATION

Due to their great importance, the therapist will find it very helpful to give special attention to the following points. The amount of curiosity, threat-anxiety, or defensiveness present in particular clients will determine to what degree the following points need to be taken into account. Unless he/she can be helped to establish a trusting, non-threatened, and non-defensive attitude toward the therapist, the client will continue to feel anxiety about guided meditation parts of this method until his/her discomfort may become so great that he/she drops therapy. Part of this risk is possibly due to the use of the power of suggestion which allows the client pleasantly to re-experience some of the openness and freedom of feelings characteristic of early childhood, but if his/her trust feelings were violated then, they will be given again now very hesitantly. It follows then that for maximum results, trustworthiness on the part of the ministering therapist is a must, but especially in clarifying any threat feelings.

   1. Special note needs to be taken of the style in which the Intensified Faith Schema is written. It is written to communicate the emotion filled vocal quality of the Schema and is intended to emphasize life-logic and its use of feeling-thought. This style is intended to aid the therapist to paint the needed imagined pictures for the client. Some points are deliberately left vague for the sake of the client's experiencing a creative, impressionistic, psychic effect. As has been amplified in the theory part, the conscious conceptual image or sign leads to the needed greater affect of the personal symbol. The image then gives rise to the more affectively charged symbols of the collective unconscious, needed for elevating the ego by Faithing Schema use into close conjunction with the Self for better ego functioning and total awareness. For this reason, voice-tone, volume emphasis, incomplete sentences, pauses, etc. should be considered as varying means of changing and intensifying the color of the vocal brush strokes which make up the symbol, thereby increasing its effect. (The accompanying tapes, if procured, illustrate the Intensified Faith Schema and other places of vocal style use and can be of help in understanding this voice emphasis and intonation device.)

2. In the Schema the therapist will note that the archetypes used in Level III, Stages 7—9 increasingly shift from visualized sensory impressions into archetypal images of a more abstract and conceptual nature. This deliberate shift of psychic process emphasis aids in intensifying alpha and theta brain wave strength, brings about increased centering of the person and also helps increase passive concentration capacities. This procedure apparently brings one's awareness of God's physical, feeling pole closer to one's awareness of God's mental, conceptual pole's grades of relevance. This is done so that the client's awareness of the grades of relevance is clearer and more powerful in his/her therapy work's valuing experience.

3. Some clients may appear to be seriously doing therapy work in the Therapy Procedures, even having especially vivid symbol activity, but getting a low yield from their entire intensified faith effort. Upon checking with biofeedback instruments such persons may show strong theta brain wave activity and practically no accompanying alpha wave production. Often upon close observation, these persons will indicate an inability (or unwillingness) to let go of overly strong body control tensions. If the client will agree, aid in accomplishing concomitant amplified alpha production may be facilitated with biofeedback training, doing Bioenergetic Therapy, or learning some simple yoga body-relaxation techniques. Also there are those who seem to evidence little imaginal ability. Help for this type of client is difficult. Most help seems to come from asking the client to "play like" he is an artist painting a picture.

4. The therapist will find the client to be simultaneously aware on two existence levels, while doing the Schema Exercise and also in the transcendent psyche state itself. The client knows he/she is in the reclining chair in the therapist's office and also knows by cosmic intuition that he/she is at the same time in an inner world, or

psyche space. When the client is doing regression work, due to some spatio-temporal distortion inherent in this part of the therapy, at times it may be necessary to clarify his/her experienced situation by asking him/her to focus attention on the "back-there, then *NOW*" and/or the "present day *NOW*" as he/she searches for behavioral correlations. The phenomenon of spatio-temporal confusion seems to stem from the timelessness and spatial infinity of the upper unconscious in which the client is working. To expect this type of perceptual intermingling needs to be made clear to the client in advance. Some spatio-temporal confusion is normal in all Guided Meditation experience, but this type of distortion generally will not continue after the special therapeutic psychic state is terminated. Such incidents need to be counseled through in the ambience of the client's conscious logical functioning, his/her usual frame of reference.

It would be difficult to overemphasize the necessity of clarifying this timelessness and spacial infinity phenomenon if the client is to use regressive, affective tone association techniques in following down a structure to abreact its traumatic parts. The intense imagery and affect elicited by the emotional pain of some past experiences can cause the client to "feel crazy" as he/she re-experiences and relives them. Consequently, while undergoing the regression experience, he/she may need strong reassurance that one is indeed sane but is simply, strongly, simultaneously aware on two levels of consciousness in the profound perception and feeling of this intensified religious experience type of therapy work.

5. When using the Schema and Therapy Procedures, the entire time span should under no circumstances be longer than two hours. If the procedure is allowed to continue past the two hour limit, uncomfortable (but not dangerous) headaches may ensue. This effect is probably due to a chemical change in the body or an overworked psyche.

6. In the Guided Meditation part of this therapy some clients will occasionally have intense feelings of bodily lightness and/or heaviness. If brought to the therapist's attention, reassurance should immediately be given that such feelings are a normal phenomenon in this process and are usually an indication that body tensions are being relaxed and muscles are at ease.

Upon feeling body lightness, some clients may have great fear of depersonalization. If so, the Crisis Intervention Technique of the

Key Word Desensitizing by Sensitizing (i.e. Stress! Key word: [Relax (name)]! Exhaust!....Smile!....Erase!....Kindle!....Beam!.... Fortress-power!....) should be used immediately and repeatedly until the causal fear and anxiety plus any residual bad feelings are relieved. Interestingly enough, the depersonalized feeling may somatize itself very shortly. Such somatization usually takes a primitive, schizoid nature such as nausea, dizziness, terror, hot flashes, or moving pains. The pains may shift with each desensitization until they arrive in the teeth or mouth and may even finally eventuate in crying or sobbing, bringing relief. Let us emphasize that this methodology offers no reason for fear of depersonalization but instead offers a solution each time such phenomena occur. Occasionally clients feeling the lightness may fear they are beginning an out-of-the-body experience. If so, the therapist quickly assures them this therapy method does not usually allow a person to produce such experiences and at its inception was actually structured away from leading a person into such a space or state. When such experiences occur, they are usually simple cosmic fantasies into which the client has allowed him/herself to drift, and all he/she needs to do is focus awareness upon the body in order to discover one is indeed still in it. However, I have had two clients who subjectively felt convinced they did experience some such out-of-the-body experiences in the Guided Meditation and told about them while they were experiencing them—even designating the spot in the office from which they said they were viewing everything. Again, the simple request to focus awareness on the body brought them back. It is of note that neither client was frightened of the experience and later claimed he/she had had such experiences on his/her own several other times in life.

7. Occasionally, rarely, the therapist will encounter a client who has a strong anxiety reaction to imagining the Sea Scene, the Mountaintop Scene or even a particular part of any scene. In such event, appropriate strongly charged affective imagery substitutions may be made. For example, the following may be used instead of a sea scene: a cool, shady spot under a giant spreading oak tree—lying upon soft grass by a gurgling, little brook—in a peaceful meadow with no threatening or harmful people, animals, plants, insects, or things about. And, instead of the mountaintop scene, the following may be substituted: a high hilltop—but not too high—looking down upon a beautiful meadow. Any reasonable substitu-

tion of appropriate symbols may be made at any point, provided the mood, thought pattern, and meaning are kept. Many times the client him/herself will be able to suggest better personal substitutions or acceptable modifications of those presented in the Schema.

8. The therapist will note that some clients will occasionally seem to drop off to sleep during the Schema while the therapist speaks. Such an incident should not be viewed as troublesome. Experience has shown that for some unknown reason (perhaps because the Self, rather than the ego, is in control) such apparent dropping off to sleep does not have a negative influence if the therapist continues with the exercise without interruption. The client will arrive at the Transcending Psyche State just as if dozing had not intervened. All that will be necessary is for the therapist gently to awaken the client's ego from the sleep-like state—but requesting him/her to keep his/her eyes closed for continued alpha-theta brainwave production. After awakening he/she should be told that dozing or sleep apparently overlaid the Schema experience, but that he/she has seemingly arrived at the right psyche state just the same. The therapist should then proceed with the therapy procedures and work just as though there had been no sleep-like intervention.

9. It is important to be informed about client drug use. Experience has shown that psychotropic drugs prescribed by physicians for mental-emotional problems generally have no overly negative effect upon this therapy method if the person has good contact with the outer world reality principle. However, alcohol or consciousness-altering substances such as marijuana, LSD, mescaline, heroin, P.C.P., cocaine, etc. will have a definite negative effect upon the brain's ability to allow the psyche to function properly. (The same holds true for most physical illness—fever, colds, etc.) *It should be clearly understood in the contract between client and therapist that these negative-effect drugs will not be used by the client at least twenty-four hours before the session.* According to consumption and type, the abstinence period may need to be longer. Past heavy use of some of these drugs may necessitate treatment and hospitalization first in order to clear up dependency and residual effects on nerve or brain tissue.

10. In order to facilitate the flow of the Schema Exercise, it will probably be more helpful to the therapist if he/she memorizes and visualizes for him/herself the Schema's archetypal imagery, belief statements, and vocal style used with the client. The words and symbols seem to paint the pictures for the client much more clearly this way rather than if done in a monotonous, unemotional reading of the Exercise. But if this vocal and visualizing procedure is followed, the therapist will have to be very careful and on guard within him/herself to keep from subjectively and experientially entering into (in a participatory and symbiotic way) the structuring of the faith operation into the transcendent psyche mood with the client. This psychic structure is personally easy to enter without being aware of it— especially if the therapist is either mentally or physically tired. A good warning signal of such symbiotic participation is for the therapist to stay aware of any feelings of drowsiness which may begin to creep in upon him/her in use of the Schema or Therapy Procedures. Additionally, a good general rule of thumb is to avoid using this method in therapy sessions beyond three or four times in any one work day. Also, even too closely listening to the Schema may draw one into the structure's personal pervading power. But this should not surprise us since its use indicates it may be a UNIVERSAL STRUCTURE. Therefore, the therapist must work to remain out of the structure even while presenting it.

11. No client should be allowed to keep a sort of magical expectation or "pink pill" concept of this therapy, though some will approach it this way. It needs to be clearly and firmly pointed out that this methodology will help him/her better solve his/her own problems, but it is not a magic type of God we worship. Rather, He/She expects us to do our own work of making it in life. We may more healthily approach life if in general we consider He/She does not do for one child what He/She would not for another. Hence, the client's task is to be responsible and autonomous in dealing with and caring for his/her own choices, decisions, feelings, and acts. He/she needs to be led to know that this is one of the major goals of therapy; therefore, he/she should take every part of the therapy in this overall context of comprehension.

Beyond the client's goal of resolving a problem he/she may have another agenda, personally chosen goals for personal, transpersonal, or spiritual growth in faith-development; however, how far one goes with these goals, beyond those which help establish autonomy, will be strictly up to him/her. If he/she chooses to continue the series of sessions primarily for help in spiritual growth (Growth Therapy) this needs to be clearly conjointly understood as the course which thereafter will be followed in the use of this methodology. Usually no spiritual growth is really adequate unless it is accompanied by increasing maturity of the client's more infantile personality patterns. It must be reasserted as often as needed that the client him/herself must accept personal responsibility if he/she is ever to become autonomous and self-confident.

12. THE MINISTERING THERAPIST MUST MAKE COMPLETELY CLEAR THAT HE/SHE IS IN NO WAY DESIROUS OF PUSHING ANY OF HIS/HER PERSONAL SPIRITUAL CONCEPTS UPON THE CLIENT. The imagery and language of this methodology for bringing about intensified faith is simply an archetypal way of establishing the needed transpersonal psyche mood with its power of creative symbolization. If there is any objection to any of the material used, the client must be assured he/she is completely free (indeed, expected) to stop any part of the process at any time and semantically clarify, reject, or personally change any doctrinally offensive or unclear construct used by the therapist. Or as an alternative, all the client has to do is "turn the therapist off within his/her own head" by his/her own ability and free choice.

13. The therapist needs to keep in mind that the goal is personal growth and expansion of the client's *personal* awareness, not to have such religious experiences as the therapist may desire for him/her. This goal is ethically appropriate no matter how right or correct certain doctrines may seem to one as a particular ministering person claiming a specific religious ideology. If the therapist has some unaware or unresolved doctrinal grandiosity or neurotic control needs, unknowingly and unintentionally he/she may let them slip into the therapy process and attempt to impose them upon the client. For this reason a practitioner of Faith Therapy should personally undergo some sort of appropriate training analysis before using this methodology. In some manner, he/she needs to acquaint him/herself well and subjectively with therapeutic guided fantasy methods and meditation techniques. Also the therapist will need to have had personal psychotherapy, preferably a type using an eclectic approach but also emphasizing Psychoanalytic AND Psychosynthesis or Analytical Psychology orientation. A therapist who has not subjectively experienced, with profound affect, the power of his own unconscious symbols will not be in a very good position to guide another.

14. While using Guided Meditation dimensions, it will be wise for the therapist never to let him/herself get so caught up into the imagery of the client that he/she cannot be completely in charge of his/her own feelings. To become too subjectively entangled with the client's images and moods is to fail oneself in retaining the needed objectivity for personal therapist safety.

15. When doing Guided Meditation parts of the therapy it is of vital importance that the therapist be aware of the occasional possibility of a client's having a large downswing of affect following any particularly high affect session, especially those involving rapturous or intensely mystical states. It is not unusual for such a downswing to take place after highly numinous experiences in a particularly fulfilling session. Of course, generally to a lesser extent, this same emotional high factor is to be found in other therapy models. But because this therapy involves relating to God in intense feelings of new vision, unity, broader perspective, overwhelming love and safety, the downswing can be more distressful in many ways. In some of the Guided Meditation parts, the points of joy and rapture sometimes are very high. (Actually the negative origin of this problem may be in the ancient confusion of religion with magic. The person falsely expects the "heavenly feelings" to abide in everyday reality.) Consequently, the therapist needs to be aware that the client's downswing may be very disturbing. Sometimes a downswing will have a delayed or time-lag effect and may take as long as three to four days for the high to wear off before the downswing occurs. It is highly advised to warn a client *in advance* about a downswing probability when he/she has experienced such a rapturous experience. In this way he/she may not feel falsely led to think such a mood is to be almost magically gained and kept all the time. Instead, it is to become a guiding part of or an incident in his/her total religious growth and consciousness-raising experience. He/she may be reminded that once having been in such a new psyche space, one now knows it exists and will never forget its inspiration, but that it is not "dished out" to him/her by God—because that would be unfair to all of God's other children.

Also in times of downswing it may be necessary for the therapist to explain to the client that in reality he/she is no worse off than before, though he/she may feel like it. The bad feeling is due to something in his/her psyche which the client would most probably have had to confront eventually in one way or another in life. Now

for the first time he/she has openly entered, and known consciously, this new space in his/her psyche. Therefore, he/she may think of
him/herself as worse off than before but actually is not in the long
run.

16. Illustration by the therapist concerning the client's progress
if he/she is unaware of it may be likened to climbing a mountain
and may be used as follows when needed: In the process of climbing any mountain, to be in a valley looks and feels the same, even if
one is at a higher elevation, if the person doing the climbing focuses his/her attention upon it. However, if another is watching from
an objective distance through a transit-type telescope, he/she can
better determine how high or low the climber has reached.

17. As previously indicated, this counseling method is exactly
the sort of I-Thou, ministering, good parenting, and friendship
model in its basic nature, and it needs to be willingly accepted as
such in advance by those who consider using it. Affective components in this methodology are usually much more intense than
those encountered in many other psychotherapy models and
demand true caring of the therapist.

However, this supportive element does not mean that the therapist accepts the childishness and overdependency of a client without question, warning, and at times blatant refusal of false demands
and expectations. This ministering method does not mean encouraging dependency as a static condition for the client. The model
aims at causing one to become realistically self-determined, self-
reliant, and autonomous.

Let the relationship between therapist and client be supportive
but not symbiotic. Let the therapist keep constantly before him/her-
self that he/she is only a shepherd lest one becomes compulsive
about getting a client "totally" well. The shepherd may oil and
bathe the wounds of the sheep, but he/she needs to realize he/she
cannot heal by his/her own power; power and province belong to
the Owner of the sheep. Ultimately all healing lies in His/Her
hands. It is enough that we, as ministering therapists, can rejoice in
being helpers to the Lord of the Universe.

18. No method of therapy works equally well for all people.
Obviously, not everyone responds well to this model. Most people
do with varying degrees of success, but some simply do not for
indeterminable reasons. When such is the case, a referral should be

made or another therapy model should be used.

19. The therapist should keep in mind, when doing the Guided Meditation part of Faith Therapy, that he/she is to include the following in each session which uses Guided Meditation with Intensified Faith and Therapy Procedures:

FOUR STANDARD USE SCHEMA REFERENTS
I.   Prayer of Commitment
II. Pre-therapy Work Check-out
III. Usual Positive Idea Use
IV. Post-therapy Work Check-out

20. While Faith Therapy, though often long range and supportive, uses only one hour a week usually in order to give enough needed growth time, the therapist may find it wise occasionally to grant two appointments in a week when such support is needed. Also there are times a client will need two successive one hour appointments. Usually this is done when very intensive and complicated regression work is to be done, when both client and therapist agree the time needed will probably be that long. Otherwise, such two hour appointments may be done with people who have to drive long distances to see the therapist. These are people who are seriously into the personality reconstruction depths of the therapy for the time being and would often need two, one-hour appointments in the week otherwise. As any client gets stronger, the appointments are made bi-weekly until he/she is ready for monthly sessions, at which time he/she may keep a monthly appointment (if indicated) or drop standing appointments and call in. This is a good weaning approach. And at the agreed upon end of therapy, clients are told that they are placed on the CAN (come as needed) basis. The therapist has a supportive dimension and is always there to be called upon when needed—like the family physician.

21. The Therapy Procedure of the "Therapist's Insight-hunch" should always be *offered* to the client but *never coerced* or pushed authoritatively. This is especially true when the client is into the Guided Meditation part of the therapy because, as the therapist must never forget, the trusting client in this mind mood may become too suggestible and could be more cooperative with the therapist than is helpful. Consequently, it is possible the client could try too hard to please the therapist without being aware of it. Personally, I am not aware of such an incident; indeed usually it takes the opposite direction. Though the client comes to feel cooperative, his/her amplified power of total will makes him/her very guarded about even wanting to please the therapist. The client is very interested at that time in his/her own needs, almost to the point of rudeness if the insight-hunch is given very insistently. However, if it is frequently adamantly refused by the client, resistance could possibly be present and needs to be checked out and worked out.

22. It is good to keep in mind what Intensified Faith Schema Level or Variation is best suited for differing ages and mental-emotional conditions of new clients. The therapist will find the use of Guided Meditation components more successful if these limits are used and advanced as clients are ready for them by their own choosing. These recommendations with limited Usual Positive Idea use will make the entire therapy more effective.

23. Many times resistance will manifest itself in this therapy method by a client's obviously striving to fill his hour with Dialogical Counseling. This is all right up to a certain point, but if it begins to get in the way of helping the client through the Guided Meditation part of the therapy, it must be confronted as the lack of trust and need of control that it is. Otherwise, the therapist is likely to feel inadequate and anxious. He/she must take care of his/her own realistic needs to do self-respecting therapy in the situation.

24. As many psychotherapists are well aware, the troubles that bring people to marriage or family counseling are frequently only symptoms. The real power components of the structures consciously manifesting themselves (often called automatic thinking) lie much deeper, down in the preconscious or deepest parts of the unconscious, and may need the Guided Meditation dimension of Faith Therapy in order to get to the roots of the problem. In such cases, the therapist needs to confront the clients early with this reality and either refer them to a therapist specializing in the more conjoint or *conscious cognitive* methods or ask them to be prepared to undergo mostly private sessions separately with some conjoint sessions from time to time, as needed.

25. People with poor imagination capacity present the greatest difficulty in the use of Faith Therapy. In such cases it would appear there was some childhood limitation placed on such right brain activity. It is likely fantasy and freedom were often overly restricted. Such an adult client will have to be trained into using his/her imaging and becoming aware of emotion-type feeling in order for the therapy to progress well. (Again, I have found the device of "painting a picture" to be of great help in training the imagination.) If one had to divide humanity into two leaning groups, obsessive-compulsives and hysterics, the hysterics would get better more quickly through using Faith Therapy's Guided Meditation dimension to full advantage.

26. A therapist using this methodology should not be disturbed if most clients are "those who more actively seek their own souls than those who seek to solve immediate problems in living." I am not sure why this is so, but it seems intense thinkers and feelers with high perception tend to be drawn to this method and are most helped by it. Apparently, it is more a therapy for people who are largely reflection-oriented. Perhaps it is that they ask the larger questions of life—questions for which Faith Therapy can help clients find personally satisfying answers, and/or a more meaningful world-view.

27. It is the admitted foremost aim of Faith Therapy to lead people primarily to know God in His/Her physical, consequent, or feeling pole, the concept of higher reality in the West, not His/Her abstract, primordial, conceptual, mental pole or the way of the East. However, such experience is not to be denied, treated lightly, or downgraded, for this experience of the Cosmos is also God. But those who founded this therapy felt that in the West our place was to share with the East, not give primacy to some of its doctrines containing dangerous concrete world and self-negating views! Such beliefs frequently make the ego world and outer reality of no ultimate value, only an illusion, and that is not our message. Our message is: "For God so loved the world (our sensory existence) that he gave his only Son (a person with a relational ego), that whoever believes in him *should not perish* but have eternal life" (Italics mine) (John 3:16 RSV). And feeling alive involves more emotion than thought in relating to our current space-time existence.

28. This point is of vital importance. In this therapy method the transference phenomenon and/or (in T.A. terms) an intense level of intimacy may be obtained much more quickly than with many methods of psychotherapy. The probable core-reason for the quick

transference or immediate intimacy phenomenon is the psychic mechanism of suggestion used in the Intensified Faith Schema and the pleasant feelings of the transcendent psyche mood. As previously stated, this entire process tends to produce rather pleasant, relaxed, unitive, and euphoric feelings. And these tend to remind the client unconsciously of pleasant childhood feelings of no responsibility plus care and protection, that is when depth security was (at least sometimes) felt, as he/she relied upon and cooperated with the parents.

Therefore, the therapist needs to take note that due to the possibility of an early and profound transference, or strong intimacy feelings, both greater rapport and greater dependency feelings are to be expected and allowed for—particularly as they manifest themselves negatively. Nevertheless, this disadvantage is usually offset by the early arrival of client and therapist at a good working point. Consequently, in many cases they also arrive at an earlier conclusion to the therapy process. It should be strongly emphasized that most of the time the transference is no problem at all because both are orienting such feelings toward the Transcendent Third.

29. The therapist needs to be alert to subtle indications (perhaps squirming) that the client may need to interrupt his/her meditation and go to the toilet. If this pressing need is not taken care of, the client will become increasingly distracted and restless, and consequently the meditation will lose its effectiveness. Even if the session must be interrupted, however, it will cause no major alteration of the mind mood. Usually, the client with ease can get back into the same psyche space and point of therapy; but if necessary, the therapist may lead the client back by retracing the last few occurrences which took place in the meditation.

30. As background information the therapist would be wise to be alert to the possibility of the client being captured by and living out some major human myth. The mega patterns of existence are so powerful that sometimes they capture and enmesh one in them and occasionally negative manifestation may be presented as a personal problem; such as, "The Cinderella Complex," "The Hero Journey," or "The Peter Pan Syndrome." The therapist may greatly help the client by inoffensively bringing this issue to light as a possible part of the current problem.

PART IV

ILLUMINATING TRANSCRIPTS

This part is intended to provide the demonstrative, illustrative concreteness of Faith Therapy in action. It will consist of four chapters, each of which is also part of a recorded verbatim of an actual therapy session (which may be procured from the author, if desired). Additionally, the transcripts will also include inserted therapist's notes and theory comments which will further clarify the session's process as presented in Parts I, II, and III.

These transcripts are not oriented toward illustrative use of *each* Procedure, though some few are deliberately included; such demonstration would be voluminous and repetitive. Beyond use of a few Procedures, these verbatims with their enlightening therapist's notes and theory comments are primarily selected to illustrate the following: expanded awareness in the Intensified Faith Schema's transcendent psyche space, its "closer-to-God" experience, Dialogical Counseling use, and communicative counseling injected into the transcendent psyche space's therapy work. In other words, the transcripts are meant to give a "feel" of Faith Therapy in its wholeness of operation, not specifics.

INTRODUCTION

In the transcripts the reader will find no illustration of the Intensified Faith Schema. Gaps in the transcriptions are used where possible for the sake of saving tape and/or manuscript space, avoiding needless repetition. Additionally, the initial use of the two Crisis Intervention Techniques, Key-word Desensitizing and Energy Transformation Switch, are briefed down and treated in this manner. The Intensified Faith Schema and Crisis Intervention Technique verbatims (and variations) in written form will be found in Chapters III and IV, and the vocal recording of them will be found in the Tapes, if procured. Some tape materials are exact copies of the original verbatims found in Part IV. Other tape materials contain recorded verbatim/demonstrations of the entire Intensified Faith Schema Exercise, its Deschematization Exercise, and Four Standard Use Schema Referents (including the three Usual Positive Ideas). They also demonstrate the Schema Variations' Special Positive Idea (Further Intensified) Meditation, and the Deschematization Exercises for it. (Again, the form and wording for all these are in Chapters III and IV.) As was stated in foregoing parts of this manuscript, there is a special vocal style used in Faith Therapy, one by which I attempt to convey more comprehensive meaning in therapy use with the audio tapes. Much of the communication in this methodology is more readily and thoroughly conveyed through emotionally rich voice tones and other nuances. For this reason vocal recording of the material was also demanded for greater clarity of the total Method.

Because of the intimate and private nature of these verbatim stories, personal permission of each client was obtained for use of the material. I am deeply grateful and trust the reader/listener is also, for the sessions would lose much central importance if taped voices and details were eliminated. These clients considered their permission an offering to God for the help of others. I have striven to handle these offerings with the reverence they are due. However, it is important to note that names and other identifying items (both in the transcripts and tapes) have been changed in order to further protect the client.*

ALSO: As before, in all these verbatims, the *therapist's notes* will be designated as "TN" and set in brackets. If longer, they will be designated as noted but indented as well.

AS MENTIONED: *Comments expressing the therapist's theory* will be made where appropriate, and these will be indicated by "COM.:" in brackets.

NOTE: Some may find the therapist's verbal interaction too intrusive; however, clients seemingly have not found it so. Dialogical Counseling, as stated, came into being as a very extrovertive method which is participatory and in a Ferenczian manner and does assert the therapist's viewpoint, forcefully but respectfully. *Listening* to the tapes will tend to bear out this factor.

*The tapes mentioned above may be ordered from the author: 4251 Berlin Drive, Jackson, MS 39211; price is subject to change. Phone: (601)362-9784.

Chapter X

∾

VERBATIM OF MITCHEL
AT GOD'S CONSEQUENT
OR FEELING POLE

Background Information

(This verbatim is of the taped session referred to in Chapter I; therefore, some additional material may be found in that section.) A few weeks prior to this session, Mitchel had had a therapy session in which the Guided Meditation components of Faith Therapy were utilized. At that time he brought to consciousness and abreacted the awareness of some of his battered child experiences. These had happened between ages two and five with his real parents and prior to his adoption. The following weeks' sessions were largely spent in counseling through and understanding these insights and experiences. This week's session on the tape starts after our getting into the office and with his coughing. However, on the way there, he had told me in the last few days he had contracted pneumonia which had not responded well to the doctor's antibiotic injections, and that the preceding night he had had a memory come to consciousness which so disturbed him he decided to come on to the session because of the memory and its distress and confusion. (Note to tape listeners: throughout this entire session Mitchel's voice is hoarse, somewhat breathless, and he is coughing frequently because of the pneumonia. Additionally, noise and radio music from the nearby waiting room sometimes render the tape difficult to understand. Also, Gene has since given up his pipe and smoking for health's sake. Besides it was frequently a means of hiding personal uncertainty.)

Session Verbatim

[COM.: DIALOGICAL COUNSELING; INTERACTIVE FRIENDSHIP.]

Gene: But at any rate, the thing that came back then with the dream was the experience (of your father's beating you at age five to make you quit coughing). What happened was that you really *relived* the experience last night in the delirium with this pneumonia.

Mitchel: Yeah! That's what it was. And, uh well, it was this morning I started coughing and coughing, and I'm kind of lucky that Evvie was [there]—she had to come back from work. She just got out there and they said, "You go home." You know, 'cause she was still sick. Anyway, I started coughing and coughing and I was freezing to death, you know, and I was running fever, you know.

Gene: Uh huh! Chills and fever together.

Mitchel: And I was holding myself and walking back, and walking and pacing, and walking. You know, just trying to keep my mind off of it some. And all of a sudden I gagged, man, to throw up, and I went lickety-split for the bathroom. And I tripped on that tile and smacked my head; and, anyhow, I mean, it just got me.

[COM: DIALOGICAL COUNSELING; USE OF A CLIENT'S LANGUAGE VERSION AND BEGINNING USE OF LIFE-LOGIC EXPRESSED IN FEELING-THOUGHT]

Gene: Damn! Everything happens at once, don't it?

Mitchel: Yeah! It sure does. It didn't leave much of a knot—but it didn't take much. I just—I just felt so bad I wanted to lay there and cry.

Gene: Yeah!

Mitchel: And I am so sore right now.

Gene: Yeah! I hear you.

Mitchel: I mean, like somebody beat me up with a baseball bat all over my body, it feels like!

[COM: DIALOGICAL COUNSELING: DEALING WITH TRAUMATIC MEMORIES CONTAINING REPRESSED AND ENCAPSULATED AFFECT.]

Gene: You know what the feeling I have [about this] is? That this may be—you remember before when we hit that, uh, business where your daddy broke your collarbone?

Mitchel: Yeah!

Gene: And you went through the pain for about a day afterwards?

Mitchel: Yeah!

Gene: And let the pain [out] that I told you, you know, was locked in.

Mitchel: Yeah! For about three days it did hurt!

Gene: Yeah! Until you worked the feelings through and the memory through like it really was. What I'm wondering is—not only is part of this (the confusion and pain) from the coughing, but if you aren't maybe feeling again what you brought up last night. You see, your daddy beating you at age five for coughing? You see, that you got all that feeling—

Mitchel: No, he beat me on the legs with a wire (a bent coat hanger). I've—

Gene: Oh! He did!

Mitchel: Yeah!

Gene: He didn't beat you on the butt?

Mitchel: Yeah! But that's when the fever came down this morning that my legs hurt.

Gene: That the legs were hurt?

Mitchel: Yeah!

[COM: DIALOGICAL COUNSELING; COGNITIVE STRUCTURING OF "STAYING WITH THE FEELINGS" OF REPRESSED AFFECT.]

Gene: Yeah! Everytime you tackle one of these things where you've got a physical hurt that you had to shut away from you to keep from, you know, just *dying* as a kid, probably you're going to feel some hurt with it. But it will leave. You know, just go on and live through it and not let it, uh, shock you.

Mitchel: Yeah! This left pretty quick. Ah, you know, it was gone by around noon.

Gene: But the association, that shows you (lights pipe) how the mind, you know, can relive for you all this crap that you can get stacked up in it. Did you have any awareness last night of how you felt about your daddy doing that? I'm wondering if the crying that you felt like you needed to do today—and the "sick"— might not have had a part to do with that?

Mitchel: It might have.

Gene: You know, a five year old kid that needs to cry, as bad as we need to cry as grownups, but five year old kids really need to.

Mitchel: You're damned right!

[COM: DIALOGICAL COUNSELING: THERAPIST USE OF THE COMMON SPEECH, COGNITIVE STRUCTURING OF TRAUMATIC MEMORY.]

Gene: And you know—you take something where you can't help it, that's like being blamed for shitting.

Mitchel: Yeah!

Gene: Or getting thirsty.

Mitchel: Yeah!

Gene: You know, it's like, and then I'm hearing, too, that you couldn't—you were not allowed to be sick.

Mitchel: Hell, no! It cost too much money. They didn't want to pay for anything.

Gene: Yeah!

Mitchel: Oh! They were really pissed. They wouldn't, you know, they kept me in the hospital for almost a year after I got my eye poked out—almost a year—because they wouldn't let me go home. Because my Dad had gone up there, and he was ranting and raving and so damned mad at the stuff that was going on, saying, "I ain't going to pay any of this old stuff." (Sniffs) And they wouldn't let me go home.

Gene: Because of him? To protect you from him?

Mitchel: Yeah! Partly that and to make sure that I got the care I was supposed to have.

Gene: Yeah! That's what I was talking about. They knew that by the way he was acting that he wouldn't see that you got the care.

Mitchel: Yeah! Because it did a whole hell of a lot of damage back in there.

Gene: How did that happen, Mitch?

Mitchel: I got stabbed with a stick.

Gene: Yeah! Well, you told me that, but I mean—

Mitchel: I was playing with a stick. I don't remember exactly. I got bumped, and it was like it was coming out of the ground. You know what I mean? Like it come—just—like a cunt hair later than you think. That's how it come.

Gene: Yeah!

Mitchel: It did that. And I think I either tripped or got bumped or something. Boy! And it went sock (gestures with hands as though holding stick thrusting in eye)! You know.

Gene: How old were you, did you say?

Mitchel: I was two, and I can remember it. I'm not kidding!

Gene: I believe you.

Mitchel: I can actually remember the stick coming straight into my eye, and then, nothing! And then this tremendous pain!

Gene: Pain?

Mitchel: God! Boy, that hurt! Well, what happened, I—I fell and hit this thing, and I grabbed it with—the only thing that kept me from getting killed is [that] I grabbed the son-of-a-bitch and fell to one side (gestures with both hands as if falling). You know the bones behind your eyeball?

Gene: Yeah!

Mitchel: I busted one of those.

Gene: It would have gone on into your brain if you had fallen—

Mitchel: By my brain.

Gene: It would have gone on into your brain if you had fallen forward on it. And you fell backwards?

Mitchel: Well, no, I fell like this (gestures as if falling to the *side*).

Gene: To the side.

Mitchel: I grabbed—it was on the ground. I was trying to pull myself up, and I just fell over and just yanked it out and threw it. And I went in the house screaming and hollering! Boy, that hurt!

Gene: Yeah!

Mitchel: (Sighs several times, lightly)

Gene: How did they react to that?

Mitchel: It scared the shit out of them at first.

Gene: Yeah!

Mitchel: Yeah! Really, it—And then my Dad grabbed me up and stopped a taxi—I think it was a taxi.

Gene: Yeah!

Mitchel: Stopped it, you know, and the guy just seen what—and, well, I was bleeding everywhere. And he jumped—jumped in the damned cab and rushed me on to the hospital. And as soon as I got in there, man, somebody was coming at me from all sides wanting to hit me with needles and shit, and that's the last I remember.

[COM: DIALOGICAL COUNSELING; THERAPIST CONFIRMING OF SOME POSITIVE AFFECT IN EARLY SIGNIFICANT RELATIONSHIPS.]

Gene: The last you remember. You know what I'm hearing in that, Mitch, is your daddy DID love you, too.

Mitchel: I think he did then.

Gene: But he was crazy, too.

Mitchel: I think he did then 'cause I can, you know, when I think about it, I can see where it [the craziness] got worse and worse and worse.

Gene: Uh huh!

Mitchel: You know! And it—

Gene: And you are the oldest. And you were the first burden, and then this happens, and that probably took a lot of expense.

Mitchel: And my mother had me when she was sixteen.

Gene: Yeah!

Mitchel: And then two months before I was born they got married.

Gene: Oh! There was a whole lot of uptight and hostility going on.

Mitchel: Yeah! Yeah!

[COM: DIALOGICAL COUNSELING; PROBING FOR EARLY GUILT TRIP AND CONFIRMING CLIENT]

Gene: Have you felt like you caused that—ever?

Mitchel: Hell, no!

Gene: You don't feel guilty for being here.

Mitchel: Shit, no!

Gene: (Laughs and slaps chair arm) Great! Man, great! By God, that's what I say—a kid's got a right to be here, you know, huh? And I—I want to bet you—let me tell you something— now, I'll bet you a full 50% of the [first born] people walking this earth, their mother was pregnant with them before they got married.

Mitchel: Before they got married! You're damned right.

Gene: You know, now nobody likes to face the truth on that.

Mitchel: Shit, yeah!

Gene: But I've married too many of them and counted too many months afterwards, you know, somebody [would say], "Oh! Did you know so-and-so had a premature baby?" and I'd [say], "Well, isn't that nice," and I just never heard anything (none of the implications behind it).

Mitchel: Four months premature, and all—

Gene: Yeah! Well, they're inviting me to play some damned game, you know. So the gal was pregnant, so what? You know, the kid's got a right to be here. They wanted to get married, you know, because of this. Well, maybe it wasn't the ideal love, but at least they loved each other enough to want the kid, you know. And, that's *something*. That ain't *nothing*.

Mitchel: Yeah! That's starting out with something.

Gene: Yeah! And I think the thing that is, you see, in your particular case, having gone through all this damned battered child crap, you see, LATER—there had to be some measure of something very reassuring to you that you were loved on one level.

Mitchel: Yeah! There really was. I mean, it was—

[COM: DIALOGICAL COUNSELING; CONFIRMING THE IRRATIONALITY OF CLIENT'S EARLY LIFE.]

Gene: That [the confusing, rapidly alternating, love/hate experiences] would make it crazy [in early childhood]. See?

Mitchel: It was *here*, and then *here*, and then *here*, and then *here*! And it was weird!

Gene: Yeah! It's a crazy world.

Mitchel: Yeah! It was like one minute (Gene lights pipe) everything looks neat, man, neat. He'd take me out fishing. We'd go down—out in the damned ocean and go fishing for a couple of days or some shit. And then the next week he'd beat the living hell [out of me]. Paranoid! (Sniffs and sighs)

Gene: Well, that's the sort of thing that gives a kid an emotional feeling early in life of everything being crazy or feeling unwanted in some way or the other, or confused between the two, you know.

Mitchel: Yeah!

Gene: And this would account for a lot of confusion and the fact that they would shut their feelings away, uh, would invite you to do a certain amount of that, too, which would account for [the] "why" [of] your forgetting some of these things. You see, like you're not supposed to know how you really feel.

Mitchel: Yeah!

Gene: Which would mean why a lot of pain would go along with that, man.

Mitchel: (Coughing strongly) [I'm] slobbering everywhere.

Gene: That's all right. You're not going to hurt anything.

Mitchel: I shouldn't even be smoking. (Sighs heavily. Rattles ashtray putting out cigarette)

[COM: DIALOGICAL COUNSELING; SUGGESTING GUIDED MEDITATION FOR CLIENT'S HEALING REST.]

[TN: We were in an office without a reclining chair, which is usually used for the Guided Meditation part of the therapy, but I thought the floor would help him relax.]

Gene: You think it would do you any good to just maybe lie down on the floor and do a little meditating without going into—(I had meant to say actual therapy work).

Mitchel: No, I can't lay down (due to lung congestion).

Gene: Oh, you can't.

Mitchel: That's what I mean.

Gene: What about if you sit up and do a little meditating, would it help you rest?

Mitchel: I don't know. I don't know if I can concentrate very good. I just—

Gene: You don't have to concentrate (meaning active—rather than passive concentration), just follow the pictures.

Mitchel: Yeah! That's what I mean. I don't know if I can do it.

Gene: If you want to try it, I was just thinking in some way it might help you relieve some of the tension.

Mitchel: Yeah!

Gene: That goes with it, you know.

Mitchel: Yeah!

Gene: O. K. Can you sit there with it, or do you want to sit in that chair over there where you can lean back a little? (My feeling was that a tilting type of chair would help the relaxation some.)

Mitchel: Yeah!

Gene: O. K. Good! Then we'll just use a, you know, we won't get into a big major level of it, or anything like that but enough to let you sort of feel some of it. I'm going to do something just a little different this time that should be very, uh, I guess what you'd say, it would have a pretty good, uh, (Mitchel coughs) it would have a sort of beneficial dimension to it by way of relaxing the muscles and also relaxing something of the emotions, too.

[COM: BEGINNING USE OF FAITH SCHEMA, MODIFIED LEVEL II, STAGE 4 WITH ITS RELAXATION RESPONSE OMITTED FOR BREVITY.]

Mitchel: (Nods yes)

Gene: O. K. All right then, Mitchel, if you will, just let yourself imagine....

[TN: We will use the Skip Technique in the written verbatim and its recording. (The written Schema form is in Chapter III.) Using the Intensified Faith Schema, Modified Level II, Stage 4, Mitchel was led into his transforming meditative space (which became transcending instead). The Schema

Level is not quite as abstract; and I, therefore, hoped he would find it restful to himself in our using the Guided Meditation Therapy Procedure's Creative Symbolization Procedures. My hope was that he would simply rest in the safety of the Circle. These Therapy Procedures had helped others thus rest in the past, but no such quietness came to Mitchel as the reader will notice. The Physical, Personal Pole of God seems more available through use of non-abstract symbols. The Holy Spirit seems to use these to overlay His/Her presence and form pictures, images, which will convey God's Presence as Person with greater ease and clarity in relating to people understandably as "at least" Person also.]

[COM: GUIDED MEDITATION: CREATIVE SYMBOLIZATION; FOREST OF LIFE, SACRED CIRCLE, KNOLL OF WORSHIP, LIGHT-OF-GOD'S PRESENCE.]

Gene: ... [Mitchel] I'd like you to imagine now being in the middle of a forest, uh, in a strange circular clearing in the middle of the forest (the Forest of Life), a—a big one, a big, circular clearing, and it's grassy, no scrub brush or anything around in it (the Sacred Circle), and the trees form a perfect circle around it. And a strange thing, in about the middle of this circle there's a rather strange looking, low hill, or a high knoll, about tree-top height, that's flat on the top. It looks a little like an Indian mound, but it's *not* an Indian mound. It's a natural phenomenon, a natural happening (the Knoll of Worship). And as I look (note therapist's use of the "*editorial I*" shifting) then, I use my imagination to imagine a strange light that is brighter than daylight itself shining down as though a spotlight right on the top of this flat part of this knoll. It's coming from somewhere up above, but you cannot tell where—a rather strange, powerful light that is brighter than day (the Light of God's Presence). Now as you stand there, and as you look around, how does the forest look to you? How does the clearing look, *and how do you feel?*

[COM: GUIDED MEDITATION; PRE-THERAPY WORK CHECK-OUT.]

Mitchel: (*In a hushed voice which lasts until the end of the Therapy Procedures*) Uh! It looks like it's a bunch of (unintelligible). It's—it's pines.

Gene: Um hum.

Mitchel: It's pines—there's no end to them, no end to them.

Gene: Um hum—just endless huge pines and what?

Mitchel: Yeah! As far as I can see.

Gene: Uh huh!

Mitchel: It looks like a—almost like a log that somebody hasn't—

Gene: Uh huh!

Mitchel: Hasn't logged it—with flowers in there.

[COM: GUIDED MEDITATION; PRESENCE OF HOPE SYMBOL OF GOD'S PRESENCE EVEN THERE (SUNFLOWERS).]

Gene: Oh! Great!

Mitchel: Sunflowers.

Gene: Um hum!

Mitchel: (Sighs. Sighs again heavily) It's—no sound.

Gene: Um hum.

[COM: GUIDED MEDITATION; GOD SYMBOL AS UNKNOWN PRESENCE.]

Mitchel: And, uh (pause and moves) it's like I was all by myself. (Pause) But, I'm not. I can't—I, I, I don't (pause) I *know* there's somebody else there but I don't know who.

Gene: All right, I want you to do something with your imagination I want you to—you said—did you say no wind or no end to the trees?

Mitchel: Oh! I couldn't tell if there was an end or not.

[COM: GUIDED MEDITATION; SYMBOL OF NO BREEZE AS SYMBOL OF LACK OF PNEUMA POWER PRESENT.]

Gene: Oh! You were talking about there was no breeze blowing.

Mitchel: No breeze.

[COM: GUIDED MEDITATION; CREATIVE SYMBOLIZATION; CHANGING THE NEGATIVE FOREST OF LIFE, USE OF LOGOS POWER.]

Gene: O. K. Now what I want you to do is to use your imagination to change that forest, like you had power coming out of your eyes so that everywhere you looked, like with magic, you could change the forest so that it became a good, healthy forest with a lot of mixed up different types of trees, you know. That, uh, evergreen forest couldn't—nothing could live much in it, could it?

Mitchel: Not very easily.

Gene: Right. So change it around. Have a few evergreens here and there of all sorts, big ones and little ones, with plenty of oaks and, uh, hardwood trees, and put some blackberry vines growing through there and a few Virginia Creepers, uh, and maybe some wild grape vines growing up trees. Maybe have some, uh, you know, hickory trees and wild pecan and maybe some wild plum around there, and just make it a good, healthy forest so that life can live in it. You know, with all sizes—underbrush and big trees—all varying sizes. And now how do you experience the forest and see and get it changed? Have you got it changed yet?

[COM: GUIDED MEDITATION; GOD SYMBOL AS PRESENT IN MORE LIFE AND PNEUMA.]

Mitchel: Oh, yeah! That's easy.

Gene: How?

Mitchel: Now I can hear birds.

Gene: Good!

Mitchel: There's a (sigh)—have you ever seen a tufted-eared squirrel? A great big bugger.

Gene: Uh huh! Yeah! Uh huh!

Mitchel: He looks like he's pissed off at me. He's settin' there—

Gene: (Laughs, coughs, laughs)

Mitchel: (Unintelligible)

Gene: Was he "cussin?" You know how they chatter. You call that "cussin."

Mitchel: Chuka—chuka—chuka.

Gene: Yeah! I used to call that "cussin."

Mitchel: Yeah! Chatter.

Gene: He really, really resents your being there. (laughs) "That's his territory," sort of thing.

Mitchel: Yeah!

Gene: O. K.

[COM: GUIDED MEDITATION; MITCHEL'S LURE TO KNOLL-OF-WORSHIP AND LIGHT OF GOD'S PRESENCE.]

Mitchel: I want to go up the hill, though.

Gene: All right. Want to go up the hill?

Mitchel: Um hum.

Gene: Did you say?

Mitchel: Yeah!

Gene: All right. You want to walk up the side of it? (Pause)

Mitchel: It's not—seems like as easy as I thought it would be. It's not, uh—it's not very easy to. (Pause)

[COM: GUIDED MEDITATION; SUGGESTION OF IMAGINED HELP.]

Gene: What do you need to get up there to it? (Lights pipe)

Mitchel: I don't know—it— (Sighs. Long silence.)

[TN: Mitchel suddenly opens his one eye, sits up and looks at

Gene with a strange, startled gaze.]
[COM: GUIDED MEDITATION; SOMEONE HEARD—APPARENTLY
    GOD SYMBOL AS "THE VOICE."]
Mitchel: *Did you say something?*
Gene: No, I just moved. Why? What—what did you hear?
    Sometimes that happens. Wait—close your eyes, lean back. Just
    go with whatever you're feeling. What—did you hear some-
    thing? What did it seem like? (Mitchel is breathing heavily.
    Long silence) I did say "it's"—you know—
Mitchel: No, that wasn't it.
Gene: It was something else?
Mitchel: I can't—I can't get it back now.
Gene: Um hum.
Mitchel: (Sighs)
Gene: Don't try.
[COM: GUIDED MEDITATION; GOD SYMBOL AS VOICE AND COM-
    PANION.]
Mitchel: I'm not. It's like somebody said—(sighs, sighs) *"No!"* But
    not like, uh, not ever, just maybe.
Gene: Um hum. Like you didn't have permission to climb any-
    more?
Mitchel: *Sounded like it was somebody said that to me! I thought you said*
    something!
Gene: Un uh! (Shakes head negatively) It was probably coming
    from inside your own head, probably it was an image inside your
    own head of self-forbidding—it may be sort of (Mitchel coughs)
    something within. It's not unusual. (Tilting chair creeks loudly)
    Sounds like something within yourself that, uh, was saying to
    you....
Mitchel: (Coughs) Well, it was getting hard to climb, and then—
Gene: That came, huh?
Mitchel: Somebody said, *"No!"*
Gene: O. K. Do you want to climb—in spite of somebody telling
    you no? (This is taking into account Mitchel's intense individu-
    ality trait.)
Mitchel: Yeah, I sort of do!
Gene: O. K. Then close your eyes and imagine being back there
    and imagine having the power in your legs to climb it anyhow,
    you know, if that's what you want to do.
Mitchel: (Sighs, sighs) (Leans back and closes his eye again)

Gene: Can you get it?

Mitchel: (Sighs) I'm having—having to try too hard.

[COM: GUIDED MEDITATION; THERAPIST'S INSIGHT-HUNCH, SUG-
GESTION OF REST.]

Gene: Don't try.

Mitchel: Just kind of—kinda goes, an' then it quits.

Gene: All right, why don't you imagine sitting down on the side of
the hill. How high up are you?

Mitchel: (Sighs, sighs)

Gene: Rest a minute. You decide what you want to do?

Mitchel: (Long silence interspersed with heavy breathing) I can't
hear anything else now.

Gene: Well, that's O. K.

[COM: GUIDED MEDITATION; GOD SYMBOL AS PENDING ENEMY OR
VOID.]

Mitchel: Now I hear this (unintelligible) and,uh,have you ever been
in a mangrove swamp, right before a tremendous storm? Or—

Gene: Um hum.

Mitchel: Something makes it silent.

Gene: Silent?

Mitchel: Nothing!

Gene: Um hum.

Mitchel: Nothing!

Gene: Sort of an ominous nothing?

Mitchel: I don't think it's so ominous. It's oppressing. Uh,uh,
now—I've—I've lost it. I've lost it.

Gene: That's O. K. You can always use your imagination just to get
it back. (Mitchel coughs) But relax to it. Don't let it, don't let it
hassle you. If you want to, just imagine yourself—

Mitchel: It's not. It doesn't hassle me. It just—

Gene: O. K.

Mitchel: (Sighs)

Gene: I'm hearing this, that there's some voice inside you sort of
saying to you, "No, you can't climb it, or you're forbidden or
something."

Mitchel: No, it's not. It's like, uh, uh, it's like, uh, it's like I *will*—
but not yet.

Gene: O. K.

Mitchel: That's the way it sounded. It sounded—

Gene: Did it sound forbidding?

[COM: GUIDED MEDITATION; GOD SYMBOL AS COMPANION.]

Mitchel: *No* uh, (pause) kind of natural, I guess.

Gene: Like sort of stating a fact?

Mitchel: Yeah!

Gene: Not either. It wasn't putting you down or putting you up either one. It was just, in friendship, saying, "Hey, this is—"

Mitchel: Yeah! It was like, right now, *NO*, you know.

[COM: GUIDED MEDITATION; THERAPIST'S INSIGHT-HUNCH, SUGGESTION TO RETREAT FROM STRESS POINT.]

Gene: O. K. Then why don't you come back down the hill? If you feel—do you feel like that's probably good advice and that's what you want to follow?

Mitchel: (Sighs, sighs) I won't tell where it is and jump and try to go on up anyway. But I—

Gene: What do you feel like *you want to do* without *anybody*, you know, *anything*, except what *you* feel?

Mitchel: I want to but, uh, uh, kinda—not necessarily afraid, but, uh—

Gene: Like something you want to get used to?

Mitchel: No! A little bit hesitant, cautious.

Gene: Uh huh!

Mitchel: I don't know. I keep losing it, I—

[COM: GUIDED MEDITATION; THERAPIST'S INSIGHT-HUNCH, SUGGESTION FOR GREATER REST.]

Gene: O.K. I tell you what. Why don't you imagine then walking back down the side of that hill and see if this lets you keep the feeling then. It sounds like walking up the hill, there might be a little uptight sort of experience—and see what happens or what you're aware of when you get back down to the bottom. (Mitchel breathes heavily, and there is a long silence) Like where is the squirrel?

Mitchel: I don't know. It, uh—I don't want to walk back down. I may just sit.

Gene: O. K. You want to just sit there—imagine sitting?

Mitchel: Yeah!

[COM: GUIDED MEDITATION; THERAPIST'S INSIGHT-HUNCH OF HELP OFFER.]

Gene: All right, can you go with that mangrove swamp feeling until it disappears? Till you can be comfortable?

Mitchel: (Sighs)

Gene: What I want you to do is to desensitize, sort of, you see, to the—the tension of that *ominous* feeling. If you want to sit there on the side of the knoll—by the hill—that's fine, you know. But there's a time to push yourself and a time *not* to push yourself, and what I'm hearing in this is sort of maybe an inner voice saying, "Hey, don't push yourself right now. Rest." But it may seem ominous to you, yet you may experience it long enough for it *not* to affect you that way longer. (Very long silence. Gene lights pipe) Anything that you want to tell me—then—you just tell me. Let it go anywhere it wants to go—the meditation, where *you* want to go.

[COM: GUIDED MEDITATION, GOD SYMBOL AS COMPANION AGAIN.]

Mitchel: I felt (pause) a comforting love feeling.

Gene: Yeah! Great!

Mitchel: I hear a jaybird somewhere and something else.

Gene: Huh?

Mitchel: You know, that squawks—

Gene: Yeah!

Mitchel: And raves and sputters.

Gene: Um hum!

Mitchel: Man, but it's still—cautious, like, uh, uh (sighs) I've lost it. I've lost it again!

Gene: That's O.K. Just get yourself back to it without trying. Remember this is non-volitional (meaning passive concentration).

Mitchel: It's like, uh, it's like, all right for me to stay where I was.

Gene: Um hum.

Mitchel: Uh, uh, it's not easy. Uh, no further.

Gene: But it feels all right now, are you saying?

Mitchel: Yeah!

Gene: It's not ominous any more?

Mitchel: No, I can stay here, but—

Gene: O.K.

Mitchel: Uh, it's like that was far enough for now.

Gene: Very good! How do you feel about it?

[COM: GUIDED MEDITATION; GOD SYMBOL PRESENT AS FRIEND.]

Mitchel: I feel like it's—*somebody* is with us. It's just like somebody was talking in my head, though. It's weird!

Gene: Uh huh!

MitchelOr somebody sitting next to me talking.

Gene: Um hum!

Mitchel: It's odd!

Gene: But you are now *not* feeling it as an ominous thing?

Mitchel: No.

Gene: You're feeling it as, uh, sort of a warning that first might be threatening and then you understand it's not a warning, it's just—say a piece of advice?

Mitchel: It's just, uh, yeah.

Gene: Healthy advice? From whom?

Mitchel: Yeah! I don't know who from.

Gene: Somebody who cares?

Mitchel: Yeah, it's just take it slow. Like, you know—

Gene: O.K. Hey, neat! (Pause) All right, how are you feeling with it? What? Did you flip out of it a minute? (Flip out of the transcendent state).

[TN: Very long silence. Mitchel again sits up with his eye open and looks around, this time incredulously. There is another long silence.]

[COM: GUIDED MEDITATION, GOD SYMBOL AS VOICE AND FRIEND.]

Gene: What are you aware of now?

[TN: Another long silence. Mitchel's eye remains open and searches around room.]

Mitchel: (In a whisper) Somebody said, "*Good!* That's enough now!"

Gene: What did you say? I couldn't understand you. What did you say? (Gene sits up *very* attentively.)

Mitchel: Somebody said, "*Good!*"

Gene: Very good! I didn't say anything.

Mitchel: I know, *it was the same voice!* Uh, it didn't, I couldn't read it. But these pictures I keep getting, uh, uh, like the maple tree, I just keep getting it. That's all. (The symbol of the maple tree, apparently his Tree of Life, had occurred spontaneously twice before in previous sessions.)

[TN:Mitchel now closes his eye and sits back.]

Gene: That's O. K. Is it like the maple tree is saying— bringing the sense of good?

Mitchel: No, uh, it was, it takes all I can—

Gene: It's O. K.

Mitchel: It's all I can visualize. It's like, uh, say—say you put two pieces of film together, and you see one thing and then, there's a zap—it's different! But it's all right.

Gene: O. K. Good! How do you feel with it?

Mitchel: I felt kindness.

Gene: Hey! Great!

Mitchel: I have a strange sense of having been comforted or—

Gene: Yeah!

Mitchel: As though I was in love.

Gene: Um hum.

[COM: GUIDED MEDITATION; GOD SYMBOL AS THE TOUCH OF LOVE AND **CONFIRMING** CLIENT.]

Mitchel: You know, like somebody loves you and they—

Gene: Uh huh!

Mitchel: Kinda rub you on the neck, or something.

Gene: Uh huh!

Mitchel: You know, just comforted! (Pause)

Gene: Sort of a warm feeling inside?

Mitchel: Yeah!

Gene: Accepted?

Mitchel: Yeah!

Gene: Like, hey you are O. K. (Lights pipe)

[COM: GUIDED MEDITATION; GOD SYMBOL AS **CONFIRMING** CLIENT'S EXISTENCE RIGHT.]

Mitchel: Yeah! Now everything's coolness inside.

Gene: Hey! Good! Hey, man, soak the feeling up real good, huh, so you can recapture it. Man, I'm—hearing this, sort of, as though it was super, super, superimposed upon the image that you have of the maple tree.

Mitchel: Yeah!

Gene: But now, as you see the maple tree you can recall this feeling that you got half-way up the hill here: "Good! Comfort! This is O. K. for now! Be here!" Am I picking it up right? What's sort of, ah, putting it together where you are experiencing it? Or am I sort of—

Mitchel: Pretty much! Pretty much! It's like when I've, uh, uh, that tree, that tree's gone; but I still, I've still got to-to feel a good deal. So I—

[TN:Mitchel opens his eye again and looks at Gene.]

Gene: O.K., good!

[COM: GUIDED MEDITATION; CLIENT'S NEED TO TERMINATE MEDITATION.]

Mitchel: I think I need to sit up, uh—

Gene: O.K., you can sit up, you know. You don't have to stay leaning back. I thought maybe you were more comfortable that way,
but you can sit up if it would be easier (Mitchel coughs). Would
you like to come down out of the meditation first, now? (Chair
squeaks) Or do you want to close your eye and try to stay with
the meditation part? If you do, it would be better to come down
out of the meditation rather than just- [open your eye without
using the Deschematization Exercise].

Mitchel: I'd rather just come down now, uh. (Closes eye again)

[COM: FAITH SCHEMA DESCHEMATIZED BUT WITH SPECIFIC POSI-
TIVE IDEA TO KEEP POSITIVE AFFECT.]

[TN:This was a *very rapid* deschematizing due to Mitchel's
condition.]

Gene: All right, I think maybe you better. You had a, had a pretty
strong experience, and this would be my feeling (too). It would
be wise to come on down now. O. K. Then be able to absorb
this feeling now that you have, and this scene of the forest and
its *aliveness*, the beauty of the grass and the birds and all the rest.
And now, using your imagination, transfer yourself as though
flying by magic, to being back on the mountain top where you
soak up this sense of God's loving you and being with you, and
giving you strength and acceptance without putting down a lot
of laws; and then by magic—as though by magic—flying back
down to the beach where you become aware that you've been
lying there and resting yourself and feeling a new sense of at-
easiness and relaxation and self-acceptance—yet alertness of
mind but able to, you know, be at ease—and—and rested—and
refreshed; then just open your eyes and sit up. (Pause)

Gene: That was neat, man. (Long pause)

[TN:Mitchel sits up, looks about, and seems somewhat confused.]

[COM: DIALOGICAL COUNSELING; POST THERAPY-WORK CHECK-
OUT.]

Gene: Do you want me to go over the diagnostic dimensions of
that with you? Or would you rather just tell me what you experienced it as?

Mitchel: Uh! (Long pause) It's kind of confusing to me. That—

Gene: Yeah! Well, you—you did a pretty profound meditation
there.

Mitchel: Uh—

Gene: Do you realize how good you are at that stuff? (Chair squeaks)

[TN:Mitchel even has a profound and insightful ability by himself and of his own accord to enter and utilize the transcendent, elevated meditative mind mood—the best such ability I have ever encountered.]

Mitchel: No, I don't really. That—

Gene: Man, you are exceptional!

Mitchel: That hadn't occurred to me.

[COM: DIALOGICAL COUNSELING; DEALING WITH THE CONFUSION ACCOMPANYING RAPID CHANGES OF CONSCIOUSNESS STATE.]

Gene: Oh! Yeah! I've told you before. Hey, you are tremendous with your meditative abilities. I have *never* had a client who was as much at home and with the meditation with themselves as you! And now, that means, also, you can work yourself harder more quickly.

Mitchel: Yeah!

Gene: You see, and that this is a sort of *confusing*, then, state—and this is not unusual for it to be a confusing state, when you first come down out of it. You know, even though you come down with no bad aftereffects. The experience of being in meditation will have been so strong for someone like *you* that it sort of, in a sense, superimposes itself for a few minutes or so, you know, maybe sometimes for a few hours even, in some measure, in diminishing degrees, over your everyday experience—a little confusion between the two realities (inner and outer) is what I'm saying.

Mitchel: Yeah, just sort of trying to beat it—

Gene: Yeah, they're both real.

Mitchel: Back and forth.

Gene: Yeah, they're both real. And it's just a matter of focusing on this (present) reality.

Mitchel: Yeah, it does. It blurs and comes back, and blurs.

Gene: It'll quit in a minute.

[TN:I meant by this remark that the dual, simultaneous awareness of both OUTER and INNER REALITIES would cease shortly of its own accord. We talked of this before.]

Mitchel: Well, it's quitting. It's just—

Gene: Yeah! Well, you see, if you weren't so doggone good at it, you wouldn't be able to get that effect. (Laughs) That's the truth. You are *that good* at it, that you can bring that reality with you, right down with you, and *do*. Each time we've done a meditation, you've, you've brought it right down with you, and you've had a little of this [effect] each time.

[COM: DIALOGICAL COUNSELING; FINDING THE RATIONAL IN THE NON-RATIONAL.]

Mitchel: Um-m-m. You know, I was sittin' there, and then somebody said, "*Good*," and then all I could see was the trees.

Gene: Um hum. (Lights pipe.)

Mitchel: And I felt like I was being comforted like (coughs).

Gene: Like being held, and loved, would you say? That's what I picked up.

Mitchel: Yeah! Like—uh, uh, like I did all right, or, uh—

Gene: Yeah! You were accepted.

[COM: DIALOGICAL COUNSELING; **CONFIRMED** BY GOD.]

Mitchel: Uh—

Gene: O. K.?

Mitchel: Yeah, I guess—it—it's hard to tell—

Gene: *Approval*!

[TN: This term is intended to convey the same meaning—a step beyond *only accepted*—meant by Martin Buber by his term "*confirmed*" in one's right to *exist*, as is. (It has ever since been added to the Intensified Faith Schema.)]

Mitchel: *Yeah! That's it!*

Gene: Which is something that people like you and me have a hard time accepting—ever saying, "You know, this is good enough."

Mitchel: But you know, I wanted, uh, I felt glad, uh. (Sighs) I still get—like the trees superimposed on things and all—like you, you know—

Gene: That's O. K.

Mitchel: Uh! Yeah! I know it's just pictures.

[COM: DIALOGICAL COUNSELING; MEDITATION AFTEREFFECTS SLOWLY DIMINISHING.]

Gene: Remember these are just images that overlay sometimes. And as long as you keep them, you know, separate in your head and know what's going on, man, don't knock it.

Mitchel: Yeah! It's—I—I know it. It's—it's all right. It's-(sigh) does it have any—some significance—or something?

[COM: DIALOGICAL COUNSELING; RABBINICAL FUNCTION; THERA-

PIST'S OFFER TO AID IN DEVELOPMENT OF THE COGNITIVE
STRUCTURING.]

Gene: Yeah! It has a great deal of significance, Mitchel. That's why
I asked you if you would like me to give you the diagnosis.

Mitchel: But you know, I feel weak.

Gene: You're tired. Do you know how tired you are.

Mitchel: I feel real weak right now.

Gene: You *are* weak and tired. You've got pneumonia, remember?
And you just tuned in on how tired you were!

Mitchel: Yeah! That—

Gene: That's why the voice came and said, "That's far enough."

Mitchel: *Oh! Man!* (Sniffs) You know, right now I just feel like I
could, I could go to sleep and sleep until Saturday, or something.

Gene: Hurray! Why don't you?

Mitchel: I could, or will. I think I'll try.

Gene: Good! See what I did was—I picked you up when you came
in tonight, I mean, my impression was, hey, you were as tense as
you could be because you'd had this hellish thing come up, you
know, memory last night with that thing. You know, on top of
having pneumonia (Mitchel coughs loudly and chair squeaks),
you know, and that means that inability to relax—you can't feel
your tiredness, and a fellow with pneumonia—

Mitchel: Yeah, I get real hyper like that.

Gene: Yeah! Well, see, *now you're not.*

Mitchel: No, now I feel like I'm—

Gene: Now you're in tune with where you are really at. See?

Mitchel: Yeah! I'm real loose *now*, this—

Gene: And if you can go home in a few minutes here and get you
some good rest, and if you can sleep til Saturday, *sleep til
Saturday, man.* They don't need you that much at work, you
know, uh, because I hear you tuning in now on your body. Now,
maybe this will—and, and opening it to the restoring, healing
powers, you know, that are present in all of us—

Mitchel: Yeah!

Gene: Now, let me tell you now what I did with the meditation.
This particular—

[COM: DIALOGICAL COUNSELING RABBINICAL FUNCTION;
EXPLAINING SYMBOLS AND MAKING THE **NON**-RATIONAL
RATIONAL.]

Mitchel: Is that what—is that what the—the—the hill is? (Gene lights pipe) That stuff?

Gene: I'm going to tell you in just a minute. This forest is the Forest of Life. Now, what we had was an evergreen forest. See, all of life seems like pictures in our head to us, and you had an evergreen forest, which is an emphasis on eternal life, and no fun in life, not real just let down and enjoying existence. No life much lives in an evergreen forest!

Mitchel: No, not much!

Gene: That's what I'm talking about.

[COM: DIALOGICAL COUNSELING; RABBINICAL FUNCTION; THERAPIST'S OFFER OF AID IN COGNITIVE STRUCTURING.]

Mitchel: Just a few birds, maybe a few deer, but not much.

Gene: Yeah, not much, you know, and there's no abundant life in it. So you see—

Mitchel: No, it's pretty sparse.

Gene: That's right. And remember what Jesus Christ said, "I have come that you might have life and life abundantly," which means that O. K., uh, from the Christian viewpoint, what he was talking about was that the forest should not be a doggone pine forest or spruce forest, or redwood!

Mitchel: Yeah!

Gene: It should be—have some in it, but it should be mixed up because these trees all represent people, and life, and uh—and fulfilling relationships. You noticed it was still and no wind was blowing. That's like the breath of God doesn't blow!

Mitchel: Yeah! I see what you mean.

Gene: You can't live there!

Mitchel: After I changed the image, uh—

Gene: You got a real, live thing.

Mitchel: Something—it cooled off, and it was nice and—

Gene: Yeah! ("Whee" sound) The squirrel cussin' (laughs), and what kind? The tufted—? (Laughs)

Mitchel: Chit, chit, chit, chit—givin' me hell.

Gene: I could practically hear it with you. You know, I really could.

Mitchel: I still could hear it! I could hear it!

Gene: Well, that's the thing about it. I go right with this stuff, you know. (I tend to sympathetically, contagiously pick up the client's image with my own pictures.)

Mitchel: It was just one of those great big old, grey, tufted-eared squirrels that you see in the Rockies or something, you know.

Gene: Yeah! I've seen—seen—

Mitchel: Great big dudes, man, delicious eating, you know.

Gene: Well, anyhow—

Mitchel: But he was giving something hell.

Gene: Well, he was giving you hell for being there, you know.

Mitchel: Could be, I don't know.

Gene: Yeah! They're always cussin' at something for—

Mitchel: Oh, yeah! Yeah! (Chair squeaks)

Gene: Well, you see, this—this magic circle in the middle of the forest is the experience of inner at-peaceness with God. In the middle of life's forest is this complete circle that surrounds us with His peace, and it's, it's—this symbol is as old as mankind. That is the first, at age three, any child does is draw a—a first form, (what) they draw is a circle.

Mitchel: Not Anthony (his three year old son).

[COM: DIALOGICAL COUNSELING; AFFIRMING THE CHILD'S DEVELOPING CONSCIOUSNESS AND EGO.]

Gene: Yeah! He would have drawn a circle first. Whether you noticed it or not (an irregular circle); that would have been the first thing that he did.

Mitchel: Well, could be. We—(Gene lights pipe)

Gene: Now, later, it gets into—you usually [first] notice it as a bunch of scratches. You have to analyze it pretty closely (draws an irregular, scratchy circle in the air with finger).

Mitchel: (Makes similar gesture mimicking son's drawings) Maybe so.

Gene: O.K. That's—that's a circle. See?

Mitchel: Yeah! I guess it is!

Gene: It's a circle. It may not be—yet—perfectly round, like we're gonna do, but you see it's a circle.

Mitchel: He draws good ones now.

Gene: Yeah! See! But it was a circle. Now, the next thing he'll draw is this plus mark thing—remember—that we used for the symbol (the "Plus-mark" in an earlier session).

Mitchel: Yeah! He's been drawing a lot of geometric kinds of stuff.

Gene: O.K.

Mitchel: Triangles, and diamonds, and squares, and circles, and such.

Gene: This is the Self-symbol—the Inner Self picture—(with finger draws in the air a circle with a plus mark and radials in it).

Mitchel: Yeah, and he does *plus*.

Gene: And zat—and that helps you grow your personality.

Mitchel: He calls them *X's*.

Gene: Yeah! O.K. Hey, and he's helping his own—see, he's helping his own personality grow with that—by doing this. Carl Jung was doing these—was drawing mandalas, they are called—he was doing them when he—when he died. But anyhow, the—we find that in the symbolism of the mind, this inner circle in this forest of life, is the point of safety and worship, which is what we mean, you know, in—regardless of how you interpret life as being—(Mitchel coughs) or if it is nothing more than a dream symbol or whether God's real or what, you know. This is it, that this is the—the sense of religious safety, or, "hey, it's safe to be in life," and when you get that forest straightened, now, you've got something. It's natural for you to want to go up that hill, and this hill or knoll is the high place in all of our collective minds where gods were worshiped, and God is symbolized by light there. And, this is what you were wanting to go towards—the experience of the Light.

Mitchel: (Sniffs) Yeah, I wanted to see what was in it.

Gene: Yeah, you wanted to see what was in it. And it is like it would have been—this was the feeling I had, without putting any words into your mouth, because you were beginning to, as you climbed to become aware of your tiredness. Now your body, it really was tired, see, like you're feeling now, and I think as you climbed and were getting Godward—

Mitchel: No, I wasn't, I wasn't aware of being tired (pause) until (pause) somebody said, "*No!*" It was like I was excited or something.

Gene: Oh, yeah, that was where you were trying it then.

Mitchel: Yeah! It was like I couldn't wait to see what that was.

Gene: Oh, yes.

Mitchel: And then somebody said, "*No!*"

Gene: "No!"

Mitchel: And then I said, "uh-h-h!"

Gene: And then the swamp feeling.

Mitchel: Yeah, just—

Gene: Like disappointment.

Mitchel: That's right. I didn't want to go back down the hill. I just wanted to sit right there.

Gene: Yeah! And why you stayed with the feeling. Why did you stay with the feeling? 'Cause, ah, very frankly, I'll tell you what I interpret the voice as. You want to know?

Mitchel: Yeah!

[COM: DIALOGICAL COUNSELING; THERAPIST'S RABBINICAL FUNCTION AS OFFERED INSIGHT-HUNCH.]

Gene: *The Voice of God!* (A verbal Self-symbol)

Mitchel: (Pause) Yeah! (Softly)

Gene: In other words, this is, it's—it has no sound, yet it seems like you should remember—

Mitchel: It was as distinct as if you said it yourself!

Gene: And yet you can't, and you can remember what it sounds like—

Mitchel: And then when it said, "Good," it was the same voice, but—

Gene: Um hum! Comforting this time.

Mitchel: I felt (pause) I felt good from it.

Gene: Yeah! It was trying to say—it was God saying, "Hey, don't push yourself up this hill of 'worship;' you're going at your speed. That's good enough for now."

Mitchel: Yeah, this is what I caught!

Gene: In other words!

Mitchel: Like—

Gene: Yeah!

Mitchel: I did all right, you know. Just cool it for now.

Gene: Cool it, man, you know.

Mitchel: Yeah!

[COM: DIALOGICAL COUNSELING; THERAPIST'S RABBINICAL FUNCTION OF OFFERING PERSONAL BELIEF.]

Gene: And this is the thing that people don't understand— that God does speak to us from our Inner Self-spark! That is the spark struck from *Him*, you know, that is ours—in us.

Mitchel: (Softly) Yeah!

Gene: And that's His love and His voice coming. Now, Jung never would *say* that this was the voice of God. He just said *people experience this* as God's voice.

Mitchel: He (Jung) calls it the *Id* or something like that?

Gene: No, he just called it the *Voice* and the self. It's a symbol of the Self, but it's a verbal symbol. It's a *communicating* symbol.

Mitchel: Yeah!

Gene: And this is God.

Mitchel: Yeah!

Gene: And the care, and then—like it was the symbol of "the Father Tree" (and/or the Tree of Life) was there, you know.

Mitchel: Yeah-h-h! (Sniffs)

Gene: Bringing with it, saying, hey, this is the way God loves. (Pause) And that's why I felt the tree kept coming in. That was *two* trees.

[COM: DIALOGICAL COUNSELING; THERAPIST'S "STAYING WITH" CLIENT'S FEELING AND MOOD.]

Mitchel: Usually when I see the tree [TN: The Tree had spontaneously appeared—but was not introjected then—in his first Guided Meditation.] it's—uh-h, it's almost a silver maple. You know what a silver maple [is]?

Gene: Yes. Uh huh.

Mitchel: You know how they ripple when the wind blows.

Gene: Oh! Yes! That's beautiful. Uh-huh.

Mitchel: Yeah! Well, it wasn't rippling. I mean I could feel the breeze; but it was like—uh—just a little sigh. Mostly it was like it was calm. (Was all this the mystery of the Pnuema?)

Gene: Not stirred up—but just, sort of, goin' with things.

Mitchel: A little bit. It—

Gene: Hey! Neat!

Mitchel: And when I seen it like that, you know, I felt all right.

[COM: DIALOGICAL COUNSELING; THERAPIST'S RABBINICAL FUNCTION OF MAKING THE NON-RATIONAL RATIONAL.]

Gene: Hey! Good! But I have to interpret this thing as from my own past experience with meditations and of dreams in all these years of research that I have done on this, you know, the empirical observation, which, you know, I research something like this by measuring it. I can't produce this for somebody. It comes in their own head.

Mitchel: Yeah!

Gene: And the response, though, is the same in everybody. Somewhere you can see it right, and if they will listen to this God-voice within them, which is where we all have heard God mostly is in the inner, quiet voice, inner still voice, and yet it is as powerful as the thunder! I don't know how to describe it. It is very calm, and it's as powerful as lightning and thunder, you know. But when it speaks, it speaks with affirmation and calm, and it's O.K. If you will stay with it, even though it may upset you, if you stay with it, you get this feeling of O. K. That's why I had you sit when you got that ominous feeling, like being forbidden. And then here was this, "Hey, man, you're loved!"

[COM: DIALOGICAL COUNSELING; THERAPIST'S RABBINICAL FUNCTION OF AFFIRMING **GOD'S CONFIRMING**.]

Mitchel: Yeah! That was what it was like! It's like—"Hey, I love you!"

Gene: (Quoting the Voice) "Hey! I love you! That's—that's far enough for *NOW*." You noticed—

Mitchel: Yeah! It's like—

Gene: You *can* do it.

Mitchel: It's like I'll be able to get there. It's just—uh, like I've gotta wait. Like I've gotta take it easy!

Gene: Right. And, you see, your own body's tiredness may have been speaking in through your very soul at that time, too, saying, "Hey, look this is no time to go through something as—quite as-as big as your experience could be with this.

Mitchel: Yeah! Well, every time I have meditated, you know, deeply, it,ah, I have always come out with—very tired.

[TN:This "tired"phenomenon often occurs when one has done a lot of *spiritual* therapy work.]

[COM: DIALOGICAL COUNSELING; THERAPIST'S RABBINICAL FUNCTION OF EXPLICATION.]

Gene: Yeah!

Mitchel: Always, I have always been very tired.

Gene: Yeah!

Mitchel: And, uh—

Gene: This comes from a lot of muscular tension a lot of times. And then the person does a lot of emotional *work*, Mitchel. A lot of people do some *profound spiritual work*, and when you do spiritual work, you do *profound emotional work*. It's like you've just been through something big, and you feel good with it, but you do feel sort of a strange tiredness at the same time.

Mitchel: Yeah! It's sort of, uh, not quite exhaustion but like—

Gene: No.

Mitchel: You had enough.

Gene: Yeah! Worked!

Mitchel: Yeah!

Gene: That's the best way I know—it's emotion—it's work!

Mitchel: It felt like—like you've just busted your ass for several hours or something, and you was tired.

Gene: Yeah! And you see, did you know a person can't stay in (Guided Intensified Faith type) Meditation—in Meditation Therapy type meditation, I don't know about other kinds—but you can't endure longer than an hour and forty-five minutes to two hours maximum without getting headaches. People do that much work. And some chemical changes occur in the body that do not occur otherwise, too, in meditation, and this is a measurable factor.

Mitchel: I didn't know that.

Gene: Yeah! And so, you see, it is—for a person who puts themselves into it, like you put yourself into it—see, not everybody can benefit themselves as much as you do.

Mitchel: I wish they could!

Gene: Oh, boy! I do, too, because they could sure get a lot out of it.

[COM: DIALOGICAL COUNSELING; THERAPIST'S RABBINICAL FUNCTION OF ATTUNEMENT TO THE "VOICE" AS POSSIBLE EARLIER VOICE OF GOD.]

Mitchel: You know, I—I can't be positive, but it seems like that was the same voice. Uh-h, I used to have an MGB (a small car) and I jacked it up and was workin' on it.

Gene: Yeah! (Chair squeaks)

Mitchel: And I looked off over like this (turns head) or somethin', and some, like some (one was)—I didn't know anybody was around—saying, "Look!" Then I looked up, man, and the damned thing was falling, and I caught it, and it pushed on my head. Well, I stayed in the hospital for several days. I thought I was going to DIE!

Gene: You told me about that before.

Mitchel: Yeah!

Gene: It didn't break your skull, but it put a lot of pressure—

Mitchel: It put a hell of a dent in it, though.

Gene: Yeah!

Mitchel: I've still got some dent there where the skull was—weird!

Gene: Was pushed, was pressed. Your skull held away the car, almost?

Mitchel: And something said, "*Look!*"

[TN:Mitchel had told me this incident previously, but not of hearing the voice—only of seeing the car falling as though in slow motion. (This is the sort of *spiritual* story a counselor using Faith Therapy hears not infrequently as clients begin to trust him and his/her honesty about the reality of a spiritual world.)]

Gene: You didn't tell me about the voice before.

Mitchel: Well, I—I didn't remember, uh, til now! (He snaps his fingers.)

Gene: Hey! Great, man!

Mitchel: Um-m-m-m. I don't know if it was the sound of it or what. It—it seems like—

Gene: The same voice?

Mitchel: And it said, "Look!" And like, "Oh, oh, my God!" And I—

Gene: That's when the time slowed down for you, didn't it?

Mitchel: Oh, you're damned right! It just seemed like it was—like that (gestures with hands and arms as though pushing weight up), and my arm kept goin' up; and I caught it, and I don't know what happened, but it just pressed on me like that, and I went, "Hell, no!" (Pushes hands up more forcefully)

Gene: And you pushed it back?

Mitchel: And I lifted that son-of-a-bitch off the ground and turned my head over and put it down (Chair squeaks, snaps fingers) and was out!

Gene: I remember you telling me about that.

Mitchel: Those two cops saw me pick the damned thing up!

Gene: And, and the cops came and, and got it off of you.

Mitchel: And they, they—

Gene: 'Cause they saw it.

Mitchel: And one of them had to lift up, and he couldn't—he didn't get the wheels off the ground. He had to just—like lift the body up some, and the other one pulled me out by the feet, and I was unconscious. This is what they were telling me about. But they were, (pause) you know like people hear of things like that happening, it's just that the shock—when you see something, you do something.

Gene: Yeah! O. K. What does that say to you, Mitchel? Who's with you, and who really loves you?

Mitchel: Uh-h. (Sighs) Somebody must—

Gene: (Laughs) Who're you O. K. by, you see?

Mitchel: Yeah.

[COM: DIALOGICAL COUNSELING; THERAPIST'S SHARING OWN RELIGIOUS CONVICTION VIEWPOINT.]

Gene: Now this is what I'm trying to say to you, you see, is simply this: remember, I'm a preacher; and I've—I've told you—

Mitchel: Oh! Yeah! I understand.

Gene: I'm talking from what my viewpoint is, but this is how I've come to experience this same sort of thing in life. That is, hey, somebody *does* love me. Now my parents weren't "that good" parents, either, you know, I didn't have a battered child syndrome background of the cruelty that you experienced; but my parents were hard and unforgiving in a lot of things, but they were good, too, like you were talking about a while ago—your daddy, you know, grabbing you up as a baby and running with you to the doctor and just *doing anything.*

Mitchel: Yeah! He nearly went nuts at the hospital.

Gene: Yeah! But, you see, he was confused. He was not strong enough emotionally to handle all of life, and this gave you the confusion. *But why did you survive in the midst of all of this?* You see, it's this inner something in you (Mitchel coughs) that got in touch, undoubtedly, (Mitchel coughs again) with—with this source of life in the universe, which I have to say is God, and manifests itself not only as, you know, as Self symbols in various ways like the star that we were talking about and the stuff that, uh, Anthony is drawing now and all on the inside, like the tree, but also manifests itself as the Voice; and when it comes as the Voice—to me it has always seemed somehow a person called God. I can't isolate It from—hey, at the center of all this power in the universe, It has personality like me and It loves me; and then It—He/She loves me or whatever, you know, because It's personness to me. I experience It that way, and I'm not going to lay that trip on anybody else, but I can't help but say this is how I've experienced It, and it's like what I experienced Jesus Christ as being like—*not* like he was always painted to me, you know, like the overlay of how my parents, when they were at their worst, were.

Mitchel: Yeah.

Gene: You know, that's all I had. The most love I had to build on was like, hey, they could take you—rush you to the doctor but also would let you get a stick stuck in your eye and put it out.

Mitchel: Yeah!

Gene: You know, or who might beat the hell out of you. That was an imperfect love; but at its best, it was a faint shadow of the love God has for us.

Mitchel: It was better than nothing at all.

Gene: Yeah! It was enough to help build on, and I think this has been—they gave you enough love to help build on—in spite of their craziness. Yeah! And this has let you open inside yourself. I'll, I'll bet you that if you could go back and remember, and say, if we had time as—as you feel better, go back far enough with your memories—as these become less fearsome—there's a very good chance that you will remember being aware of that Voice very early in your life.

Mitchel: Could be! (Tape fades)

END

[COM: THIS ENTIRE SESSION WITH GUIDED MEDITATION SEEMED TO CONTAIN MUCH PERSONAL TYPE SYMBOLIZATION, AND I CONCLUDE ITS PLACE WAS AT GOD'S PERSONAL OR CONSE-QUENTIAL POLE. I LATER LOST CONTACT WITH MITCHEL, BUT THE LAST I HEARD OF HIM HE WAS RUNNING A MOUNTAIN RETREAT CENTER FOR CHURCH YOUTH. THAT SEEMED APPRO-PRIATE GROWTH FOR HIM.]

Chapter XI

VERBATIM OF DENNY IN SELF-DIRECTED THERAPY AT MODIFIED LEVEL II, STAGE 4

Background Information

Denny (a nickname) is of a semi-rural background from a skilled tradesman's family in which he is the youngest of five children, three boys and two girls. His parents had grade school or less education and were poorly emotionally adjusted, although the client has an I.Q. of 147 as indicated by psychological testing, but it still seemed strange in view of his background and current behavior. Perhaps he had lived more by perceptions than by *organized thought* before now.

He is in his mid-twenties, and after high school graduation had all but "dropped out." He is an excellent musician (guitarist), who spent several years "fooling around" with all sorts of drugs, did some odd jobbing (mostly musical and welding), was highly irresponsible and highly dependent, and had become filled with existential despair. Approximately three years prior to this session he had met and married a divorcee with three children, had difficulty assuming family responsibilities but began to do so reluctantly, and constantly fought an inner battle to "drop it" and escape alone. However, he found through his counseling that he had grown to enjoy the success he discovered through self-respect and acceptance of responsibility at work (his first stable job). He was given a supervisory position as he manifested his inborn caring and creative leadership capacities.

Upon the birth of his own son some several months prior to this session, he had undergone a severe attack of regressive emotional problems, though he continued to function well at work. The birth of his son had again emotionally brought to the foreground his own inadequately parented child type of problems, this time on a deeper level. This led to a return to weekly therapy sessions, with considerable additional work given to striving to overcome his personality problems. At the time of this session, he had been my client off and on for approximately three years; and though he originally claimed atheism (his upbringing had given him no formal religious training whatsoever), he had been willing to utilize Faith Therapy's Guided Meditation component in spite of its religious base simply because of its ability to help him get into his own head without drugs. A sort of slow development of self-chosen Christian beliefs began to develop about one year prior to this tape, but the development was strictly on his terms and with his own insights, which did not reflect my current personal convictions (though mine had been similar in my own faith development). A warm, personal friendship grew between the client and me as the client was convinced that no private beliefs would be pushed upon him in the therapy process. However, he felt that if his personal symbolism led him in a religious direction, that fact would be acceptable to him.

Denny is another client who has a high personal aptitude for entering the transcendent mind state by his own volition. This seems to be due to his rich imagination and symbolic visualization capacities. He is the rare type of client who apparently, of his own volition and with the therapist's request that "he close his eyes and enter his own desired meditative state," can do so at will within a few minutes. Therefore, much work has been accomplished in this manner. However, there are times when he desires the Faith Schema or the therapist's help be used to lift him to a higher level of meditative capacities, such as in this particular session. For persons of this sort, who have a strong capacity to enter the transcendent psyche space upon their own after initial help from the therapist, a very brief additional Schema Form is usually most adequate. Furthermore, they seem to have an ability to know inwardly in advance to what faith level they need to proceed. The particular matter which had brought Denny to therapy at this time was a very disturbing dream from a couple of nights before. It was of an old house or school out in a rural section, abandoned, and in a dilapidated state with the roof crumbling in. He had found himself inside the house with the roof about to fall on him and had felt himself terrorized. Later, in doing Dialogical Counseling about the dream, he had an intuitive flash which visually symbolized the terror to him as a huge, giant woman standing behind him with a large foot about to crush him.

It may be of interest to the reader that following the current session Denny took another powerful step forward in integration of his personality with a much higher level of improved self-image and personality functioning.

The tape and verbatim begins at the conclusion of use of the Intensified Faith Schema, Modified Level II, Stage 4.

Session Verbatim

Gene: Now in the name of the Father, the Son, and the Holy Ghost. Amen.

[COM: GUIDED MEDITATION; SELF-DIRECTED THERAPY. THERE WAS NO OPPORTUNITY FOR A PRE-THERAPY WORK CHECK-OUT SO THE THERAPIST "STAYS WITH" THE IMAGERY AS IN "STAYING WITH" THE FEELINGS.]

Denny: Uh! There's an image that come up.

Gene: O.K.

Denny: I was viewing it as though I was some fifty feet up in the air.

Gene: Um hum!

Denny: I saw a stretcher; and my body was lying on the stretcher, and there was a woman walking around, uh, translucent.

[TN: This seems to be the appearance of the basic Existential Threat of Non-being. In Jungian concepts it would be his negative anima bewitching his consciousness and ego with his Self looking on objectively and from above. Remember from the relevant dream matter that this was the "giant woman with the big foot and about to step on me." Now please take note of how the psyche, as a self-regulating entity, and through the unifying center of the Self, resolves the conflict and brings it to consciousness as the therapy work proceeds.]

Gene: O.K.

Denny: Uh, long robe.

Gene: Long robe?

Denny: Yeah.

Gene: O.K.

Denny: And, uh, she was just walking around the stretcher.

Gene: Uh huh!

Denny: And, uh, she was drawn to my face, like, [she] kept moving toward my face. And, uh, my spirit or whatever it is that was viewing the body—

Gene: Um hum!

Denny: And there's, there's the body.

[COM: GUIDED MEDITATION; THERAPIST ALERT TO PRESENCE OF POSSIBLE UNCONSCIOUS SUICIDAL FEELINGS SO THERAPIST GOES ON "STAND-BY" HELP ALERT.]

Gene: Um hum! (Pause) All right! What are you feeling with that? Can you be there with that and see what that feeling is saying to you? Is it better to be above it, or better again, or better to be down (pause) with it—which way would you feel most comfortable with what's going on?

Denny: Uh!

[COM: GUIDED MEDITATION; THERAPIST GOES WITH THE FLOW OF SELF-DIRECTION (WITH HOPE).]

Gene: Or where do you want to be?

Denny: Well, my body rises from the stretcher and goes back to where I was to begin with.

Gene: Oh-h-h! Hey!

[COM: GUIDED MEDITATION; POSITIVE HEALING IMAGERY STARTS TO WORK.]

Denny: And the woman is still walking around the stretcher and just (pause) fades away.

Gene: Oh, neat! (Laughs) Like she's just gone?

Denny: Huh?

Gene: Like she's just gone?

Denny: Uh, everything's gone.

Gene: O.K. Where are you then?

[COM: GUIDED MEDITATION; CLIENT'S CHOICE OF THERAPY OPERATIONAL LEVEL AND STAGE.]

Denny: I'm standing on my (pause) cliff. (Apparently at the Faith Schema Mountain-top Scene.)

Gene: O.K.

Denny: Right at the edge but not feeling threatened.

Gene: O.K. (Pause) I like what you did with connecting yourself back to your body. Now, you see, you separated off from the ego, which is represented by the body (pause) into your Real Self, God-spark Self, and then you brought it back together.

That's good! That was good perspective to be able to do it, though. (Pause)

[COM: GUIDED MEDITATION; CLIENT "ASKING GOD" AND PERSONAL PRAYER ANSWER.]

Denny: Also, while I am standing on the edge, I (pause) don't know what to do, so I just asked God, you know, "Where do I go from here?"

Gene: O.K. Good!

Denny: And I'm awaiting for the answer. (Long pause) And, uh, the answer that comes back is that, "You're already there."

Gene: (Pause) Hey!

Denny: And I see (pause) I'm picturing myself—on the cliff, and again I'm viewing it from far away.

Gene: O.K.

Denny: As though I'm (pause) as though I *am* with God, you know, looking down.

Gene: All right!

[COM: GUIDED MEDITATION; CLIENT AWARENESS OF "SELF-EGO PSEUDOPOD" EXISTENCE.]

Denny: A higher scene (pause) not that I've separated myself!

Gene: No! I'm hearing you're, you're able to go between the two, and that's good! You see, that's the *transcendent* and the *transforming,* [Faith Schema Levels] like the ego's on the transforming level, and the [Self] above is the transcending and it gives an overall viewpoint. What I hear you doing is tying both together.

Denny: O.K. It seems that I've gone to a higher level again.

Gene: O.K.

Denny: And I've gone about a mile. I left myself at that cliff. And now, I'm at another cliff.

[COM: GUIDED MEDITATION; THERAPIST AWARE OF SELF'S OBJECTIVE OBSERVER NEED FOR RESOLUTION.]

[TN: It seems Denny has many "selves," "multiminds," or personality fragments, which his Self must integrate or otherwise deal with constructively. Sometimes the Self will choose the best way unassisted.]

Gene: O.K.

Denny: Much higher! (Pause) And I'm in a white robe.

Gene: All right!

Denny: Oh, man! Now (pause) there's, uh, blood coming from the backs of my hands. [TN: Indication of Christian concept of cross-like suffering in life.]

Gene: Blood?

Denny: Yeah!

Gene: O.K. You want to look at it and see what it looks like? How do you feel about it?

[COM: GUIDED MEDITATION; CLIENT PRAYER—"ASKING GOD" AND ANSWER.]

Denny: Well, I don't understand it. I mean, why would I have blood there, I'm asking God, "Why do I have blood there?"

Gene: Very good.

Denny: He said, "I've got my own damned," well, he didn't say "*damned*"—I added that, because I felt that. "I've got my own cross that (pause) I have to be nailed to." (Pause)

Gene: (Quietly) Um hum.

[COM: GUIDED MEDITATION; CLIENT AWARENESS OF NEGATIVITY TOWARD PERSONAL SUFFERING.]

Denny: Which, uh, you know, I don't want to be nailed to no cross. (Sniffs)

Gene: Uh huh.

Denny: (Pause) But the blood's on the back of my hands—not in the palms. An' I don't understand it. (Pause)

[COM: GUIDED MEDITATION; THERAPIST ON "STAND-BY" USES DIALOGICAL COUNSELING TO CLARIFY AND HELP IF NEEDED.]

Gene: I don't either. Whether—can you get—? I guess what I'm being confused by is the difference between the symbolism of carrying a cross, and there is some suffering in life—or being killed. I'm getting—

Denny: I'm bogged down.

Gene: It's a, it's a confused picture of what you're—

Denny: Now, what I'm feeling is—it's, it's changing, it's kind of frightening.

Gene: O.K.

[COM: GUIDED MEDITATION; DREAM-LIKE SYMBOLISM CHANGES ITSELF WITH SOME PURPOSE.]

Denny: But the cross is now a knife, and sticking up in the ground, and a—I'm attached to it. And I'm (Pause—)

Gene: Oh!

Denny: Uh, drawn away, I'm drawn away from it. And there's this great big—I'm real little, *real little*, about yeah high (Gestures with fingers). [TN: His real ego?]

Gene: O.K.

[COM: GUIDED MEDITATION; NEGATIVE ANIMA APPEARS AGAIN.]

Denny: And, uh, there's this big towering figure (pause) with this *big foot*. (Huh!)

Gene: O-O-O. K-K-K. H-e-y! Stay with it, now, I think you got to it automatically, didn't you?

Denny: Yeah!

Gene: Is that the feeling you were looking—that we were talking about?

Denny: Yeah, that's what triggered me. But I'm viewing it from the—

Gene: The perspective of above.

[COM: GUIDED MEDITATION; CLIENT GAINS SELF-DESTRUCTIVE INSIGHT.]

Denny: Yeah! And not—I *am* the, the actual person that's threatening to stomp on—the *little* me.

[TN: Perhaps also, this is a projection upon his own infant son as well as his attitude towards his own ego.]

Gene: *You're* the person that's threatening to stomp—stomp the little— n-e-a-t! O.K.! Where is that sort of crap coming from?

Denny: (Pause) I don't know. I can't get out of the big person because I'm, I'm wanting to stomp the little—*of course!* I want to stomp the little person, don't I?

[COM: GUIDED MEDITATION; THERAPIST'S USE OF *CLIENT'S LANGUAGE VERSION*, THERAPIST'S USE OF THE INSIGHT-HUNCH.]

Gene: Uh-h, that's what you said. (Long pause) Sounds like you hate yourself, and I'm wondering why. [TN: Therapist's insight-hunch] Or, I don't know, don't let me lay a trip on you. (Pause) That's—(pause) Where did that come from? Where the hell did that come from?

Denny: Well, I actually, you know, *hate* the little person. That's what I'm seeing.

Gene: Oh-h-h! You do?

[COM: DIALOGICAL COUNSELING; CLIENT GAINS PERSPECTIVE, OFFER FOR CREATIVE SYMBOLIZATION HELP.]

Denny: But I'm at a different level than—than I normally am because I normally *am* the little person.

Gene: All right, do you want to do something therapeutically right there that can be helpful?

Denny: Uh-h!

Gene: Do you want some feed-in from me? [TN: Therapist's Insight-hunch offering.]

Denny: Hold off for just a second. (Said smilingly)

Gene: O.K.! Tell me if you want it.

Denny: Well, not right now. (Smiles) You just back off. But I picked up—I don't, I don't stomp him.

Gene: Very good.

[COM: GUIDED MEDITATION; SELF-DESTRUCTIVE URGE BECOMES SYMBOLICALLY VERY REAL.]

Denny: And, he's a—it's a crucifix. And, oh man, it's no longer an act or myself.

Gene: Um hum. Um hum.

Denny: I kiss it.

Gene: What happens? (Long pause)

Denny: I put it back down on the ground. (Long pause) And then I turned away from it, and just walk off sadly, I might add. (Pause) And I'm really feeling (pause), uh, really, really feeling bad (pause) that I feel that.

[TN: Note the personality equity need injected by the Objective Observer dimension of Denny's Self.]

[COM: DIALOGICAL COUNSELING IN GUIDED MEDITATION.]

Gene: That—you regret the fact that you walked away?

Denny: Yeah! Yeah! I feel like I'm going to walk away.

Gene: O.K.

Denny: Now I've got to turn, you know, turn my back on him.

Gene: You've *got* to, *or* is that a choice?

Denny: It's a choice.

Gene: Yeah! How can you make that choice? I'm not—

Denny: It's a choice.

Gene: Huh?

Denny: It's my free choice.

Gene: O.K. I'm not going to say that I think it's wise—

Denny: But the question now would be, that comes to my mind, why would I turn back on a small crucifix and walk away?

Gene: Um hum.

Denny: And, I'm just walking slowly up the hill? (Long pause) When I turn back the crucifix is not a crucifix, it's a—it's a marker on a tombstone.

Gene: O.K.

Denny: A marker on a grave, rather. (Pause)

Gene: Anything written on it? (Pause)

Denny: *Death*. It just says—death! (Pause) I'm, I'm really confused walking uphill. I don't know which direction to go or what to do. (Looks really distressed)

[COM: GUIDED MEDITATION; THERAPIST'S DIRECTION, CREATIVE SYMBOLIZATION OF "LOGOS-POWER" USE.]

Gene: All right. Do you want some help and guidance on it?

Denny: Yeah!

[COM: GUIDED MEDITATION; CREATIVE SYMBOLIZATION OF "FEEDING THE WEAK OR MONSTEROUS".]

Gene: O.K.! Let me make a suggestion, that you turn around then go back, pull up the tombstone, throw it away, dig that little *you* (that is on the crucifix) *up*. Then touch it with a sense of *powerful touch* (more than yourself)—*Logos-power* and restore it to life. Take it off the crucifix. *Now, what does this little you need?* It needs some sort of nurturning, or something given to it—it sounds like to me. Some sort of—is it hungry? What is it it desires?

[TN: Logos-power (the speech with creative-meaning power) as conceived of in these therapy procedures is a creative-person-thought-feeling which may be used to change and transform things. Also, it may be defined to clients as "the creative-person-thinking-feelingness which was in Christ, and since we, too, have a spark of God's life in us, we, too, can use it with imagination in therapy fantasies."]

Denny: Uh, it's hungry for just plain love and nothing else.

Gene: O.K. Now what I'm hearing is that's, that's why it's little. It's symbolized by the lack of food. I suggest to you then that you just have with you, just almost by magic, the—the sort of food that "little you" needs and everything else—and start feeding. (Pause) Now just keep on feeding—til there's no, no further desire on the "little you's" part and see what happens. (Long pause)

[COM: GUIDED MEDITATION; STRENGTHENING SELF-EGO AXIS (FEEDING IS THE BASIC WILL'S ACT TO BESTOW LIFE AND GOOD UPON.)]

Denny: Well, coming from the "little me" directly toward the "big me" it's a (pause) a real feeling that I'm gonna like you. I love you.

Gene: O.K. Good! Keep feeding it.

Denny: But it's helpless. It's feeling helpless.

Gene: Yeah! Keep feeding it. That is, you've got all the food you want, anything that you need, that it needs. Just keep feeding it.

Denny: (Pause) That's, it's somewhat bigger than it was.

Gene: Good! It should be growing. That's good. That's right. It's going in the right direction. (Pause)

Denny: Now, what I'm feeling for it, it's a (pause) well I'm kinda saying,

[TN: Termination bell sounds]

[COM: THERAPIST IGNORES BELL. SURGEONS MAY NOT STOP IN MID-OPERATION.]

Denny: Look, I know, man, I know how it is.

Gene: Uh huh!

Denny: I love you, but—hell, what can we do about you? You know, I've got—myself to take care of. I can't, and I have nothing to give you except this food that's—that's here.

Gene: That's all right. Just keep right on feeding it. Now let you—let yourself stay with this guided, directed therapeutic fantasy just to keep feeding it and letting it grow. You've got an inexhaustible supply.

Denny: Uh, I'm feeding it. Now, I'm not handing him food. He's—

Gene: Good.

Denny: I'm placing it by his side.

Gene: O.K. Keep right on feeding him.

Denny: (Pause) O.K., and he keeps growing.

Gene: O.K. Good! Good! Just keep right on. Stay right with that.

Denny: Well, I'm—Uh, I'm feeling a little fear here with it. Uh—

[COM: GUIDED MEDITATION; CLIENT BECOMES AWARE OF EGO INFLATION FEAR.]

Gene: Yeah!

Denny: If I let him eat all he wants, then he's gonna be bigger than me.

Gene: Yeah.

[COM: GUIDED MEDITATION; CLIENT FEAR OF EGO AND COWARDICE EVIDENCING ITSELF.]

Denny: In fact, he's taking the—he would take the form of a chicken, a big chicken, and that's—I don't want him to turn into a big chicken.

Gene: Maybe—I mean, does he have to take the form of a big chicken? Does he, he doesn't have that sort of form now. He started off as a little—

Denny: Yeah, but that's what I think he's gonna take the form of.

Gene: (Pause) I don't know that he is.
   [TN:Therapist's encouragement—faith in the client's increased health.]
Denny: Huh?
Gene: I don't know that he is! I don't know that he is going to take any form at all—other than that which he has. If he does, it's most unusual.
[COM: GUIDED MEDITATION; CLIENT BECOMING AWARE OF EGO DEVELOPMENT AND MATURING PROBABILITY.]
Denny: O.K. It's, it looks like about a twelve-year-old child now.
Gene: Neat! That's O.K. if a twelve-year-old child's a chicken. Huh?
Denny: No, he's not a chicken.
Gene: O.K. (Laughs) That was what I just picked up, that that was a background symbol that flashed through. You know, because we're all chicken. We've got a "scared kid" down deep somewhere. But it doesn't mean we *are* a chicken, does it? (Pause)
Denny: He's still there, that's it, he's got all the food around him that he needs, but he doesn't want any more.
Gene: O.K. Then fine. Just stop it right there. Now, how do you feel toward him, and how does he feel toward you?
[COM: GUIDED MEDITATION PLUS DIALOGICAL COUNSELING; CREATIVE SYMBOLIZATION OF LOVE-CYCLE FLOW.]
Denny: Well, I feel toward him, it's, uh (pause) yeah, I love him.
Gene: Good! How does he feel toward you? You fed him.
Denny: All right. He smiles. He feels—the same.
Gene: Good! Excellent! Now, you've got it. (Pause) Sort of let that soak up, that flow, back and forth, of love.
Denny: (Pause) Boy! That's how I'm feeling. I actually *want to* take him and take care of him.
Gene: Good!
[COM: GUIDED MEDITATION; CREATIVE SYMBOLIZATION OF SELF-EGO AXIS GROWTH.]
Denny: But, uh, I don't believe we could do that. That would make us both a bunch of sick—a couple of sickies.
Gene: You're right. Sounds like it—sounds like these are the two parts—
Denny: So—
Gene: Of your person that need to be equal, and equally powerful.
[COM: GUIDED MEDITATION; CLIENT'S INCREASING MATURITY

FEELINGS.]

Denny: But, he is actually grown into about a sixteen-year-old now

Gene: O.K.

Denny: Without eating any more. But he, uh (pause) you know, I feel secure enough to leave him there with all the food he needs- secure that he will get what he needs.

Gene: O.K.

Denny: And, uh, I gotta turn around and start going back up the hill. It's not a steep hill though, it's just slightly inclined.

Gene: Um hum.

[COM: GUIDED MEDITATION, CLIENT ACCEPTANCE OF SELF AND EGO SEPARATE FUNCTIONING EMPHASIS.]

Denny: And he doesn't try to follow or anything. He (Pause) he accepts it.

Gene: O.K., just like it's all right? He's gonna have to take care of himself.

Denny: Well, he would like to go, of course, but he does accept it.

Gene: O.K., like you're on sort of two levels; but it's, both of you are O.K. now?

Denny: Yeah.

[COM: GUIDED MEDITATION; THERAPIST CHECKING TIMER BELL AWARENESS AND NEED TO CLOSE SESSION.]

Gene: O.K. are you at a place where you feel like you're ready to end it?

Denny: Yeah!

Gene: O.K. Then bring—

Denny: Recall some scenes later—like if I keep walking up the hill?

Gene: Well, you said—

Denny: Well, I shouldn't want to keep walking there.

Gene: Huh? That's sort of what I was feeling right there, that you're at a point where you can stop; but it's good, too, because we need to stop from the time element, too, before the buzzer (if the secretary should buzz that next client is present). Uh, I think you got a real good picture there. Now then, just feel that *close-ness* in the love flow, and then let yourself imagine—(*client*— while still *into* the transcendent mind state).

[COM: GUIDED MEDITATION; DESCHEMATIZING INTENSIFIED FAITH STATE, BUT WITH A GROWTH SURPRISE OF IMMEDIATE NEW AFFECT.]

Gene: You've got your eyes open, old buddy—is there any reason for that?

[TN: This sort of incident is usually due to some sort of irruption of *highly* numinous material into consciousness and *must* be immediately acknowledged—and questioned about—by the therapist.]

Denny: (Pause) No, they're just open. I wasn't even thinking about it. (Closes them again)

Gene: O.K. I don't want you to put too quick (an end to this transcendent mind mood) to stop the alpha waves (needed for deschematizing the mind mood), you know, 'cause we want to deschematize this thing before we do. All right, then be back atop the mountain, soaking up that sense of well-being—

Denny: I'm having a hard time keeping my eyes closed. (His eyes open again.)

[COM: GUIDED MEDITATION; NECESSARY RAPID DESCHEMATIZING DUE TO NEW AFFECT.]

Gene: O.K. Just soaking that up, feeling the power of "loved in spite of yourself and because of yourself," unconditionally, soak that well-being up with no bad aftereffects.

Denny: (Laughs—his eyes pop open again)

Gene: What is it? Is there something happening?

[TN: I am suspicious that a spontaneous, numinous symbol may have suddenly visualized itself.]

Denny: Uh, I don't know, I just can't keep them closed. (Grinning and laughing)

[TN: I decide to make the deschematizing *very rapid* because of the eye opening—knowing client *may* have some mind mood fuzziness, but also knowing that the eye opening phenomenon needs immediate, *ego (consciously logical) attention.*]

Gene: All right! Fly right back down to the beach. Be aware that you've been lying there resting, renewing and restoring yourself—with no bad aftereffects—easily remembering all this. Now you open your eyes and sit up—just do so. (Coughs) You know what I had the feeling of—as you were opening your eyes?

[COM: DIALOGICAL COUNSELING; THERAPIST HELP IN COGNITIVE RESTRUCTURING AND USING THE INSIGHT-HUNCH AND POST-THERAPY CHECK-OUT.]

Denny: What?

Gene: A new aliveness in you.

[TN: This sort of spontaneous therapist's Insight-hunch

offering type of personally relating is part of the "I-Thou" approach of the Dialogical Counseling Method of relating—used also (as shown) in the Guided Meditation part. It represents a contribution given to the other which he/she may accept as helpful guidance—or may totally reject it. The therapist must be *confirming* enough to accept the client's position lovingly whether the hunch is accepted or rejected.]

Denny: (Laughs) Maybe!

Gene: I don't know whether, whether that was, whether I was picking up something—

Denny: *That was s-t-r-a-n-g-e*, Gene!

Gene: Yeah! I know it was. You just fed the thing that you thought was your monstrous self.

[COM: DIALOGICAL COUNSELING; SPIRITUAL HIGH AFTEREFFECTS APPEAR. ALSO, THERAPIST ADDS HIS CONFIRMING OF (APPARENT) NEW EGO STRENGTH AND BETTER SELF-IMAGE.]

Denny: (Laughs)

[TN: This type of "fun-sounding" laughter, for some people, happens frequently in this accompanying counseling approach after a particularly powerful meditation. To me it seems to have a certain glossalalia-like, charismatic, child-like quality, and seems to take place with a certain "holy high" feeling. Also, it is pleasingly contagious for the therapist whose usual response is one of feeling inwardly spiritually fulfilled. Notice how the rest of the session is interspersed with it.]

Gene: See what you've been doing, you've been trying to stomp yourself with your spiritual self. It wasn't God's foot, it was yours. (Denny laughs) You came up with it, you know. And, hell, you were just gonna nail it on a cross and all that stuff (Denny laughs) and, uh—

Denny: I'm a mean bastard, ain't I?

Gene: Yeah! You're mean to yourself. What I heard was, you know, what I heard was very much that you regard yourself, you know, on your ego level like this (Denny continues laughing) as, as, a—as being a worthless son-of-a-bitch.

Denny: Shit! (Continues giggling)

Gene: A worthless—worthless little fart that isn't good for anything but putting on a cross and burying, you know, and that's, that's bullshit.

Denny: Yeah, it is.

[COM: DIALOGICAL COUNSELING; DREAM INTERPRETATION INSIGHT-HUNCH.]

Gene: That's really a spiritual screw-up on the, on the deeper dimension. Now, hey, that would go with that, you know, sagging-in roof of a house sort of thing. (Reference to his terrorizing dream he had—of his "life-house" being old with his early learning experience, and the roof sagging so badly it was about to fall in with him inside. Recall that the residual feeling of the dream had brought a conscious vision with it of a giant woman standing behind him with a huge foot and it poised to step on him. It was this feeling which made him set up a special session with me.)

Denny: Um hum.

Gene: You know, now that, that just connected for me, you know. Somewhere there's the sick learning, about—(unintelligible because microphone was bumped—but my concluding words were—"religion and God").

Denny: Um hum.

[COM; DIALOGICAL COUNSELING; RABBINICAL FUNCTION OF SHARING OWN RELIGIOUS VIEWPOINT.]

Gene: And that's it because that was teaching you, hey, you little fool, go crucify yourself. That what was Jesus. . ."Hey, he ain't crucified me (the therapist). I, I can deal with it, but I ain't supposed to crucify myself." *He* didn't want to get crucified. So, what I was hearing was a sickness about some early religious teaching that was—had so affected your spiritual selfhood that you were ready to just "kiss yourself off." Bury you! Dead!

Denny: Yeah.

Gene: You know, and you really were ready to stomp, and uh, what you do in a case like this is, uh, you know, enter into the right sort of therapeutic maneuver for yourself—and you did it just exactly right—it's Feed the Monster sort of thing. And I think we did that once before in the Childhood Meadow. I don't remember, maybe we did and maybe we didn't. I don't remember what the monster was, but it's the same principle. You know, like it's got a right to be. You know, so there was the digging it back up, bringing it back to life. Maybe that's why the eyes flashed open. I don't know.

Denny: I—something's—something's—

Gene: Something's going else. Anyhow, the feeding and it's growing up, and your letting it grow up and your being able to love
yourself, you know. Love your neigh—love God, love your
neighbor as you love yourself, and that's what you're doing, and
the feeding is the first loving we get (Pause) that's it.

Denny: Good!

Gene: Oh man, that sounded good.

Denny: I've got to go!

[TN: He was under a time bind, and now I was, too; but in
circumstances like this, for the therapist's sake, the client *must
not* be allowed to leave without the therapist having some
feeling of client closure. And, he also is not to leave without
an adequate feeling of reassurance of care and protection
coming from the therapist. The surgeon cannot stop the
operation just because his operating room time is up either.]

[COM: DIALOGICAL COUNSELING; THERAPIST'S NEED FOR CLO-
SURE IN CLIENT UNDERSTANDING IN ORDER TO GIVE POST-
THERAPY PROTECTION.]

Gene: Yeah! I've got to, too, but I want, I want to get to whatever it
is that you're with right now.

Denny: Something's happened. Something's—I don't know, it's,
something that we've overlooked is, is—

Gene: Is hanging?

Denny: Yeah! It's—

Gene: Scary or what?

Denny: Exciting! (Smiles broadly)

Gene: (Pause) O.K.! What I'm picking up is, it's like it wasn't
chicken. See, that was a symbol-fear.

Denny: Yeah!

Gene: Of the *word*, of being scared. Like it's not 0. K. to be a scared
kid, and, uh, when you dismissed the idea of actually its being a
chicken, and it's 0. K. to *be* "chicken," it's O.K. to be a scared
kid—?

Denny: Yeah!

Gene: And when it's O.K. to be scared, and while, golly, it's
courage, you know, the right to decide, to think things through,
decide to choose; and I'm wondering if that's—that has to do
with *action*, see, that leads on over towards *action*, and I'm wondering if it's a—a sort of a new Self level in here.

Denny: Yeah.

Gene: Meaning it might be sort of an *exciting desire to act.*

Denny: Um hum. Yeah, that's—

Gene: That could be the smile? (Long pause) I don't want to leave anything that you may *need to touch.*

[COM: DIALOGICAL COUNSELING; THERAPIST'S CHECKING FOR GOOD CLOSURE—SELF PROTECTING ALSO.]

Denny: Yeah. Un uh! (Faraway look in his eyes.)

Gene: Briefly, you know, *at least.* 'Cause if it's at all disturbing, now that—there could be the danger of jumping off into something too quick!

Denny: Yeah.

Gene: Like the sixteen-year-old?

Denny: No, it's not that.

Gene: What? It's not that. You've got it, O.K.?

Denny: I don't know. I've seen something that I want. (Still with faraway look)

Gene: O.K.

Denny: (Long pause) Uh, I've seen it *unconsciously,* anyway. I don't know what it is.

Gene: Does it symbolize itself in any way to you? If it does—

Denny: The main thing is that I've opened my eyes.

Gene: I, I—the—the—that's, that apparently was what was going on. It was like you couldn't keep your eyes closed, or something.

Denny: (Laughs) Yeah, but it'll come up by itself.

Gene: It will? O.K. (Denny assured me next that if it did disturb him when it came up, he would contact me by phone, briefly, to clarify any disturbing emotion.)

[COM: DENNY WENT ON TO FULFILL HIS NEW POSITIVE SELF IMAGE, BECAME A RESPONSIBLE FATHER AND HUSBAND, WAS PROMOTED AT WORK, WENT ON TO ANOTHER COMPANY AND MANAGER'S JOB, JOINED THE CHURCH, AND EVEN BECAME AN OUTSTANDING SUNDAY SCHOOL TEACHER.]

Chapter XII

❦

VERBATIM OF SPECK'S EXPERIENCE OF GOD AS A CORE OF LIGHT AND FATHER OF LOVE, FORGIVENESS

Background Information

Speck is a distribution route salesman, has a marriage problem and in Transactional Analysis language has a "Please-me" Driver concerning his vocation and wife, an I.Q. of 144, is a college graduate, no children, one brother and one sister who are younger. He comes from a family of excellent intelligence but poor family emotional adjustment patterns. His wife is a college graduate and teacher. The wife is more strongly religiously oriented, and the husband is strongly interested in religion but not as actively so. Speck illustrates well one of those occasional people who can participate in this therapy model with such intensity as to have a profound mystical experience directly with God.

This session and its tape begin at the close of the use of the Intensified Faith Schema, Modified Level II, Stage 4.
NOTE: The tape of this session was not of the best quality but is clear enough that none of its content is lost. I use it because of the unique nature of this session.

Session Verbatim

Gene: Now in the name of the Father, Son, and Holy Ghost, Amen. O. K. Speck, how're you feeling?
[COM: GUIDED MEDITATION; PRE THERAPY-WORK CHECK-OUT, CLIENT IS TO IMAGINE BEING INTO THE TRIGGER INCIDENT WITH WIFE.]
Speck: (Long pause, clears throat) Very relaxed, right now.
Gene: O. K., now, use your imagination then to, uh, get this feeling

like you had of being in the *game* (with wife in a T.A. Persecutor/Victim hassle) and feeling empty that you were talking about, was it last night?

[TN: This is a check to see if he is still experiencing the feeling as described on his usual mind level or to see if *new* insight is perhaps already available in the transcendent psyche state. If so, the more fitting feeling should be sought out and defined.]

[COM: GUIDED MEDITATION; THERAPIST TRIES TO GET CLIENT INTO THE TRIGGER.]

Speck: Huh? (*Really* into his transcendent psyche state and following his own *zazen*-like awareness-though he had wanted to do some therapy work.)

Gene: Is that the way it feels, like *empty*?

Speck: O. K. (Returns to being "*with*" therapist for guidance.)

[TN: We will use the Skip Technique on the Key-word Desensitizing Exercise in both the taped audio recording and written verbatim in order to save space and prevent repetitious boredom. The written form may be found in Chapter IV.]

Gene: O. K., all right. Stress! Key Word; [Relax Speck]!.... Exhaust!.... Smile!.... Erase!.... Kindle!.... Beam!.... Fortress-power!.... O.K., imagine being in the same situation now (pause) and how does it feel? How does it hit you? (Pause) Or what do you think or what comes to you? Whatever *you* are aware of is central.

[COM: GUIDED MEDITATION; THERAPIST CHECK ON TRIGGER FEELING. IT SEEMS GONE.]

Speck: (Long pause) It's not there.

Gene: All right. What is there?

Speck: It's going over "blah." (Not causing him an angry affect any more so that he feels desensitized to the "game" itself and can place his attention on what is really going on with his own and his wife's feelings.)

Gene: How does it feel?

Speck: Nice.

Gene: Good! That's a positive feeling then, huh?

[COM: GUIDED MEDITATION; THERAPIST'S FURTHER CHECK ON TRIGGER FEELING.]

Speck: Um hum.

[COM: GUIDED MEDITATION; CHECK ON TRIGGER ANXIETY ABOUT SELF-ASSERTIVE CONFIDENCE.]

Gene: Good. All right, next, I'd like us to take this fear/excited feeling that you've got right now of acting altogether on your own—stepping out with this new confidence. Have you got it? (Long, long pause) (He had just quit an excellent job in which he was unhappy and which was driving him frantic. Though he was a top salesman, the job kept him away from home too much and saddled him with many greatly disliked duties. In a session two weeks prior he had in regression work discovered a feeling tone and memory chain of awareness, in using the Desensitizing Procedure, which had caused him to realize he was staying with a job he hated so his father would not reject him as a failure, and this insight gave him the self-confidence to quit.

However, he was now aware of a combined fear of failure, plus excited feelings about going into a business he liked, on his own. The feeling and its associated relations were unclear and he wanted to use the Desensitizing Exercise to get some new insight. As the reader will see, the result of even preparing for it was surprising to us both.)

Gene: If you'll think of a situation, a specific situation—

[TN: If a person has difficulty while in the transcendent mind state in recalling a "triggering" feeling itself, asking him/her to remember a specific situation in thought will usually allow him/her to recapture the accompanying feeling. Sometimes it is necessary to go below the intellect further by asking for "the feeling which produces the thought" (or becomes a thought).]

[COM: GUIDED MEDITATION; THERAPIST TRIES TO GET CLIENT TO IMAGINE THE TRIGGER—CLIENT SEEMS DISTRACTED.]

Speck: I've got company.

Gene: You'll get the picture. You've got it? Let's see what company is here. It's all right. You're safe—in God. It's O. K. for anything.

[TN: It is frequently necessary to *reassure* people from time to time at some seeming block-point in the various Therapy Procedures, that they are now in the safety of God's presence and that, therefore, it is safe to let themselves now know consciously any feeling or thought they may have formerly kept hidden from themselves.]

[COM: GUIDED MEDITATION; BECOMES INFUSED WITH DIALOGI-
CAL COUNSELING FROM HENCEFORTH.]

Speck: Boy, He's, uh (long pause) He's with me.

Gene: Who is he?

Speck: God.

[COM: GUIDED MEDITATION PLUS DIALOGICAL COUNSELING;
THERAPIST TRIES TO CLARIFY SPONTANEOUS SITUATION.]

Gene: All right, excellent! Is He in an image form or are you perceiving Him as a symbol, an image, or a picture, or as the awareness—

Speck: Glow.

Gene: Oh! Glow? What sort of glow?

Speck: Just a brightness.

Gene: Oh. You say, "He." Does it feel like a, like a person? Or—

Speck: Um hum!

[COM: GUIDED MEDITATION PLUS DIAGLOGICAL COUNSELING;
THERAPIST EXPRESSES NON-INTERFERENCE FOR CLIENT'S
EXPERIENCE]

Gene: What? Because it's totally your experience, now I can't lay a
trip on you with this.

[COM: GUIDED MEDITATION PLUS DIALOGICAL COUNSELING;
CLIENT SEEMS TO BE HAVING A PERSONAL EXPERIENCE (MYSTI-
CAL UNION) WITH GOD.]

Speck: (Long, long pause) I don't know, it's just so, so *good* right
here.

Gene: How would you describe the good? (Pause) Is a value a good

[COM: GUIDED MEDITATION PLUS DIALOGICAL COUNSELING;
CLIENT'S EXPERIENCE WITH GOD SYMBOLIZED IN COSMIC
FEELING-THOUGHT PATTERNS AS: LIGHT, CLEANLINESS, AND
WARMTH—CLIENT'S VALUE OR PRECIOUSNESS TO GOD.]

Speck: Um hum. (Pause) It's—it's bright. It's clean. (Pause) It's
warm, and it's, it's just, you know (pause). I feel (pause) like I'm
floating, I mean, it's just—

Gene: Um hum.

[COM: GUIDED MEDITATION PLUS DIALOGICAL COUNSELING;
CLIENT'S EXPERIENCE WITH GOD AS SHARED SPACE (GOD
IMMANENT?), SYMBOLIZED AS CORE OF LIGHT AND HIMSELF AS
HAVING AN "INNER BODY" (ALSO OF LIGHT?).]

Speck: There's not a—I know that I'm sitting in the chair but my
Inner Body is, is absorbed in this brightness, of this Light, and
there's a core, a center to this. [TN: Is this the "spiritual body"
Paul spoke of?]

Gene: Um hum.

[COM: GUIDED MEDITATION PLUS DIALOGICAL COUNSELING; CLIENT EXPERIENCES GOD AS FORGIVER, LOVE, AND COMPANION/FRIEND—ALSO INTO THE SAFE-SECURE AFFECT.]

Speck: And I keep getting the feeling of—(pause) of saying (pause) there's the *Forgiver*, [Source] of *Love*. (Pause) "I'm with you."

[COM: GUIDED MEDITATION PLUS DIALOGICAL COUNSELING; THERAPIST PROBES FOR MORE OF GOD-EXPERIENCE—GOD AS CORE (CENTER?).]

Gene: You're saying it, or is someone saying it or what?

Speck: It's coming from the *Core*.

Gene: All right, is it like words or is it like a thought or what (Pause) Very good, you're very well into it.

[COM: GUIDED MEDITATION PLUS DIALOGICAL COUNSELING; CLIENT'S EXPERIENCE OF GOD *COMMUNICATED BY FEELING* (WAS SCHLEIERMACHER RIGHT?).]

Speck: *It's more of a feeling*. It's being (pause) transferred, uh (sighs). [TN: Note the pattern of meaning-filled feeling-thought given the client by God. (Is this the *base* for language?)]

Gene: Good. Go right ahead, you're doing well with it.

[COM: GUIDED MEDITATION; CLIENT EXPERIENCES "SPINNING".]

Speck: (Pause) I'm riding that spinning wheel again. (The client had in a previous session experienced a feeling of rapid, circular motion with which he had to use the Key Word Exercise in order to stop the feeling so that we could proceed with the therapy.)

[COM: GUIDED MEDITATION; CLIENT "STAYS WITH" FEELING UNTIL IT ABATES.]

Gene: O. K.

Speck: But it feels *good*!

[TN: This sensation of spinning, spiraling, or circling, is not infrequent in the transcendent mind mood. It may sometimes stop of its own accord if the client can endure in a relaxed way. However, if it becomes uncomfortable and threatening, it should be terminated by *repeated use* of the Desensitizing Exercise (the briefer forms) or *panic* may ensue for the client.

I, as elsewhere stated, have no good explanation for the spinning phenomenon. No one has been able to conceptualize it adequately. However, perhaps it is an experience in the Void, for the person almost always experiences it *in blackness* (if the feeling is not projected onto a sensation of the spinning

of the recliner in which they are sitting). Also, it is the movement—not the blackness—that disturbs. Another characteristic is that it is *never vortex-like*. The most I have to offer is
God as the Void and the spinning as the Principle of Life and
Motion. Perhaps it is the *primary* experience of the human
monad itself. This remains a mystery and we can only speculate.]

Gene: All right. Very good. (Pause) I hear your feelings becoming
words, and though I'm not projecting into what you're, what
you're talking about—

Speck: It's, well (pause) I'm (pause) oh, it's that I—I have a sensation in my *body* but (pause) then there's, uh, this area that I'm
just, it's just nice.

Gene: O. K.

[COM: GUIDED MEDITATION PLUS DIALOGICAL COUNSELING;
    CLIENT APPARENTLY EXPERIENCING HIS *SELF* AS SOUL-CEN-
    TER.]

Speck: It's (pause) it's a place within my *own mind*.

Gene: Sure.

[COM: GUIDED MEDITATION PLUS DIALOGICAL COUNSELING;
    CLIENT AGAIN EXPERIENCES GOD AS IMMANENT.]

Speck: (Pause) That He shares and (long pause)—

[TN: Note, the "seeming" paradox of God and Self sharing in
    client's psyche space. God and Self seem always in
    relation/connection, separate/together. (God as immanent
    and transcendent.)]

Gene: Good!

[COM: GUIDED MEDITATION PLUS DIALOGICAL COUNSELING;
    CLIENT EXPERIENCES GOD AS TRUST-IN, NO FEAR, AND FAITH-
    IN.]

Speck: Just got—I feel that it just keeps, you know (pause) just, just
Not Fear—and [is] Trust.

Gene: Um hum. (Pause) It's *without* fear and *is* trust? Did you say—
is that what you said?

Speck: Yeah. *No fear* in it (pause).

Gene: And it *is Trust*? Is that what you are saying?

Speck: Yeah!

Gene: Is it the same as what you call *faith*?

Speck: Yeah. (Pause)

Gene: Good. Hum! Excellent.

[COM: GUIDED MEDITATION PLUS DIALOGICAL COUNSELING;

CLIENT EXPERIENCES GOD AS ABSOLUTE ASSURANCE GIVER.]

Speck: Everything's going to be all right!

[TN: Note, the *safe-secure affect* as FAITH known as TRUST on this transcendent level.]

[COM: GUIDED MEDITATION; THERAPIST CHECKS CLIENT'S FEEL-INGS.]

Gene: Excellent! Well, do you need to, uh, (laughs) do anything further, then, on this business of fear "back on your own?" (Laughs) It sounds like you got your answer, or are you still spinning?

[COM: GUIDED MEDITATION; THERAPIST ERRONEOUSLY CHECKS CLIENT FOR "SPINNING".]

Speck: Yep! Here we go!

Gene: All right. (Pause) What's the feeling?

Speck: Oh, about ninety miles an hour.

Gene: Scary or—

[COM: GUIDED MEDITATION; THERAPIST CHECKS FOR CLIENT'S DESIRE TO DESENSITIZE THIS TIME.]

Speck: W-e-l-l, no! It's making my head feel real light.

Gene: O. K. (Pause) How would you feel about desensitizing to the spinning part of it?

Speck: I wouldn't mind that.

[COM: GUIDED MEDITATION; THERAPIST USES KEY WORD TECH-NIQUE—BRIEFED DOWN THIS TIME.]

[TN: Some variation of a particular "command word" and its phraseology content may be used in preference over others. Word use is according to the therapist's discretion and his perception of the client's particular and most outstanding desensitizing need on the occasion of the use of the Exercise.]

Gene: O. K. Good. Get the spinning feeling, *STRESS*! [Key Word:] Relax, Speck!.... Exhaust!....Smile!....Erase!....Kindle!... Beam!....Fortress-power!....

Gene: (Pause) All right. How does it feel now?

Speck: Good. Strong!

Gene: O.K. That's what I'm hearing, that now it's turning into strength.

Speck: Um hum.

Gene: O. K. Feel like you're ready to come out of it?

Speck: Huh? Um hum.

[COM: GUIDED MEDITATION; CLIENT DESCHEMATIZED.]

[TN: Skip procedure used here in verbatim for
Deschematizing.]

Gene: All right just open your eyes and sit up. How're you doing?
(Chair creaks. Long, long pause) You were quite into it!

[COM: THERAPIST DOES POST THERAPY-WORK CHECK-OUT.]

Speck: (Whistles)

Gene: (Laughs) What does that mean? (Long pause. Chair creaks.)
Is that powerful or something?

Speck: Um hum.

[COM: DIALOGICAL COUNSELING; THERAPIST USE OF RABBINICAL
FUNCTION TO CLARIFY CLIENT'S CONFUSION IN CLASPING
AND UNCLASPING HIS HANDS AND STARING AT SPACE
BETWEEN THEM.]

Gene: What, you're feeling it between your hands, or something?

Speck: Um hum.

Gene: Are you aware of your aura? Can you see it now? That's the
(spiritual) power emanating from us.

Speck: Um hum.

[TN: (His spiritual "hang-over" lasted about five more minutes in which he was so energized he took a few minutes to do
some exercises. Also, we went over his experience until he had
it all in a properly understood rational position but with new
room in his thinking for his seemingly *non*-rational experiences of intense emotion in experiencing God and religious
phenomena.)]

[COM: THE MARRIAGE ENDED IN DIVORCE, BUT SPECK MOVED TO
ANOTHER CITY AND TOOK A JOB WITH A LARGE INDUSTRY AND
HAS DONE WELL AS OF MY LAST INFORMATION.]

Chapter XIII

❧

VERBATIM OF THE CLIENT WITH "BURN-OUT"

Background Information

This client is in his mid-fifties, has an I.Q. of 149, and is married. He holds a doctorate in his field in the health professions in which he is well-established. Brought up in a small county seat town, his personal family history background was culturally religious, but not so much so on an experiential level. He has one married daughter living in another city. The problem was a case of increasing depression (partially related to a long-lasting viral infection), existential despair, and loss of enjoyment in his professional work. I had been seeing the client one hour weekly for approximately six weeks and the negative dimensions were steadily decreasing with an accompanying renewal of enjoyment of life and work. However, this portion of this session presents an excellent indication of the Crisis Intervention Technique, Energy Switch, and of learning to identify emotional feelings, instead of sensation feelings primarily, from the level of the five basic body-based emotions (this unclarity had led to fatigued over-work). While his capacity for entering an intensified faith psyche state was not as great as many, the verbatim and tape demonstration illustrate well the capacity of anyone who enters this Schema's Intensified Faith experience to benefit from whatever inherent or developed state specific faith development stage at which he/she has currently arrived in life thus far. In Jungian concepts this client's personality would be considered largely sensation and thought centered. This verbatim and tape pick up after the session has proceeded into his personal transcendent mind mood capacity at Intensified Faith Schema Level III, Stage 9.

Session Verbatim

[COM: GUIDED MEDITATION; THERAPIST PROBES FOR FURTHER
TRIGGER AWARENESS.]

Gene: Sort of get into it.

Client: Cut maybe an hour or better a day off on the standing. (His
profession called for him to be on his feet a lot.)

Gene: Um hum. That sounds like taking as intermittent breaks like
that, that it might help do the trick with the plain muscle fatigue
in those knees. That's what I'm hearing. And it sounds like that's
what it is, from what your awareness is.

Client: Well, I—it's—I think it's s-s-some, uh, physical muscle
fatigue and I think some of it's, uh, a mental state, too. You
know that it's—like well—not wanting to—you might call, uh,
uh, hating the fact that it's necessary to do it, so to speak, in
order to live you know, being—

Gene: All right

[COM: GUIDED MEDITATION; THERAPIST BECOMES AWARE OF
"BURN-OUT" DEPRESSION.]

Client: Just like I'm sure you have some people you have to deal
with that you don't want to deal with but you feel like, well,
(pause) that it's necessary to reality of life. If you want to eat and
to provide for your family, you've got to put up with the bitter
with the sweet, you know.

Gene: Right. (pause) How would you do it—you took that attitude,
now, I hear you in contact with it—that feeling, "I got to put up
with it." Got it?

Client: Yeah!

Gene: O.K. Then, again, let yourself wallow in it. (He had already
been told to imagine the scene as he spoke of it.) Just sort of let
yourself just wallow in that feeling, "I've got to put up with the
bitter with the sweet." And now, SWITCH/"CLAP." Release
energy from ego's will-to-power...; sensitive to spiritual
valence...; switched across and up/"Clap" to God-spark Center
and into Will-of-wills...; transformed upward into your good/
"Clap," free/"Clap," powerful/"Clap."

Gene: [Return to the same scene] and tell me about it—how it feels
different.

[COM: GUIDED MEDITATION; THERAPIST CHECKS FOR VARIATION
IN FEELING.]

Client: Well, it's a good feeling to know that—that it isn't going to go on for too long a time and there will come an end to it, unpleasant thing you might be faced with, and something else is gonna come up that will probably make—be more enjoyable to have to treat or take care of.

[COM: GUIDED MEDITATION; THERAPIST CHECKS FOR TYPE OF BASIC FEELING.]

Gene: Uh huh. All right, what's the *feeling* with it? *Sad, mad, glad, scared, excited*—the basic feeling? I heard anger before—or mad.

Client: It's a glad feeling to know that it ain't goin' on forever (laughs).

[COM: GUIDED MEDITATION AND DIALOGICAL COUNSELING; CLIENT'S PHILOSOPHICAL COGNITIVE STRUCTURING OF LIFE'S NATURE.]

Gene: (Laughs, too) O. K., that sounds pretty healthy to me (laughs).

Client: Glad, too—

Gene: Because there are some things that are negative. There are evils in the world, and that's all, or negatives to us; what—whatever it may be, it's evil to me, isn't it?

Client: Um hum.

Gene: And some of it must be endured. I guess that's what we call character development or suffering.

Client: Yeah.

Gene: And you can sort of take that attitude in going through it.

Client: Ummm. You have to endure some things, all right.

Gene: Yeah, and see, this gives you a freedom in undergoing it, is what I'm hearing, to keep developing this track of, well, it isn't going to last forever. It's a very healthy way of reducing the uptightness that's caught up in it. (Pause) Does that feel right, what I'm saying?

Client: Yeah! Uh—

[COM: THE REST OF THE SESSION WAS IRRELEVANT FOR ILLUSTRATION PURPOSES AND THUS IS NOT INCLUDED HERE. THE CLIENT DID BEGIN TO IDENTIFY BETTER HIS ANGER AND OTHER *EMOTIONAL* FEELINGS. HAVING RECOGNIZED THEM AND TRANSFORMED THEIR POWER UPWARD, HE COULD DEAL WITH THEM FIRMLY AND HONESTLY. THIS LED TO SOME CONFRONTIVE *ACTION* WHICH BROUGHT GREATER COMFORT AND TENSION REDUCTION AS WELL AS HELPING RELIEVE THE DEPRESSION.]

Chapter XIV

∾

FIRST SESSION: MITCHEL AT GOD'S PRIMORDIAL OR MENTAL POLE

Background Information

Inasmuch as Mitchel's relevant matter is included in Verbatim Number One and his story in Chapter I, there is no need to repeat it here. The only major note is the fact that, viewed from the position of process metaphysics and theology, the client seems to be experiencing things at God's more abstract, formal, and mental pole (as compared to the opposite, His/Her physical or feeling pole) than in Chapter I. This current session was the client's first experience with the Guided Meditation dimension of Faith Therapy while the former verbatim and tape of his experience was his third. Also, this recorded part of the session started after use of the full Faith Schema, Level III, Stage 9, while the other verbatim used the briefer Schema, Modified Level II, Stage 4.

Session Verbatim

[COM: GUIDED MEDITATION; CLIENT BECOMING FAMILAR WITH TRANSCENDENT PSYCHE SPACE (DUE TO MITCHEL'S PRIOR STATED ATTITUDE ABOUT RELIGIOUS MATTERS, MOST OF THE PRE-THERAPY WORK CHECK-OUT WAS DONE RATHER INFORMALLY).]

Gene: O.K., Mitchel, you're in the, uh, meditative mood, and all you have to do now—you might want to examine it and see how you feel.

Mitchel: I should. I sure can right now.

Gene: O. K. Any comment you care to make about it?

[COM: GUIDED MEDITATION; CLIENT'S PERSONAL DESCRIPTION

OF TRANSCENDENT SPACE—HIS PERCEPTION.]

Mitchel: (Clears throat) Um—I don't know. Uh—I just feel like—I feel lighter! (Archetypal UP?)

Gene: Uh-huh.

Mitchel: You know what I mean?

Gene: Yeah! Like—it's almost a little like you might float.

Mitchel: Yeah!

[COM: GUIDED MEDITATION; CLIENT'S AWARENESS OF BODY LIGHTNESS SENSATION]

Gene: Your body feels a little heavy—but you—

Mitchel: No, my body even feels lighter.

Gene: Oh! Sometimes people's body feels heavy and they feel light.

Mitchel: Oh, I feel light all over, I mean—

Gene: That's good!

Mitchel: Inside and out.

Gene: That's good unity.

Mitchel: Uh! I don't know, uh, I'm still kind of lost here.

[COM: GUIDED MEDITATION; THERAPIST GIVES ASSURANCE OF PRESENCE AND HELP IF NEEDED.]

Gene: That's all right, I'm with you. Anything you need to ask me, ask me.

Mitchel: I mean not big questions or something. I mean in, well, well, feelings that I'm getting.

Gene: All right. Do you want to just examine those feelings or what? Just sort of sit there and talk about them, if you would like.

[COM: GUIDED MEDITATION AND DIALOGICAL COUNSELING USED TOGETHER FOR CLIENT CLARITY IN COGNITIVE STRUCTUR-ING.]

Mitchel: Well, it's—I would say—well, I mean, it's not—you know what I mean by *talkable feelings* or—and primitive, it's more the primitive. It's like you can't explain it, but it's there. (Language is often inadequate to describe experience in this psyche space.)

Gene: Yeah!

Mitchel: Can 'ya understand?

[COM: GUIDED MEDITATION PLUS DIALOGICAL COUNSELING; THERAPIST'S ACCEPTANCE OF CLIENT'S AWARENESS OF COGNI-TIVE BUT UNEXPRESSABLE FEELINGS.]

Gene: Yes, I sure do! It's there, and it's good.

Mitchel: That's the way—Yeah! That's the way I've always felt about things.

Gene: Yeah!

Mitchel: It's more like that I couldn't ever explain, why—but I did.

Gene: Some things you just have to sort of make pictures of as you talk about them to people because they don't—

Mitchel: Yeah! I-I make—

Gene: It's the only way they can be understood. Symbols, they're called.

[COM: GUIDED MEDITATION PLUS DIALOGICAL COUNSELING; THERAPIST'S EXPLICATION OFFERED.]

Mitchel: Well, like I can picture how I feel in my mind.

Gene: Uh-huh.

Mitchel: But the picture that I get, I can understand, but it would be something like—just like Salvador Dali painted.

[COM: GUIDED MEDITATION PLUS DIALOGICAL COUNSELING; THERAPIST ACCEPTANCE OF CLIENT'S EXPERIENCE WITH PSY-CHE SPACE CONTAINING FORMS AND ARCHETYPAL SYMBOLS—VISIONARY EXPERIENCE.]

Gene: Yeah!

Mitchel: Just like that! It's like I understand it, but nobody else really would.

Gene: Um-hum. Are you aware—

Mitchel: But it's so hard to explain.

Gene: Yes, it is. (Laughs)

Mitchel: Because there's so much detail in it.

Gene: It's more there than you can get.

Mitchel: And I can see the detail.

[COM: GUIDED MEDITATION PLUS DIALOGICAL COUNSELING; THERAPIST'S ASSERTION OF PSYCHE SPACE AS LIKE L.S.D. TRIP TO INSIDE WORLD BUT WITHOUT DISTORTION.]

Gene: Now, you see what I mean now about it's being like an "acid trip" except that you don't have the images distorted? And that, you know, [is] sort of out of place?

Mitchel: That's true.

Gene: And so, it's a better way—

Mitchel: But I'm getting the same, well, the only thing I can say is— togetherness.

[COM: GUIDED MEDITATION PLUS DIALOGICAL COUNSELING; CLIENT HAD EXPERIMENTED WITH MIND-ALTERING DRUGS AT ONE TIME.]

Gene: Yes, uh-huh! It's that unique—

Mitchel: It's that I did with that—I'm getting the same thing without any distortion.

Gene: Um-hum. This is the way many people have described it.

Mitchel: That's—that's what I would say—its, its, togetherness in it.

Gene: Yeah, a real unity!

[COM: GUIDED MEDITATION PLUS DIALOGICAL COUNSELING; CLIENT HAS REAL EXPERIENCE OF PARTICIPATION MYSTIQUE.]

Mitchel: It's like everything's *right there!*

[COM: GUIDED MEDITATION; THERAPIST HAD FORGOTTEN "WHO IS IN CONTROL" QUESTION SO IT IS DONE NOW.]

Gene: Um-hum, yeah! (Pause) I know what you're talking about. Do—are you aware of quote who is in command and who is in control? Are you in control or am I? (Laughs)

Mitchel: No, I am. I can control however it goes.

[COM: GUIDED MEDITATION; CREATIVE SYMBOLIZATION WITH USE OF PLUS-MARK PROCEDURE—DESCRIBING IT STEP-BY-STEP.]

Gene: Good. Very good. Man, you've done good, you've gotten into a good mood. All right, let me help you then with a, a symbol or two that will, uh, probably be very helpful and meaningful to you, and then afterwards we will explore their meanings. Uh, what I would like for you then—[to do] is to use your imagination to imagine a huge, white, plus mark, and tell me when you've got it.

Mitchel: (Long pause) O. K.

Gene: O. K. Now, Mitchel, you've seen, uh, you know, like sliding doors—how they would close over the door opening?

Mitchel: Um-hum.

Gene: I'd like for you to imagine that there is a sort of line that's transparent, but a brilliancy of almost blue-white light moving at the same rate of speed from all four corners of this plus mark, slowly toward the center. So that as these lines move toward the center, they leave behind them this trail of blue-white light that zips [by] about as fast as, uh, oh a fluorescent bulb with a pulsation of power of some sort from the outer edge of the mark toward the line as it moves. Are you getting it?

Mitchel: Yeah-yeah! That's easy.

Gene: All right. Very good. Then, what I would like you to do then is to watch those lines continue to move together until they converge and overlap, and where they overlap you have such an intense core of powerful, churning, transforming energy that literally, it explodes in a sunburst of radiance constantly, like a star.

Mitchel: (Unclear)

Gene: Yeah, so that now what you should have would be sort of this huge, white plus mark with the blue-white zips of light and power coming to this powerful, transforming core that radiates constantly like a star.

Mitchel: Yeah.

Gene: Got the whole picture?

Mitchel: Oh, yeah!

[COM: GUIDED MEDITATION; CLIENT'S CREATIVE SYMBOL INTRO-JECTION/ASSIMILATION.]

Gene: Very good. O. K., now, what I want you to do is to absorb that into yourself with your imagination just as though, you might say, you were a sponge absorbing a drop of water—just sort of soak it into yourself and tell me when you've got it absorbed.

Mitchel: (Pause) Well, I think that—that I can see—see it. I have to have it absorbed.

Gene: All right. O. K.

Mitchel: To be able to see it.

Gene: All right. Can you put your hand on your body at wherever you're feeling it? (Pause) The center-most power. Very good!

Mitchel: Right here. (Places hand over heart)

Gene: All right. Now what does it make you—

Mitchel: But, uh—

Gene: Good, now, concentrate then on what your feelings are.

[COM: GUIDED MEDITATION; THERAPIST'S CHECK-OUT OF CLIEN-T'S UNITY AFFECT.]

Mitchel: I just feel good.

Gene: O. K.

Mitchel: Just like it's spreading out—all over.

Gene: Um-hum, sort of warmth from over your heart there in general?

Mitchel: Like, like warm water—

Gene: Yeah!

Mitchel: Like warm water, all, you know, it's going everywhere at once.

Gene: O.K. Let's see, if you think of yourself, for example, this is what a symbol is—it can get distorted, you know, like with "acid," etc., but this is a symbol of your inner, God-spark Self.

You see, it's even to the plus-mark, positive side; and, uh—if you imagined yourself then, you see, as being like this—this symbol, the plus-mark, this is your personality—whatever might hit it, you can take by the spiritual power within you, which would be those zips of blue-white light, pull it to the center of your own decision and choosingness and core—like the center of a star. Change it! Transform it in whatever way and radiate this same energy out transformed into something better for you and others, even. Does that explain? This is an explanation I've come out with over all these years with what people have put together as their experience of that.

Mitchel: Well, yeah (pause) except that, that warmth, you know, has reached like all over my body, and I can feel a pulsing.

Gene: Yeah!

[COM: GUIDED MEDITATION; CLIENT AWARE OF HIS ATTUNE-MENT TO COSMIC RHYTHM.]

Mitchel: Uh! Not—sort of, not, not a throbbing but (pause) a pulsing.

Gene: A rhythmical power?

Mitchel: Yeah! Just—

Gene: From within you.

Mitchel: Yeah! It's from me.

Gene: That's it.

Mitchel: But I can feel it all over—even into—into my toes.

Gene: Very good.

Mitchel: I can feel it.

Gene: Very good. How do you feel? The main thing is the sense of unity that it gives you—the ability to choose within yourself, your own sense of inner power, that whatever hits you, you can deal with it.

Mitchel: Oh, yeah!

Gene: It's a good, powerful feeling, usually.

[COM: GUIDED MEDITATION; CLIENT AWARENESS OF WILL-OF-WILLS POWER FROM SELF]

Mitchel: Yes, I've gotten it extremely, well, not power conscious.

Gene: Um-hum.

Mitchel: Uh! (Pause) I don't know. It's like I don't feel like anything is impossible.

Gene: Um-hum.

Mitchel: ANYTHING!

Gene: Um-hum. (Pause) See, it is at the center of the God-spark itself.

Mitchel: It's like it's all in the same rhythm as this pulsation that I'm getting.

Gene: Um-hum.

Mitchel: It's just that I get this pulsing all over.

Gene: Very good.

[COM: GUIDED MEDITATION; CLIENT AWARENESS OF COSMIC UNITY—CONSCIOUSNESS RAISING.]

Mitchel: And, oh, it just feels nice.

Gene: Very good. And, see, if you'll notice, too, the amount of sensibleness that comes with it, too. O. K. You know all this power, but it is—there's no reason there to prove it or to do anything stupid or foolish with it. It sort of has a wisdom with it.

Mitchel: Yeah! It's like—

Gene: Are you feeling in it? It's like I say, I'm just— (Undistinguishable)

[COM: GUIDED MEDITATION PLUS DIALOGICAL COUNSELING; THERAPIST CHECKS FOR CONCEPT CLARITY AND AWARENESS OF POWER AND WISDOM OF INDIVIDUALITY.]

Mitchel: Now it's like—it's like—it's like—Yeah! It's like-I know, that, I mean—even things that I believe are impossible (pause) that—if I could keep this pulsing, or make it stronger or something, I could do even things that I believe are impossible. It's weird, this, I mean, that's the kind of a power I feel.

Gene: Yeah! It is a kind of very powerful—

Mitchel: It's like (pause)

Gene: You don't really want to.

Mitchel: I don't really feel like doing it.

Gene: Uh-huh! What's the need of it? (Pause) You see it's real freedom inside, that's the marvelous thing about it.

Mitchel: Yeah!

Gene: You don't have to prove anything; you don't have to disprove anything. It's just—hey, I'm here.

Mitchel: Yeah! Yeah! That's it! That's it!

Gene: I can cope with whatever comes.

Mitchel: Here I am!

Gene: Yeah! I can cope with whatever comes.

Mitchel: Right.

[COM: GUIDED MEDITATION; THERAPIST USE OF A SPECIFIC POSI-
TIVE IDEA.]

Gene: Hey, good man! O. K. Try to keep the feeling of that, then,
you know, on the conscious level—-everyday consciousness,
adult level—when you come down out of the meditation, so that
reimagining this picture, you can let yourself reexperience this
sense of unity, that anytime you need to, just closing your eyes
and imagining it and feeling this sense of unity. All right . . . .

[COM: THIS WAS NOT THE CONCLUSION OF *THIS* SESSION WITH
MITCHEL, AS THE STORY IN CHAPTER I INDICATES; THE
RECORDING TAPE RAN OUT AS WE WERE SUCCESSFULLY DOING
TWO MORE SYMBOLS FOR HELPING BETTER STRENGTHEN THE
CONSCIOUS PERSONALITY. HOWEVER, THIS MUCH OF THE
TAPED PART OF THE SESSION GIVES THE NEEDED ILLUSTRA-
TION OF A PERSON AT INTENSIFIED FAITH SCHEMA LEVEL III,
STAGE 9, WITH GUIDED MEDITATION EXPERIENCING BEING AT
GOD'S MENTAL OR CONCEPTUAL POLE. BY HEARING THE SAME
INTELLIGENT AND ARTICULATE PERSON AT BOTH OF GOD'S
POLAR EXTREMES, IT GIVES GREATER INSIGHT INTO THE
POWER OF THE GUIDED MEDITATION DIMENSION OF FAITH
THERAPY. I HOPE THIS WILL BE OF AID TO ANYONE DESIRING
TO PRACTICE THIS THERAPY MODEL.]

SUMMARIZING CONCLUSIONS

Much research remains to be done as Faith Therapy continues to develop. The therapeutic potential for group participation in such settings as retreats, public worship service, and group psychotherapy is one area that needs thorough exploration. My brief excursions into group work has yielded some significant success. A skilled group therapist who is also religiously qualified might well develop this potential.

As ongoing research on the brain and neurological systems continues to reveal new information, new theorizing remains a challenge for the developers and practitioners of this therapy method. These new psychobiological insights will continue to advance the effectiveness of Faith Therapy, particularly in its Theory and Guided Meditation expressions.

Another area for exploration in use of this methodology is its application to the lives of the terminally ill. I believe that discreet use of the Christ Symbol Procedure could be of great comfort to Christians in these situations, if they are not too heavily medicated.

Some skeptics or detractors hold that since suggestion is used in arriving at the Intensified Faith Schema's transcendent psyche state, this method is merely hypnosis and the transcendent planes are only hypnoidal states. Repeated practice, however, will show that a person arrives at a psyche space where "The Holy" is experienced and interpreted using Christian concepts. To consider this experience as simply hypnotic is to be grossly reductionistic as it ignores the distinguishing spiritual aspect of the process. The simple fact is that this method works. It leads one into better awareness of inner and outer reality. Such awareness promotes psychic growth, healing, and spiritual development, regardless of the means used in arriving at the transcendent state.

Since Faith Therapy began its development by using the practices and beliefs of the Church, it is meant to bring its adherents needed psychic growth and healing, both in the worship experience and in personal ministering. However, in some measure, use of the Intensified Faith Schema and Guided Meditation points beyond itself to a larger and more encompassing concept of Deity. The Meditations of various clients obviously contain some universal religious experiences, although they use Christian interpretive schemes of the mind in order to understand the experience. As I have pointed out to many of these, there are various paths up the Cosmic Mountain where persons contact Ultimate Reality; but because of our culture and background, we are following the Christian interpretive path to that psyche space. Perhaps our assumptions derive from Christ's saying that there were "many dwelling places" (John 14:2 NRSV) in the Father's house, and that gives us, as Christians, an exclusivistic mindset about being with God. But Christ did not say there was *only one* dwelling place. It is probably easier to reach this heaven-like experience with an understanding of God as Person in Christ because we have experienced total dependent life while infants as safe with the protecting persons of our mother and/or father. However, even when we have "found Christ" and have experienced the "safe-secure" affect, we are left trying to explain the mystical state's All-encompassing Love.

As is generally known, throughout the world the highest common religious experience of most great mystics, regardless of Faith group, is that *God is Love.* In our present world, religious pluralism surrounds us so we, while using the Church's orientation and the Christian mystical religious experience as a guide, need to see beyond our somewhat parochial concept of Ultimate Reality and open our minds to additional facets of God's Being. Perhaps this was the direction toward which Paul Tillich was leading us at mid-century when he spoke of our need to have "absolute faith" which was directed toward "the God beyond the God of Theism" who "is present, although hidden, in every divine-human encounter."[1]

This view does not negate the Christian experience. James Fowler's discoveries of stages in faith-development have acknowledged the above truth when he writes of persons who live in the

Stage Six faith area (highest in all religious). These Universalizers spend themselves trying to transform present reality to a higher level. Their faith position concerning their particular religious conviction is a sort of "sacred idolatry." Such persons realize "...absoluteness of the divine character can come to expression in different forms and in different contexts, with each of these instances bearing the full weight of ultimacy."[2] Therefore, the more sincerely and devoutly we practice and follow the transcendence of our particular Faith's direction, the closer we come to God as Ultimate Reality, embracing all that exists.

Psychologist Robert Ornstein has said that humanity has developed the mind's structured survival patterns to the fullest extent of which we are currently aware. Further he has stated, "There will be no further biological evolution without conscious evolution." He sees our need to be aware of unconscious parts of ourselves as our capacity to change ourselves and our world to meet an ideal of "global patriotism." To accomplish this goal, we need to concentrate on providing better formative environments for infants and toddlers in their critical period as well as for youth in their adolescence when there is a second mental system refinement for adulthood. Additionally, we need to accept responsibility for humanity's well-being as a group; showing compassion for others has a positive influence on the functioning of the immune system. Ornstein does not propose a life of asceticism, as some religious people try to practice in order to suppress parts of their being, for all of a person's differing "selves," such as "multiminds" and "simpletons," serve some purpose and have evolved in our brain largely as built-in systems of adapting for survival. Most of these selves are still helpful at times, and we need to become consciously aware of their presence, especially when they spontaneously take over and our actions may become maladaptive. He also believes that as humans we are "one step beyond straightforward biological altruism...." It is this inborn capacity that causes us to bond together into "something greater that seems to be important," and this innate quality has made possible the religions of the world. Thus even our moral and spiritual potential has its base in our earthly being. It would appear then that further development will be spiritual, consciousness raising, and awareness expansion, which will allow humanity to know and better control its inner nature.[3]

Our need to express greater altruism for our species' survival and growth is a developmental matter for each individual. This development starts with the early family as parents interact with their children individually and later as they model close relationships. It continues as the child is subject to family and society's modeling. But the most vital impact is made by the parents who, one hopes, cherish the baby.[4] All these influences shape our capacity to relate intimately and positively with God throughout our lives. The position of this book is that whether the early period of one's existence has much negativity within it because of poor parenting, or whether the "trust set" is positive, any problems may be corrected or faith enhanced through Faith Therapy and its Guided Meditations. Such therapeutic correction and self-acceptance can increase our spiritual growth and altruistic feelings by letting us consciously know and guide our "multiminds." We can begin to relate more idealistically to ourselves and to all other human beings. And this can be done by expanding our awareness of God's unconditional love through mystically experiencing our personal value to Him/Her.

Let me emphasize that, as a rule, Faith Therapy's mystical experiencing of the safe-secure affect in God's Presence does not *immediately* cause one consequently to relate to everyday living on a higher faith development stage beyond one's usual, or recently improved, orientation. The encounter with Ultimate Reality brought about by use of the Intensified Faith Schema and Guided Meditation does bring new hope and spiritual growth, but it is usually only to a higher expression of one's present faith development stage. Within the process of Faith Therapy's continuing work, however, one may *ultimately* grow into a higher stage, but Faith Therapy does not lift one to a higher rapturous state where he/she may permanently dwell. While it does improve one's faith growth in resolving reality's problems, the total experience is finally very down-to-earth. Speculatively, in space-time, human experience has an evolutionary purpose (perhaps it is a "sort of" training school) which finds its ultimate meaning beyond the present with its "tuned-into" awareness of the NOW; therefore, life with its usual consciousness seems to provide some knowledge essential to fuller life beyond present existence. BUT IT IS TO CURRENT REALITY WE RETURN FORM OUR TRANSCENDENT EXPERIENCES with renewed faith, hope, and love to labor in this vineyard until our allotted time on earth has expired.

Faith Therapy began with a concern for members of local churches who were searching for more fulfilling lives. Because that concern relates to universal human problems, this method has brought them help. Pierre Teilhard called for the development of a new mysticism which would not be typical of the old forms of either East or West; it would be one which would fill the need for a *personal* relating to God. He contended that the new mysticism would need to be oriented around experiencing a new "universal quasi-presence" which is the "Ultra-human" seeking to be newly born into our noospheric existence. Further, he expected this mysticism to come from the West.[5] Faith Therapy, oriented as it is toward a new and more practical approach to mysticism, seeks to meet such a need.

NOTES

[1] Tillich, *Courage*, pp.186-7.

[2] Fowler, *Stages*, pp. 200-9.

[3] Ornstein, *Evolution*, pp. 267-79.

[4] Morton Hunt, *The Compassionate Beast: What Science Is Discovering About the Humane Side of Humankind* (New York: William Morrow, 1990), pp. 101-11.

[5] Pierre Teilhard de Chardin, *Let Me Explain*, ed. Jean-Pierre Demoulin,trans. by Rene Haque (New York: Harper and Row, 1970), pp. 116-19.

GLOSSARY

ACCOMMODATION An organism's inner, reinforcing feedback limit to assimilation of the environment. This limiting is an adaptational and closure function.

AFFECTIVE-TONE The subjective, vaguely aware, but *experienced* feeling or emotionally charged state of a person. Usually it is not consciously focused upon but forms a sort of energetic background in the psyche.

AGAPE Love which finds its satisfaction in selflessly meeting the legitimate needs of another or doing good without expectation of reward.

ALTERED STATE OF CONSCIOUSNESS An identifiable level of specific mental functioning caused by ingestion of chemical substances (such as alcohol or abuse of psychotropic drugs) and which causes hallucinogenic and/or non-natural mental functioning—*not* to be confused with STATE-SPECIFIC STATE OF CONSCIOUSNESS.

ARCHETYPE An inherited, basic representation, pattern, or model which abides in the collective unconscious, and which has reasoning and structuring force when activated in the individual.

ASSIMILATION The method by which an organism "takes in" its needs from the environment.

ATTITUDE A relatively stable pre-disposition or valued outlet for the expression of feeling.

COLLECTIVE UNCONSCIOUS That part of the unconscious which is the genetically inherited past of all mankind, origin of the individual psyche, and that which has been determined by nature as humanly adaptive.

COMPLEX An emotionally highly charged psychic structure, held together by associations of similar affective tones, split off from conscious control, and seems to have a will of its own.

CONSCIOUS That of which one is most immediately aware.

COSMIC (UNITIVE) INTUITION A special perceptive force drawing one toward direct and immediate knowing (unity with) of that which tends cosmically to fulfill life. It is chiefly intended ultimately to lead one Godward and is experienced within as a sort of depth, restless desire for some final and ultimate fulfillment.

CRITICAL PERIOD That time in human development extending diminishingly from birth to puberty when the brain's basic unconscious and preconscious neurological behavior patterns are formed. These patterns underlie all later life. The most powerful patterns, however, are fixed in the prefrontal lobe in life's first two years and are caused by environmental adjustments and the quality of parenting. These fixed neuronal connections are most difficult to change later and may lead to maladjustment.

EGO The *usual* and spatio-temporal center or focal point of conscious awareness, I-am-ness, or existence and the center of secondary process mentation and field of consciousness referred to in this work as the "self."

ENGRAM A neural pattern or electrical circuit in the brain cells which accounts for memory, habit, learning, etc.

EQUILIBRIUM The organizing and balancing intelligent function which shares with assimilation and accommodation in the organism's optimal adaptation to its internal and external needs and the changes in both.

EROS Love which seeks personal fulfillment of needs for life and pleasure for oneself—unifying desire energy.

ETERNAL NOW The inner psychic state of awareness of space-lessness and timelessness.

EXECUTIVE FUNCTION That psychic ability, interactive in the total will, which produces final decisions.

FAITH OPERATION The initial *action* pattern of life or love energy, which also structures into itself in a process manner the psychic attitudinal components of hope and love, thus bringing the basic life-building function of faith into existence.

FAITH SCHEMA The mental pattern followed by the interact-ing, structured process of faith, hope, and love (as attitude and energy). This process increasingly intensifies faith's psychic reaching action toward more successful living and higher states of consciousness.

FEELING-THOUGHT Well equilibrated patterning of the psy-che's action so that both content and form are balanced in the ongoingness of life in the process of assimilation and accommo-dation.

IMAGE A psychic representation or likeness of something not present.

INTELLIGENCE The capacity to know and do successful prob-lem solving.

KNOWING Cognition. To have an understanding of, intellectual and emotional awareness of.

LIBIDO The life-energy, or love-energy, which surges through every part of a person with longing for pleasure, satisfaction, life, and fulfillment of personal being.

LIFE-LOGIC The mental organization which leads one to an accurate understanding of daily, human life experienced as a meaningful and purposeful process and which also searches for life's ultimate meaning. It is more attuned to the full livingness of the present moment than to Aristotelian logic's correctness of thought.

MIND That which is the non-physical activity of a person. See psyche.

OBJECTIVE PSYCHE See Collective Unconscious.

OPERATION A type of internalized action or psychic pattern, which is reversible and tends to eliminate errors through feedback. At times the process undergoes transformations from within and can also combine with other complementary organizations which enhance its functioning.

PERSONAL UNCONSCIOUS That part of the collective unconscious which belongs to an individual subject alone. It is made up of one's private experiences and potentialities and contains the person's individual pre-conscious (middle unconscious), lower unconscious, and upper unconscious.

PRECONSCIOUS That part of the unconscious (including many of the cognitive structures themselves—which can never be conscious) which is currently out of awareness, but some of which (presumably) can be made conscious by focusing attention upon it. Since it houses much of one's past individual experience, it is also that part of the psyche which pre-shapes or pre-interprets the material arriving in consciousness.

PRIMARY PROCESS MENTATION Inner mental activity, which is present from infancy and is illogical (in the Aristotelian sense), symbolic, and unconscious.

PSYCHE That which is the non-physical aspect of a person. See Mind.

REASON The principle which supports, justifies, or explains a fact or properly evaluates feeling energy. In this manuscript, it is also viewed as a major attribute of God which serves to advance life.

REPRESSION To shut away from consciousness feelings and thoughts of which one would be ashamed, or subjectively feel so frightened by as to hinder adequate functioning. This is done unconsciously through guilt, shame, or inferiority.

SCHEMA The logical outline of the internal organization and dynamics of behavior.

SCHEME A pattern of organized actions.

SECONDARY PROCESS MENTATION Mental activity oriented around outer, sensory reality. In the sense of Aristotelian logic, it is logical, coherent, and conscious, and develops from the necessity of dealing with outer reality in order to gain satisfaction from it.

SELF (High Self, Soul-center, "God-spark", Inner Self). The human monad. Man's basic subjective sense of being, existence, or I-AM-ness. The ultimate structuring, reasoning, and activating aspect of a person.

SET A psychic inclination or predisposition toward specific action, a relatively fixed attitude.

SIGN A mental representation which is consciously and culturally constructed and for humanity is (usually) more thought than emotion oriented.

SOUL The spiritual force-field or animating principle which carries out the designs of the Self in humans. Soul is also operative in all animals, but it does not have a center of self-aware awareness.

STAGE A step or unit in developmental progress.

STATE-SPECIFIC STATE OF CONSCIOUSNESS An identifiable and somewhat lasting level of specific mental functioning with personal, ego awareness; e.g., one's usual outer world awareness level, hypnotic trance, mystical stages, heightened physical awareness conditions, metapeak experiences, etc. This state is not caused by ingestion of any mind-altering substance.

STRUCTURE A related grouping of psychic phenomena which is bound together by the concepts of wholeness, transformation, and self-regulation.

SUBCONSCIOUS That which is out of conscious awareness, more oriented around instinct and memory.

SUPEREGO The *ought-to* and *ought-not* faculty of the mind, which through its guilt functions, safety standards, and perceptive activity, aids in keeping one's ego and consciousness adequately functional in meeting personal needs arriving from both the inner and outer worlds of reality. This psychic faculty contains the critical or judgment factors and the Self's spatio-temporal expression of the moral sense. In general, this whole psychic faculty roughly may be thought of as akin to the conscience.

SUPPRESSION To choose consciously not to act upon some thought or feeling arriving from the unconscious because such an urge or impulse is deemed unworthy of oneself or threatening to one's continued existence.

SYMBOL A mental representation which elicits or stimulates both feeling and thought but whose origin usually lies closer to the unconscious, affective meaning.

THE HOLY A term used by Rudolf Otto and this manuscript to describe in general the human universal experience of God, or as the case may be, the gods, that which is the fascinating, dreadful and most powerfully mysterious.

TOTAL SELF That which encompasses all which is sensed as belonging to the human subject, both in actuality and potentiality.

TOTAL WILL (WILL) All aspects of intentionality, purpose, choice and goal-seeking decision:

Will-of-Wills (Ultimate Will) That part of the will which unitively seeks the most equitable good for God, self, and neighbor and is construed as most operative in the Self.

Will Power The part of the will which is primarily active as a part of the ego and strives to lead one toward action which will overcome feelings of inferiority and enhance one's potentiality and coping ability.

Will-to-Power In this work it is conceived as an *overly active will power*, which grows out of overly severe guilt or inadequacy feelings and tends to fixate one at some stage of egocentrism.

TRANSFORMATION To convert or change into a new cofiguration, usually to a higher level.

TRANSPERSONAL Above and beyond the usual personality.

Spiritual. That area of development including the ego but centering upon a more advanced center of being and including some awareness of one experiencing beyond space-time.

UNCONSCIOUS The parts of the psyche which are beyond the usual field of consciousness and contain the cognitive structures themselves.

Upper That part more oriented around altruistic and spiritual aspects.

Middle Source of specifically humanistic mental activity and much of preconscious mentation.

Lower Origin and location of life-energy, instincts and animal-nature needs.

VALUE One of consciousness' two psychic rational, evaluating (Jungian) functions. One involves *thought*, to put into correct order, relation, or place. The other involves *feeling*, to give a sense of specific emotional importance or worth.

BIBLIOGRAPHY

∿

Aaronson, Bernard. "Psychosynthesis As System and Theory." *The American Journal of Clinical Hypnosis.* Vol. X. No. 4 (April, 1968).

Ahsen, Akhter. "Image for Effective Psychotherapy: An Essay on Consciousness, Anticipation and Imagery." *The Potential of Fantasy and Imagination.* Edited by Anees A. Sheikh and John T. Shaffer. New York: Brandon House, Inc., *circa* 1979.

American Association of Pastoral Counselors. "The Efficacy of Pastoral Counseling." *Pastoral Counseling: A National Mental Health Resource.* Fairfax, VA: *circa* April, 1993.

Anderson, Camilla M. *Beyond Freud.* New York: Harper and Brothers, 1957.

Arasteh, A. Reza. "Final Integration in the Adult Personality." *Frontiers of Consciousness.* Edited by John White. New York: Julian Press, 1974.

Arieti, Silvano. *Interpretation of Schizophrenia.* 2nd ed. New York: Basic Books, 1974.

Arnold, M. B., and Gasson, J. A., S. J. "Feelings and Emotions as Dynamic Factors in Personality Integration." *The Nature of Emotion.* Edited by Magda B. Arnold. Baltimore, Md.: Penguin Books, 1968.

Assagioli, Roberto. "Dynamic Psychology and Psychosynthesis." Greenville, Del.: Psychosynthesis Research Foundation, 1959.

Assagioli, Roberto. *Psychosynthesis: A Manual of Principles and Techniques.* New York: Hobbs, Dorman and Co., 1965.

Assagioli, Roberto. "Self-realization and Psychological Disturbances." Greenville, Del.: Psychosynthesis Research Foundation, 1961.

Besmer, Beverly. "An Interview with Roberto Assagioli." "Psychosynthesis: Height Psychology—Discovering the self and the Self." New York: Psychosynthesis Research Foundation, 1975.

Birkman, Roger W. "Evangelism through Small Groups." *Pastoral Psychology.* June, 1968.

Birkman, Roger W. "Perception as a Unifying Theory." *An Approach to Mental Health and Spiritual Growth.* Manuscript, Houston, Tex.: Birkman and Associates, Inc., 1962.

Birkman, Roger W. *The Birkman Method: Manuals of Description and Instruction.* 3 vols. Houston, Tex.: Birkman and Associates, Inc., 1952, 1967, and 1970.

Boisen, Anton T. *The Exploration of the Inner World.* Philadelphia, Pa.: University of Pennsylvania Press, 1936.

Bonhoeffer, Dietrich. *The Cost of Discipleship.* Trans. by R. H. Fuller, 2nd ed. New York: Macmillan, 1963.

Brenner, Charles. *An Elementarv Textbook of Psychoanalysis.* 2nd ed. Garden City, New York: Anchor/Doubleday, 1974.

Brill, A. A. "Introduction." *The Basic Writings of Sigmund Freud.* New York: Random House, 1938.

Brown, Robert McAfee. *Theology in a New Key.* Philadelphia, Pa.: Westminister Press, 1978.

Buber, Martin. "Distance and Relation." "Elements of the Interhuman." "What is Common to All." "The Word that is Spoken." *The Knowledge of Man.* Trans. by Maurice Friedman and Ronald Gregor Smith. Edited by Maurice Friedman. New York: Harper and Row, 1965.

Buber, Martin. *The Way of Man: According to the Teaching of Hasidim.* New York: Citadel, 1966.

Buber, Martin. *I and Thou.* Trans. by Ronald Gregor Smith. 2nd ed. New York: Charles Scribner's Sons, 1958.

Campbell, Joseph. *The Masks of God: Primitive Mythology.* Vol. I. 3 vols. New York: Viking, 1969.

Carney, Frederick S. "On Frankenna and Religious Ethics." *The Journal of Religious Ethics.* 3, 1 (Spring, 1975).

Chardin, Pierre Teilhard de. *How I Believe.* Trans. by Rene Hague. New York: Harper and Row, 1969.

Chardin, Pierre Teilhard de. *Human Energy.* Trans. by J. M. Cohen. New York: Harcourt Brace Jovanovich, Inc., 1962.

Chardin, Pierre Teilhard de. *Let Me Explain*. trans. by Rene Hague. Edited by Jean-Pierre Demoulin. New York: Harper and Row, 1970.

Cirlot, J. E. *A Dictionary of Symbols*. Trans. by Jack Sage. New York: Philosophical Library, 1962.

Clift, Jean Dalby. Core Images: A Symbolic Approach to Healing And Wholeness. Three lectures to Southeastern Region of American Association of Patoral Couselors, Hendersonville, N.C., October 18, 19, 1991.

Clift, Jean Dalby and Wallace B. *Symbols of Transformation in Dreams*. Melbourne, Australia: Collins Dave, 1989.

Clift, Jean Dalby and Wallace B. *The Hero Journey in Dreams*. New York: Crossroad, 1988.

Cobb, John B., Jr. "Alfred North Whitehead." *Twelve Makers of Modern Protestant Thought*. Edited by George L. Hunt. New York: Association Press, 1971.

Collingwood, R. G. "Faith and Reason." *Faith and Reason*. Edited by Lionel Robinoff, Chicago: Quadrangle Books, 1968.

Cousins, Ewert H. Editor. *Process Theology; Basic Writings*. New York: Newman Press, 1971.

Crampton, Martha. *An Historical Survey of Mental Imagery Techniques in Psychotherapy and Description of the Dialogic Imagery Method*. Rev. ed. Montreal, Quebec, Canada: Canadian Institute of Psychosynthesis, Inc., 1974.

Crampton, Martha. "Some Principles and Techniques of Energy Transformation at Psychological Levels." *Transcript of Psychosynthesis Seminar*. April, 1973. New York: Psychosynthesis Research Foundation, 1973.

Deikman, Arthur. "Bimodal Consciousness." *The Nature of Human Consciousness*. Edited by Robert E. Ornstein. San Francisco: W. H. Freeman and Co., 1973.

Desoille, Robert. *The Directed Daydream*. Trans. by Frank Haronian. New York: Psychosynthesis Research Foundation, 1966. (The current address by which one may order Psychosynthesis reprints of booklets is Psychosynthesis Institute, 3352 Sacramento St., San Francisco, Cal. 94118.)

Dictionary of Pastoral Care and Counseling. Nashville: Abingdon, 1990.

Draper, Edgar. "Religion as an Intrapsychic Experience." *Cincinnati Journal of Medicine*. V. No. 5 (May, 1969).

Droz, R. and Rahmy, M. *Understanding Piaget*. Trans. by Joyce Diamont. New York: International Universities Press, Inc., 1975.

Eberhart, John J. Letter to American Association of Pastoral Counselors, May 18, 1970.

Edinger, Edward F. *Ego and Archetype*. Baltimore: Penguin, 1974.

Elliott, Charlotte. "Just As I Am," *The Cokesbury Worship Hymnal*. Nashville: Methodist Publishing House, *circa*: 1938.

Erickson, Milton H. *Life Reframing in Hypnosis*. Edited by E. L. Rossi and M. O. Ryan. Vol. II, 2 vols. New York: Irvington, 1985.

Evans, Richard I. *Dialogue with Eric Erickson*. New York: Harper and Row, 1967.

Evans, Richard I. *Jung on Elementary Psychology: A Discussion Between C. G. Jung and Richard I. Evans*. New York: E. P. Dutton and Co., 1976.

Fordham, Frieda. *An Introduction to Jung's Psychology*. 3rd ed. Baltimore: Penguin Books, Ltd., 1966.

Forest, Izette de. *The Leaven of Love*. New York: Harper and Brothers, 1954.

Fowler, James W. *Faith Development and Pastoral Care*. Philadelphia: Fortress Press, 1987.

Fowler, James W. *Stages of Faith: The Psychology of Human Development and the Quest for Meaning*. New York: Harper and Row, 1981.

Fowler, James W. "Stages in Faith: The Structural-Developmental Approach." *Values and Moral Development*. Edited by Thomas C. Hennessy, S. J. New York: Paulist Press, 1976.

Fowler, Jim. "Life/Faith Patterns: Structures of Trust and Loyalty." *Life Maps: Conversations on the Journey of Faith*. By Jim Fowler and Sam Keen. Edited by Jerome Berryman. Waco, Tex.: Word Press, Inc., 1978.

Frank, Jerome D. *Persuasion and Healing: A Comprehensive Study of Psychotherapy*. Revised ed. New York: Schocken, 1974.

Frankl, Viktor E. *The Doctor and the Soul*. New York: Alfred A. Knopf. 1955.

Freud, Sigmund. *An Outline of Psychoanalysis*. Trans. by James Starchey. New York: W. W. Norton, 1949.

Freud, Sigmund. *Civilization and Its Discontents*. Trans. and ed. by James Starchey. New York: W. W. Norton, 1962.

Freud, Sigmund. "The Interpretation of Dreams." *The Basic Writings of Sigmund Freud*. Trans. and ed. by A. A. Brill. New York: Random House, 1938.

Friedman, Maurice. "Introductory Essay," in Martin Buber, *The Knowledge of Man*. Trans. by Maurice Friedman and Ronald Gregor Smith. Edited by Maurice Friedman, New York: Harper and Row, 1965.

Friedman, Maurice S. *Martin Buber*. New York: Harper and Brothers, 1955.

Fromm, Erich. *Psychoanalysis and Religion*. New Haven, Conn.: Yale University Press, 1950.

Fuller, B. A. G. "Leibniz," "Santayana." *History of Philosophy*. Vol. II, 2 vols. 2nd ed. New York: Henry Holt and Co., 1945.

Gerard, Robert. "Symbolic Visualization—A Method of Psychosynthesis." Greenville, Del.: Psychosynthesis Research Foundation, 1961.

Green, Elmer and Alyce. "Update from Elmer and Alyce Green." Association for Transpersonal Psychology Newsletter (Summer, 1977).

Hall, Calvin S. *A Primer of Freudian Psychology*. New York: New American Library, 1954.

Hall, Calvin S. and Nordby, Vernon J. *A Primer of Jungian Psychology*. New York: New American Library, 1973.

Hall, Elizabeth. "A Conversation with Jean Piaget and Barbel Inhelder." *Psychology Today*. Vol. III, No. 12. May, 1970.

Haronian, Frank. "The Repression of the Sublime." New York: Psychosynthesis Research Foundation, 1972.

Horner, Althea J. *The Primacy of Structure: Psychotherapy of Underlying Character Disorders*. Northvale, New Jersey: Jason Aaronson, 1990.

Houston, Jean. "Forward" *Physicians of the Soul: The Psychologies of the World's Great Teachers*. By Robert M. May. New York: Crossroad, 1982.

Howe, Leroy T. "Jean Piaget's Theory of Cognitive Development: An Overview and Appraisal." *Perkins Journal*. XXXI, No. 1 (Fall, 1977).

Howe, Leroy T. "Piaget's Theory of Cognitive Structures as a Resource for Conceptualizing Religious Understanding." Paper presented at the Seventh International Conference on Piagettian Theory and the Helping Professions. Los Angeles, Cal.: *circa* January, 1977.

Hunt, Morton. *The Compassionate Beast: What Science Is Discovering About The Humane Side of Humanity*. New York: William Morrow, 1990.

Jacobi, Jolande. *The Psychology of C. G. Jung*. Trans. by Ralph Manheim. 6th ed. New York: Yale University Press, 1962.

Jaffe, Anelia. *From the Life and Work of C. G. Jung*. Trans. by R. F. C. Hull. New York: Harper and Row, 1971.

"James Fowler Constructing Stage Theory of Faith Development." *Harvard Divinity Bulletin*, IV, No. 5 (February, 1974).

James, Muriel and Jongeward, Dorothy. *Born to Win: Transactional Analysis with Gestalt Experiments*. Reading, Mass.: Addison-Wesley Publishing Co., 1973.

Johnson, Raynor C. *Nurslings of Immortality*. New York: Harper and Brothers, 1957.

Johnson, Stephen M. *The Symbiotic Character*. New York: W. W. Norton, 1991.

Journal of Mental Imagery. Brandon House, Inc., P. 0. Box 240, Bronx, New York 10471.

Jung, C. G. *Aion*. 2nd ed. Trans. by R. F. C. Hull. Bollengen Series XX. Princeton, N.J.: Princeton University Press, 1959.

Jung, C. G. *Analytical Psychology: Its Theory and Practice*. New York: Random House, 1968.

Jung, C. G. "Foreword." *An Introduction to Zen Buddhism*. By Daisetz Teitaro Suzuki. New York: Grove Press, Inc., 1964.

Jung, C. G. *Mandala Symbolism*. Trans. by R. F. C. Hull. Princeton: Princeton University Press, 1972.

Jung, C. G. *Memories, Dreams, Reflections*. Trans. by Richard and Clara Winston. Edited by Anelia Jaffe. Rev. ed. New York: Random House, 1961.

Jung, C. G. "The Transcendent Function." *The Portable Jung*. Trans. by R. F. C. Hull. Edited by Joseph Campbell. New York: Viking Press, 1971.

Jung, C. G. *The Undiscovered Self*. Trans. by R. F. C. Hull. New York: New American Library, 1957.

Jung, Carl Gustave. *Psychology and Religion.* New Haven, Conn.: Yale University Press, 1938.

Jung, Emma. *Animus and Anima.* Trans. by Carey F. Baynes. New York: Spring Publications, 1957.

Kamasatsu, Akira and Hirae, Tomio. "An Electroencephalographic Study on the Zen Meditation (Zazen)." *Altered States of Consciousness.* Edited by Charles T. Tart. New York: John Wiley and Sons, 1969.

Kasbab, F. Paul. "Imagery Techniques in Psychiatry." *Archives of General Psychiatry.* Vol. 31 (September, 1974).

Kellogg, Rhonda and O'Dell, Scott. *The Psychology of Children's Art.* New York: CRM-Random House, 1967.

Kepler, Thomas S. Editor. *Fellowship of the Saints.* Nashville, TN: Abingdon-Cokesbury, 1948.

Klaus, Marshal H. and Kennell, John H. *Maternal-Infant Bonding.* St. Louis, Mo.: C. V. Mosby Co., 1976.

Kretschmer, Wolfgang, Jr. "Meditative Techniques in Psychotherapy." *Zeitschrift Für Psychotherapie und Medizinische Psychologie.* Trans. by William Swartley, Vol. 1., No. 3. (May, 1951) Greenville, Del.: Psychosynthesis Research Foundation, *circa* 1956.

Leuner, Hanscarl, M. D. and Kornadt, H. J., Ph.D. "Initiated Symbol Projection." Unpublished manuscript. Translated, edited, and amplified by William Swartley, Ph.D. Greenville, Del.: Psychosynthesis Research Foundation, *circa* 1958.

Levinson, Daniel J. *et. al. The Seasons of a Man's Life.* New York: Alfred A. Knopf, 1978.

Livingston, James C. "Rudolph Bultman." *Modern Christian Thought.* New York: Macmillan, 1971.

Lowen, Alexander. *Bioenergetics.* New York: Coward, McCann and Geoghegan, Inc., 1975.

Lowen, Alexander. *The Language of the Body.* New York: Collier, 1971.

McBride, Alfred. "Reaction to Fowler." *Values and Moral Development.* Edited by Thomas C. Hennessey, S. J. New York: Paulist Press, 1976.

McLaurin, Elizabeth. *The Nature of Belief.* New York: Hawthorn Books, 1976.

McMillin, R. E. *Handbook of Cognitive Therapy Techniques.* New York: W. W. Norton, 1984.

Maltz, Maxwell. *Psycho-cybernetics*. Englewood Cliffs, N. J.: Prentice Hall, 1960.

Maslow, Abraham H. *Religious Values and Peak-experiences*. New York: Viking, 1970.

May, Gerald O. *Addiction And Grace*. San Francisco: Harper, 1988.

May, Rollo. *The Cry for Myth*. New York: W. W. Norton, 1991.

Neibuhr, H. Richard. *Radical Monotheism and Western Culture*. New York: Harper and Row, 1960.

Neibuhr, Richard R. *Experiential Religion*. New York: Harper and Row, 1972.

Ornstein, Robert E. *The Evolution of Consciousness*. New York: Prentice Hall, 1991.

Ornstein, Robert E. and Sobel, David. *The Healing Brain*. New York: Simon and Schuster, 1987.

Ornstein, Robert E. and Sobel, Daivd. *Healthy Pleasures*. New York: Addison-Wesley, 1989.

Ornstein, Robert E. *Multimind*. New York: Doubleday, 1986.

Otto, Rudolf. *The Idea of the Holy*. Trans. by John W. Harvey. 2nd ed. New York: Oxford University Press, 1950.

Outler, Albert C. *Psychotherapy and the Christian Message*. New York: Harper and Brothers, 1954.

Pannenberg, Wolfhart. *Metaphysics and the Idea of God*. Trans. by Philip Clayton. Grand Rapids, Mich.: William B. Eerdmans, 1990.

Patton, John. *Pastoral Counseling: A Ministry of the Church*. Nashville: Abingdon, 1983.

Pesso, Albert. *Movement in Psychotherapy: Psychomotor Techniques and Training* . New York: New York University Press, 1969.

Pey, Pythia. "The Changing Face of Death." *Common Boundary*. Vol. 9, No. 1. January/February, 1991.

Piaget, Jean. *Play, Dreams, and Imitation in Childhood*. Trans. by C. Gattegno and F. M. Hodgson. New York: W. W. Norton, 1962.

Piaget, Jean. *Structuralism*. Trans. and ed. by Chaninah Maschler. New York: Harper and Row, 1970.

Piaget, Jean. *The Child and Reality*. Trans. by Arnold Rosin. New York: Grossman, 1973.

Piaget, Jean. *The Moral Judgment of the Child*. Trans. by Marjorie Gabin. New York: Macmillan, 1965.

Piaget, Jean and Inhelder, Barbel. *Memory and Intelligence*. New York: Basic Books, 1973.

Piaget, Jean and Inhelder, Barbel. *The Psychology of the Child.* Trans. by Helen Weaver. New York: Basic Books, 1969.

Polster, Erving and Polster, Miriam. *Gestalt Therapy Integrated: Contours of Theory and Practice.* New York: Vintage Books, 1974.

Post, Laurens van der and Taylor, Jane. *Testament to the Bushmen.* New York: Viking Penquin, 1984.

Psychosynthesis Research Foundation. "Introduction to the Techniques: Working Draft." Greenville, Del.: Psychosynthesis Research Foundation, *circa* 1955.

Rahner, Karl. *I Remember.* Trans. by Harvey D. Egan. New York: Crossroads, 1985.

Rizzuto, Ana-Maria. *The Birth of the Living God: A Psychoanalytic Study.* Chicago: University of Chicago Press, 1979.

Rossi, Ernest Lawrence. *The Psychobiology of Mind-Body Healing: New Concepts of Therapeutic Healing.* New York: Simon and Schuster, 1987.

Russell, Stanley C. "Coping with Stress—Christ's Way." *The Christian Counselor* (Spring, 1986).

Russell, Stanley C. "Mental Illness: A Conceptual Model." Manuscript, Jackson Miss.: University of Miss. Medical Center, 1986.

Sanford, John A. *Dreams: God's Forgotten Language.* New York: Crossroad, 1984.

Sanford, John A. *Dreams and Healing: A Succinct and Lively Interpretation of Dreams.* New York: Paulist Press, 1978.

Schaeffer, Brenda. *Is It Love or Is It Addiction?* New York: Harper and Row, 1987.

Schiff, Jacqui Lee, *et. al. Cathexis Reader.* New York: Harper and Row, 1975.

Schlauch, C. R. "Empathy as the Essence of Pastoral Psychotherapy." *The Journal of Pastoral Care.* Vol. XLIV No. 5 (Spring 1990).

Schleiermacher, Friedrich. *The Christian Faith.* Trans. by H. R. MacKintosh and J. S. Stewart. New York: Harper and Row, 1963.

Sheikh, Anees A. and Shaffer, John T. Editors. *The Potential of Fantasy and Imagination.* New York: Brandon House, Inc., *circa* 1979.

Shorr, Joseph E. *Psycho-imagination Therapy.* New York: Intercontinental Medical Books Corp., 1972.

Skinner, B. F. *About Behaviorism*. New York: Alfred A. Knopf, 1974.

Smidt, Paul F. "Factual Knowledge and Religious Claims." *Religious Language and the Problem of Religious Knowledge*. Edited by Robert E. Santoni, Bloomington, Ind.: Indiana University Press, 1968.

Spence, Donald P. *Narrative Truth and Historical Truth: Meaning and Interpretaion in Psychoanalysis*. New York: W. W. Norton and Co., 1982.

Spring: An Annual of Archetypal Psychology and Jungian Thought. Spring Publications, P. 0. Box 222069, Dallas, Tex., 75222.

Stanton, Martin S. *Sandor Ferenzi: Reconsidering Active Intervention*. Northvale, New Jersey: Jason Aronson, Inc., 1991.

Steiner, Claude M. *Scripts People Live: Transactional Analysis of Life Scripts*. New York: Grove Press, 1974.

Tart, Charles T. "States of Consciousness and State-specific Sciences." *The Nature of Human Consciousness*. Edited by Robert E. Ornstein. San Francisco: W. H. Freeman and Co., 1973.

Tillich, Paul. *The Courage to Be*. New Haven: Yale University Press, 1952.

Tillich, Paul. *The New Being*. New York: Charles Scribner's Sons, 1955.

Tillich, Paul. *The Shaking of the Foundations*. New York: Charles Scribner's Sons, 1948.

Trueblood, David Elton. *The Logic of Belief*. New York: Harper and Brothers, 1942.

Wallace, Lee. *Stories That Heal: Reparenting Adult Children of Dysfunctional Families Using Hypnotic Stories in Psychotherapy*. New York: W. W. Norton, 1991.

Wallace, Robert Keith and Benson, Herbert. "The Physiology of Meditation." *The Nature of Human Consciousness*. Edited by Robert E. Ornstein. San Francisco: W. H. Freeman and Co., 1973.

Welch, Mary. *What Wilt Thou?* Henderson, Tex.: Park Printing Company, 1952.

Whitehead, Alfred North. *Adventures in Ideas*. New York: Free Press, 1961.

Whitehead, Alfred North. *Process and Reality*. New York: Free Press, 1929.

Whitehead, Alfred North. *Religion in the Making.* New York: New American Library, 1926.

Whitehead, Alfred North. *The Function of Reason.* Boston: Beacon Press, 1929.

Wicks, Frances G. *The Inner World of Choice.* New York: Harper and Row, 1963.

Wink, Walter. *Transforming Bible Study.* Nashville: Abingdon, 1980.

Winson, Jonathan. *Brain and Psyche: The Biology of the Unconscious.* New York: Vintage, 1985.

Wise, Carrol A. *Pastoral Psychotherapy.* Northvale, New Jersey: Jason Aronson, 1983.

Wolberg, Lewis R. *The Technique of Psychotherapy.* Vol. 1. 2 vols., 2nd ed. New York: Grune and Stratton, 1967.

Wolpe, Joseph. *The Practice of Behavior Therapy.* New York: Pergamon Press, 1969.

Zig, Jeffrey K. *Eriksonian Psychotherapy: Structures.* Vol. I, 2 Vols. New York: Brunner/Mazel, 1985.

Zig, Jeffrey K. *Eriksonian Psychotherapy: Clinical Applications.* Vol. II, 2 Vols. New York: Brunner/Mazel, 1985.

INDEX

∾